Esfir Shub

Esfir Shub

Pioneer of Documentary Filmmaking

Ilana Shub Sharp

BLOOMSBURY ACADEMIC
NEW YORK • LONDON • OXFORD • NEW DELHI • SYDNEY

BLOOMSBURY ACADEMIC
Bloomsbury Publishing Inc
1385 Broadway, New York, NY 10018, USA
50 Bedford Square, London, WC1B 3DP, UK
29 Earlsfort Terrace, Dublin 2, Ireland

BLOOMSBURY, BLOOMSBURY ACADEMIC and the Diana logo are trademarks of Bloomsbury Publishing Plc

First published in the United States of America 2022
This paperback edition published 2023

Copyright © Ilana Shub Sharp, 2022

For legal purposes the Acknowledgements on p. x constitute an extension of this copyright page.

Cover design: Ilana Shub Sharp

All rights reserved. No part of this publication may be reproduced or transmitted in any form or by any means, electronic or mechanical, including photocopying, recording, or any information storage or retrieval system, without prior permission in writing from the publishers.

Bloomsbury Publishing Inc does not have any control over, or responsibility for, any third-party websites referred to or in this book. All internet addresses given in this book were correct at the time of going to press. The author and publisher regret any inconvenience caused if addresses have changed or sites have ceased to exist, but can accept no responsibility for any such changes.

Library of Congress Cataloging-in-Publication Data

Names: Shub Sharp, Ilana, author.
Title: Esfir Shub : pioneer of documentary filmmaking / Ilana Shub Sharp.
Description: New York : Bloomsbury Academic, 2021. | Includes bibliographical references and index.
Identifiers: LCCN 2021018363 (print) | LCCN 2021018364 (ebook) | ISBN 9781501376511 (hardback) | ISBN 9781501376504 (epub) | ISBN 9781501376498 (pdf) | ISBN 9781501376474
Subjects: LCSH: Shub, Esfir Ilinichna, 1894-1959–Criticism and interpretation. | Women motion picture producers and directors–Soviet Union. | Documentary films–Production and direction–Soviet Union.
Classification: LCC PN1998.3.S4755 S58 2021 (print) | LCC PN1998.3.S4755 (ebook) | DDC 791.43023/3092–dc23
LC record available at https://lccn.loc.gov/2021018363
LC ebook record available at https://lccn.loc.gov/2021018364

ISBN: HB: 978-1-5013-7651-1
PB: 978-1-5013-7648-1
ePDF: 978-1-5013-7649-8
eBook: 978-1-5013-7650-4

Typeset by Deanta Global Publishing Services, Chennai, India

To find out more about our authors and books visit www.bloomsbury.com and sign up for our newsletters.

For Denise J. Youngblood

Contents

List of Illustrations	viii
Acknowledgements	x
Note on Translation and Transliteration	xi
Introduction	1
1 Shub and the Art of Montage: Soviet Style	7
2 Esfir Shub and the Constructivist Avant-Garde	35
3 *The Fall of the Romanov Dynasty*: Shub's Constructivist Paradigm for Nonfiction Film	61
4 *The Fall of the Romanov Dynasty*: The Theory, the Politics and the History	93
5 Only Newsreels: Shub's Triumphant Way Ahead	127
6 Shub's Final Silent Documentary: *Today*	147
7 *K.Sh.E.*: Shub's Conversion to Sound	185
8 Shub's *Spain*: The End of the Line	217
Conclusion	253
Notes	265
Esfir Shub: Filmography	304
Select Filmography	308
Bibliography	310
Index	321

Illustrations

1	Esfir Shub, a leading editor at the Third Film Factory	16
2	Esfir Shub with the great composer Dmitry Shostakovich	19
3	The panoramic majesty of *Wings of a Serf*, 1926	21
4	Tina Modotti: *Elegance and Poverty*, 1928	26
5	The influence of Esfir Shub on *Strike*: the grid and the factory	31
6	Alexander Rodchenko: *The Constructivist Party*, 1926	39
7	Aleksei Gan: *Constructivism* [Konstruktivizm], 1922	49
8	Esfir Shub: the only female in the frame	58
9	Marching in the streets on International Women's Day, February 1917 in *The Fall of the Romanov Dynasty*	71
10	V. M. Purishkevich in *The Fall of the Romanov Dynasty*	74
11	An arms factory: white crosses on shell casings in *The Fall of the Romanov Dynasty*	76
12	The Tercentenary Celebrations of the Romanov Dynasty 1913 in *The Fall of the Romanov Dynasty*	79
13	The hand of power and the orb in ruins in *The Fall of the Romanov Dynasty*	81
14–15	At Labour and at Play in *The Fall of the Romanov Dynasty*	87
16	Pretension and Privilege in *The Fall of the Romanov Dynasty*	88
17	The original poster for *The Fall of the Romanov Dynasty* 1927	101
18	Barrel of a ship's cannon: 'workers and peasants become the Red Fleet' in *The Great Way*	131
19	The personal touch: Lenin in Gorki with Nadezhda Krupskaya, 1922 in *The Great Way*	140
20	Lenin in conversation: filmed in his office at the Kremlin, 1921 in *The Great Way*	140
21	Lenin appears in the official car, surrounded by supporters in *The Great Way*	140
22	Lenin's name is in lights in *The Great Way*	144
23	Veiled in sunlight and shadow in *Today*	152
24	Another veil – the same time but another place: the USA in *Today*	152
25	A Soviet girl smiles, happy in her new environment in *Today*	153

Illustrations

26	One of her playmates, in the same apartment complex, shyly averts her gaze from the camera in *Today*	153
27	Let the tractor race begin! *Today*	155
28	The unselfconscious beauty of a young Soviet woman is shown to perfection in *Today*	156
29	The Reapers in *Today*	157
30	Constructivist imagery and the poetry of the crane in *Today*	159
31	A trio of comrades in *Today*	161
32	A diligent factory worker at her daily toil in *Today*	174
33	The young look forward to tomorrow with optimism in *Today*	178
34	Nato Vachnadze being filmed as she gives the signal in the recording studio in *K.Sh.E*	192
35	Shub filming at the Dneprostroi Dam in *K.Sh.E*	194
36	A stark Constructivist grid seemingly out of place in the arid countryside of Armenia in *K.Sh.E*	197
37	A filmed radio interview with Marietta Shaginyan in *K.Sh.E*	198
38	No Pasarán! 'La Pasionaria' (Dolores Ibárruri) addresses the people in *Spain*	229
39	Franco's fascist army in *Spain*	232
40	Yet again, Shub's images speak for themselves in *Spain*	233
41	Supporting the Republican cause: the *Zyrianin*, a Soviet ship docks in Barcelona's harbour in *Spain*	234
42	A young soldier with the International Brigades in *Spain*	235
43	Her fighting comrade, a member of the socialist UGT [the General Union of Workers], in *Spain*	236
44	In Madrid, children wait apprehensively in an underground shelter in *Spain*	237
45	Grief and darkness fall on an underground shelter in *Spain*	238
46	Homage to Rodchenko: his Constructivist graphics live on in *Spain*	241

Acknowledgements

My immense gratitude goes to Denise J. Youngblood, mentor extraordinaire, for her unfailing support and encouragement. Without her, this book would never have been written.

Graham Roberts deserves my appreciation for his invaluable advice and kindness.

Grateful thanks are extended to James Donald and Antonio Traverso, who helped me take my first steps on this journey with the completion of my doctoral thesis.

Additionally, my thanks go to Birgit Beumers for the bountiful fruits of her shopping expedition in Moscow.

Alexander Lavrentiev, the grandson of Varvara Stepanova and Alexander Rodchenko, is worthy of acknowledgement for his extraordinary generosity regarding an image used in this book.

Thank you to Katie Gallof, my helpful and patient commissioning editor at Bloomsbury.

Furthermore, thanks to Greg Loftin for fuelling my curiosity long before my quest began in earnest.

Finally, no words can adequately express my infinite thanks to Jem, who makes all things seem possible.

This book is in memory of my beloved paternal grandfather Moshe Shub.

Note on Translation and Transliteration

Transliteration is the bane of every author writing in English on a Russian subject. Strict adherence to the Library of Congress system satisfies the specialist but will look somewhat odd to the Anglophone reader who does not speak Russian. Transliteration in this book is, therefore, a hybrid: I mainly adhere to the LC system but with the following exceptions to facilitate pronunciation: *ya* instead of initial and final *ia* (Yakov, Tolstaya); *ye, yu* instead of initial *e, iu* (Yekaterina, Yutkevich); *y* instead of final *ii* (Shklovsky). The silent soft and hard signs are omitted. Occasional inconsistencies are hard to avoid; for example, spellings well established in English are retained: Leo Tolstoy, Sergei Eisenstein, etc.

Introduction

> Preserving the past is a moral duty . . . people may want to know how we used to live.
>
> Yakov Tolchan 1992[1]

This book is the first full-length and detailed analysis of the oeuvre of Esfir Shub (1894–1959), a major Soviet filmmaker who was the founder of the compilation documentary. She was also the first woman both to write critical texts on cinema and then to practically apply her theories to her own films. Her syncretism of cinema theory and praxis inspired her to ask questions regarding both the nature of nonfiction film, such as the problem of authenticity and reality, and the function of the artist in society – issues which are still relevant in contemporary discussions about the documentary film. Yet, although scholars of early Soviet cinema have conceded her genius in a perfunctory manner, her work has never been afforded the continued, in-depth critical focus paid to leading male directors in her coterie, like Dziga Vertov or Sergei Eisenstein. With the recent renewal of interest amongst academics and critics in pioneering women directors, there has been some indication over the past five years that this attitude is changing, but Shub studies are still in a nascent stage. My objectives for this work are to establish Shub's diverse contributions not only to Soviet but also to world cinema, as well as to demonstrate the ongoing significance of her work and the rationale driving it.

Shub was born Esfir Ilinichna Roshal on 16 March 1894 (Old Style) into a Jewish family in the provincial town of Surazh within the Pale of Settlement.[2] Surazh was in the Chernigov district of Ukraine, Russian Empire.[3] Although she wrote a memoir, she was extremely reticent about her private life, of which we know little. Indeed, her two published volumes, *My Life – Cinematography* [Zhizn moya – kinematograf] and *In Close-up* [Krupnym planom], are essentially anthologies of her published journal articles on film, essays on influential figures in her clique and commentaries and letters concerning her work in the film industry. However, we are aware that in the 1910s, she attended the Women's Institute of

Higher Learning in Moscow, after an intervention by her father, needed because of the Jewish quotas that existed at the time. There, Shub immersed herself in her books; Russian literature was her primary focus, specifically Dostoevsky and Pushkin, but she was also an avid reader of Dante and Heine. At some juncture, she married Isaak Vladimirovich Shub, with whom she had a daughter, Anna. Later, she married Aleksei Gan, the high-profile avant-garde Constructivist theorist, who receives only oblique mention in her memoir and is not named.

After the Bolshevik Revolution, in autumn 1918, Shub began to work directly for Anatoly Lunacharsky at the People's Commissariat of Enlightenment [Narkompros], which would prove to be an advantage due to Lunacharsky's connections in Soviet cinema of the 1920s. Her entrée into the avant-garde art circle was facilitated by her next position with the famed theatre director Vsevolod Meyerhold at the Theatre Department of Narkompros [TEO]. Her film career began in 1922 when she was appointed to Goskino, the state film trust, later renamed Sovkino (cinema was nationalized in 1919). She worked as a film editor until 1924, re-editing foreign films to make them appropriate for the Soviet public. From 1924 to 1925 she assisted Sergei Eisenstein with both the film script and the editing of his groundbreaking first film *Strike* [Stachka, 1925].[4] In 1926 she was the editor of both Yury Tarich's *Wings of a Serf* [Krylya kholopa] and Oleg Frelikh's *A Prostitute/ Crushed by Life* [Prostitutka/Ubitaia zhizn'iu]. Hence, Shub had a solid foundation working on the feature-length acted, staged fiction film, or *igrovaya filma*, to build upon before embarking on an independent career as a maker of non-acted, unstaged nonfiction film, or *neigrovaya filma*.

Accordingly, this work seeks to demonstrate Shub's dominant position as both a leading documentarian and a valued member of the early Soviet avant-garde. Until now, Shub's positioning as a central figure in the annals of cinema history has not been fully acknowledged. My book attempts to redress this imbalance. Shub deserves recognition both as the founder and ardent promoter of the compilation film genre *and* as a pioneer of the theory and practice of documentary filmmaking.[5]

Organization

Chapter 1 demonstrates that montage was a fundamental building block, structurally the filmic foundation, of the Soviet avant-garde filmmakers of the 1920s. It was emblematic of these practitioners both in nonfiction films as exemplified by Shub and in the fiction films of Eisenstein. The distinctive stylistic roots of Soviet montage sprang from such diverse artistic sources as Kazimir Malevich, Vsevolod Meyerhold, Vladimir Mayakovsky and Lev Kuleshov. Accordingly, these origins are explored fully in this chapter due to their catalysing effect, propelling the modernist ideals of the vanguard to unique forms of experimentation.

Chapter 2 situates Shub firmly within the heart of the avant-garde Constructivist movement. Indeed the creed of Constructivism was at the ideological core of Shub's methodology as she shaped her nonfiction films. The first film in her trilogy, the pioneering *The Fall of the Romanov Dynasty* [Padenie dinasty Romanovykh, 1927], epitomizes the theoretical underpinnings of this revolutionary group.[6] The chapter includes the first of several critiques of this documentary in the book. Controversial though this may appear, it is also demonstrated why it was Shub and not Dziga Vertov who was the leading Constructivist filmmaker. Crucially, I claim that the contribution to film history of Shub's Constructivist-based cinematic practice was far-reaching in its impact. The unacknowledged influence on documentarists who followed her, decades later, makes Shub worthy of an elevated place in the world of cinema.

The next six chapters showcase Shub's principal achievements in film, chronologically. Chapter 3 seeks not only to highlight this unprecedented documentary work, the first full-length compilation film internationally, but also to contrast it against Eisenstein's drama *October*, a fascinating work of fiction loosely based on fact. This exegetic reading serves to contextualize Shub's position in the milieu of the avant-garde as the leading Constructivist filmmaker. *The Fall of the Romanov Dynasty* is shown to be a remarkable contribution to the utopian project of Soviet cinema of the 1920s.

Chapter 4 continues the analysis in Chapter 3. It ends the appraisal of *The Fall of the Romanov Dynasty*, a prime example of Shub's filmic achievement. This work is a seamless dovetailing of Constructivist art and technology, using newsreel footage, to promote the evolving socialist path forward. Chapter 4 concentrates on questions of Party propaganda and ideology, historical truth and the authenticity of the raw material. Added to these challenges of truth, objectivity and the notions of reality was Shub's initial and problematic issue of authorship.

Chapter 5 concerns *The Great Way* [Veliky put, 1927], the sequel to *The Fall of the Romanov Dynasty*. Its focus is not only on Lenin as the guiding light after the toppling of the darkness of Tsar Nicholas II's regime but it is also a discourse on the evils of the capitalist West. The latter's decadence, greed and exploitation of its working class is juxtaposed with the glorification of the virtues of the nascent socialist state. In contrast to *The Fall of the Romanov Dynasty*, made solely from archival footage, in *The Great Way* Shub films sequences partially due to the paucity of material. As in *The Fall of the Romanov Dynasty*, Shub's intention is to raise the political consciousness of her audience. There is no chapter on *The Russia of Nicholas II and Leo Tolstoy* [Rossiya Nikolaya II i Lva Tolstogo, 1928], the other film in her trilogy, because, unfortunately, not one complete copy of this film is extant.

Chapter 6 introduces the First Five Year Plan. Shub's last silent film, *Today* [Segodnya, 1930] develops the thematic threads of *The Great Way*. Known as *Cannons or Tractors?* when screened overseas there is continued emphasis on promoting the might, progress and successes of the newly created Soviet Union and the industrious nature of its proletariat, building a shining future through enthusiastic labour. This is compared with the United States, which is found lacking in every sphere of its society and culture. Shub extols the virtues of the socialist state seen against a background of discord, privilege and inequity in the United States. Although her ideological narrative toed the Party line to perfection, promoting the victorious modernizing of the Soviet Union at record speed, Shub's work met with severe criticism in the press. The documentation and relay of history were amongst her objectives, as she presented her films to her audience. Worryingly, the changing political climate heralded the emergence of a precarious positioning for Shub's nonfiction film.

Chapter 7 is her wholehearted immersion into the wonders of sound technology in all its aspects. Its application within the framework of her first sound film, *K.Sh.E.* (Komsomol Patron of Electrification) [Komsomol-shef elektrifikatsy, 1932], is a successful endeavour, filled with joy and hope. There is a comparison between her film and Vertov's initial foray into sound, *Enthusiasm: the Symphony of the Donbass* [Entuziazm: Simfoniya Donbassa, 1931]. Despite the chaos in the Soviet film industry and a deficiency of basic equipment, which was often of an inferior standard, Shub continues to highlight the triumphs of Soviet industry in its technological progress. Living within a repressive regime creating increasing levels of fear and uncertainty, Shub was also battling immense frustration and lack of opportunity within her chosen genre. She almost begged for work and saw projects such as her highly innovative film script for 'Women', which could have brought her far-reaching critical acclaim, rejected and then discarded onto the scrapheap of film history.

Chapter 8 relates to *Spain* [Ispaniya, 1939]. This is the last film deserving of international stature in Shub's oeuvre. Thus, it is appositely the final chapter in the book. *Spain* is a largely forgotten documentary of the Spanish Civil War.[7] Its brutal subject matter aside, it is also a documentary of considerable fascination, vibrancy and beauty. The narrative catalogues the conflict from the Republican faction's point of view. Additionally, this chapter seeks to explore Shub's successful preservation of the myths surrounding the Soviet presence in Spain, and Stalin's contribution to the war effort, while simultaneously creating a film of value. Joris Ivens's *The Spanish Earth* is viewed in tandem with *Spain* because its format and approach to the same subject are very different from that of Shub's. *Spain* was the effective end of Shub's career, and as her last major work, it is a fitting tribute to Shub's oeuvre in its most evolved manifestation.

This work, together with the other four major films critiqued within these pages, deserves to be included in every tertiary cinema study course across the globe. Shub's documentaries should be accessible to all. Indeed it would be an appropriate and lasting tribute to her as, during her lifetime, it was her aim to reach as diverse and large an audience as possible. These five nonfiction films follow the shift from the utopian dreams of the avant-garde to its collapse and the increasing subservience of all art forms to Party dogma in the 1930s. After all the frustration and disillusionment of this decade of political turbulence, after *Spain*, Shub's career declined rapidly and her work faded from memory.[8]

It must be recorded that my intention is to engage a broad spectrum of readers. This mirrors and pays homage to Shub's objectives for her documentaries, where she aimed at intelligibility and accessibility. This was cinema for a cross section of the populace. Hence this book is multidisciplinary and traverses, even blurs, the boundaries between cinema, art, history, politics and women's studies. In addition there is a tendency within the text towards the melding of a theoretical core with a narratively and descriptively based approach, reflecting in part some of Shub's aims for nonfiction film. In this way, I hope to honour both her documentaries and her philosophy of filmmaking.

1

Shub and the Art of Montage: Soviet Style

Montage was pivotal to Soviet film theory and practice in the 1920s. Therefore, this chapter is an exploration of the theoretical centrality of montage as a key identifier of avant-garde cinema in this era. It addresses the structural elements that underpinned Shub's nonfiction film through her utilization of the revolutionary principles of montage, unique to the Soviet silent films of the vanguard.

Through its revolutionary political and aesthetic structure, Esfir Shub, Lev Kuleshov, Sergei Eisenstein and Dziga Vertov attempted to create a dramatic new reality. Each of these four filmmakers made key contributions through their own highly individual interpretations of montage, which they had identified as a crucial element upon which their cinematic philosophies were based. Indeed, Shub's interlocutions with the avant-garde consisted of an interchange between the alternating voices of montage, Constructivism and nonfiction film. While Constructivism lay at her filmic foundation, Shub's ideological montage (in symbiosis with Constructivist principles) was a means of mapping and unifying the structure and meaning of her raw material.

Soviet Montage: Its Origins and Specificity

'Montage was a staple of Berlin Dada long before Eisenstein theorized about it in Mayakovsky's[1] journal *LEF* the acronym for Left Front of the Arts [Levyi front iskusstv] in 1923.'[2] Although this statement cannot be denied, the historian Robert C. Williams, in *Artists in Revolution*, fails to acknowledge the impact of the Russian avant-garde artists in general (and Kazimir Malevich in particular) prior to the Revolution. Montage was a revolutionary expression of cinematic art in the newly emergent socialist society. It was itself a collage constructed from the following expressions: the artworks of Malevich circa 1914; the poetry of Velimir Khlebnikov, Alexander Kruchenykh, Vladimir Mayakovsky and the futurists; formalist literary theory; the photomontage of Aleksei Gan, Gustav Klutsis and Alexander Rodchenko; and the theatre of Vsevolod Meyerhold.[3] In fact, montage was born out of Malevich's nonsensical juxtaposition of visual images and also, its poetical equivalent, the literary trans-sense [zaum] of Khlebnikov and Kruchenykh in 1913. Added to this was the surreal emphasis of the artist Marc Chagall,[4] the formalists' defamiliarization [ostranenie] and the futurists' displacement [sdvig]: all were captured in the kaleidoscopic world of Malevich's artworks.[5]

Therefore, in opposition to Williams, I argue that the foundation of montage in the Soviet Union owes far more to the blooming of avant-garde art in the early twentieth century (before the upheaval of October 1917) than to Dadaist photomontage in 1918. The roots of montage lie embedded in the cultural soil of tsarist Russia, specifically in the work of Malevich, which in turn influenced Raoul Hausmann, Hannah Höch, John Heartfield and Kurt Schwitters.[6] Interestingly, there is a powerful connection between Shub's work and that of Höch's.

Photomontage had its genesis in Malevich's *Lady by the Advertising Pillar* [1914], *Warriors of the First Division* [1914] and *Darkness in Parts, Composition with Mona Lisa* [1915–16]. These mixed media artworks used collage and incorporated photographic images, creating an early synthesis of art and technology. While Hausmann and his Weimar colleagues were creating this new art form, the Constructivists Klutsis and Rodchenko were at the forefront of the advancement of photomontage and photography in the Soviet Union. Five years after Malevich's groundbreaking artworks of photomontage, exhibited three years before the Revolution, Klutsis's work, *The Dynamic City*, of 1919 is claimed to be the first example of Soviet photomontage: although Aleksei Gan is thought to have been exploring this genre as early as 1918.

Just as Höch and Heartfield used photomontage as a political weapon, Klutsis defined photomontage not 'merely [as] the expressive composition of photographs. It always includes a political slogan.'[7] Undeniably, *The Fall of the Romanov Dynasty* was the cinematic realization of Klutsis's earlier objective, as it was a chronicle of moving photographic images punctuated by political slogans. Using Constructivist rhetoric, Klutsis claimed further that 'photomontage ... is closely related to the development of industrial culture and forms of art for mass propagation ... it represents a new art of the masses, because it represents the art of Socialist Construction'.[8] In terms of the purely productive, functional and political aspects of her filmic constructs, Shub made her mark on the development of this aesthetic. She would echo Klutsis's philosophy as she transformed this concept into her nonfiction films.

However, apart from the photomontage works on paper by Klutsis and Rodchenko, the evolution of the distinctively Soviet form of montage was further influenced by the stagecraft of Meyerhold and Mayakovsky. While Shub promoted the weighty issues of the USSR through her documentaries, she was well aware that the principles of Soviet montage, which she observed so seriously, were in fact derived from sites of laughter and merriment: the circus and the theatre. Indeed, both Meyerhold's and Mayakovsky's revolutionary experimentation in the theatre was to have a significant impact on (and be a vital rehearsal ground for) the montage practice of the young filmmakers.

Meyerhold and Theatrical October: Innovation and Montage

The influence of popular theatre on Soviet film and Constructivist art was substantial. Georg Fuchs's *The Theatre of the Future* [Die Schaubühne der Zukunft], published in Leipzig and Berlin in 1906, was a catalyst for revolutionary artistic processes that began with Meyerhold's observations on theatre and ended with the Constructivists. In his book, Fuchs expressed his belief that 'dramatic art . . . should utilise the techniques of carnivals, acrobats, circuses, and the Japanese Kabuki and Noh theatres'.[9] Fuchs's volume was instrumental in the clarification and development of Meyerhold's experimental and theatrical pathway, inspiring revolutionary methods of 'circusization' of the theatre and of biomechanics.

In 1921, Sergei Yutkevich and Sergei Eisenstein both became avid pupils of Meyerhold. As Yutkevich wrote, he and Eisenstein 'were both crazy about the circus' and each wished to become a *metteur en scène* under Meyerhold's tutelage.[10] Meyerhold's emerging methodology would have a profound effect on Yutkevich and Eisenstein, and on Sergei Radlov and his Popular Comedy Theatre in Petrograd. In his position as a leading theatre director and mentor, Meyerhold would also play a vital role in the theoretical and practical development of the emerging filmmakers at the heart of experimental Soviet art and cinema.

Just prior to the February Revolution in 1917, Meyerhold launched his production of Mikhail Lermontov's *Masquerade*. According to the Soviet theatre critic and historian Konstantin Rudnitsky, this interpretation was to have a profound influence on the repertoire of Russian theatre. Meyerhold perceived *Masquerade* as 'a tragedy within the frame of a carnival'.[11] This was high art dressed in the garments of popular culture. Together with Mayakovsky, who extended this philosophy in his political satire *Mystery-Bouffe*, Meyerhold was creating a framework for the avant-garde filmmakers and the Constructivists (Shub, of course, being a member of both circles).

From a viewing perspective, the drama of *Masquerade* was highly filmic. Alexander Golovin, renowned for his artistry, replicated features of the interior design of the theatre on the stage thus creating visual continuity, a total entity.[12] Meyerhold and Golovin had suspended multiple curtains, which could be brought down smoothly and swiftly at varying points on the stage. These drops were utilized to slice and thrust the action forward with rapid cutting between various scenarios. A curtain would lift at the back of the stage resplendent with a different set, acting would then recommence, the curtain would fall and the drama and the actors would be propelled elsewhere so that the rhythmic pace could continue.[13] Meyerhold also broke up the text: a soliloquy would start in one location and then the actor would move in front of another curtain closer to the audience, and this scenario, in turn, would eventually be resolved on another section of the stage. Together with this editing was the corresponding optical montage. Meyerhold was forcing scenes to quickly flicker in front of the eyes of the spectators, cutting up the performance not just visually but also in terms of the rhythm and dialogue. The curtains were controlled like cinema frames. Meyerhold choreographed the actors' body movements with precision, heralding his theory of biomechanics, which he was to utilize in his Constructivist theatre productions in the early 1920s. Thus, with the staging of *Masquerade*, a theatrical antecedent of filmic montage was already unfolding in early 1917.

Like his student Radlov with his Popular Comedy Theatre, Meyerhold's emphasis on the circus and the music hall in order to create theatre for the populace was to have an immense bearing on Eisenstein in *Strike* and Yutkevich (and therefore Yutkevich's fellow FEKS [Factory of the Eccentric Actor] collaborators, Grigory Kozintsev and Leonid Trauberg).[14] Moreover, Kozintsev recalls that over and above Meyerhold, their 'dominant influence was Mayakovsky'.[15] The anti-art stance of FEKS is reflected in their manifesto 'Eccentrism' [Ekstsentrism] published in Petrograd in 1922. This document clearly demonstrates not only their passion for popular culture, in particular music hall revue, pantomime and the circus, but even more significantly, it contains a denunciation of traditional figurative painting. Yutkevich, Kozintsev and Trauberg urge artists to 'leave the picture frames and move towards . . . the object' . . . 'texture is a degree of tension in the treatment of the raw material'.[16] Importantly, these are Constructivist sentiments and an indication of the allegiance of FEKS to the avant-garde in art and film.

In a less spectacular fashion than FEKS, Shub was to make her own contribution to the world of the circus. Before she resigned from TEO to embark on her film career, Shub wrote a pantomime script for the leading actor-clown personalities of the Moscow State Circus. Reviewed by the theatre critic P. A. Markov, Shub noted modestly, 'it was well received. Markov commended the performance in the *Theatre Courier* [Vestnik teatra].'[17] As Shub recounts: 'the Moscow State Circus . . . contained famous dynasties of actors whose whole life was spent in close contact with the people. Socially relevant, acute and sometimes political scripts were heard from the circus stage, even in the blackest days of reaction.'[18] Shub was nominated to its board of directors: 'once a week I attended a meeting and an evening performance. . . . In this way, I supplied Meyerhold with precise knowledge about the working of Moscow's circuses.'[19]

The influence of the circus aside, Kozintsev, who, like Trauberg and Yutkevich, later became an established filmmaker, reflected that 'the Soviet cinema learned much more than the Soviet theatre, from the brilliant work of Meyerhold'.[20] Kozintsev was referring to the October Revolution and Meyerhold's corresponding *Theatrical October* [Teatralnyi Oktiabr]. Shub expands on this assertion: 'What was typical of *Theatrical October*? . . . Constructivism in the design of the "ground" (as they called the stage) and an enthusiasm for biomechanics. Also required from the actors, was an almost acrobatic mastery of movement. The theatre was expected to approach the dynamism of the circus with the showiness of the music hall.'[21]

Like his comrade Mayakovsky, Meyerhold was committed to the aims and principles of the Revolution. On 4 February 1918 (O.S.), *Pravda* described the demise of the 'aristocratisation of theatre' in favour of 'carrying it out into the street' with Meyerhold 'working with a feverish intensity' to make this a reality. Moreover, as *Pravda* added: 'he is turning his aspirations directly to the people, who can create their own original theatre.'[22] Thus began the collaboration between Meyerhold and Mayakovsky, with the latter bringing his drama *Mystery-Bouffe* for Meyerhold to direct. *Mystery-Bouffe*, with costumes by Malevich, was performed at the close of 1918 and again, in revised form, in 1921. Within the duality of *Mystery-Bouffe*, Mayakovsky wove the poetic with the primitive, the circus with class struggle and buffoonery with the medieval mystery play. The production portrayed the Old Testament and religion as opposing socialism.

It is fascinating to note that it was not just the hand of Meyerhold but also the powerful fist of Mayakovsky that was apparent in the evolution of Eisenstein's bold stamp on Soviet montage theory. Like Eisenstein's *Strike*, Mayakovsky's much earlier *Mystery-Bouffe* also revolved around the fairground, clowns and the clearly delineated caricatures of the capitalist bourgeoisie. Similarly, Mayakovsky portrayed the proletariat as a collective rather than as an individual: as the unified embodiment of a heroic working class. Mayakovsky's approach to characterization and theme is embodied in the basic structure of *Strike*.[23] Meyerhold and Mayakovsky's experimental theatre tied political agitation to art without pretension and elitism. Theirs was a type of propaganda art specifically created for the workers, and this was to be Shub's aim in her nonfiction films.

In her memoirs Shub discloses that she began to rigorously hone her montage craft with the laborious 'editing of two hundred fiction foreign films and dozens of Soviet ones . . . but I wanted my first independent work to be made from non-acted historical footage'.[24] Her painstaking work experience was invaluable. Added to this were the colourful, ebullient and dramatic transformations of Mayakovsky and Meyerhold, Kuleshov's theoretical and practical investigations (not in theatre but in film), which inspired, stimulated and opened new avenues of cinematic expression to Shub.

Lev Kuleshov as Founder of Montage Theory: His Influence on Shub and Her Comrades

Made when Kuleshov was only eighteen, *Engineer Prite's Project* [Proekt inzheniera Praita], which according to him was 'the first Russian film made according to the conception of montage', was completed in '1917 before the October Revolution'.[25] Through his film, Kuleshov introduced to Soviet film theory the notion of montage as the essential principle that underpinned cinematic structure. As he succinctly defined it: 'joining together the fragments that constitute the film is called montage'.[26] Obviously, for Kuleshov, Shub, Eisenstein and Vertov, montage was far more than merely the simplistic splicing together of two pieces of film.

Writing in 1917 Kuleshov believed, as did the Constructivists, that it was imperative that filmmakers were able 'to renounce the rules and conventions of easel and stage-set painting' and move forward, leaving behind the traditionally held canons of theatre and fine arts.[27] Even more central to the specificity of cinema was that, at its very core, 'everything is based on composition'.[28] He continued to develop his theory of the centrality of montage in *Cinema Gazette* [*Kinogazeta*] and, in March 1918, stated that 'montage is to cinema what colour is to painting' and that 'this method of expressing an artistic idea is provided by the rhythmical succession of individual still frames or short sequences conveying movement'.[29]

Yet, rather than Shub merely applying Kuleshov's written theoretical principles of montage construction, his influence on her was based instead on direct work experience. Early in her career, Shub would often travel to Kuleshov's studio to participate in his laboratory exercises where he would willingly spend time with her experimenting with the techniques of montage. Shub remembers how she would

> visit him in the evenings after our working day. I would often find him with his Kinap Projector, through which he would run small rolls of twenty-five, and sometimes fewer metres, experimenting, trying different montage possibilities, while I rearranged and changed this or that montage étude on the spot. This was a practical school of montage. Kuleshov had the ability to translate simultaneous events . . . to create an impression of unity of place with frames filmed in different places, to find montage connections. He had an amazing sense for the correct length of alternating frames, taking into account the movement within the frame as the basis for rhythm and pace.[30]

Remembering their obsessive devotion to their vocation, Shub emphasized that 'we were absorbed in only one thing – the desire to work in the cinema outside the traditions of the old cinematography, and to prove with our work that cinema was a new field of art'.[31] Referring explicitly to Kuleshov's delightful satire *The Extraordinary Adventures of Mr West in the Land of the Bolsheviks* [*Neobychainye prikliucheniya Mistera Vesta v strane bolshevikov*, 1924] and his undoubted masterpiece *By the Law* [*Po zakonu*, 1926], Shub confirmed that these two films 'were received as the beginning of a new development in cinematography'.[32] Significantly, Kuleshov's explorations in his earlier films would be expanded in Eisenstein's *Strike* several years later. However, this film was to become so heavily over-layered with Eisenstein's montage of attractions (with the addition of Shub's ideological montage), as well as a myriad of other cinematic and symbolic devices, that Kuleshov's more straightforward emphasis on montage was obscured.

In a crucial statement in 1922, Kuleshov declared: 'the method of transcending cinematic raw material, the essence of cinema, lies in composition, the change from one filmed fragment to another.'[33] In Kuleshov's terminology, the word 'composition' was synonymous with 'montage', and Shub's compilation genre was to become an illustration of this meaningful combination of fragments, which gave sense to the totality of the work. Kuleshov stressed the links in the chain of montage to the film's entirety: 'the way these fragments relate to one another . . . the juxtaposition and the interrelationships . . . the significance of each element in isolation and of the construction as a whole.'[34] He viewed this 'essence of cinema', namely montage, as an assemblage of cinematic segments that informed and transformed the raw material. In fact, *The Fall of the Romanov Dynasty* structurally exemplified Kuleshov's reflections on montage where Shub, as she phrased it, aspired 'to gather these facts and to organize from them pieces that are socially connected'.[35]

Moreover, Kuleshov compared the construction of montage to a child's set of jumbled alphabet blocks: squares that were rearranged so that nonsensical signs were then reconstructed to form words and thereby create meaning. By extension, in order to construct coherent visual sentences, 'the director must compose the separate filmed fragments, disordered and disjointed, into a single whole and juxtapose these separate moments into a more . . . integral and rhythmical sequence'.[36]

Although the famous 'Kuleshov effect' has been fully detailed and documented in a plethora of film texts, there is merit in acknowledging it because of its influence on Eisenstein, Vertov and Shub's film craft.[37] The 'Kuleshov effect' is used with particular power in the montage composition of *Strike*. While Eisenstein would later extend Kuleshov's montage theory using elements of collision and conflict to create new meaning, what is noteworthy is that the specific manipulation by Kuleshov of two consecutive unrelated frames had produced a startling new reading for his audience. Through this filmic syntax, Kuleshov constructed expressly staged camera shots in a particular sequence that suggested a connection. Through the clues given by the context, the audience would decode the cinematic communication by putting these blocks together to form an entirely fresh reading, thereby constructing a different narrative and eliciting an emotional response.

The 'Kuleshov effect' was an obvious catalyst for Shub, Eisenstein and Vertov. They were influenced by Kuleshov's exploration of the emotional and the atmospheric, working in amalgamation with his formulation of meaningfully compiled communicative visual phrases. Thus, while Kuleshov fully deserves the soubriquet 'founder' of Soviet montage, it was the work of Shub and her comrades that further developed his theories and their practical application.

In a reinforcement of Kuleshov's principles of montage, Eisenstein writing in 1924 stressed that the use of 'montage (in the technical, cinematic sense of the word) is fundamental to cinema, deeply grounded in the conventions of cinema and the corresponding characteristics of perception'.[38] Furthermore, just as Meyerhold's productions in the theatre had been a springboard for the younger artists, so too had Kuleshov's passion for and dedication to experimentation in film. It helped to propel and encourage the emerging filmmakers to take a step forward into the vibrant cinematic world of the avant-garde.

While Kuleshov used his innovative technique for fictionalized drama, Shub would effectively employ the same strategy for nonfiction film in *The Fall of the Romanov Dynasty*. Discussing the central role that Shub's ideological montage played in the success of *The Fall of the Romanov Dynasty*, Kuleshov declared that

> the main virtue of Shub's film is the highly technical quality of its montage . . . used not as an aesthetic device to transmit the subjective emotions of the editor, but as a means to express . . . the material, to bring out its thematic essence . . . it is only through montage and the skilful choice of material that *The Fall of the Romanov Dynasty* could have been made into such a significant film.[39]

Clearly, ideological montage was a serious business for Shub. According to her: 'montage tasks involved a focus on the facts, not only on showing the facts but also on making people examine them'.[40] In addition, Shub and her co-workers had to 'organize the material in categories of meaning, association and generalisation that convey to the viewer the relationship of the author with the given facts'.[41]

Esfir Shub: 'The Magician of the Editing Table' [Volshebnitsa montazhnogo stola][42]

In 1959 Sergei Yutkevich assessed Shub's notable role in promoting the primacy of montage in the 1920s as follows: 'This word [montage] during the early years of our cinematography was of almost magical importance. It was spoken as

Figure 1 Esfir Shub, a leading editor at the Third Film Factory. While Shub examines the film, seated in the foreground is her colleague 'the young montage worker Tatiana Kuvshinchikova'. *In Close-up*. Tatiana Kuvshinchikova is listed as an assistant director on Shub's *The Great Way*.

an incantation that could open the caves of cinema treasures. And the owner of these secrets was the magician of the editing table, Esfir Shub.'[43] Likewise, writing almost thirty years later than Yutkevich, the film scholar Vlada Petric asserted Shub's 'method of editing had a substantial influence on both Vertov and Eisenstein'[44] (Figure 1).

Shub's contribution to Soviet montage was not merely via her films and her published works on filmmaking but also through an influence not as easily quantified. Working for the collective good, Shub, in fact, encouraged, advised and taught montage to many young filmmakers. According to Yutkevich, 'the Vasilev brothers [they were not in fact brothers][45] considered themselves to be pupils of Esfir Shub. There was no young cinematographer during that period, who had not asked for her advice.'[46] Moreover, even with failing health, early in the year of her death, Shub was still in demand as an authority on cinema. This is clearly evidenced by a letter sent to her in 1959 by Medvedkin, who wanted her opinion on his latest endeavours: 'I always remember you as my well-wisher and friend and sincerely wish you a speedy recovery . . . I am working on a comedy script for Mosfilm and once it's written, it will be my pleasure to pass it on to you for a critique.'[47]

Pointing both to himself and to Eisenstein, Yutkevich acknowledged that 'Shub taught both of us editing.'[48] Furthermore, in Yutkevich's introduction to Shub's

My Life – Cinematography we are afforded an insight into a young filmmaker's initiation into the mysteries of montage. In 1927, Yutkevich was attempting to edit *Lace* [Kruzheva], his first film, in a poky room situated inside the First State Film Factory. Overawed by the notion of working in illustrious company, he was to exclaim that 'this is where Soviet cinema was born, on this very spot! Just here, in a small pavilion with a glass roof – *Strike, Battleship Potemkin* . . . were shot!'[49] Initially, Yutkevich struggled with the basic laws of montage: 'I rotate the winding wheel. I am confused.' Fortunately for him, in an adjoining room is Shub 'bending over the frosted glass of her editing table and examining pieces of film. . . . Like me, she is working late into the night . . . from her . . . I will study all the secrets of the mystical and powerful process that is called montage.' Yutkevich asks Shub: 'why should I place this shot here, but not there? How long a segment should I cut off . . . one or two metres and why as much as you advise? Divulge the secrets that you know so well.'[50] Shub responds: 'there are no secrets, nor are there any rules. One only needs to master the feeling of a piece – the sense of the parts within a whole.' The following day, when Yutkevich views his endeavours, he verifies that 'Shub was right. You can feel the internal rhythm of the scenes only when you analyze them not only as the author, but also as the first viewer. Only at this time is your attention sharp enough to discover the structure of the assembled piece.'[51]

Also, Shub the mentor was deeply touched when Eisenstein paid tribute to her, in front of all his students, by publicly acknowledging her crucial supporting role in his formative film years. In 'Sergei Mikhailovich Eisenstein' [Sergei Mikhailovich Eizenshtein], Shub recalls:

> Sergei Mikhailovich invited me to attend one of his lectures and, indicating the exact time for me to arrive, added sternly 'Don't be late!' Arriving at the agreed time, I was confused by the fact that the class had already been in progress for some ten minutes. I knew how Eisenstein disliked being interrupted. Nevertheless, I risked opening the door, going into the lecture theatre and . . . I occupied a seat next to the entrance. Suddenly, with a smile, he addressed his students: This is the film director Esfir Shub . . . stand up and welcome her! I received my first roll of film from her hands and she taught me my first lessons in montage.[52]

'The students rose to their feet and applauded me . . . I was flustered and happy. This was also the case of "the pupil surpassing the teacher." Sergei Mikhailovich had taught me so much, and my relationship with him had enriched me so.'[53]

In fact, even when they were both established filmmakers, Shub and Eisenstein continued to bolster each other through both thwarted dreams and triumphs.

When Eisenstein was appointed to head the Directors' Course at VGIK [All-Union State Institute of Cinematography] in September 1932, he invited Shub, whose star was also on the wane, to take the position as teacher and supervisor in montage studies. In addition, Shub also held workshops within Eisenstein's department from 1933 to 1935. This period coincided with her unsuccessful struggle to produce her film on the women of the Soviet Union. As Shub notes, at this time she not only 'served as a consultant for the graduates' director scripts' but 'was also a member of the government exam committee'.[54] She adds that she 'worked with Eisenstein harmoniously and happily because our points of view were often similar and he worked with me in a very trusting way. Our joint work enriched me.'[55] Shub and Eisenstein's relationship was built on reciprocity, and Shub was the professional colleague and trusted friend that Eisenstein consistently summoned to critique his works in progress. As she recalls,

> Sometimes Eisenstein would ring me and ask me to come to the editing room or to a viewing hall so that I could check a finished episode . . . He demanded a strict evaluation. He would screen the sequence over and over again and he would impatiently make me discuss everything – the factors that I thought indisputable and those, which were not clear to me, and that I needed to think through.[56]

As a consequence of her time at Goskino and then at Sovkino, which superseded it, Shub's growing familiarity with the techniques of montage had given her not only an advanced level of expertise but also a crucial foundation for her filmmaking career. Consequently, Shub became adept at montage through experiment and wide-ranging experience:

> Watching films in the viewing hall and then analysing them at the editing table, I gradually acquired the knowledge necessary for every director. I learnt to correctly judge the technical execution and composition of the shot. Slowly I developed the capacity for memorizing each frame, a sense of its inner content and movement, for its rhythm and pace. Then a moment always arrived when I began to feel sure at what point it was necessary and justified to cut from a wide to a medium shot, or from a medium shot to a close-up and vice-versa. Finally, I became aware of the magical power of the scissors . . . I began to strive for indiscernible transitions, for a fluid, dynamic change from one shot to another.[57]

While Shub learnt montage by trial and error, allied with technical skill, she recognized the unmistakable impact (on herself and the avant-garde) of Mayakovsky's poetic underlay within montage. This is made apparent in the chapter of her book, *In Close-up*, which she dedicated to him.[58] In confirmation of this, Petric assessed Mayakovsky as having also been an influential and prominent force in the work of both Eisenstein and Vertov.[59]

Eisenstein, for example, acknowledged that in Mayakovsky's poetry, he 'chops up the line in the way that an experienced montage editor would do it, arranging a typical scene of confrontation . . . first one and then the other. Then a clash between them.'[60] Shub divulges that it was not just Eisenstein and herself but also Vertov who 'was inspired by Mayakovsky' and was influenced by the structural design of his verse.[61]

Shub's avid interest in music and melodic form since childhood gave her insight into Vertov's creative framework (Figure 2).[62] She discloses that Vertov 'had musical talent, and was particularly interested in symphonic music: the powerful richly layered orchestral sound, the music, the rhythm and the tempo.'[63] This fascination with sound, this essential musicality, precisely identified by

Figure 2 Esfir Shub with the great composer Dmitry Shostakovich, 1948, *In Close-up*.

Shub, can be readily indicated within the cadences of Vertov's film segments and his use of montage. What Shub labels as the 'expressive content of the frame within the film's rhythm and pace' in Vertov's cinema can be traced back directly to Mayakovsky's poems with their atypical structure of strangely fragmented lines and phrases, and rhythmic sound patterns.

Additionally, in her essay 'My School of Cinematography' [Moya shkola kinematografy], Shub paid tribute to the substantial effect of Mayakovsky not only on the world of art in general but also on her nonfiction film in particular. To give a concrete example of this, Shub quotes the stanzas of his rousing verse *Kiev* on the power of the people, 'which reflects thoughts and feelings close to all of us at that time'.[64] In reality, Mayakovsky's poem mirrored Shub's compilation of sequences in her ideological compositions for *The Fall of the Romanov Dynasty*: through its montage of fragments, juxtaposition of politically charged shots and linguistic visual displays of textual splintering.

Nevertheless, while embarking on the initial stages of *The Fall of the Romanov Dynasty*, she was made the editor of Yury Tarich's historical fiction drama *Wings of a Serf* [Krylya kholopa, 1926], a film that was the antithesis of what was to become Shub's restrained genre of choice. *Wings of a Serf* premièred in November of that year and Viktor Shklovsky was one of the scriptwriters.[65] This fiction film was markedly different in style, content and intent from every cinematic work that Shub would then go on to direct.

Tarich's captivating film is sumptuous and painterly with its richly textured canvas and exquisite detail of tone, achromatic colour (seductive even in its subtle gradations of neutral blacks, greys and whites), harmony and contrast.[66] I concur with the historian and film scholar Denise Youngblood in her appraisal of the enchanting *Wings of a Serf* as not only a 'minor masterpiece',[67] but also as 'an extraordinary example of the historical genre . . . the best of its kind made in the silent period'.[68] Additionally, *Wings of a Serf* was more complex but just as spellbinding as the delightfully clichéd costume epics starring Douglas Fairbanks. Set during the reign of Ivan the Terrible [Ivan Grozny], it relates the sobering and cautionary tale of Nikita, a serf, who not only builds a flying machine but also learns to fly. The story of his subsequent fall from grace and his murder in one of the tsar's dungeons has obvious parallels with both the legend of Icarus and the darker side of the Soviet regime: Nikita flew too close to the sun both symbolically and literally.

There was an ingenious segment in *Wings of a Serf*. In his introduction to Shub's memoirs, Yutkevich was to describe an inserted visual motif of striking cinematography in Tarich's film. Here Yutkevich relates how Shub's ability as an editor was based on far more than just a reputation for technical excellence. Consequently, he cites a lesser-known facet of Shub's attributes: a quality of true originality and sophistication, which she revealed with such flair in *Wings of a Serf*. Recording his assessment of Tarich's production, Yutkevich emphasizes Shub's power to influence the very creative fabric and emotional texture of the film's reading through the nuances of composition, in her montage structure (Figure 3).[69]

Indeed, with reference to this specific factor, Shub expressed her abiding gratitude to Tarich: 'for believing in my capacity to contribute, for trusting me ... for permitting me, in essence to reformulate the montage of his film ... entrusting me with a director's function. This was the beginning of a very important stage for me.'[70] During the production of *Wings of a Serf*, Shub worked closely with Shklovsky 'on the direction of the story board to this or that episode of an upcoming shoot.'[71] Yet, it was Shub's inclusion of footage of a brooding Ivan the Terrible, played by the distinguished Moscow Art Theatre's Leonid Leonidov, that was memorable. He portrayed the contradictory character of Ivan, both as a ruthless Machiavellian schemer and as a pious upholder of the traditions of the church, with the utmost

Figure 3 The panoramic majesty of *Wings of a Serf*, 1926.

mastery. Leonidov's unforgettable performance was greatly enhanced by Shub's innovative use of montage. Shub's specific treatment of a series of abandoned shots of Leonidov, which she repeated and intercut dexterously at appropriate moments in the film, served to accentuate and personify the character of Ivan. In her memoirs, Shub recounts how she deliberately ignored the advice of Tarich. He had instructed her to disregard the rushes of Leonidov squinting into the camera, as worthless celluloid. Shub's incorporation of this rejected close-up footage became an arresting and evocative cinematic inlay subtly interspersed within the framework of the film. Shub documents the incident as follows:

> I remember how, while viewing all the shot frames of ... Leonidov ... I was strongly impressed by the expression in his eyes. Or rather, by the invariably menacing expression on his face – a slight squinting of one of his eyes at the moment when the filming started and the lighting equipment flared up. This was the initial 'working' frame sequence that was discarded during the montage process. I thought of inserting this facial expression ... to add meaning to various moments of the film. Leonidov's attitude to this idea remained to be seen ... thoroughly rehearsed before shootings, creatively demanding of himself ... he took an acute interest in the montage ... I was extremely pleased when he not only accepted, but also enthusiastically approved my use of these frames not visualised by the director. Indeed, the result was a complementary, very specific variation of the conceptualised image.[72]

Shub's editing of *Wings of a Serf* was praised by Yutkevich as she cut the whole work not only skilfully and with fluidity but also imaginatively. Other directors were impressed by Shub's ability, as exemplified by her part in the initial success of this mesmerizing film. Consequently, some of them, including Kuleshov, who was then shooting *By the Law*, invited her to be present on set as an unofficial advisor (a role which she often fulfilled for Eisenstein). In fact, Youngblood considers Shub as 'arguably the best editor of the 1920s'.[73] *The Fall of the Romanov Dynasty* aside, purely on the strength of Shub's contribution to the enthralling *Wings of a Serf*, Youngblood's pronouncement is easily substantiated.

Unfortunately, *Wings of a Serf* was to become problematical in the eyes of the authorities and therefore was to be attacked severely. Yet Shub made the decision to dedicate her career to an even more challenging genre.[74] Therefore, despite the obvious artistic exhilaration and freedom afforded to her in *Wings of a Serf*, Shub elected to embark on a far more restrictive cinematic path, with a complete change of focus. As she remarked in 'The Path toward Choosing a Profession' [Put k vyboru professy]:

> Nobody could persuade me to make a film with actors. I was interested in authentic people, with no acting involved. Noting their behaviour, selecting for filming those moments which captured their true characteristics – this was my joy if the filming was successful and my regret if the camera lens disrupted people's natural behaviour. These people's activity, their participation in social life, their work, spoke of the new era in the clearest way.[75]

Moreover, with the advantage of her long-standing familiarity with montage, Shub was able to pinpoint the critical disparity between what she deemed as the authenticity of non-acted nonfiction film and the artificiality of acted fiction film. In addition:

> One more thing became clear to me – the need for a specific, non-theatrical behaviour on the part of the cinema actor in front of the camera. The rules of facial expression and body language, the movement within the frame are different, and so are the behaviours in a given environment – with partners at work or play, or with things. Everything is different – the expressivity and the means of achieving effects. Montage remains the strongest tool for realising all that is woven into the filmed material.[76]

Therefore, with this aspect of fiction film and the power of montage at the forefront of her mind after working on *Wings of a Serf*, Shub's introduction of the Constructivist compilation genre through *The Fall of the Romanov Dynasty* necessitated a highly specific form of montage structure, one that would support the didacticism of socialist ideology. In an exegesis of the montage in Shub's final major film, *Spain* [Ispaniya, 1939], the film theorist Marcel Martin observes:

> What interests us here is not the usual narrative montage, a consequence and corollary of cutting, but expressive montage, above all ideological . . . It is natural that the country where the first theories of montage were formulated, accords a leading position to the compilation film as an ideological weapon . . . Montage rests fundamentally on the interaction of the images . . . ideological montage aims at a precise political and moral point in putting together images which have no strictly causal or temporal relationship.[77]

As Marcel Martin's assertion confirms, Shub's use of ideological montage is prevalent throughout her oeuvre. This is illustrated from the earliest years of her career through her contribution to Eisenstein's *Strike*, followed by her major body of work commencing with her compilation trilogy and ending with her film about the Spanish Civil War at the close of the 1930s. Setting aside her involvement in the making of *Strike*, Shub's participation in the production of

Wings of a Serf was not her only contribution to dramatized fiction film. In the same year as *Wings of a Serf*, Shub edited Oleg Frelikh's socially conscious drama *A Prostitute*. With a screenplay written by Shklovsky, according to the film scholar David Gillespie, *A Prostitute* 'demonstrates the link between social deprivation and prostitution'.[78] That year Shub began constructing her first nonfiction film and, from henceforth, devoted herself to the discipline of documentary. Unlike Vertov, she was not tempted to veer from that rigid path.

In direct contrast, through the lens of Mikhail Kaufman (Vertov's cameraman and brother), Vertov aimed to create a world 'showing everyday life' with Rodchenko's eye-catching photography influencing the startlingly bold high- and low-angled shots that were to become a feature of Kaufman's style.[79] Much of Vertov's work was indisputably expressive. As a consequence, by the very nature of his work, unlike Shub, and for all his loud proclamations, Vertov was unable to adhere to the principles of the non-acted documenting integral to nonfiction film.[80]

However, despite this, Shub was in agreement with Vertov's belief that

> it was not enough to use montage to connect separate moments and episodes into one film, uniting them under a more or less successful heading. It was necessary, by taking unexpected events and occurrences and juxtaposing them, to find the organic relationship between them, to reveal their true essence.[81]

Vertov's pronouncement, this revelation of truth through montage, was precisely what Shub sought to accomplish in *The Fall of the Romanov Dynasty*. By means of her dynamic insertion of ideological montage, through the juxtaposition of dissimilar and often contradictory images, Shub promoted the socialist themes of her film. Interestingly, Vertov's idea that the effect of montage is 'to reveal [its] true essence' also uncovers a conceptual bond between Shub and the prominent Berlin Dadaist Hannah Höch through their use of montage and photomontage, respectively.[82]

The parallel between the photomontage of Höch and the nonfiction films of Shub that I am suggesting here is a significant one. In *cut with the kitchen knife: the weimar photomontages of hannah höch*, cultural historian Maud Lavin discusses the symbiotic relationship between the vanguard in the arts and popular culture during the period of the Weimar Republic. She indicates that for Höch 'the mass media served not only as an archive and resource fuelling her avant-garde production, but the *Workers' Illustrated Newspaper* [the Illustrierte] also offered her a panoply of images'.[83] Similarly, several years later Shub was engaged in the compilation of archival newsreel images, which were then collated to be used in the construction of her ideological narratives. Together Shub and Höch utilized and manipulated snapshots of society, both contemporary and archival, through their application of film and photography respectively. As this book argues, for Shub this was a realization of her Constructivist philosophy. Similarly, Höch and the Dadaists (in particular Hausmann, Heartfield and Schwitters) embraced the homage to modernity and 'art into life' philosophy inherent in Russian Constructivism.

Shub and Höch's other common bond was their specific investigations into montage in the visual media, through celluloid (Shub) and through paper (Höch). However, Shub and Höch diverge in the intent behind their work. Through the application of photomontage Höch created stylish and political images. Her cleverly juxtaposed pictorial reproductions raise questions not only about the role and identity of women in the Weimar Republic but also about the dynamics of female sexuality, in their exploration of pleasure, desire and violence. While the work of Höch centres on the problematic nature of the representation of the female self, showcasing the New Woman, Shub's films paint a broader political canvas no less revolutionary but with a differing emphasis. Shub's context is historical, ideological and political whereas Höch's is feminist and centres on sexual politics. Significantly, even here, there is an implied intersection underpinning this. In constructing images for the Soviet Union and the Weimar Republic respectively, Shub's films and Höch's artworks on paper share a significant subtext. Both these women possessed an unwavering conviction in the possibility of transforming the future through their societal documentation of the past and present: an archetypal utopian vision.

It is noteworthy that the revolutionary idealism and the concept of photomontage that defines Höch's art (and also that of Schwitters, Heartfield and Hausmann) are rooted in the innovations produced by the Russian art movements during the late tsarist epoch in the first decade of the twentieth century. In fact, Höch and her compatriots were specifically inspired by the early paintings of Malevich, together with the Russian futurist notion of 'displacement' and the formalist 'defamiliarization' in the years before the Revolution. Such influences are evident in the work of these Weimar artists. Similarly, it was from the birth of these Russian visual and literary elements of contraposition and conflict that the montage theory of firstly Kuleshov and later Eisenstein emerged. These essential principles were also carried forward in the theoretically informed practice of both Shub and Vertov.

Shub's montage was overtly ideological. Additionally, unlike Höch and Rodchenko, whose photomontage was defined by deliberately cut-out and collaged construction, Shub's conflicting images were assembled seamlessly. In this sense, the technique of another woman, the photographer, social documentarian and political activist Tina Modotti, possesses a marked correlation to Shub's approach. Modotti produced a work of photomontage in which the joining of her two images is imperceptible. Indeed, her motivation (both artistically and politically) is uncannily similar to Shub's. This can be observed, for example, in her photomontage *Elegance and Poverty* [1928], which provides a disconcerting and bleak statement about the inequalities in society (Figure 4).

Like both Kuleshov and Shub before her, in *Elegance and Poverty* Modotti brought together two distinctly unrelated shots in order to offer an entirely new reading. Thematically it is an image that, if adjusted visually to fit Shub's earlier era, would not have looked out of place in *The Fall of the Romanov Dynasty*. Just as *The Fall of the Romanov Dynasty* concerns the injustices and repression leading

Figure 4 Tina Modotti, (1896–1942): *Elegance and Poverty*, 1928. Gelatin silver print, printed 1976 by Richard Benson, 9 15/16 x 6 1/2"(25.2 x 16.5 cm). Courtesy of Isabel Carbajal Bolandi (SC1976.280). New York, Museum of Modern Art (MoMA). © 2020. Digital Image, The Museum of Modern Art, New York/Scala, Florence.

to the February Revolution of 1917, so Modotti's photomontage is infused with the same form of social commentary. *Elegance and Poverty*'s juxtaposition of two disparate visual elements to produce new meaning is reminiscent of Shub's earlier and more prolonged montage sequences in *The Fall of the Romanov Dynasty*. The name of Modotti's piece, like Shub's intertitles, leaves the viewer in no doubt of the intended message. Both Shub's and Modotti's didactic engagement with ideology and politics remained at the forefront of their art.

This philosophy is also dominant in Eisenstein's first major work, *Strike*, and before Shub commenced her compilation trilogy, she had worked closely with him on this film. Shub had first met Eisenstein in 1922 and their professional paths intersected when he came to TEO. He decided to leave his experiments on the stage for more theatricality within the versatility of the cinema. Just as Shub analysed the work of Vertov and her professional relationship with him, so too did she not only explore and interpret the oeuvre of Eisenstein but also reveal details of their enduring friendship. Shub's succinct appraisal of Eisenstein as a filmmaker was that:

> Sergei Mikhailovich ... an outstanding artist ... was a great worker with a fiery imagination: a discoverer and a researcher, with the ability to contrast events synthetically and analytically and then to summarise them. This ability of his made others think of him as a cold, intellectual. ... But, to me, he was always an artist with an enormous burning incandescence. I was not the only one who thought so.[84]

These key elements of Eisenstein's talents and passion, outlined by Shub, would help him formulate his investigations and initial theories on montage, which were evident in the composition of *Strike*.

New Formations: Rebellion, Soviet Montage and Shub's Contribution to Eisenstein's *Strike*

The freshness and experimental approach to socialist drama first came to cinematic fruition in Eisenstein's *Strike*. The specificity of Russian montage is reflected in this revolutionary work, which not only heralded the beginning of new forms in Soviet film but also embodied a nascent avant-garde cinema. As such, it is a prime example of early montage investigations into fiction film. This most overtly political and ideological of socialist filmic narratives is also important contextually because of Shub's collaboration with Eisenstein both at the initial scriptwriting stage and during the later montage process. In addition, Shub added her signature not only to the script and the ideological montage but also to two major thematic and visual symbols of the film, namely the wheel and the grid, which bear the hallmarks of Shub's Constructivist influence.

Strike, a fictional, historical re-enactment, was moulded from the pages of Bolshevism's rise. Besides being an impressive mélange of the experimental, both in terms of content and form, the film introduces us to a world transported from the theatre of Meyerhold. Indeed, *Strike* abounds with both Radlov's and FEKS' clowning antics, fights, hot pursuits and bloodthirsty *Grand Guignol* influences. Underpinning this roller coaster of gasps, laughter and pantomime is a serious tale of class struggle.

Both structurally and thematically it forged new paths. With overt didacticism, *Strike* is almost a call to arms. It serves also as an epitaph for all those in the proletariat who sacrificed their lives for the socialist cause before the Revolution. We are not told when and where this particular strike occurred, but it serves as a symbolic representation of all historical conflict brought about by social divisions.

In other words, *Strike* is a tribute to the awakening of class-consciousness amongst the ill-educated, downtrodden masses. This involves the wrestling of the ownership of the means of production from the hands of the privileged few into the communal control of the proletariat (which is still in a nascent stage). As a result, the ruling class is seen in the film as savagely aborting the workers' bid for power. Consequently, the audience of *Strike* is simultaneously stirred by the struggle for liberation and shaken by the rapid cutting of climactic and shocking effects. As *metteur en scène*, Eisenstein was setting the visual changes in pace and mood with a dizzying speed. Through their montage technique, he and Shub, working in conjunction with each other, skilfully coloured the political, ideological and emotional agitation represented on screen. *Strike* is permeated with ideological slogans that are woven into the very fabric of the plot. This format will set the tone for *The Fall of the Romanov Dynasty*.

At this juncture it should be noted that when Eisenstein started to work on *Strike*, his first feature film, he had almost no knowledge of the techniques of cinema (apart from *Glumov's Diary*, a film insert of several minutes in duration).[85] Shub, on the contrary, was by then regarded as an experienced editor and had already fulfilled an important function as Eisenstein's tutor in this field.

Therefore, it is understandable that he asked Shub to be his technical advisor and collaborator when he embarked on his preparations for *Strike*.

Indeed, in his book of essays, *Film Form*, Eisenstein himself readily acknowledged Shub's pioneering role as one of the first great 'master [sic] film editors'.[86] Also, Yutkevich stated that 'Sergei Eisenstein, who in the beginning of the 1920s' was only just becoming acquainted with the new art, spent day and night with Shub in her editing room'.[87] In 1924, Shub worked side by side with Eisenstein, producing the shooting script for *Strike*. As she recalls, 'We worked on *Strike* in my house for at least two uninterrupted months'.[88]

However, as a result of political wrangling with the 'Proletarian Culture Organization' [Proletkult], who were the producers of *Strike*, Shub's crucial collaboration in the formation of the script with Eisenstein and her subsequent role as co-editor with him was omitted from the credits.[89] Instead, Valerian Pletnev, the national president of Proletkult, who had neither general expertise in filmmaking nor any technical knowledge of film editing, was boldly acknowledged as the film's editor; his name appearing above that of Eisenstein in the opening credits. Pletnev's problematical control was to lead to an acrimonious split between Eisenstein and the organization.

Prior to the making of *Strike*, Shub had reconstructed Fritz Lang's thriller *Dr. Mabuse* in order to render it ideologically sound for Soviet audiences. It was then renamed *Gilded Decay* [Pozolochennaya gnit]. According to Yutkevich, 'Shub . . . had to re-edit the film and Eisenstein appointed himself her voluntary assistant in order to be able to study the construction of Fritz Lang's montage.'[90] Additionally, as R. C. Williams asserts, 'after Eisenstein watched Shub re-edit *Dr. Mabuse*, within a few months Eisenstein and Shub went on to create a film of their own, *Strike* for Proletkult . . . Shub did most of the editing at her home during the autumn of 1924 while Eisenstein directed the shooting.'[91]

Although Williams notes that Shub co-edited *Strike*, he neglects to mention that she also devised the script with Eisenstein. Additionally, he makes no reference to the influence of ideological montage and Constructivist philosophy, as principal theoretical and aesthetic foundations of *Strike*. Shub's demonstration of her editing skills to the inexperienced Eisenstein is further substantiated in a footnote in *Film Form*, where its translator into English, Jay Leyda, states that 'the first time Eisenstein ever joined together two pieces of "real film" was while assisting Esther [sic] Shub in the re-editing of Lang's *Dr. Mabuse*'.[92] Shortly after the completion of this expurgated version of *Dr. Mabuse* for Soviet audiences, Eisenstein and Shub began their preliminary work on *Strike*.

Despite Shub's contribution to *Strike*, she and Eisenstein were to choose radically different directions in film. Nonetheless, Eisenstein always remained not only an intimate friend but also a steadfast supporter of her work.[93] According to Shub, by the time she had worked with him on *Strike*, they 'were already good friends. Our shared views on cinematography brought us even closer.'[94]

Towards the end of Shub's career, in an essay of 1937 Eisenstein praised the ideological montage in her 'remarkable films'.[95] In this paper he discussed the fragmentation, juxtaposition and amalgamation characteristic of montage construction found in the poetry of both Stéphane Mallarmé and Mayakovsky.[96] Significantly, Eisenstein also referred to the poetic methodology of the cento (derived from the Latin *centó* meaning 'patchwork'), which he linked to Shub's montage technique. He elaborates:

> the so-called 'cento', is even closer to montage. Its basis is an interesting method of assembling and juxtaposing literary fragments from various sources with the aim of lending a new meaning to the resultant compilation. The remarkable films made by Esfir Shub are essentially 'cine-centos'; in her work, the use of this aspect of the potentialities of montage is displayed in its purest form. Sequences from newsreels shot in the context of *one* set of events – indeed, within one ideological system – are totally transformed, in both senses of the word, by new juxtapositions and combinations with other fragments of *other* events and stories. (Particularly striking is her use of tsarist newsreels in *The Fall of the Romanov Dynasty*).[97]

Here Eisenstein is reinforcing the comments of both Mayakovsky and Kuleshov about *The Fall of the Romanov Dynasty*, in the sense that Shub's montage craft involves the transformation of unconnected raw newsreel scraps, which are sewn together impressively into an ideological quilt. Apart from the shooting script, Shub's hands-on contribution to *Strike* was her methodology, used in the editing phase, of stitching together the pieces of narrative fabric in order to form a meaningful sociopolitical statement.

In contrast to Shub's commitment to the principles of Constructivism, when she commenced her compilation trilogy, Eisenstein clearly stood at the opposite end of the filmic divide. He was the epitome of the Renaissance man, far removed from Shub's no-frills documentation of reality and politicizing of art. Indeed, when writing about his apprenticeship in cinema, in *Notes of a Film Director*, over twenty years later, Eisenstein bemoaned the fact that 'All around was the insistent demand to destroy art, substitute materials and documents for

Figure 5 The influence of Esfir Shub on *Strike*: the grid and the factory: the Constructivist beauty of utilitarian forms. Film reflects both art and life in the work of, on the left, Liubov Popova, *Spatial-Force Construction*, 1921, Oil and wood dust on plywood, 71 × 63.9 cm., MOMus - Museum of Modern Art - Costakis Collection, Thessaloniki and a still from the film *Strike*, 1925 on the right.

the chief element of art – the image [and to] put Constructivism in the place of organic unity, replace art itself with practical and real reconstruction of life'.[98] Eisenstein was never a member of the Constructivist movement, whose utilitarian philosophy was the antithesis of all that he stood for in art (Figure 5).

Nonetheless, for all its spectacular and stellar forays into new and revolutionary paths of cinematic exploration, *Strike* was not an astounding success at the box office. This was a film that would only strike a chord with highly educated spectators, who were willing to read and process more complex cinematic codes and messages. Although Eisenstein's film was an ode to the working class and dedicated to their struggle, the working-class viewers themselves were singularly unimpressed. Denise Youngblood uncovered a 'report of audience response to *Strike*' from which she translated the observations of an S. Dashkevich, who detected that 'when shown in Red Army clubs at the time, it held attention for a mere twenty-five minutes before restlessness and chattering began'.[99]

Unfortunately, for the majority of Soviet citizens, the structural, theoretical and thematic concerns addressed through the montage of films such as *Strike* and *The Fall of the Romanov Dynasty* were completely indecipherable. In a purportedly classless socialist society, only an avant-garde audience could appreciate such works. As the film scholar Richard Taylor discovered, experimental montage and the problems of its reception were being articulated in *New Spectator* [Novyi zritel] as late as 1927: 'The perception of montage raises a very serious question: the rural audience cannot grasp alternating parallel montage. Thus the movement is perceived but the essence of the action is lost; often rapid movement provokes laughter. Films for the countryside require re-editing and adaptation to the perception of the peasant.'[100]

This issue was to lead to bitter disputes that raged between the vanguard adherents of a vanishing revolutionary montage and those in the film industry who supported intelligibility through fictitious drama or comedy narratives. In the early 1930s the advent of sound and the approach of Socialist Realism hastened the inevitable outcome. As a film director, Shub was faithful to her commitment to both ideological montage and Constructivist nonfiction film, despite the possible professional consequences of this stance.

In retrospect, pondering on her non-inclusion on the final film credits of *Strike*, Shub was to conclude: 'I was saddened . . . Now I think that this might have been a good thing. What interested me most of all in art was everything connected with our reality, everything that reflected and supported it. I was seeking my own way.'[101] This attitude by Shub epitomized her outlook on Soviet film. The fact that her substantial involvement in the making of *Strike* was not acknowledged and added to this that she was never to work on another of Eisenstein's projects was deeply regrettable. In spite of this, she was not deterred from her overriding purpose: documenting Soviet society. Consequently, Shub's then unique cinematic practice, that is, her ideologically based Constructivist compilation nonfiction film, was to become firmly established. Filtering into mainstream cinema, a variant of this specific format of the compilation was later to become the norm in documentary film throughout the world.

In 'The Art of Montage: Soviet Style' it has been maintained that the inspiration given by avant-garde artists (such as Malevich, Meyerhold, Mayakovsky and Kuleshov) in the first two decades of the twentieth century to the early Soviet filmmakers such as Shub (Eisenstein and Vertov) was instrumental in forging the period's unique experimentation into montage. Specifically, it has been contended that Shub's involvement in its development, from the initial scriptwriting stage to the final editing process, helped towards making *Strike* an important and committed agitational document. In addition, Shub was the most sought-after editor of her era. The stimulation that she gained through her collaboration with Eisenstein in *Strike*, a defining example of montage in early Soviet film, was beneficial in crystallizing her chosen path and indeed her faithful promotion of non-acted film. Accordingly, ideological montage was the pivot upon which Shub's Constructivist nonfiction film would revolve. This factor was most evident in her compilation trilogy, particularly *The Fall of the Romanov Dynasty*, a paradigm for both nonfiction film and Constructivism.

2

Esfir Shub and the Constructivist Avant-Garde

This chapter defines Constructivism as the aesthetic and ideological force from which the nonfiction films of Shub emerged. It will address her dedication to the methodology of Constructivist art underpinning her oeuvre. As Shub and her Constructivist works should not be viewed in isolation, it is important to situate her within the context of the artistic avant-garde and the iconoclastic platform that Constructivism was based upon. Thus, I will claim that Constructivism was the foundation upon which Shub as a cinematic practitioner shaped her documentaries, as she forged utilitarian productions for the film factory.

The Fall of the Romanov Dynasty, her resultant groundbreaking compilation film, can be seen as an illustrious milestone signposting the way to the modern documentary. Hence, there will be an analysis of a segment of *The Fall of the Romanov Dynasty* epitomizing the theory of Constructivism and its practical applications.

Shub and the Roots of Constructivism

As Constructivism was the foundation for Shub's film practice, it is necessary at this juncture to trace the origins of this movement by outlining the germination of ideas that influenced Constructivist theories both before and directly after the October Revolution. The avant-garde of the early twentieth century, of which Shub was to become an active member, was born of the political turbulence and uncertainty of the second half of the nineteenth century and consequently shared much of its reforming zeal.

Although they comprised of only a small band of creative individuals, nonetheless the Peredvizhniki [the Wanderers], a group of figurative painters, had energized society with their critical stance while focusing on the cultural transformation of feudal Russia. A breakaway movement of fourteen artists, from the staid confines of the Imperial Academy of Fine Arts in St. Petersburg, they took art to the people for the first time in Russian art history.[1] Yet although stylistically the Peredvizhniki cannot be read as avant-garde, they nonetheless risked their careers in order to facilitate change in the 1860s. They were rebelling against the rigid academicism and privilege attached to the Imperial Academy of Fine Arts, a bastion of conservatism. Ironically, although the Peredvizhniki had once shocked society by their rebellion, at the time of Shub's studies at Women's Institute of Higher Learning during the second decade of the twentieth century, they were being emulated as the standard in art.

Significantly, 1863 had seen both the publication of Nikolai Chernyshevsky's groundbreaking political novel *What Is To Be Done?* [Chto delat?] and the revolt of the Peredvizhniki. *What Is To Be Done* was to have a major impact on the political thought of the intelligentsia of the day, also becoming a catalyst for early feminism. It was in fact read avidly by Shub fifty years later.[2] The Peredvizhniki, like most idealists of their era, had been influenced by Chernyshevsky's novel, and in serving art and society, they organized travelling exhibitions that wandered through the Russian countryside. Chernyshevsky and the Peredvizhniki promoted the notion that art should be in communion with the everyday world and everyday people. Shub embraced this in the century that followed, as she aimed to make her films accessible to Soviet society in both urban and rural areas.

In addition, the Constructivist movement in the 1920s would underscore this motif of art as a part of life. However, for Shub and the Constructivists their *raison d'être* was more than just an expression of art. They aimed to provide art with a social and political function. In a unification of art and life, Constructivism was to meld with socialism. Nevertheless, just like Shub, Vertov, Mayakovsky and Meyerhold in the twentieth century, the Peredvizhniki wanted to rid art of elitism by making it easily available (and comprehensible) to the masses. Reinforcing and shaping these attitudes, Chernyshevsky's writings not only inspired the intellectuals of his day but they also served this new eagerness, initially by a handful of artists, towards a conscious awareness of the needs of society. In his 1855 essay *The Aesthetic Relations of Art and Reality*, Chernyshevsky had boldly proclaimed: 'Art does not limit itself only to the beautiful. . . . It embraces the whole of reality . . . the content of Art is life in its social aspect.'[3] This statement would be refashioned and magnified in the creed of Shub and the Constructivist movement as a whole.

The ideals of the Peredvizhniki were accentuated and carried forth in the revival of Russian folk arts and crafts in the artists' colonies at Abramtsevo and

Talashkino founded in the 1870s and 1890s respectively. For both artisans and artists alike, these two communes were to sow the seeds for a revolution in the arts in Russia that flowered in the early twentieth century (prior to the Bolshevik Revolution of 1917). These hives of industry aimed for the resuscitation and preservation of the rich traditions of ceramics, embroidery, woodcarving, furniture making and architecture.[4] Their emphasis was on the utilitarian aspect of art. Furniture making and embroidery stitching rather than easel painting, earthy majolica-ware rather than Sèvres, theatre design in place of a portrait in a gilt frame were to be extended and radicalized by the Constructivists in the early 1920s. Unlike the work of the Constructivists, however, these functional objects were often exquisitely decorated: adornment was part of their craft. Moreover, the unswerving belief of the communities at Abramtsevo and Talashkino was that art should be couched in terms of social purpose for the betterment of society. Modernization and industrialization had driven peasants into the city, and, inevitably, the subsequent rejection of their mores also hastened the loss of folk art due to this machine age of mass production.

In order to counteract this, the wealthy and influential patron Savva Mamontov, inspired by the Arts and Crafts philosophy of the English socialist, conservationist and designer William Morris, had not only established the colony at Abramtsevo in order to reawaken these traditions but had also built a school and a hospital for his community. In fact, as Mamontov expressed it: 'I deeply believe that art will play an enormous role in re-educating the Russian people.'[5] This was also the philosophy that would be furthered by Shub and the Constructivists after the October Revolution.

Importantly, a fusion of ideas pertaining to art and life percolated through from the Peredvizhniki, Abramtsevo and Talashkino to the avant-garde artist Mikhail Larionov and the writer Ilya Zdanevich. In 1913 they collaborated on 'Why We Paint Ourselves: A Futurist Manifesto'.[6] Here, in this cementing of the avant-garde in the arts they were to propound:

> We have joined art to life . . . life has invaded art, it is time for art to invade life . . . we do not aspire to a single form of aesthetics. Art is not only a monarch but also a newsman and a decorator. We value both print and news. The synthesis of decoration and illustration is the basis of our self-painting. We decorate life and preach.[7]

The idea of art being 'a newsman and a decorator' (the emphasis on popular culture rather than high art) was added fodder for the Constructivists and the concept of art as utilitarian design. Vladimir Tatlin was then to develop this notion and is credited with inventing the motto of the Constructivists: 'art into life'.[8]

Significantly, one essential source of Constructivist influence in Shub's formative period was her close alliance with that conspicuous troika within Constructivism: Aleksei Gan, Alexander Rodchenko and Varvara Stepanova.[9] Admittedly, there were four other participants in the inaugural Working Group of Constructivists: Konstantin Medunetsky, Karl Ioganson and the Stenberg brothers (Vladimir and Georgy). Despite Maria Gough's foregrounding of Ioganson, the trio of Gan, Rodchenko and Stepanova still remain the most prominent and publicized figures in the Constructivist movement.[10] The latter three were all intimately connected with Shub and are seen with her in Rodchenko's charming and evocative photograph, which he labelled *The Constructivist Party* (Figure 6).

Shub quoted Anatoly Lunacharsky, who 'believed and repeatedly stated that the proletariat would develop their own intelligentsia in the arts, which together with the workers of the old pre-Revolutionary theatre, would build the new'.[11] Shub was to recall that in these early days: 'the new spectator, truly of the people . . . enthusiastically embraced the culture of the theatre.'[12] 'Theatres were subsidised by the government. At first they were free of charge' and complimentary theatre passes authorized by Shub 'were distributed among Moscow plants, factories and institutions.'[13]

Importantly, aside from Gan, Rodchenko and Stepanova, the other central foundation for Shub's Constructivist inspiration can be ascribed to her working relationship with Vsevolod Meyerhold. This revolutionary director was the instigator of 'Theatrical October'. Just as Shub would later perceive her Constructivist documentaries, 'Theatrical October' was seen as a form of creative provocation and political education after the Revolution. This was a role to be assumed increasingly by the cinema, initially with the commissioning of agit-films (agitational films). In this respect, Shub clarifies Meyerhold's policy of 'Theatrical October': it 'set a truly Marxist approach to art . . . completely rejected traditionalism, pre-revolutionary theatre and art, and anything unable to reflect the new revolutionary epoch'.[14] Similarly for Meyerhold's collaborator Mayakovsky, who fully embraced and breathed the aims and principles of the Revolution, only rebellion against all art forms would be acceptable. Thus, Mayakovsky proclaimed: 'we do not need a dead mausoleum of art where dead works are worshipped but a living factory of the

Figure 6 Alexander Rodchenko: *The Constructivist Party*, 1926. Shub is placed second from the right and is seated next to her friend, the Constructivist artist Varvara Stepanova (who is closest to the camera). On the left, the Constructivist Aleksei Gan is almost obscured by the photographer Alexander Rodchenko, who appears in the left foreground. In the centre is Yevgeniya Sokolova-Zhemchuzhnaya, who modelled Stepanova's Constructivist sports clothing and, at that time, was the partner of the Constructivist theatre director and critic Vitaly Zhemchuzhnyi. Sitting between Zhemchuzhnaya and Shub is Rodchenko's mother Olga, the subject of one of his most delightful portraits, *Mother Reading* 1924. Courtesy of A. Rodchenko and V. Stepanova Archive, Moscow.

human spirit – in the streets, in the tramways, in the factories, workshops and workers' homes.'[15]

Indeed, the theory of 'Theatrical October' was strongly related also to the avant-garde in art and film. Essentially, the vanguard declared war against the culture of the past and was led by the left: the radical, the revolutionary in all spheres of art. This was epitomized by LEF, spearheaded by Mayakovsky, and enthusiastically supported by Shub and other members of the avant-garde.[16] Mayakovsky's faction, with their publication *LEF*, was the mouthpiece for the Constructivists. As Mayakovsky was to explain: 'LEF does not caress the ear or the eye and substitutes the art of representing life with the work of constructing life.'[17] Furthermore, Mayakovsky's dominance over these artists was considerable. As Shub evaluated it in 1922, at the beginning of her career in the film factory: 'during this period, people from LEF attracted my attention. I believed that only such a direction in art could express the revolutionary enthusiasm of those years . . . Mayakovsky was the bearer of the banner of this movement.'[18]

As if to confirm Shub's judgement, late in that year, Mayakovsky visited Paris where he met with the intelligentsia and leading French artists of that era.[19] Indeed, he announced proudly:

> For the first time, not from France but from Russia, a new word in art has come: Constructivism. . . . Not the kind of Constructivism that constructs unnecessary little instruments out of good and necessary wires and sheet metal. But the Constructivism which conceives of the artist's formal work as engineering only, essential for the shaping of our practical lives.[20]

Mayakovsky's allusion to 'unnecessary little instruments out of good and necessary wires and sheet metal' was a barbed reference to the Constructivist artist, designer and maker of models Vladimir Tatlin. For Mayakovsky as for Shub, Constructivism was focused on the purity of the unadorned and functional object, the construction of art into everyday life. In Shub's case this was exemplified by her dedication to nonfiction film and to the ideals of the new socialist state. Therefore, in her own words: 'it is imperative that the author of non-acted cinema can rise to the level of cultural tasks proposed by the Revolution.'[21]

In the same year as Mayakovsky's journey to Paris there were others similarly dedicated to supporting an 'actorless' reality, utterly opposed to the use of thespians and staged cinema. The vociferous Aleksei Gan edited the nonfiction film mouthpiece, the journal *Cinema-Photo* [Kino-fot]. Its first issue was issued in late August 1922. A few weeks earlier there had been an article published in *Hermitage* [Ermitazh] written by Lev Kuleshov, who was to become a renowned theorist and filmmaker, on the 'reality' of cinema. Like Shub, Mayakovsky and Gan, Kuleshov rejected the theatricality of the stage, the artificiality of theatre and painting, in favour of the reality of the cinema. In his essay of August 1922, 'Cinema as the Fixing of Theatrical Action' [Kinematograf kak fiksatsiya teatralnogo deistviya], Kuleshov argued for the solidity and integrity of real objects as opposed to the artifice of painted props and canvas. He viewed the latter as mere symbols, poor substitutes for the authentic vision, the real thing. Kuleshov compared 'real objects' on a film set with the artifice of replicated objects placed in a scene's backdrop having been painted in a photo-realistic manner. Similarly, he broached the subject of the validity of filming documentary as opposed to clichéd and false drama: 'Experiments in filming artificial and real objects . . . "real" people and *actors*, always produce the same result: artificial people (actors) *do not come out well*.'[22] Shub was to put these elements into practice in *The Fall of the Romanov Dynasty*.

In addition Aleksei Gan wrote 'The Cinematograph and Cinema' [Kinematograf i kinematografiya], which appeared in the August edition of *Cinema-Photo* in 1922. It encapsulated the basic doctrine of members of the avant-garde. He viewed filmmaking 'as the product of industrial culture . . . a technological phenomenon'.[23] Gan equated the cinématographe (the privately owned cinema theatre) with all that was bourgeois, tsarist and subsequently allied with 'the capitalist system of exploitation'.[24] Cinema as a productive and mechanized form of proletarian labour, on the other hand, was a product of Bolshevik culture and was therefore indubitably the way forward: 'the path for tomorrow'.[25]

This of course was to be Shub's path. In 'And Again – the Newsreel' [I opiat – khronika] 1929, she asserted that 'my goal was to select material that I could recycle and make meaningful'.[26] Referring to the films in her trilogy, Shub claimed eagerly that 'they have enormous value not only as historical cinematic documents, but also as a wonderful visual history of the newsreel'.[27]

The Fall of the Romanov Dynasty fulfilled the primary function of Constructivism: the construction of material, in this case newsreel, to form a utilitarian art product. This principal documentary compilation was a readily accessible mass-produced record of tsarist and Soviet rule. Moreover, in her 1928 essay 'First Work' [Pervaya rabota] Shub's belief was 'that if the attempt to make a historical film on the basis of authentic material succeeded, this would be the most convincing agitation in favour of nonfiction film, in favour of the need to keep, organize and study the collected material'.[28] For her 'such a film must convince those who doubt, and those who bow before fiction film, that newsreels are not just material for gluing together "cinema journals" but material from which it is possible to create works of great thematic development'.[29]

To further reinforce the value of nonfiction film and its sources, Shub considered the worth of news footage and its fledgling form after the Revolution with optimism: 'What was best at expressing our era in art form? . . . Newsreel was the answer . . . It focused on a whole series of historical events of universal importance honestly and truthfully . . . in an unassuming way. October, the Civil

War, the reconstruction of the people's economy, the social and political life of the Soviet Union.'[30]

Shub, in her naive claims for nonfiction film, seemed oblivious to the fact that her genre (unlike the vastly more popular dramatized fiction film) had a limited audience. Evidently, as did many others, Lenin had no illusions about what he firmly believed was the lack of allure presented by nonfiction film. In comparison with its profitable cousin fiction film, nonfiction film was neither commercially successful nor popular entertainment. The prominent literary critic and left-wing intellectual Osip Brik pinpoints the major obstacles for Shub: unlike nonfiction film, 'fiction film . . . has at its disposal factories, scriptwriters, money . . . nonfiction film feeds on the leftovers'.[31] In the under-funded, under-resourced nonfiction film, Shub had her work cut out for her.[32]

Unfortunately, despite Shub's promotion of nonfiction film, the general public was to find it inaccessible and was ultimately to reject this genre in favour of the more entertaining and comprehensible fiction film. They simply wanted straightforward images in art and uncomplicated entertainment in film, as was to be offered by Soviet Socialist Realism. Unsurprisingly, only a minority of the population had fully embraced Constructivist objectives and radical exploration in film: namely the avant-garde and their followers.

Consequently all the hope, vitality and experimentation associated with the Constructivist movement and the vanguard was to splinter and disintegrate by the end of the 1920s. In addition the official sanction of Socialist Realism in the 1930s, as prescriptive of the only way forward, signalled the end of the revolution in the arts. As an art form, Socialist Realism made a significant contribution to the rewriting of history, the personality cult of Stalin and the literal death of the real in artistic representation.[33]

This was the end of the road for Constructivism and the avant-garde. Paradoxically, artistic expression was to turn full circle as the traditional Peredvizhniki, once the rebels of the nineteenth century, became the paradigm for Socialist Realism (both in content and in style) with their easily readable and conventional renditions of life.

High Art or Constructivism: 'Shakespeare or a Pair of Boots?'[34]

Unlike the Peredvizhniki, Constructivism implied a denunciation of the concept of the inspired creative artist associated with figurative art and easel painting – repudiating the mystical role of the artist-priest in favour of the artist-engineer. Vasily Kandinsky exemplified the sacred artist-priest whose paintings in the Symbolist tradition, steeped in romanticism, emotion and sheer beauty, were destined for the refined spaces of art galleries.[35] Shub, on the other hand, personified the artist-engineer in her utilitarian approach to her raw material and her compilation films were intended for mass public screenings.

Therefore, Constructivism promoted the production of functional works using industrial materials in the place of traditional representational art. Thus, it discarded ornamentation in favour of a practical methodology. The rallying cry of Constructivism was an invitation for Soviet artists to abandon their easels and embrace industrial constructions. Consequently, Shub and her comrades in this avant-garde movement believed in the combining of art with industry, technology and politics. Ideologically committed, their objective was to transform their society through Constructivism, thereby constructing an ideal socialist way of life. In their view, this philosophy of social transformation was not reflected in the contemporaneous sculptures and spatial constructions that, for example, Naum Gabo and Antoine Pevsner created exclusively for the art gallery or the museum space. Shub's motivation, as encapsulated by her compilation trilogy, was in stark contrast to Gabo and Pevsner, who could not accept the aesthetic rebellion implicit in the Constructivists' anti-art stance and their passionate utopian vision for the emerging socialist state.

Prior to the publication of the art historian Christina Lodder's book on Russian Constructivism, there was a widespread misinterpretation regarding the principles of this movement. According to Lodder, unlike its reincarnation in the West solely as an art movement, Russian Constructivism was the province of a utopian avant-garde inextricably allied with the ideology of socialism. Vlada Petric reinforces the misconception held regarding Constructivism in his seminal work on Dziga Vertov, where he states that 'perhaps the most articulate definition of Constructivism was put forth in the famous "Realist Manifesto" [1922] issued by the brothers Naum Gabo and Antonin Pevsner'.[36] This document, more commonly referenced as 'The Realistic Manifesto', was, contrary to Petric's assertion, written solely by Gabo, with Pevsner merely being a solidarity signatory. In addition, the document was neither a Constructivist manifesto nor was it produced in 1922.[37] Published in August 1920, Gabo's text embodies elements of previous Rayonist and Suprematist declarations, rather than influencing and contributing to the theoretical texts of the era. As a result, 'The Realistic Manifesto' ('Realistic' denoting the essence of reality) adds nothing of significance to the existing literature and more crucially, nothing to Constructivist thought. It should not be seen as a mouthpiece for Constructivism. In fact, Gabo and Pevsner always vociferously dissociated themselves from the Constructivists destruction of 'bourgeois' art.[38] Gabo and Pevsner would always create site-specific artworks for a gallery space. In direct opposition to Shub's Constructivist nonfiction film, form was everything to them and there was little place for function in their aesthetic objects and beautiful constructions.

In the introduction to her text on Constructivism, Christina Lodder states that 'Russian Constructivism posited an entirely new relationship between the artist, his [sic] work and society'. What is more, she adds: 'this radical reassessment of artistic activity was a direct response to the experience of the Russian Revolution of 1917 and the ensuing Civil War.'[39] Yet, despite Lodder's assertion, art in Russia prior to 1917 was ripe for Constructivism. For example, Malevich's extraordinary *Black Square* [circa 1914 to 1915] was often believed to have left avant-garde art with nowhere to go. *Black Square* heavily influenced the principles of Constructivist art with its startling use of minimalist abstraction and the paring away of the superfluous and the decorative.[40] The works of not only Alexander Rodchenko but also three prominent woman artists – Liubov Popova, Olga Rozanova and Varvara Stepanova – were at the forefront of Constructivist art, and they strongly reflected the influence of Malevich's dynamic and revolutionary geometric forms.[41]

Furthermore, the search for a new visual vocabulary to symbolize their new world propelled these artists along the road to modernism. Technology and the machine age joined with socialism and produced the utopian projects of Constructivism. Shub's non-acted film, as illustrated specifically in *The Fall of the Romanov Dynasty*, is a triumph of cinematic compilation and construction, incorporating all the fundamental tenets of Constructivism.

Apart from Constructivism's forays into theatre, architecture, cinema, photomontage and typography (the latter two being successfully used in both agitational posters and silent nonfiction film), the theoretical treatises of the Constructivists did not always translate into reality. While Vladimir Tatlin, the acknowledged father of Constructivism, faded from view, Shub took this movement to another level. Significantly, Shub achieved what Tatlin had only been able to promise. Tatlin's proposed glass and iron skyscraper, the *Monument to the Third International*, can be viewed as a metaphor for his Constructivist oeuvre. It was to become an enduring emblem of the avant-garde and a bitter reminder of their failed utopian dreams. Ironically, Tatlin's *Monument to the Third*

International was to be a symbol of the feat of twentieth-century technological mastery, and yet it was economically and architecturally unfeasible, just as his later flying machine *Letatlin* was incapable of being airborne. Where Tatlin's *Monument to the Third International* was not realized as a fully integrated architectural structure and remained an intricate model on display, Shub's compilation trilogy was the manifestation of pure Constructivist art with *The Fall of the Romanov Dynasty* becoming accessible to millions of cinemagoers throughout the Soviet empire.

Additionally, Pablo Picasso's 1912 collages of throwaway junk and recycled objects had been catalysts for Tatlin's work with *objets-trouvés* (and also for Marcel Duchamp's 'ready-mades').[42] Indisputably, the strategy of incorporating found objects into a work of art can be compared to Shub's utilization of newsreel.[43] She discovered chaotic heaps of unlabelled film reels abandoned in dank basements in Leningrad and retrieved this footage for the construction of *The Fall of the Romanov Dynasty*. Shub recalled that the 'places' were 'so horribly humid that the emulsion was trickling down from the films'.[44]

Correspondingly, Tatlin's mantra of 'real materials in real space' (which referred to his relief constructions, the three-dimensional structures that he made before the Revolution) can be translated from sculptural form into cinema as it describes Shub's compilation trilogy.[45] Shub took authentic (Tatlin's 'real') raw material, and reframed and reconstructed it cinematically to reveal the history of her Motherland.

Hence, Constructivism was to be art for the people, art on the factory floor. It was not just an expression of the proletariat but demanded their involvement in Constructivist projects. In fact, in *The Fall of the Romanov Dynasty* the proletariat is featured throughout Shub's film and is heralded as the architect of political and social change. As Stephen Bann maintains: 'the notion of Constructivism as the art devised for, and in some respects by, the masses had its notable successes – in the "actorless" documentary films of Esther [sic] Shub.'[46]

Furthermore, Aleksei Gan, as a founding member of the Constructivist movement, had stated this even more forcibly than Stephen Bann, writing on *Constructivism in the Cinema* nearly fifty years earlier. In this journal article, Gan emphasized 'the vitality of the ciné platform of Constructivism' and viewed Shub as being at the forefront of Constructivist film.[47]

Gan was a passionate and vociferous champion of both nonfiction film and Constructivism. Hence, he declared it was his sincere belief that 'the historical truth of the Revolution was demonstrated' through Shub's use of 'genuine ciné documents'.[48] Her methodological approach was in evident contrast to the practices of fiction filmmakers. They were described scathingly by Gan as mere 'art makers' who attempted 'to re-create historical events by mobilizing all the magic forces of idealistic art'.[49] This heated polemic and competitive jousting between advocates of nonfiction film and its opposing faction of fiction film was characteristic of this period. Thus Gan claimed that 'despite the unequal conditions in production and the disparity in material resources', Shub's film was the resounding 'victor in this unfair competition'.[50] He was merely reinforcing a fact that was public knowledge amongst the film community, namely that nonfiction film was the poor relation of fiction film.[51] In reality, there were serious problems for documentary filmmakers like Shub. Confirming this, writing in 1929, Shub was desperate for facilities and support:

> We must agitate in defence of the newsreels of our days . . . and must consider this not just one moment of agitation. When we talk about acted and non-acted film, we are not talking about denigrating acted film at all. We see that in acted film there are enormous resources, the best and most highly skilled people work there. . . . Meanwhile we have a small factory, no [camera] operators, and no enthusiastic people with ideas. And in the absence of all of this, we can do nothing at all.[52]

Shub emphasized that 'Lenin's idea of proportion [a balanced percentage between fiction film entertainment and nonfiction film propaganda] must not be a footnote but an effective policy.[53] Only after these conditions are met will non-acted cinema budge from its current deadlock.'[54] Accordingly, Shub proposed viable and well-considered solutions:

> Author-directors, camera operators, montage specialists and laboratory workers are needed in non-acted cinema, now more than ever. We must use the experience of the pioneers in this field and create a special course on non-acted film within GTK [State Cinema Technical Institute]. There have been attempts to this effect before . . . at two GTK conferences in December 1928. On those occasions, they proposed to organize individual workshops within GTK, and a department for research work on non-acted film. . . . This would afford us the opportunity to transmit our experience and work methods to the younger generation. . . . Filming laboratories and experimental ateliers should help restore the production of non-acted cinema. We need to understand that, instead of actors, we must have filming and lighting equipment of the highest technical quality.[55]

Yet, in spite of these challenging impediments, Shub's nonfiction film was at the apex of Constructivist art. For Jaroslav Andel, 'Soviet cinema of the 1920s' represents perhaps the most successful materialisation of the Constructivist programme.'[56] At the forefront of this accomplishment stood Shub's directorial début, which saw the unveiling of her experimental compilation genre. According to the cinema scholar Graham Roberts, compilation films such as Shub's *The Fall of the Romanov Dynasty* are at the 'pinnacle' in addition to being 'an early standard setter, in the history of the genre'.[57] Undeniably, the structure and fully realized cinematic motivation of this film can be viewed as an ideal of the Constructivist art form. The fusion of factual compilation montage together with its ideological content permeates its structure and creates an archetype.

Consequently, *The Fall of the Romanov Dynasty* can be seen as encapsulating the defining triad of fundamental principles for a work of art as formulated by the First Working Group of Constructivists. These three central materials of industrial culture were labelled tectonics [tektonika], construction [konstruksiya] and facture [faktura]. Shub's filmic constructions faithfully adhered to Constructivist doctrine, as her archival material was 'consciously selected and appropriately used for a particular purpose without arresting the . . . construction and without constraining its tectonics – indeed preserving all this'.[58] The Constructivists were to define 'facture' as the manner of making an art object, the use of the materials and the quality of its execution. All of these regulations were encapsulated within the structure of Shub's compilation trilogy. The art historian Maria Gough, in her work on Russian Constructivism, interprets facture as that which 'refers to the overall handling or working the material constituents of a given medium . . . the process of production in general'.[59] Gough's understanding of this terminology therefore encompasses not just the plastic arts and applied art but also literature and film. Facture can be seen therefore as the exploration of form and analysis of materials started in Tatlin's painterly and counter reliefs of 1914 and 1915, developed in the constructions of Alexander Rodchenko, Vladimir and Georgy Stenberg, Konstantin Medunetsky, and the Latvian artists Gustav Klutsis and Karl Ioganson.[60] Shub later took these central components to their most fully realized expression in her documentaries.

During one of the initial meetings of the First Working Group of Constructivists, Aleksei Gan asserted that facture was far more than Tatlin's earlier considerations of facture simply as surface or texture: 'insofar as you are a Constructivist, you are making *faktura* . . . you are working the material and not just treating its surface'.[61] Thus, Gan's facture is the process of making and producing a material structure; either a spatial construction by Rodchenko or a compilation film by Shub. Furthermore, *The Fall of the Romanov Dynasty* epitomized 'the best use of the materials' with an 'absence of any superfluous elements' as viewed by Constructivist theory.[62] Shub's utilization of preserved newsreel footage, transforming this material into a product of art (nonfiction film) with which to instruct the new socialist society, encompassed all of the major components of the mission and blueprint for Constructivism.

With the declaration by Rodchenko that 'construction is the system by which an object is realised from the utilisation of material together with a predetermined purpose' we also see the erasure of the traditional notion of the spirituality, subjectivity and individuality inherent within the artist.[63] This can be summarized in the following terms: construction equals 'utilisation of materials' [facture] and hence Shub's use of raw archival newsreel thereby creates an 'object', that is, *The Fall of the Romanov Dynasty*. Therefore, Shub's 'predetermined purpose' is to educate and entertain the proletariat through Constructivist film. In turn, this implies the repudiation of the artist-priest's inspiration exchanged for the artist-constructor's industrial production. The factory supersedes the temple.

Moreover, the critic Boris Kushner, a champion of the Constructivists, asserted that 'to the socialist consciousness, a work of art is no more than an object'.[64] Osip Brik echoed this notion; as for him 'not ideas but a real object is the aim of all true creativity'.[65] Brik stated that art workers must create 'not idealistic vapours, but material objects' and his 'idealistic vapours' were exhaled directly at Kandinsky's intuitive, subjective, spiritual and idealist approach to art.[66] The Constructivists saw Kandinsky's work as ideologically incompatible with their definition of art as utilitarian and productive. Art's mission was to construct useful objects. Kandinsky's artist-priest seeking inspiration in her or his ivory tower was in direct opposition to the practical artist-engineer working in a factory as an instrument of production.

The concept of art as an object of production was clarified by Gan's vigorous treatise on Constructivism. In 1922 his zealous rhetoric was translated into a daring dissertation, a book with the simple title of *Constructivism* [Konstruktivizm]. This was the first formal illustration and presentation of the ideological position of Constructivism in text form. Its pages are punctuated by pithy slogans. The cover of this publication, also designed by Gan, is functional and to the point. Emblazoned on a cream background with no added ornamentation, Aleksei Gan's name appears (larger than life) printed in red,

Figure 7 Aleksei Gan: *Constructivism* [Konstruktivizm], 1922. This was the only book that was devoted to Constructivist theory and its cover design, devoid of embellishment, reflects the philosophy of the movement and the ego of its author. The words 'Aleksei Gan' swamp the title! Book with letterpress cover. Page (each): 9 5/16 × 7 5/8" (23.7 × 19.4 cm); overall (closed): 9 5/16 × 7 15/16 × 1/4" (23.7 × 20.1 × 0.6 cm). Published by Tverskoe izdatel'stvo, Tver in an edition of 2000. Gift of The Judith Rothschild Foundation. Digital Image © The Museum of Modern Art/Licensed by SCALA/Art Resource, NY.

sans serif, and the modestly sized title is a horizontal block of black on cream (Figure 7).

The typography is effective in its simplicity of style. Within its covers, the layout of his pages is dynamic. Words are printed in bold type with heavy underline while whole paragraphs appear in upper case. The phrases are often placed on the diagonal, bombarding the reader with the zigzag of agitational language. The text is electric with fervour. For example, Gan declares: 'Art is indissolubly linked with theology, metaphysics and mysticism . . . it was artificially reheated by the hypocrisy of bourgeois culture, and finally, crashed against the mechanical world of our age. Death to art! . . . Art is finished!'[67]

Gan equated art tradition with the 'bourgeois' excesses of the past, especially with the decadence and corruption of tsarist rule. Art in the new socialist state was, for him, art of and for the proletariat. It was definitely not Gabo and

Pevsner's art in a gallery space catering for a privileged minority but rather Shub's instructive compilation film directed at the working masses. Constructivism was provocatively and vehemently anti-art: it announced the end of representational easel painting and promoted the triumph of popular culture over high art. Proclaiming the death of art also spelled the demise of mysticism and symbolism, thus silencing the spiritual and inspirational voice of traditional art. The artist as a lone individual was now being replaced by the artist as part of a collective: that is, as a maker of products in the community. Gan perceived painting and other traditional art forms as feudal and anti-socialist, whereas Constructivism fused with Marxism, modern technology and the new proletarian order. In Gan's words: 'dialectical materialism is, for Constructivism, a compass that indicates the paths and distant objectives.'[68]

Additionally, science, technology and socialist thought were to depose the methodologies of art and art criticism. Commenting on this issue in 1926, the art theorist Yakov Tugenkhold observed that 'the fundamental methodological aspiration of Marxist art criticism is the affirmation of a scientific approach to art'.[69] By the same token, Shub wanted the authentic subject matter of nonfiction film to be found in the 'real world' of the Soviet Union: in 'the natural and technological environment in which we live ... the events of the day ... people equipped with and pushing forward scientific knowledge, people struggling heroically to subdue the natural elements. All this, is the material for our films.'[70]

In Shub's view, socialist newsreel was the substance of art. Art was understood as a communal and productive enterprise. The Constructivists promoted the ideological base of their functional art form, which at its nucleus spoke of both societal change and the desire to work with real materials. Yet, when Gan, the *enfant terrible* of Constructivism, declaimed with great conviction in his book that art was finished, warning bells should have rung for Shub and the avant-garde.

With many Constructivists becoming increasingly reliant on photomontage, photography, posters and typography in order to eke out their living throughout the 1920s, they significantly turned from their three-dimensional utilitarian constructions back towards two dimensions. The real object and real materials in real space transmuted into the real image of photography, photomontage and finally film. Simultaneously, Socialist Realism was to arise from the conventional and traditional art forms, supported by the Party. These had flourished throughout the 1920s in opposition to Constructivism. With realism in art, particularly in painting, being the preferred choice of Stalin and the majority of the populace, the death knell of Constructivism was sounded.

Writers and filmmakers of the vanguard were denounced publicly and accused of the crime of 'formalism'. Gan and Klutsis, who were both outspoken Constructivists and would not toe the Party line, were imprisoned and died in the Gulag.[71] In addition, a staunch ally of the Constructivist movement, Vsevolod Meyerhold (a friend and mentor to both Shub and Eisenstein), was later executed as an enemy of the people.[72] This was the fate suffered also by playwright, scriptwriter and founding LEF member Sergei Tretiakov and the novelist, dramatist and scriptwriter Isaac Babel, also close associates of Shub and Eisenstein.[73]

The Emergence of the Constructivist Filmmaker: Shub and *The Fall of the Romanov Dynasty*

Although she is never mentioned in Christina Lodder's otherwise comprehensive book on Constructivism, Shub is an ideal example of the extension of Constructivist ideology, methodology and critical practice into film. Successfully reaching a far wider audience than Meyerhold's theatre productions in Moscow, her work was agitational, sociopolitical and utilitarian. Using the latest technology, images made by a machine for mass production, Shub produced cinema in the form of factual documents. Her unadorned nonfiction film recorded the real world's objects and people with neither actors nor staging of events. As Shub herself exclaimed, in nonfiction film 'we do not need studios, actors, decorators and props . . . we have nothing to learn from the composition and colouring methods of fine arts'.[74]

In fact, affirming her position as a committed devotee of Constructivist doctrine, Shub explains why she built the structure of her first compilations wholly from newsreels:

> Why do I constantly return to the old material? Because I work within the limits of a particular school, the school of Constructivism. The task of this cinematographic school is to work on authentic, not dramatised material. We are deeply persuaded that only newsreel, only live material can adequately reflect the great era in which we live, and the real people that create and exist within it.[75]

This promulgation attests to Shub's passionate adherence and commitment to the aims of Constructivism (as encapsulated by nonfiction film), something that is apparent in her use of document. Shub produced important historical filmic journals that recorded the Russian and Soviet way of life, through her use of recycled newsreels and her avoidance of actors and staged events. Her first compilation is a perfectly realized expression of this film form, which laid the theoretical foundations for early nonfiction film and the modern documentary. In addition, it is apposite to note the didacticism inherent in Shub's endeavours to record historical reality on film, as she attempted to educate the masses through the promotion of the utilitarian message of the Constructivists. Furthermore, *The Fall of the Romanov Dynasty* could be seen to exemplify what Walter Benjamin (the influential Weimar philosopher, literary critic and theorist) would refer to, in the 1930s, as the mass production of popular culture. According to Benjamin, this negated the uniqueness and privilege afforded by high art. Thus, by utilizing new technology in a format both accessible and easily comprehensible to the masses, Shub was a maker of art for the proletariat: a montage engineer armed with the weapons of Marxist ideology.

Within *The Fall of the Romanov Dynasty*, Shub's long segment on World War I is a perfect example of the Constructivist model, and it occupies a massive forty-five minutes of the total ninety-minute film. This prominence, although highly significant in terms of Shub's theme – that is, salient factors responsible for the Revolution – may also be due to practical considerations. There was such a paucity of authentic newsreel footage available to Shub on the narrative leading to the February Revolution of 1917. Shub bemoans this lack of raw material in her film memoirs. There were obviously far more reels showing World War I at Shub's disposal, and hence perhaps this accounts for the slight imbalance of visual emphasis in *The Fall of the Romanov Dynasty*.

Indeed, as a piece of cinema, Shub's film was a logical extension of the concept of Constructivist photomontage as socialist campaigning, a form that can be traced back to the posters of Alexander Rodchenko, Gustav Klutsis and El Lissitzky.[76] Unlike 'capitalist' posters, which were used primarily for advertising commodities, Constructivist posters in the Soviet Union were designed as a means of propaganda. Thus, they aimed to rouse the political consciousness of the proletariat through the use of agitational photographic stills and modern technology. Hannah Höch, John Heartfield and the photomontagists of the Weimar Republic are obvious exceptions to this categorization of all-Western poster art as consumer driven. Although the European 'Constructivists' appropriated some of the basic principles of Russian Constructivism, the European variant was essentially an artistic exploration devoid of the sociological and political context of its Soviet counterpart. The latter was inspired and driven by the utopian ideals of the Revolution.[77] Thus, Maria Gough was to appraise Russian Constructivism as the 'most groundbreaking development in the visual arts in the decade or so following the October Revolution of 1917'.[78]

Accordingly, Shub was to develop this industrialization of ideological, educational and Constructivist art further than Varvara Stepanova and Alexander Rodchenko (and other members of their clique) in the cinematic images of *The Fall of the Romanov Dynasty*. Her sparing use of factographical text, in her intertitles, not only propelled the agitational action forward but also illustrated and instructed in terms of Marxist doctrine. The World War I component of *The Fall of the Romanov Dynasty* exemplifies this developmental shift as it shapes its socialist platform through the didactic use of words on the screen, followed by the reinforcing photographic image in motion. Shub divides this commentary into segments, which are thematically germane to both Russia's involvement in the war and the inevitable consequences for its empire. In her integration of technology, art and archival documentary film, Shub builds within *The Fall of the Romanov Dynasty* a paradigmatic emblem of Constructivism.

In her cinematic depiction of armed conflict, Shub's framework is clearly delineated. Firstly, we have the prelude to war: a socialist film essay on the role of the institutions of capitalism fuelling the conflict, with a Marxist subtext that capitalism can only be eradicated by revolution. This motif will not only become glaringly apparent in Shub's dénouement but will also be merged with the earlier narrative in *The Fall of the Romanov Dynasty* (occupying the first twenty minutes of the film), concerning the repression of the masses by both the Tsar and the privileged upper classes.

Fittingly, Shub appraises the design of her Constructivist endeavour with precision: 'by connecting loose pieces of film, separate events, with meaningful montage, *The Fall of the Romanov Dynasty* became an authentic cinematographic document of the recent past.'[79] In this 'recent past' we watch the prologue to World War I, which will be followed by the Russians making ready for war, the mobilization, the battles and finally the unfolding of the aftermath. Shub's structure aimed to lead the viewer of the day to conclude without doubt that with the combination of these factors, revolution was inevitable. Her intertitles read:

> In those days in EUROPE
> Organizers of the worldwide slaughter
> Capitalist plunderers fighting for markets

Accordingly, Shub exposes the excesses of the West with an image of the imposing classical pillared stock exchange in Paris (La Bourse). Shots of its clamouring shareholders and scenes of massive vaults piled high with gold bullion follow. The specific use of shots of the imperial Parisian exchange (rather than New York or London, for example) is then reinforced in a later segment when we learn from Shub's intertitles that at 'a military review in honour of the President of France [who was visiting Russia] in exchange for French loans – cannon fodder'. Next, we are shown richly gowned ladies wearing splendid millinery, escorted by gentlemen in shiny top hats, as they alight from a coach pulled by horses. Now that we have seen the capitalists fuelling big business and cavorting in their leisure time, Shub introduces us to 'those who do their bidding'.

The parade of heads of state and policymakers begins with Shub introducing the French contingent: the military hero General Joseph Joffre; the Minister for War Alexandre Millerand; Raymond Poincaré, their President; and the Prime Minister Aristide Briand. We observe Millerand and Briand climbing into their open carriage. A flunkey then rushes over and covers their knees with a rug before they are driven off. It is a perfect image of master and slave in the decadent West.

The footage moves to London where King George V travels to the state opening of parliament in an ornate gilt Cinderella-style coach. After the British monarch, the elderly Franz Joseph, Emperor of Austria, struts into the frame. Franz Joseph wears an absurdly over-feathered ostrich plumed hat and is filmed taking the salute. Shub then cuts to Kaiser Wilhelm II of Germany, who, dressed in military garb, reviews his troops.

Now she presents us with the reality of the situation: away from the pomp and public parades, we are taken to a stark shot of ordinary soldiers drilling and bayoneting sandbags. The audience watches while the Russian proletariat in the factories manufacture ammunition, such as shell casings, bombs and bullets. There are row upon row of shells stretching endlessly across the screen. As Shub pithily phrases it in her intertitle: 'the hands of the workers were preparing death for their brothers.' She then shows these weapons being used on the field of battle, in the air, at sea and on land.

This is also a filmic chapter of contrasts. We see the sailors of the fleet scrubbing the decks, while their officers, dressed in immaculate whites, relax at dinner with the lower ranks as servants in attendance. The dining table is set with silver and fine crystal goblets on white linen napery. Following this, Shub displays the turbulent seas, a metaphor for all involved in the war. After frames of the cold and choppy ocean, her intertitles read:

> READY FOR THE EXPLOSION
> Under steam, the fleet
> Was awaiting the order

We see all the battleships flying the Tsar's ensign. However, as images speak louder than captions, Shub shows us two priests showering hapless troops with holy water without any accompanying text. There are shots of Tsar Nicholas II and his generals in jovial mood, laughing and chatting with much hand shaking and head nodding. The Tsar directs proceedings and talks strategies from a position of safety, well away from the battlefield.

Furthermore, in the summing up of this footage of World War I, Shub takes us through ravaged land and strife-torn battlegrounds. Shub comments on the aftermath of the hostilities in the straightforward non-emotive mode of her genre:

> Killed, wounded, maimed
> In the World War
> 35 MILLION PEOPLE

These are typical scenes of war and not a jingoistic display of patriotism and heroism, as Shub is not screening an advertisement for the glories of battle. It is instead a Constructivist catalogue of facts with the clear-cut and understated intertitle headed: 'Faces of War'.

Exhausted soldiers numbly walk past the dead bodies of their comrades. The intertitle 'Peaceful settlements and towns destroyed' appears on the screen. Whole villages are decimated, and amidst this wanton destruction and suffering, a woman sits in disbelief on a pile of rubble that was once a dwelling. 'The retreating armies burned the grain fields', Shub observes in her intertitle. The shots that accompany this illustration of a scorched earth policy, depriving the enemy of food supplies, hold immense tragic stillness and power. We see nothing but waste and desolation. Friends and family carry the injured, taking them for medical treatment. Refugees with their meagre possessions trudge helplessly along a never-ending road of misery. Later, there are further scenes of heartbreak as the camera pans over graves littering the countryside, followed by official mass funerals for those who gave their lives for Mother Russia and the policies of the Tsar.

In light of this cavalcade of authentic images, Lev Kuleshov summarized Shub's Constructivist objectives and praised her for them: 'Shub's triumph is the triumph of cinematography relying on real material . . . the material of cinema is not acting, not theatrical productions, but reality: newsreels . . . real events, real things, real people, and the demonstration of their behaviour in the daily life that surrounds them.'[80] Shub's own writings mirror Kuleshov's observations on her methodology and abound with similar hopes for nonfiction film.

Additionally, Kuleshov wrote glowingly of *The Fall of the Romanov Dynasty* and believed that it had created a major 'cinematic impression' viewed with 'unwavering interest' by the public.[81] Consequently, he claimed that Shub's nonfiction film was more 'interesting, truthful and convincing' than any fiction film.[82] Why was this so? It all hung on Shub's Constructivist mission: her complete reliance on the raw material in order to form her work and her use of archival newsreel to construct cinema for the masses. *The Fall of the Romanov Dynasty* constituted a socialist document of facts about the recent past and the struggles towards the goal of a Soviet state.

Kuleshov confirms the above assertion when he declares that 'newsreel must show events correctly, and the form of the montage of the newsreel is defined not by the author, but by the material'.[83] Moreover, as a leading filmmaker, Kuleshov was eminently qualified to assess that technically speaking with *The Fall of the Romanov Dynasty*: 'the material out of which Shub had to make the film was cinematographically very poor: badly shot, badly preserved, extremely mixed up . . . the work she has done in selecting the sequences is the basic achievement of the editor.'[84] Thus, Shub had created a documentary of great worth using rusty unlabelled tins of damaged footage and thereby shown her considerable editing skills.

After an enthusiastic critique of prominent scenarios in *The Fall of the Romanov Dynasty*, Kuleshov is led to the conclusion that 'cinematographically, the strongest part of the film is the war. It is edited not as chaos or as a sum of expressionist impressions, but as a logically developing process.'[85] Admittedly, Kuleshov's statement has validity. Shub's montage in this section of the film successfully proceeds in an unfolding of all the factors influencing and then prolonging Russia's active participation in World War I. However, unlike the ironic segments on the Tsar and his retinue, as well as on the Governor of Kaluga and his wife in the preceding footage, parts of the war segment (although thematically significant) seem interminably extended.[86] They would have benefited from some radical filmic pruning. Although it must be acknowledged that the sombre narrative pertaining to World War I is pivotal to an understanding of one of the catalysts that lit the fuse of the Revolution, Shub does pelt us with too many protracted sequences of battle in a case of visual overkill. Yet, in spite of this minor criticism, there are scenes of true poignancy as we view soldiers frozen to death in the snow with their animals, and we witness the wounded and the plight of the escaping refugees. Thus, despite the excessive length of this section, the overall impression of World War I that Shub transmits to us (with her characteristic thoroughness) serves the socialist explanation for reform and the rise of Lenin and the Soviet Union. This was Shub's uncomplicated approach to Constructivist film, and yet the same could not be said about her comrade Dziga Vertov.

Shub as the Pre-Eminent Exemplar of Constructivist Filmmaking

LEF deemed Shub's *The Fall of the Romanov Dynasty*, a synthesis of documentation assembled into a coherent cinematic construction, as an ideal manifestation of nonfiction film. Yet conceptually, to some extent, Shub was in harmony with Vertov's 'Film-Truth' [Kino-pravda]. Nevertheless, she labelled her more stringent adherence to his film truth, authentic [podlinny] material. As she observed, 'authentic material is something that gives life to a documentary film, regardless of the fact that it might be composed of archival footage, or film shot by the filmmaker' (Figure 8).[87]

The structural and visual austerity marking *The Fall of the Romanov Dynasty* made Shub the Constructivist filmmaker par excellence for Mayakovsky, Brik and other members of the avant-garde. Although both Shub and Vertov held firmly to a utopian vision of their society through nonfiction film, their focus was radically different. Unlike Shub, and for all his loud proclamations to the contrary, Vertov did not adhere to the principles of the unstaged documenting of actuality. He sometimes staged and often distorted his work to create aesthetic fragments of artifice. Shub's strict adherence to the rules of Constructivist documentary cannot be reconciled with Vertov's 'interpretation of images'.

Figure 8 Esfir Shub: the only female in the frame. The lone woman filmmaker photographed with her colleagues. The caption reads: 'A group of Soviet film workers go to Berlin in May 1929. In line from left to right, Ilya Trainin, Natan Zharki, Esfir Shub.' Wearing a beret, Vertov is standing directly behind Shub. *In Close-up.*

On reflection, in 1979, the cameraman Mikhail Kaufman offered a fascinating insight into these fundamental differences between the filmic philosophy of Vertov and that of Shub the ultimate Constructivist. Speaking for Vertov and himself regarding nonfiction film, Kaufman considered that

> With Shub, you somehow still have a connected plot, an accessible story, which develops gradually. . . . We [Vertov and Kaufman] felt that when working with documentary material one shouldn't follow a standard narrative; it was extremely important to piece facts together and unite everything in a single thrust. Actually, we felt that the point of editing, in the full sense of the word, was not only to have an image in every frame but to produce . . . *an interpretation of images* [the italic emphasis is mine].[88]

In line with their differing viewpoints and strategies for nonfiction film, Shub criticized Vertov's dismissal of precise, factual detail in his films in favour of blurring the edges, thereby privileging Vertovian creativity over authenticity.

Shub's specific methodology for nonfiction film was to document the historical reality of Soviet society. Her engagement with authentic documentary, the actuality of socio-historical reality, was to fit Constructivist ideals like a glove. As a result, it must be noted that *Constructivism in Film*, the very title of Vlada Petric's book on Vertov, is a misnomer. None of Vertov's full-length feature films could be characterized as examples of Constructivism. Petric refers to 'Vertov's creative imagination', and 'creative imagination' was the antithesis of every concept upheld by Constructivism.[89] Shub's *The Fall of the Romanov Dynasty* with its stark, factual presentation of archival material is Constructivism fulfilled. It is indubitably the most resolved embodiment of the movement's objectives.

The Fall of the Romanov Dynasty adheres to all the criteria for nonfiction film. It is synonymous with the principles of Constructivism in its most developed form. Thus, Shub's film constitutes a fusion of Soviet technological art and socialist ideology with its firm emphasis on social reality. Shub's mass-produced machine-driven art was factual, intelligible cinematic ideology, propaganda for the proletariat.[90] While the earliest expressions of the Constructivist movement, namely, the abstractions of Rodchenko, Ioganson, Medunetsky and the Stenberg brothers had been both inaccessible and incomprehensible to the masses, *The Fall of the Romanov Dynasty* blurred the boundaries between traditional high art and popular culture in its quest for Constructivist objectivity through nonfiction film. Shub's philosophy mirrors that of Walter Benjamin. Like Benjamin, Shub was convinced that 'the tiniest authentic fragment of daily life says more than painting' and consequently, for her, nonfiction film was an everlasting historical document of incalculable importance.[91]

Therefore, *The Fall of the Romanov Dynasty* represented a textbook example of contemporary documentary and, as Shub was to declare emphatically: 'nothing can be more persuasive than fact'.[92] Her work not only sought to be a true to life Constructivist interpretation on film, but it also structured its documentary material to reveal the ideological, political and social landmarks of her era.

What is more, I have claimed that Constructivism was the scaffolding upon which Shub built her work, and this has been demonstrated through an explanation of the background and creed of the Constructivist movement and Shub's engagement with their radical practice. Hence, it is necessary to reinforce the notion of Shub's leading role as a dedicated practitioner of nonfiction film. This was a genre that exemplified the doctrines of Constructivism and also one that married with the critical cinematic debates and theories of Shub (and the avant-garde) brought to fruition in her Constructivist film philosophy. In fact, by selecting raw material in the format of discarded fragments of newsreel footage,

Shub produced meaningful sociopolitical, historical documents. Repudiating 'art', through this Constructivist negation, Shub aimed at creating a practical product that was unadorned. Additionally, she was concerned with a collective approach for the benefit of society pertinent to the objectives of Constructivism. This was evinced by her compilation trilogy, specifically *The Fall of the Romanov Dynasty*, a pioneering utilitarian Constructivist nonfiction film project in which the purposeful use of materials aimed to give instruction and meaning to the life of the proletariat.

In summary, Shub's *The Fall of the Romanov Dynasty* indisputably constituted a Constructivist engagement with the events leading to the collapse of the House of Romanov and the resultant revolution. The film was never intended to foreground Shub's signature as an individual filmmaker but rather to construct a reproduction of Soviet historical reality. Shub's compilation genre spoke of historical research, the collecting and collating of film facts, and the archiving of genuine newsreel footage. In its production, Shub chose to remain an invisible presence: a Constructivist power driving the documentary in the film factory.

Hence, in order to illustrate Shub's adherence to Constructivism, the following chapter is an exegesis of *The Fall of the Romanov Dynasty* contrasted with the opposing genre of acted film drama as exemplified by Sergei Eisenstein's *October*.

3

The Fall of the Romanov Dynasty: Shub's Constructivist Paradigm for Nonfiction Film

Shub's *The Fall of the Romanov Dynasty* was the embodiment of both Constructivism and early Soviet nonfiction cinema. Her archival documentary was a political, didactic tool: a juxtaposition of contrasting newsreel images in order to promote a Marxian dialectic of her society. Thus, it is contended that, through *The Fall of the Romanov Dynasty*, Shub was to set a blueprint for Constructivist nonfiction film.

Not only does the following commentary demonstrate the specificity of Shub's nonfiction film but also it accentuates the incompatibilities between her genre and Sergei Eisenstein's mode of fiction film. Therefore, in order to place *The Fall of the Romanov Dynasty* in the context of its cinematic milieu, it is critically examined against a variant form of fiction film: as typified by Eisenstein's *October* [Oktiabr, 1928].[1]

Fact versus Fiction: Shub's Actuality or Eisenstein's Ingenuity

Despite their divergent cinematic interpretations and methodologies, *The Fall of the Romanov Dynasty* and *October* were nevertheless shaped upon variations of the same ideological maquette: the glorification of the Bolshevik Revolutions of February (Shub) and October (Eisenstein) 1917. In fact, in addition to being linked by their subject matter, these films were connected by a need to communicate the essential credos of Marxism and the new, revolutionary state. Yet despite these similarities, the essential attribute that differentiates Shub's film from that of Eisenstein's is that while *October* was a dramatized narrative (fiction film) interspersed with historical fact, *The Fall of the Romanov Dynasty* was composed solely of newsreels (nonfiction film). Thus, a Constructivist approach to documentary was the specific element that made Shub distinctive amongst the filmmakers of her generation in the late 1920s. It was her pioneering role in nonfiction film, specifically through her adherence to genuine archival footage without the embellishment of actors and staging, which made Shub's compilation film, and the trilogy in which it belongs, unique.

Accordingly, with *The Fall of the Romanov Dynasty* Shub was striving to elevate nonfiction film to the same standard of success, prestige and popularity enjoyed by fiction film. Nonetheless, as a committed Constructivist she aimed also to make her film ideologically significant. As Shub clearly articulated: 'our task is not simply to produce a film . . . let acted film do that. We think that cinema must be an organising force, an agitator and communicator of propaganda.'[2] In *The Fall of the Romanov Dynasty* Shub demonstrated her role as a propagandist through the controlled manipulation of her material, by means of which she contrasted seemingly disparate events that were then combined didactically in her specific form of ideological montage. To this effect, Shub explains her methodological approach towards *The Fall of the Romanov Dynasty* as an attempt 'to avoid looking at the newsreel material for its own sake, and . . . to maintain the principle of its documentary quality'.[3] In addition, Shub's preservation of the integrity of her archival material was combined with the doctrines of Marxism: *The Fall of the Romanov Dynasty* cinematically highlights the essence of Marxist class struggle and proletarian revolution using genuine newsreel footage. Shub's application of historical materialism becomes apparent, for example, in the film's depiction of the events leading to the collapse of the royal House of Romanov, as they unfold in chronological sequence from Tsar Nicholas II's despotic reign to his spectacular demise in 1917.

Indeed, as the leading Constructivist Aleksei Gan declared in *Cinema-Photo*: 'the basic task of Soviet cinema [. . .] is the task of fixing revolutionary life on the screen.'[4] Shub was not only to fulfil this proclamation but, with *The Fall of the Romanov Dynasty*, she also assembled a Constructivist synthesis of art, industry and ideology. Indeed, *The Fall of the Romanov Dynasty* was avant-garde and politically based nonfiction film, which was constructed in a film factory. In other words, Shub was ideologically and politically endorsing a revolutionary project that was not only embedded in a Marxist discourse but also upheld the experimental principles of Constructivist art.

As a result, when *The Fall of the Romanov Dynasty* was initially released, amidst the festivities commemorating the first decade after the Revolution, both LEF (representing the avant-garde) and the Party gave it their seal of approval. Viewed in its day as epitomizing realism on the screen, the film fulfilled not only

LEF's marked preference for authentic newsreel-based nonfiction film but also the regime's official version of events. For a short period of time, the avant-garde and the State saw eye to eye.

A realistic and often stark Soviet documentary, thematically Shub's film is divided into three major, intertwined chronicles. The first part concentrates on Russia under the yoke of Nicholas II and depicts the system (the crown, the church, the state) pitted against the common people. In the second segment we learn about the advent of World War I and its terrible toll. The final episode centres on the February Revolution of 1917: mass demonstration, the abdication of the Tsar and the ensuing rise of the Bolsheviks under Lenin. The dénouement of Shub's film shows us the proletariat triumphant in their liberation. Shub repeatedly makes the viewer aware of the inequality, repression and hardship in Russian Tsarist society before the ascendancy of the Bolsheviks. In order to accentuate and reinforce her message, Shub exposes these binaries in filmic juxtaposition: placing two unrelated scenarios side by side. For example, images of the Governor of Kaluga and his wife sipping tea while comfortably seated in the shade of their garden are contrasted with women reapers labouring in a field.[5] In this way, the audience is directed to decode Shub's ideological montage as the representation of an imbalance in society: the injustice of privilege. This method of contextualizing her didacticism through contrast prevails throughout *The Fall of the Romanov Dynasty*. With her agitational montage being organized by the formalist principles of Shklovsky's 'defamiliarization' [ostranenie], Shub uses this element in order to give meaning to her work and as a most effective tool for espousing and reinforcing her political message.

Shub described *The Fall of the Romanov Dynasty* and the other two films in her compilation trilogy as a lasting monument to her epoch, unlike dramatizations covering the same era. While she saw played, fiction films on the same subject as becoming dated, her 'three historical documentary films' had for her a perpetual quality.[6] From Shub's viewpoint: 'only this material has the potential to bring the period of Tsarist Russia and the heroic years of the Civil War and the October Revolution back to life.'[7] Presenting social and political history through a montage of documents, the genre of nonfiction film was for Shub the way to demonstrate the authenticity of documentary film.

Fiction film, on the contrary, could be a factually based narrative and yet contain a large proportion of fictitious material in order to accentuate an element of drama. Thus, while Shub's *The Fall of the Romanov Dynasty* is based on archival newsreel documents, Eisenstein's referent for *October* is John Reed's subjective account of the events of 1917.[8]

After the release of *October* in March 1928 (exactly a year after the première *The Fall of the Romanov Dynasty*), Shub had postulated a succinct and valid case for fact over fiction, in 'This Work Cries Out' [Eta rabota krichit], by using Eisenstein (and Grigory Aleksandrov) as her points of reference. She had asked rhetorically 'have they given us *Ten Days That Shook the World*?'[9] The implication of this question was that, like John Reed's book, Eisenstein's film was a romanticized, idealized and therefore subjective interpretation of the Revolution. However, in common with *October*, *Ten Days That Shook the World* was generally accepted as an accurate and authentic depiction of the events of October 1917. By basing his script on Reed's work, Eisenstein was dismissing Shub's historical reportage and use of newsreel footage as factual evidence in favour of Reed's impressions. In this sense, what Reed had accomplished with great success was a vivid and inspiring encapsulation of the zeitgeist, and this is precisely what Eisenstein wished to achieve with his choreographed performance of events. However, as Shub reminds her readers in 'This Work Cries Out':

> Have they [Eisenstein and Aleksandrov] forced people and objects to go back ten years and convince us that that was precisely how *a fact of world significance* – the conquest of power by the workers and peasants – happened ... You must not stage a historical fact because the staging distorts the fact. ... You must not make millions of peasants and workers who did not participate in the struggles, or our younger generation ... think that the events of those great days took place exactly as they happened in ... *October*.[10]

Continuing her argument for nonfiction film, Shub asserts that 'in such matters you need historical truth, fact, document and the greatest austerity of execution: you need newsreel'.[11]

Conversely, Eisenstein was clearly more interested in dramatized nonfiction film than factual documented footage. In *October*, he further manipulates and embellishes Reed's text to astonishing effect. For instance the image of Alexander Kerensky dissolving into the mechanical peacock is a glittering and brilliantly conceived fantasy scenario (with connotations that couldn't be more obvious). Likewise, the references to Kerensky's supposedly Napoleonic aspirations are cleverly orchestrated. Yet Eisenstein unfairly adds to the melodrama by having the actor playing Kerensky portraying him as an ineffectual and simpering idiot. To add to the effect of ridicule, Kerensky is farcically filmed burying his head under the pillows in the Tsarina Alexandra's boudoir. This is an outrageously exaggerated distortion of the man even though it adds to the drama.[12]

On the other hand, Shub presents Kerensky in *The Fall of the Romanov Dynasty* by showing authentic newsreel of him without resorting to the use of an actor, histrionics or a fictitious mise en scène. Shub's Kerensky is featured after an intertitle declaring him to be one of 'the leaders who had been pushing the masses towards a compromise with the bourgeoisie'. In Shub's film, rather than a quivering weakling, Kerensky is portrayed as he was photographed in the film news of the day. The historian Richard Abraham reinforces Shub's evaluation when he comments that Kerensky 'was a moderate who accepted the current Marxist orthodoxy suggesting that Russia was unripe for socialism'.[13] In the Provisional Government, 'the liberal Kadets and the Mensheviks both agreed that the government following the overthrow of tsarism must be a "bourgeois" government'.[14] Kerensky appears only once more in *The Fall of the Romanov Dynasty* just prior to Shub's triumphant epilogue. After a shot of Kerensky and before presenting the film's climax with Lenin's inspiring 'Peace! Bread! Freedom!' speech, Shub juxtaposes the fall of Kerensky with the rise of Lenin. Thus, she reminds her audience of Kerensky and the Provisional Government's ill-advised urging to continue to send Russian soldiers to the front. With a once enthusiastic public now believing that World War I was a futile and disastrous exercise, Kerensky's downfall was hastened by his misguided sustained engagement with the war effort (and therefore his insistence on continuing support for the Allies). Shub's intertitle informs us that 'War Minister Kerensky himself visited the front in order to inspire courage in the hearts of the glorious defenders of freedom'. In order to convey that this is not what the proletariat were seeking, Shub shows workers demonstrating in the street.

Thus, while Shub constructs her compilation from authentic material, in *October* Eisenstein alters and recreates the historical narrative radically. Being forced to comply with orders from Stalin himself to remove all references to Trotsky, instead, Eisenstein decides to use the actor playing Trotsky to discredit him thoroughly. Although Trotsky was seen as one of the seminal figures during both the Revolution and the Civil War, Eisenstein besmirches his achievements in what is a brutal character assassination. Trotsky is shown as cowardly and vacillating and worse still, a traitor to the Bolshevik cause. In a blatant fabrication of facts, he is portrayed not only as being in conflict with Lenin but also as cowering behind the door of the Menshevik office with his equally pusillanimous cohorts.

Where Shub sought to document historical events with accuracy to substantiate her accounts, such as her brief insertion of information pertaining to Kerensky, Eisenstein had no such restrictions in the more creative environment of fiction film. In fact, his vast intellect and fertile imagination were even more effective when, instead of distorting historical truth, he introduced poetic imagery with clear literary origins. Thus, Eisenstein used powerful metaphors: for instance, an audience could watch spellbound as a dead white horse literally plummeted earthwards out of the heavens. This spectacular and enduring image of portent does more than merely herald and indicate the bloodshed of revolution. The film theorist Yuri Tsivian has interpreted this apparition as a symbol of apocalypse. As Tsivian conveys it: 'Bely [stated] that film in general meant the end of art, film as apocalypse of art. . . . A falling white horse announced the end of our culture.'[15]

Shub was thoroughly versed in the works of the leading Russian Symbolist poets (such as Andrei Bely and Alexander Blok), and, like Eisenstein, she was well aware of the significance of this horse from the sky.[16] Yet, unlike their Symbolist forbears, Shub and the Constructivists promoted this idea of the death of traditional art as a necessity for the ongoing cultural revolution, and they did so with strategies markedly different from those of Eisenstein. Indeed, Eisenstein's arresting apocalyptic allegory demonstrates his ability to intercut the real with the fictional, the diegetic with the non-diegetic, thus interweaving extraordinary elements with the everyday. What did a white horse, a peacock or a statue of Napoleon infer? What significance could the viewer attach to this textual and cinematic imagery imbued with mythology and symbolism? Such questions represented the latitude allowed by fiction film, where inventiveness and creativity of style were without boundaries.

Additionally, in R. Bruce Elder's *Harmony + Dissent: Film and Avant-Garde Art Movements in the Early Twentieth Century*, Elder's persuasive positioning of Eisenstein as a disciple of mystical thought (Madame Blavatsky's Theosophy, Rudolf Steiner's Anthroposophy and Rosicrucianism) adds another dimension to Eisenstein's attraction to myths and fables.[17] Elder believes that Eisenstein was influenced by Rosicrucianism to such a degree that the doctrines of this brotherhood, particularly the centrality that they afforded to alchemical states of being and becoming, informed Eisenstein's film theory and practice. Obviously, an involvement with the workings of this occult sect was totally incompatible with the fundamental tenets of Constructivism as was Eisenstein's undeniable fascination with the Russian Symbolists (and by extension, the white horse of the apocalypse which appears with such compelling effect in *October*).

However, in spite of this opposition between Shub and Eisenstein stylistically, there was a point of intersection between nonfiction and fiction film. With Shub's constant parallel cutting between the proletariat and the monarchy, the church, the bourgeoisie and the capitalists, her audience similarly would need to decode her messages of hierarchical structure and the gross imbalance in their society. Within the construction of nonfiction film, Shub balanced and weighed fact against fact, or compared two seemingly unconnected documentary fragments to persuade the viewer to perform a new reading. Through this filmic structure, Shub overturned the inherent isolated meaning of the frame and constructed an ideological position.

We watch, for example, the frivolities of the privileged Romanovs whiling away the hours in pleasure, dancing the mazurka without a care in the world. In counterpoint, Shub unveils the wretched life of the manual labourers who are toiling in the blazing sun.[18] The audience sees the various elements of the staggering inequity of wealth and status created from two sources of film: firstly from the Tsar's private family films chronicling average days in the life of the Romanovs, and secondly from the unstaged newsreels of daily rural life. What is unique about this insight into two strata of tsarist society, namely, its zenith and base, is that Shub's motivation for the inclusion of the Tsar's personal film footage was so vastly dissimilar from its original intent. Thus, Shub used these authentic film fragments in ironic contrast with one another to construct her ideological montage. Meanwhile, Eisenstein employed a fictional strategy loosely underpinned by historical fact, juxtaposing and colliding shots, which were composed from the staging of often fabricated, dramatized action. While both Shub and Eisenstein believed, as Yuri Tsivian observed, that 'history could be edited without betraying its real essence', *October* was nonetheless far removed from Shub's documentary structure.[19] *October* was a mélange of staged, dramatic realism together with ersatz documentary: a pageant of acted historical events interspersed with symbolic tropes and overlaid with intellectual montage.

'The Ambiguity of Reality' in Shub's Historical Documentary

Shub's editing of her documentary compilations was in direct contrast to Eisenstein's editing of history. Shub would take a frame of authentic newsreel and add a political intertitle, while Eisenstein took a staged drama and then embellished it by combining elements of fact and fiction. Shub's montage involved the assemblage of actuality footage, thus preserving the original image in its basic form: shots of peasants reaping the harvest, the tercentenary celebrations of the Romanov Dynasty, processions of priests, members of the Duma, women demonstrating in public and Lenin conversing with the converted. Consequently, it was her Constructivist methodology, and therefore the realistic style of her nonfiction documentation, which made Shub rather than Eisenstein LEF's filmmaker of choice. For LEF, *The Fall of the Romanov Dynasty* represented cinematic authenticity, while *October* (in which Eisenstein creates a fictional narrative embellished with rich metaphors and ornate symbols) was seen as its antithesis.

Indeed, with *October*, Eisenstein was seen as straddling two genres, and, despite some powerful moments of acted realism, his film form and methodology fell heavily onto the side of fiction film. Vertov's cutting dismissal of him as a maker of 'fiction pictures in documentary trousers' underlined the avant-garde's criticism aimed at Eisenstein's approach.[20] For the leaders of LEF, there was a marked dichotomy between Eisenstein's symbolic and dramatized approach to realism, and Shub's preserving of historical truth through documentary. It was what LEF alleged was the contrived choreography of Eisenstein as opposed to what they identified as the documenting of reality in the cinematic works of Shub.

In contrast to *The Fall of the Romanov Dynasty*, Eisenstein's *October* was perceived as a work that André Bazin perhaps would have described as 'the pseudo-realism of a deception aimed at fooling the eye (or for that matter the mind)'.[21] This evaluation of *October* is exemplified not only by Eisenstein's re-staging of the seizing of the Winter Palace but also by his use of the non-professional actors Vasili Nikandrov and Nikolay Popov to play the roles of V. I. Lenin and Alexander Kerensky respectively.

Simultaneously, LEF recognized Shub's *The Fall of the Romanov Dynasty* as a film that served to 'embalm'[22] her epoch, to borrow Bazin's terminology again, through the documenting of a cinematic 'objectivity in time'.[23] LEF's argument, problematical though it may appear today, claimed that the image Shub displayed for her audience was not the staged reproduction of an event but an authentic moment captured by the camera: their conclusion being that she presented reality directly on the screen. Although Bazin's notion regarding the relationship between film and the real may be interpreted as a form of naive realism, in his observations about Italian neorealism he speaks of 'the ambiguity of reality'.[24] I would suggest that this expression is applicable to both Shub's and Eisenstein's cinematic representations of the Russian Revolution, in the sense that theirs are subjective responses to a momentous year in world history.

Shub's images of the events leading to the February Revolution have become (over a hundred years later) priceless snapshots of the beginning of the twentieth century. This is so in spite of the fact that, just as all documentary makers, she edited her film sequences to convey a specific sociological, ideological and political agenda. Shub's characterization of women in *The Fall of the Romanov Dynasty* further confirms the principles of nonfiction film in the presentation of straightforward, non-dramatized and candid newsreel images. The film scholar Martin Stollery remarks on issues of gender in *The Fall of the Romanov Dynasty*. He maintains that 'what would now be recognised as feminist preoccupations . . . were not central to Shub's work'.[25] The overriding issue is more complex. In summation 'in Leninism, class was privileged, not gender. Feminists were persecuted'.[26] As Denise Youngblood has observed regarding the 'woman question' in the USSR:

> The Bolshevik leadership paid lip service to women's rights but looked askance on feminists in their ranks, the best example being Alexandra Kollontai, whom Lenin thoroughly despised and crudely vilified. 'Marxist feminism' is an oxymoron: Marxists believe that class determines power relations, while feminists believe that it is gender. Stalin was more overt than Lenin in his patriarchal views on women, but they shared the same basic outlook. The Bolsheviks did expand 'women's place' to most sectors of the workforce, but any sector that was significantly feminized (like the medical profession) had low status in Soviet society. (All surgeons, hospital directors, medical school professors were, however, men.) Women might be tractor drivers, but they were still expected to do all the work at home.[27]

These sobering facts aside, with the empowering agitation in the latter nineteenth century by the Russian feminists and the more extremist elements of the women's movement (some of them had made the ultimate sacrifice and had been executed for terrorist activity), the way was paved for Shub and her female contemporaries in the early twentieth century. This crucial change opened the door for women in terms of education, career opportunities, equality and financial independence.

Shub came to Moscow to commence her university studies before the Revolution. At this time, the long and difficult struggle of the women's movement in Russia had already given way to a degree of emancipation, notably in the arena of higher education and this was a major liberating force. Shub was living proof of all its hard-fought-for gains.

Nonetheless without declaring it overtly, Shub was a feminist in the way in which she conducted her life and career. Significantly, there seems to be no feature by which to clearly differentiate the work of Shub as a woman filmmaker, from that of her male counterparts of the period. As the director of factual nonfiction film, Shub needed to be hidden from sight: 'impartial' and invisible. Yet this unobtrusive and seemingly anonymous method of cinematic presentation may be the very point. As a filmmaker, Shub was both indistinguishable from and the equal of any man. She stood shoulder to shoulder with Vertov as the leading documentary maker of her era.

However, the viewer can witness women from every stratum of society presented within the context of Shub's thesis on the disparity between the nobility, the bourgeoisie and the proletariat. They are presented within the context of the authoritarian tsarist hierarchical class structure (and hence Marxist theory) rather than as part of a discourse on the question of gender and women's rights prior to the socialist era. Consequently, there are archival shots of the Tsarina, the upper-class ladies at court and the Governor of Kaluga's wife all portrayed amidst scenes of idleness and wealth. In opposition to the privileged upper classes, we also observe peasant women involved in backbreaking agricultural work in the fields and their counterparts in urban areas engaged in manual labour clearing snow from the roads or employed in the factories.

Hence, with reference to this, in Shub's section on World War I, there is the following intertitle: 'the government replaced the mobilised workers with women.' The accompanying images show the female proletarian workforce in charge of machinery, making armaments and on a production assembly line. Out of necessity, due to the extraordinary circumstances of military conflict, they have temporarily been placed on an equal footing with their male co-workers. There are groups of women in the street using shovels, digging the snow and ice from under the wheels of vehicles. Shub's corresponding intertitle reads: 'The weather was severely cold. It was too much for them to struggle against the snow drifts.'

Later, we deliberate on the collective power of the women's movement when hordes of their members take to the streets celebrating International Women's

Figure 9 Marching in the streets on International Women's Day, February 1917 in *The Fall of the Romanov Dynasty*.

Day in March 1917 (February O. S. and henceforth known as the February Revolution) (Figure 9). Amongst the marching throng, Shub's text informs us of the presence of 'Vera Figner – an old revolutionary, a member of the People's Will Party'. We then witness priceless slightly blurred footage (possibly the only shots now in existence, apart from a fleeting shot in *The Great Way*) of Vera Nikolaevna Figner (1852–1943) ringing a bell and yelling encouragement from the open back of a vehicle. In the mid-1870s, this legendary activist had abandoned her medical studies for a committed role in terrorist activities against Alexander II. After the Tsar's assassination, she was imprisoned for twenty years having had her sentence of execution overturned. Figner was seen as a political legend and a radical feminist role model and was free at last to join the march with her socialist sisters.

Yet, despite the stirring footage of women joining forces (presented so vividly on screen by Shub), the only textual commentary for the whole of this segment is the short intertitle giving us Vera Figner's name and a phrase describing her importance. Shub could have enlightened her viewers further in her intertitles because this protest was in fact far more than merely a public symbol of liberation. It was not only a rousing parade but also a mass demonstration where women workers, appalled by the interminable bread queues and the crippling cost of living, combined their strength in solidarity with other members of the sisterhood from all walks of life. Later that day male workers and factory employees went on strike. Spilling onto the streets, they swelled the ranks of women demonstrators. The theme became a torrent of 'Down with the Tsar!' This march in Petrograd on Nevsky Prospekt was a catalyst for the February Revolution. Women agitators and their demonstration played an important role in sparking the events that triggered the collapse of the Romanov Dynasty.

Shub's panoramic sweep illustrates, through the evidence of clearly documented newsreel, her commitment to the cause. It can be seen that while Shub and Eisenstein worked in different genres and with antithetical methodologies, they were both idealistic political filmmakers, who used agitation to stir feelings of collective patriotism within the environment of the cinema. As far as they saw themselves as revolutionary film artists, Shub and Eisenstein were aiming for an awakening of political consciousness as a result of their respective filmic representations of reality, in order to effect a transformation of Soviet society.

In light of this fact, it is not surprising that for all its spatial and temporal discontinuities (and its dominating non-diegetic symbols) there is a memorable and patriotic scene of played theatrical realism in *October*, namely the filmic reconstruction of the storming of the Winter Palace. In fact, the film scholar Richard Taylor examines this controversial issue of Eisenstein's historical re-enactment of October 1917 as a purported first-hand record of events.[28] Even though his tableau depicting this spectacle illustrates Bazin's critique of 'pseudo-realism', Eisenstein's orchestrated and highly charged cinematic performance of this incident has been viewed and accepted as reality by audiences far and wide. His electric mise en scène in *October* was to be seen as a worthy substitute for the real thing. Hence, it is perhaps because understandably no documentary footage was shot of this event that Eisenstein's recreation has been transformed into historical evidence. Ironically, Eisenstein's thrilling staged dramatization of the October Revolution has come to be accepted as a genuine eyewitness sequence, whereas Shub's comparatively far less sensational historical documentation of the circumstances leading to the February Revolution in *The Fall of the Romanov Dynasty* has slipped into comparative obscurity.

Instead of Eisenstein's exhilarating drama, Shub continually offers us facts and figures. Early in *The Fall of the Romanov Dynasty*, in Shub's introductory intertitles, the spectator is informed that 'Obedient to the Tsar, the State Duma was in session in St. Petersburg'. There follows a long shot of the Duma and then another intertitle which, through its statistics, presents us with the striking imbalance of representation. The privileged classes are governing the country.

The champions of the populace are shown to be grossly outnumbered. As Shub notes with clarity in order to educate her viewers:

'Representatives of the People'
Out of the 445 members of the State Duma
Landowners – Gentry 241
The bourgeoisie 79
Priests 43

We then see an interior shot of the Duma in session with the camera lingering on a commanding full-length portrait of the Tsar. Shub wants to leave no hesitation in the mind of her audience about the supreme power wielded by the absolute ruler, Nicholas II. By extension, she is preparing her spectators with the utmost clarity for the outcome of this intolerable situation for the subjugated masses. This is part of Shub's well-tabulated evidence, in her comprehensive argument, which gradually develops her proof and thereby anticipates the inevitability of what she describes as the 'complete disintegration of the monarchy'.[29]

In this segment of *The Fall of the Romanov Dynasty*, Shub's focus is fixed firmly on the personalities who exercise political sway in this repressive tsarist era, through their wealth, influence and seats in the Duma. Therefore, her objective of preserving historical truth through the unadorned use of archival film documents can be further appreciated in her subtle reference to the politician and influential friend of the Tsar, Vladimir M. Purishkevich. Although Shub never directly mentions her Jewish heritage in *My Life – Cinematography*, she demonstrates her abhorrence for the notorious extreme right-wing and anti-Semitic 'Black Hundreds' [Chernosotenetsy] organization.[30] Justifiably, in her written text Shub describes the hate-filled and murderous Black Hundreds as 'the greatest disgrace in all of Russia'.[31] This is reiterated in the most understated manner when Shub lingers on shots of what appears to be an ordinary, inoffensive looking and well-dressed official (wearing prim gloves and a bowler hat). He is seen leaving the Duma and stepping into his carriage. This man is V. M. Purishkevich the virulent extremist, well-known anti-Semite and the fervid supporter and organizer (with Dr A. I. Dubrovin), of the Black Hundreds (Figure 10).

Unlike other members of the Duma, whose names are fleetingly mentioned before we briefly observe their faces, this man is fully described in one succinct sentence laden with subtext. Shub uses no emotive language. Instead, on the screen we simply read a direct statement: 'Purishkevich leader of the monarchist Black Hundreds – pogromshchiks.' This label is, however, pregnant with

Figure 10 V. M. Purishkevich in *The Fall of the Romanov Dynasty*.

meaning, as are the seemingly commonplace images of Purishkevich. Although, textually, she gives us the barest of facts, just enough to record whom this man is and what he does, Shub's understatement holds immense power. For her, without doubt (as she notes in her memoirs), the name 'Purishkevich was one of the most offensive words imaginable' and yet her message has been conveyed with subtlety.[32]

Additionally, Shub emphasizes the Tsar's complicity in not only the senseless slaughter of countless Jews during the pogroms ('a regular technique regularly applied'),[33] directly attributed to the Black Hundreds, but also in the justification for these unprovoked attacks through anti-Semitic propaganda in Romanov-funded daily newspapers.[34] To this end, Shub photographs the front page of one of these publications, resplendent with the prominent image of a religious work of art, an icon, boldly centred on the page and surrounded by text, as if to declare that there is room for only one religion in Russia. Yet, Shub's intertitle consists of just three telling words enclosed by ellipses: '... the pogromist press ...'.

In order to further underline Tsar Nicholas's connection with the 'pogromist press', in the following statement Shub postulates: 'All are LOYAL subjects of "his majesty": The First Nobleman and Master of Rus.'" Her intertitle thus leaving us in no doubt as to who is driving this campaign of vilification in the print media. For further emphasis, Shub deliberately chooses *The Russian Banner* [Russkoe znamya], a daily newspaper published by Purishkevich's ally, Dr A. I. Dubrovin. It is known as being both anti-revolutionary and anti-Semitic and is the mouthpiece of the Black Hundreds. The image, from *The Russian Banner*, in Shub's film is of an unambiguous signifier: a sacred Christian artwork emblazoned across the centre of the front page. The icon represents Holy Mother Russia and the Orthodox Church allied in every way to Nicholas II, a union that is encapsulated by their guiding motto: One Russia, One Tsar, One Creed.

Consequently, in *The Fall of the Romanov Dynasty* Shub continually contrasts the conflicts of the monarchic past with the February Revolution of 1917 and the resultant surge in social consciousness. She shows the old feudal system in the guise of the monarchy and the church being supplanted by the new and the modern. This change of paradigm is illustrated by the rise of the Bolsheviks, who ostensibly herald the demise of oppression and the promotion of atheism and freedom. Thus, thematically and structurally, *The Fall of the Romanov Dynasty* propounds the constant opposition of these two contradictory forces through Shub's montage: the evils of tsarism balanced against the virtues of the new socialist order. Accordingly, through both its didactic commentary and visual montage, Shub's Constructivist film of 1927 encapsulates the liaison between the flowering of the social, the political and the artistic revolutions of the Soviet Union in the 1920s.

Despite its dual emphasis on historical factography and ideological agitation, *The Fall of the Romanov Dynasty* is not devoid of humanity. On the contrary, this film in Shub's trilogy not only transfers onto film a record of revolutionary times but also depicts the hopes of the people for a just society in their brave new world. As an example, the film's lengthy focus on World War I, discussed in the previous chapter, forces the viewer to reflect on the senseless brutality of battle, driven by the heads of state and their generals who needlessly sacrifice the lives of the populace. On the screen, we read a document that will prove to be the final nail in the coffin for the reign of Nicholas II. This edict will have a profound impact on the inhabitants of Tsarist Russia, thereby hastening the fall of the Romanov Dynasty:

To the War Minister:

Having recognised it as necessary to bring the army into a war posture, as per the instructions given by ME to you, we enjoin you forthwith to make all pertinent arrangements.

July 17, 1914 is to be designated the first day of mobilisation.

Nicholas

Figure 11 An arms factory: white crosses on shell casings in *The Fall of the Romanov Dynasty*.

Correspondingly in the segment on World War I Shub presents nothing but ruin, devastation and destruction. We see the factories that belch forth not just smoke but weapons of death, and the vehicles that carry these military armaments. Later, we observe the factory workforce making weapons: shots of row upon row of shells, which look like tombstones in a graveyard with their casings even marked with crosses (Figure 11).

At this point, Shub introduces a shot of the smug self-satisfied 'Vtorov owner of the largest armaments factory', who, in Marxian terms, is represented as a capitalist exploiter sacrificing the life of the proletariat for the sake of greed and profit.[35] As Shub so aptly phrases it in her intertitles:

Those to whom war was necessary: Vtorov . . .
Those who would be sent to the slaughter . . .
The hands of the workers were preparing death
For their brothers.

Just as Shub attacks the capitalists who profit from war, neither the Russian Orthodox Church nor the bourgeoisie emerge unscathed. We watch the clergy solemnly walking along a line of bedraggled, weary troops dispensing prayers and sprinkling them with holy water. There is an opulently robed priest making the sign of the cross with an elaborate gold bejewelled crucifix. After close-up shots of two bandaged soldiers, the ranks line up while their officers pin meaningless medals onto their miserable chests. Representatives of the charitable middle class then munificently bestow food parcels upon the demoralized rank and file. Shub derisively summarizes the empty and sombre ritual. Her cutting Marxist ideology is well to the fore in an incisive appraisal, succinctly expressed within the text of her mocking intertitles:

> The 'holy fathers' tried to prop up the troops' fighting ability
> with the word of Christ.
> The authorities conferred them with little crosses.
> The bourgeoisie rewarded them with 'little somethings'.

Furthermore, in this segment of the film we also read the following text: 'Mobilization was taking the workers away from their machines... and the peasants from the fields.' The image that seems to correspond with this text is, however, not of soldiers but of a woman openly sobbing. This is followed by shots of crowds farewelling their loved ones. The woman is weeping and being comforted and her 'performance' is not aimed at the camera lens. Consumed by emotion, she appears totally unaware that filming is taking place. Shub is presenting us with grief as the inevitable consequence of war, which in turn is presented as the effect of capitalism.

It is also visibly shocking to watch 'Cannon fodder... being drilled'. Schoolboys in uniform armed with bayoneted rifles (as large as themselves) solemnly march past us on the screen. This piteous sight of children, some looking as though they are no more than ten years old, serves to emphasize further the horror and tragic waste of war. Shub's poignant but controlled intertitle reads: 'they formed regiments of toy soldiers.' The use of the specific phrase 'toy soldiers' underscores yet further the connection between childhood games of make-believe and the loss of both innocence and young lives.

Interestingly, in the opening chapter of *The Fall of the Romanov Dynasty* we see a small lad gazing in wonderment at the Tsar's soldiers practising their drills within the walls of the Kremlin. In a later shot, in the section on World War I, Shub shows an image of a woeful little boy who has been wounded, wearing his army uniform and sporting an enormous bandage wrapped around his head. These thought-provoking images of children's involvement in war are extremely effective as they are presented as lambs being led to the slaughter. Taken directly from newsreel footage, their pathetic faces were emblematic of senseless human sacrifice in the name of the Tsar, and as such, these shots had the potential to exert a powerful emotional reaction.

Realism, Identification and the Representation of Historical Reality

Shub's film was the newsreel documentation of not only pathos-filled war footage but also a recording of everyday life. Even though 'The Work of Art in the Age of Mechanical Reproduction' was not written until the middle of the following decade, in this groundbreaking study Walter Benjamin echoes much of Shub's filmic philosophy. He considered that 'For the film, what matters primarily is that the actor represents himself [sic] to the public before the camera, rather than representing someone else'.[36] Added to this, 'the newsreel offers everyone the opportunity to rise from passer-by to movie extra. In this way any man [sic] might even find himself part of a work of art [and] lay claim to being filmed.'[37] With Shub's non-acted cinematic documents there was always the potential for people to identify with her images. In her films they could see themselves (or people like themselves) either in close-up or in scenes in the fields, factories, mines, in army barracks, peasant market places or walking through a provincial town in their Sunday best. By the same token, through the genre of nonfiction film, Shub acknowledged the sacrifices of the common people in their struggle for freedom. For the first time, peasants and factory workers were given a voice and a significant role in Russian society; *The Fall of the Romanov Dynasty* reinforced this view in its representation of the proletariat as actively participating in the construction of their history.

However, *The Fall of the Romanov Dynasty* was not just a series of often touching shots of the proletariat; there are also authentic scenes from the lives of their aloof Romanov rulers. Shub even shows at first-hand irrefutable evidence of the disabling haemophilia endured by the Tsar's small son Aleksei. There is poignant footage of him pitifully but bravely limping along and trying to keep pace with his father, who is reviewing the sailors on the deck of a ship from the Romanov fleet. There is another image of a lame Aleksei (wearing a sailor's suit) being carried by a burly retainer in the long procession of dignitaries during the tercentenary celebrations. He is situated behind the Tsar and Tsarina, who are placed in the centre of the shot. Significantly, Nicholas and his wife walk in humility behind the Procurator of the Holy Synod, in a perfect union of the church and the monarchy (Figure 12).

As these candid shots showing Aleksei with his father on the Royal naval vessel and again in the public procession with his parents attest, *The Fall of the Romanov Dynasty* is more than merely a synthesis of newsreel fragments. Supplementing this

Figure 12 The Tercentenary Celebrations of the Romanov Dynasty 1913 in *The Fall of the Romanov Dynasty*.

fundamental element, the film often displays more personal insights and moments of human interest, within a framework of convincing and authentic footage.

Furthermore, *The Fall of the Romanov Dynasty*'s historical accuracy and textual economy is exemplified in the following intertitle where Shub displays an extract from an authentic political document filled with urgency. It is a heart-wrenching cry for support and direct action:

> We are perishing. We are starving. . . . We are dying in the trenches.
> To be silent is impossible. Everyone onto the streets . . .
> Everyone under the red banners of the Revolution!
> *From a proclamation of the Central Committee of the Bolsheviks,*
> 25 February 1917.

Shub's narration continues: 'the combat force discontented and embittered, had been suffering defeats and was falling to pieces. They were leaving the front lines.' The wretched and appalling accompanying images are of dead men and dead animals lying frozen in a deep blanket snow at the front. In typical Constructivist style, Shub uses actual war footage combined with a direct quotation from a genuine historical declaration. Her presentation of stark, authentic images of death on the battlefield, accompanied by text from the pages of history, constitutes a compelling cinematic attempt to bring the real drama of their recent past to the attention of the audience.

Moreover, unlike the fiction film of *October*, *The Fall of the Romanov Dynasty*, as actorless nonfiction film, is teeming with genuine images of Shub's society, directly constructed from archival footage. As Walter Benjamin states: 'some of the players . . . in Russian films are not actors . . . but people who portray themselves'.[38] By using 'people who portray themselves' Shub strives to heighten a sense of authenticity in the documented historical reality presented in her film. This is epitomized by the motifs and structure of her film's introduction and conclusion, analysed in the following section.

First and Last Images: Signs and Meanings

Both Shub and Eisenstein's two cinematic interpretations of the Russian upheaval in 1917 have filmic beginnings and endings that befit their different genres. The pseudo-realism of *October* is filled with often complex metaphors and abstruse codes. Yet like Shub, Eisenstein begins and ends his film with visual and ideological clarity conveyed through readily identifiable signs and signifiers. Starting with the statue of Nicholas II's father, Tsar Alexander III, followed by its destruction, the last image in *October* is that of the Smolnyi Institute at night, ablaze with electric lights.[39] Eisenstein gives, in this way, an excellent summary of the October Revolution itself: as the first images in *October* depict the toppling of despotism, the last frame gives a satisfying concluding picture of the heralding of the new power. We go from backward tsarism to the advancement of the technological age, with the 'light of modernity' attributed to socialism. Eisenstein has Lilliputian-sized peasants swarming over the gigantic sculpture of Alexander III, hauling it down on ropes and thus destroying the massive machinery of Tsardom, as they peel away its artifice. There is adherence to historical truth behind this scenario because the statues of the old regime were actually destroyed. In accordance with the facts, Shub shows genuine shots of the demolished symbols of monarchy lying in ruins in *The Fall of the Romanov Dynasty*. Where Eisenstein provides us with theatre, Shub produces real footage, as we view the actual emblem of the hand of power broken on the ground and yet defiantly still clutching the orb (Figure 13).

The structure of *October*'s introduction and conclusion is identical to that of *The Fall of the Romanov Dynasty*'s. As the latter was released the month before Eisenstein had even started filming; it is feasible that *The Fall of the Romanov Dynasty* would have been an influence on *October*.[40] Shub commences her work with a filmic paragraph, which like Eisenstein signifies the end of the old order.

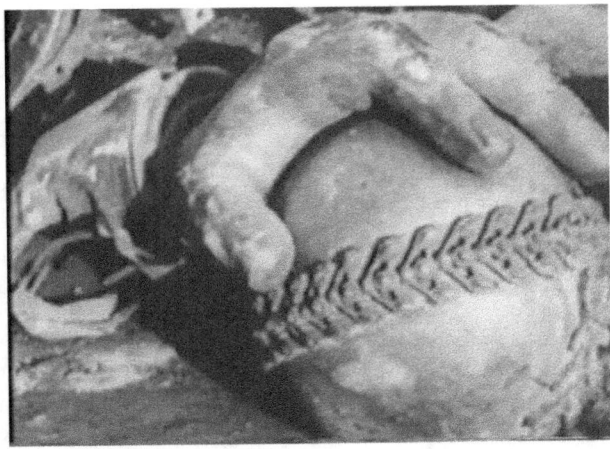

Figure 13 The hand of power and the orb in ruins in *The Fall of the Romanov Dynasty*.

She begins with an architectural shot, whereas Eisenstein ends his film with one. Her initial intertitle ushers in her opening chapter: 'Tsarist Russia in the years of the black reaction.' The next frame reads: 'The Kremlin of the Romanovs.' After this text the first image follows: the wondrous symmetry and beauty of the towers of the Romanovs. These three steeples reach skywards like the points of a crown as they hover above the nation. While in general they symbolize the trinity of crown, church and state, they particularly signify the height of Romanov power. As if to accentuate this, the central and highest of the spires is topped with the imperial double-headed eagle of the House of Romanov, a dynasty founded in 1613.

From the pale verticals, Shub then cuts directly to a giant dark cannon within the Kremlin walls and presents us with the Romanov's military might. We have just observed how high their dominance stretches. To further accent their supremacy, this menacing cannon symbolizes the breadth of their strength as its powerful horizontal image commands the frame.

Finally, in this triptych we see the leading imperial subjects who are instruments of this authority. After the height and the breadth, we are now shown the depth of tsarist rule. Firstly and most importantly, there is an impressive and lengthy column of priests wending their way in a seemingly endless procession: a hypnotic and highly influential band within the court of the Romanovs. Like the Romanovs, the clergy strike awe and fear into the hearts of the common people.

This powerful brigade of clerics is followed, not by an intertitle but by vividly contrasting images of army regiments drilling and marching within the

Kremlin. Their dark, austere winter uniforms are in direct counterpoint to the light-coloured and sumptuous robes of the priests: the Tsar's ermine-draped guardians. However, the soldiers and the priesthood both serve a common purpose. It is not only to support the Tsar physically and spiritually but more significantly to act as instruments of control. These two pillars of officialdom (the two lesser spires of the first image) protecting the Romanov pinnacle, the heart in the centre, are the military and religious defenders of the realm.

Shub continues to document the dominion of the Romanov Dynasty over its subjects. Apart from the church and the army, there are the police, the politicians, the gentry and the landowners. All these factions, who exercise power over the proletariat, are featured in *The Fall of the Romanov Dynasty*'s first visual chapter.

Moreover, Shub subtly juxtaposes the opening images of the powerful tsarist-controlled clergy with corresponding shots in the film's closing segments, sending an altogether different concluding message to the audience. At the beginning of the film, the priests are observed striding confidently towards the camera; they are an imposing and controlling presence. In the film's finale, just before a sequence in which Lenin addresses the people, we see the clergy for the last time. On this occasion, however, they are a fading image. Portrayed in a never-ending snake-like procession, these once influential and supremely self-assured men are now dwarfed by the Kremlin Wall (this sequence lasts about seven seconds). What is telling here is that these upholders of the faith are no longer giants in the foreground. They are, at this point in time, disclosed as small, indistinct, modest and insignificant shapes fading from sight as they walk away from the lens. Just as the camera pins the priests against the wall and then banishes them from view, thus negating their power, so Lenin will dispense with religion. Shub's visual statement is apparent: the Kremlin citadel is to become synonymous with the Soviet government, and there will be no place for the church in this new socialist world.

Consequently, in the concluding chapter of *The Fall of the Romanov Dynasty* before ushering in the towering figure of Lenin, Shub heralds the finale of her film with a vigorous political poster:

DEMONSTRATION TODAY!
Neither a separate peace with Wilhelm, nor a secret treaty with the French and English capitalists!
BREAD! PEACE! FREEDOM!
Central Committee,
Russian Social Democratic Workers' Party.

Shub's intertitles at this juncture become slogans. Used dynamically, they are instructions to the defiant masses, a succinct call to arms, which serves to enhance the corresponding images:

> Proceed in orderly ranks along the streets of the capital
> Declare your wishes with calmness and sureness:
> DOWN WITH THE COUNTER-REVOLUTION!
> DOWN WITH THE TSARIST DUMA!
> DOWN WITH THE STATE COUNCIL!
> DOWN WITH THE 10 MINISTER-CAPITALISTS!

Exclamation after exclamation is superimposed over the images of the marching crowds with their banners unfurled. The text on the screen seems to signify the slogans on the standards carried by the demonstrators. Apart from Lenin's speech, which is to follow, this is the only time Shub breaks with her convention of placing an intertitle before the image. Conspicuously, in this case, the political text seems to envelop the people; thus, the working class is represented as being at one with the Revolution.

The final shots of *The Fall of the Romanov Dynasty* are thus devoted to Lenin and the advancement of the downtrodden proletariat. Where Eisenstein shows the Smolnyi, Shub gives us the man himself. A massive demonstration is taking place on the streets; there are banners aplenty. We behold a sea of jubilant faces. These are the faces of the people and their champion Lenin is addressing them. The multitude – entranced soldiers and sailors – listen to his every word. In this closing scene, Lenin lectures and motivates the crowd, stirring the thousands of loyal members of the proletariat gathered to listen. Shub now transforms her intertitles into a dynamic use of political slogans: 'All power to the Councils of Workers', Soldiers and Peasants' Deputies!' The text is bold, short and sharp, and it merges in unison with the rare newsreel footage of Lenin.

The rapturous crowds wave, cheer and applaud as Lenin continues with his socialist sermon. Finally, he concludes his inspirational pulpit oratory with further declamations: 'Revise "The Declaration of the Rights of the Soldier"! Abolish Orders against Soldiers and Sailors!' To emphasize her thesis of the unification of the proletariat with the doctrines of Lenin and socialism, these concluding two lines of his speech are also superimposed over the masses of people in the throng, the camera's focus being mainly on soldiers and sailors in their uniforms. The final shots in *The Fall of the Romanov Dynasty* portray a triumphant Lenin, promising hope for the future of the Soviet Union and its populace through the creed of socialism.

Visually, Shub's agit-poster filmic construction, with its rousing battle cries, the text on screen and actual footage of the crowds and Lenin, illustrates her adherence to Constructivist principles. The effectiveness and simplicity of this unembellished, utilitarian art form was perfectly suited to the compilation film genre and to nonfiction film. *The Fall of the Romanov Dynasty* begins with depictions of the despair of subjugation in the Romanov past and concludes with an image of rose-tinted optimism for a future utopia. Thus, in her film, Shub is promoting the deeply held belief of Constructivism that, through the participation of the proletariat, the emancipation of art would lead to the emancipation of society.

Ideological Montage in *The Fall of the Romanov Dynasty*

The social and political commentary that documents the historical events in *The Fall of the Romanov Dynasty* encapsulates Shub's filmic aspirations for nonfiction film. Her Constructivist chronicle depicts priests, landowners and aristocrats startlingly contrasted with the downtrodden workers and their supporting champions, as well as significant milestones in the events leading to the overthrow of the imperial family and the rise of Lenin. Interwoven with these epoch-changing events, she displays vignettes of ordinary life from her era. Accordingly, as she expresses it, Shub illustrates by her seamless combinations of short fragments, how 'the shaping of the film structurally derives from the raw material'.[41]

Consequently, by 'choosing this material in a conscious way', Shub was to transpose home movies belonging to the Tsar and his family into an alien context, thus utilizing this footage to drive forward her ideological montage.[42] With this aim in mind, in one scene of *The Fall of the Romanov Dynasty* Shub introduces the Tsar, his family and his entourage as they perform a perfunctory dance during a period of empty diversion on a royal ocean liner. Her intertitle reads: 'Their "honours" were pleased to dance the mazurka with their "highnesses" . . . until they perspired.' Shub discovered this sequence, of the Romanov party dancing on the deck, in a reel of the Tsar's home movies. Over sixty years later, Chris Marker would use it imaginatively in his film *The Last Bolshevik*.

On board, the women are resplendent in summery gowns with posies on their waistbands and ornate sprigs of silk flowers decorating their hats. Their male partners are attired in dazzling snowy-white jackets. After a 'fatiguing' display on the dance floor, one of the females is seen fanning her face vigorously. Somewhat flushed, a noble lady dabs perspiration from her face with a flimsy handkerchief.

A member of the royal entourage is then filmed adjusting her hat and patting her coiffure back under it. As she disappears, exiting to the right of the frame, the next image is of the work party. The gestures of a peasant, seen prominently in the foreground, correspond to the end of the previous sequence. Shub has intentionally parallel cut images of good breeding and refinement with a shot of grimy peasants digging a ditch and sweating profusely. The workers in their dirty, crumpled rags do not have dainty lace-edged handkerchiefs at their disposal and instead mop their faces with their shirtsleeves.

Shub's ideological montage continues to alternate between the aristocratic women under the shade of the awning on deck wearing their exclusive millinery and the labouring workers. Some of these men, including a peasant in the foreground, are bareheaded. The few of them fortunate enough to have work caps emphasize yet another underlying difference between the two classes. The labourers wear headgear that is cheap and purely functional, whereas the expensive artistic creations of the upper crust are primarily for ornamentation. The glaring inequality of the privilege of nobility set against the bondage of the rural labourers could not be stated more transparently.

Through such fragments in her film, Shub demonstrates her role as agitator through the contrasting of two seemingly dissimilar incidents. She also includes another more subtle parallel between masters and slaves. There is a mimetic motion which links the refined lady, sweeping her fingertips across her eyes and perspiring brow, patting her slightly dishevelled coiffed hair into place and tucking it under her pretty broad-brimmed hat, with two of the peasants. Firstly, in the centre of the frame, a man momentarily stops digging to push a shock of hair off his brow and wipe his dripping face, before rolling up his sleeves, then scratching his chest and returning to his labours. Following this shot, almost out of the frame on the extreme far right, one of the workers adjusts his greasy locks, which are falling into his eyes. Flicking the sweat away from his eyes with the back of his hand, he removes his utilitarian worker's cap. He then runs his hand through his hair, brushing it back as he replaces his headgear. In this subtle comparison of gestures, Shub is yet again juxtaposing the body language of the nobility with the actions of their underlings.

Moreover, in another startling example of societal division and contrast in the stratified world of the *ancien régime*, Shub again accentuates the reason for the destruction of the royal lineage and the rise of the Bolsheviks. As Shub makes it clear in her intertitles:

> The landowner's lands covered enormous expanses
> The rich estates of the landowners
> And next to them – land-short, poverty-stricken villages

Instead of the frivolity of the Romanovs, Shub now features the wealthy Governor of Kaluga. We see him, a rotund man, with his equally amply proportioned wife as they regally descend the staircase of their massive palatial mansion. This shot is a close-up of the imposing multi-storied residence that Shub had shown us earlier, as she panned slowly across vast, rich tracts of fertile land. In a vista stretching as far as the eye can see, there are never-ending abundant fields and fruit trees heavily laden with blossom. The scene finally leads us to a bower-like avenue and then draws us towards the Governor's dwelling. At this moment, Shub beckons her audience inside with an interior shot of the Governor's splendid drawing room. There is antique furniture upholstered with costly brocade, an exquisite tapestry draped across the wall and a classical marble bust artfully positioned to the right of the screen.

From the magnificence of this living room, Shub cuts to the abject poverty of the peasants' hovels, thatched with straw, in an area of wasteland totally denuded of trees. In pride of place is not an art treasure from antiquity, but an outdated communal pump situated in the bare earth village 'square' which is surrounded by dwellings. We watch as the women draw water from this crude device.

This image of primitive water usage is then cleverly compared with the Governor of Kaluga and his wife about to enjoy a civilized afternoon tea in a leafy arbour on their gigantic property. After the scene where they leave their mansion with a sturdy little white bulldog gambolling at the heels of his mistress, the camera rests on their idyllic ornamental lake where swans and cygnets glide gracefully past. Bringing the pair and their pet back into the shot, we view them as they amble through the splendour of their grounds to a grove of shady trees. Here we see a charming table, laid out with refreshments. To bring us back to earth with a thud, Shub then abruptly inserts an intertitle: 'The peasants labour under the yoke on the landowner's land.'[43] The idyll has been broken: we see women hard at work in the fields under the scorching sun; they are gathering grain and bundling it into sheaves (Figure 14). This is parallel cut with the indolent pair sitting at their dainty table without a care in the world. They sip their tea from delicate cups and saucers (Figure 15).

Shub now cuts to show us contented, well-fed cows feeding on pasture and lazily chewing their cud by the riverbank. At this point, she pans gradually to the left. The inference is only too clear, with the contented well-fed Governor and his wife grazing idly and living off the fat of the land. We return once again to the duo finishing their tea. She plays with their dog, her husband tweaks his moustache and then she drinks the last dregs from her china cup. They rise

Figures 14 and 15 At Labour and at Play in *The Fall of the Romanov Dynasty*.

from the table and stroll out of the frame. Enter the staff, the maid and the manservant. He wears immaculate white gloves. Ridiculously, it takes two of them to clear away the paltry handful of insubstantial dishes. Shub pounds home her ideological message with a final scene of peasant women lifting massive and heavy stacks of hay. However dissimilar this latter image may seem from the gloved manservant and the maid who carry light and fragile crockery, they are all enslaved – whether through the burden of toiling in the fields or in service in the residence of a high-ranking official.

From the kerchiefed women hoisting hefty bundles of grain in the fields, Shub transports us to 'the nobility at court'. In their lavish ceremonial dress they look suspiciously like strutting peacocks (Figure 16). These cocky aristocrats are reminiscent of Eisenstein's brilliantly conceived theatrical projection (in *October*) of Kerensky melting into the dazzling mechanical peacock with all the obvious connotations of preening, vanity and conceit. However, where Eisenstein's Kerensky is a cleverly dramatized caricature played by an actor, Shub's mocking images are genuine newsreel footage of the upper classes on parade.

These popinjays exemplify Shub's Constructivist understanding of nonfiction film as both art and agitational propaganda – an understanding often laced with irony to accentuate her message. Shub's powerfully observed presentations of the life of the privileged in Tsarist Russia, such as the tercentenary celebrations and the Royal Family dancing on their ocean liner, are subverted and used

Figure 16 Pretension and Privilege in *The Fall of the Romanov Dynasty*.

satirically as a critical judgement of Russia prior to October 1917. Likewise, this is graphically illustrated in the segment featuring the Governor of Kaluga and his wife. Shub's straightforward intertitles serve to underline, through the use of derision, a visual comparison between the portly Governor of Kaluga and his plump wife and the satisfied, carefree cows in their pasture.

It is pertinent to recognize in a similar vein Shub's witty textual statement about the demise of Tsar Nicholas II, in which she holds the ineffectual and incompetent ruler and his impressive titles up to ridicule:

> Emperor and Autocrat
> of All Russias
> Tsar of Poland
> Grand Prince of Finland
> and so on and so forth
> Nicholas the Second . . .
> and last . . .
> . . . was solemnly celebrating the
> Three-hundredth Anniversary of the House of Romanov.

The segment prior to this one has revealed bleak images of the Alexandrov Central Prison. Shub again utilizes parallel cutting in order to place yet another conspicuous contrast before the viewer. The political prisoners seen here are casualties of Nicholas's reign of brutal repression, as Shub's text informs us:

> The tsarist regime dealt with
> those who rose up and fought
> by means of prisons . . .

A pan across the vast expanse that is the Alexandrov Prison complex is followed by a caption: 'penal servitude and exile'. After viewing prisoners loading a boat with cargo, Shub whisks us off for a tour of the opulence and excess at the House of Romanov's gala. Again, we have been shown cruel punishment and bitter hardship (those incarcerated for political agitation and social reform) alongside sheer wasteful luxury (the lavish festivities for Nicholas and Alexandra). From behind the barriers, the congregation of plebs watch with appropriate deference as the regal anniversary procession of hundreds of dignitaries dressed in their rich finery (followed by the Royal Family and their retinue), solemnly and self-importantly amble by. This is a fitting finale of overindulgence and extravagance, as the upper echelons of Russian society parade to applause in what will be the final major public commemoration honouring the reign of the Romanovs. It is clearly a prelude to the abdication of the last Tsar and the fall of the Romanov Dynasty.

Thus, Shub continually invites her spectators to deliberate on the specificity of her ideological montage, while implying the viewer's outrage at the injustices of tsarist society. Commenting on this very aspect of Shub's montage, the film scholar Jay Leyda contends that

> in her first three precedent-forming films her cutting ideas [montage] usually combined a forcefully simple logic with a minute study of the formal elements in the available footage; the ideas were often built on contrasts that seem obvious now – but it took imagination to dig them from her raw material.[44]

Hence, in Shub's deft hands, her ideological montage construction sought to inform the viewer of the major causes of the Revolution, showing why the decadent Romanov Dynasty was finally defeated. In her film, socialism supposedly redressed the yawning divide between the various levels of society that had existed during the regime of Tsar Nicholas II, as it replaced discrimination with equality for all. Sadly, Shub was soon to understand that, to paraphrase Orwellian doom, under socialism, all people were equal, but some people were more equal than others. This unpalatable truth was one that Shub and her comrades were forced to stifle during the period of Stalinist rule.

In summation, as a prime example of Shub's cinematic praxis, *The Fall of the Romanov Dynasty* was an assemblage of utilitarian visual forms, which sought to replicate pre-Bolshevik aspects of Russian life through the machinery of modern visual technology. In fact, the structure of Shub's film reflected the function and application of industrial art in the mass production of entertainment, propaganda and information. Accordingly, as the first part of Shub's trilogy of compilation film, a genre that she was instrumental in founding, *The Fall of the Romanov Dynasty* needs to be seen as a major development in early historical documentary. In reality her distinctively Constructivist approach, which set Shub apart from such celebrated contemporaries as Eisenstein, is arguably the epitome of early nonfiction film.

The Fall of the Romanov Dynasty was constructed as an ideological illustration of the birth of socialism in the Soviet Union. Indeed, the film sought to not only represent events in the lives of the people but also to characterize what their future expectations should be, as a result of an evolving political consciousness. Furthermore, in the late 1920s *The Fall of the Romanov*

Dynasty played a significant role in LEF and the avant-garde's utopian project to attempt a transformation of their society through Constructivist art. In fact *The Fall of the Romanov Dynasty* was a defining moment in the historical development of documentary cinema. It is an exceptional and memorable work that epitomizes the tenets of both Shub's film practice and her method of ideological montage.

Acknowledgement

A version of Chapter 3 was first published in 2008 as Ilana Sharp (née Shub), (2008), 'The Fall of the Romanov Dynasty (1927): A Constructivist Paradigm for *Neigrovaia Filmá*', *Historical Journal of Film, Radio and Television*, 28:2,195–217, DO1:10.1080/01439680802077238. © IAMHIST & Informa UK Limited, trading as Taylor & Francis Group reprinted by permission of Taylor & Francis Ltd, http://www.tandfonline.com on behalf of IAMHIST & Informa UK Limited, trading as Taylor & Francis Group.

4

The Fall of the Romanov Dynasty: The Theory, the Politics and the History

Shub's Constructivist compilation film genre conveys the conflict between nonfiction film and Soviet Socialist Realism as different strategies of documenting political, cultural and social history. Her contribution to the new order as a revolutionary artist was first and foremost expressed by her participation in the allied avant-garde movement. Therefore, her utilitarian and instructive filmic collages not only challenged conventional notions of authorship but also epitomized Constructivist principles. Beyond the specific aim of ideological agitation, they positioned the mass production of nonfiction cinema as the ultimate expression of the fusion between art and technology. Underpinning this theoretical position, Shub had aimed to introduce a genuine societal record providing photographic evidence of 'life with all its diversity, complexity and contradictions . . . everyday situations that could be significant material [to be used] in the construction of non-acted pieces'.[1] Indeed, it was what Osip Brik called the 'authenticity with which the raw material is communicated' that gave *The Fall of the Romanov Dynasty* its powerful sense of actuality.[2] Furthermore, commenting on the influence of this film specifically and the compilation genre in general, Lev Kuleshov foresaw that Shub's production 'should be seen as one of the steps forward in our cinematic culture'.[3]

'*The Fall of the Romanov Dynasty*: The Theory, the Politics and the History' complements the analysis of *The Fall of the Romanov Dynasty*, realized in the previous chapter, by considering the film's historical context. Thus, the aim is to illustrate how this work encapsulated the function of nonfiction film in the construction of historical meaning and, consequently, how *The Fall of the Romanov Dynasty* articulated nonfiction film as a dialectics between historical truth and propaganda in the early Soviet documentary. Accordingly, it is maintained that, despite the unmistakable role of ideological agitation in Shub's first compilation, this work constituted itself as a foundation for early nonfiction film's project of the documentation of historical reality.

Ideology, Propaganda and the Power of the State

In Bill Nichol's treatise on the documentary film, he argues that 'the filmmaker was always a participant-witness and an active fabricator of meaning'.[4] If Nichol's observations were to be applied to the Soviet Union, there would be another dimension to be added: that of an overriding, unspoken compliance with the standpoint imposed by its socialist government. As in all documentaries, ever-present in *The Fall of the Romanov Dynasty* was the conflict between a purported objectivity and the inherent subjectivity of the director. Within the study of early Soviet film, this needs to be examined in light of the demands imposed by the regime on nonfiction film (and its filmmakers) to spread and reinforce Party doctrine.

A year after the release of *The Fall of the Romanov Dynasty*, as was clearly documented in the Party's Cinema Conference Resolution in 1928, it was established that without doubt 'Cinema . . . must occupy an important place . . . as a medium for broad educational work and Communist propaganda'.[5] On reflection, in order to accentuate this dictum, Shub assesses and reinforces the Party's approved place for propaganda in cinema in her essay 'On the Creative Method' [O tvorcheskom metode]:

> Suddenly it is as if everybody has agreed at the last conference that propaganda films have a colossal importance. Besides, no matter how much we like to close our eyes and talk about the relevance or irrelevance of the acted method [fiction film], the fact remains that 90 per cent of propaganda films are made following the non-acted method [nonfiction film]. That is why we must pay such attention to these films.[6]

Accordingly, Shub continues with her observations on the Conference and the altogether gratifying realization: 'Now that we have received instructions from the Party and RAPP [acronym for Russian Association of Proletarian Writers] to put on screen real people, real life, real construction and concrete heroes with names and surnames, the role of non-acted film is rather current and meaningful.'[7]

In this context, particularly in light of the 1928 Conference's endorsement of the value of propaganda in nonfiction film, Shub's Constructivist theories (allied with her ideological montage in *The Fall of the Romanov Dynasty*) had become, albeit temporarily, the perfect vehicle for the articulation of the creed of the Bolsheviks. In fact, Shub interpreted truth and reality through the prism of the dominant socialist system. Film, as exemplified by *The Fall of the Romanov Dynasty*, had the power to reach the widest possible audience (including those who were illiterate) while spreading the socialist message. Indeed, nonfiction film was the ideal tool to express this ideological discourse, and in *The Fall of the Romanov Dynasty* Shub illustrates segment by segment how class-consciousness is outwardly transformed into class conflict and, ultimately, into social revolution.

Therefore, Shub's film offers a diachronic nonfiction narrative, which contrasts and compares two dynasties. It is a politico-historical portrayal of the changing structure of her society as wholly fettered by the last Romanov Tsar and then liberated by the reign of Lenin, who is depicted as the people's saviour. However, to the contemporary viewer, the irony associated with the substitution of Nicholas II, a feudal oppressor, for Lenin, a modern despot, is self-evident. Thus, while the cruelties during the repressive reign of Nicholas II were well documented, the brutality unleashed upon Lenin's opponents was a different matter altogether. As a consequence, *The Fall of the Romanov Dynasty*, and indeed any film from that era depicting Lenin, shows only a sanitized portrait with no signs of the tyrannical Lenin who exiled the intelligentsia and murdered his rivals.[8] In conjunction with this blind faith in the events and prominent figures of the Revolution, as re-presented by Shub, she would have become increasingly aware of the force of censorship as the 1920s drew to a close.

Thus, as a result of this constraint, if one were to compare the mode of her documentary schema with the dramatic approach of Robert Flaherty, the so-called founding father of documentary, Shub's style of manipulation of her material can be labelled austere. Indeed, free from political restrictions, Flaherty manipulated both the Inuit in *Nanook of the North* [1922] and later the islanders in *Man of Aran* [1934], endangering their lives in order to add atmosphere, dramatic tension and, paradoxically, a greater sense of authenticity. Ironically, Flaherty utilized the tools of fiction film, and thus stepped away from reality, in order to create a work that was perceived as genuine nonfiction.[9] Indeed, this was exactly what Eisenstein had created with the storming of the Winter Palace in *October*.

In contrast, while shooting very little new material, and constructing her early films principally from genuine newsreel, the crux of Shub's method of filmmaking revolved around her specific selection and manipulation of the archival footage through ideological montage. This process resulted in not merely a gluing together of small and unrelated scraps of film but the creation of a coherent whole from this disarray of often discarded images. In *The Fall of the Romanov Dynasty* Shub gives order to the chaos of revolution through the thematic unity of her documentary structure. Through this framework, Shub's objective was to construct a foundation for nonfiction film, built, as she was to declare, 'not on artifice, but on authentic materials'.[10] In this context, the austerity of Shub's compilations offered the Bolsheviks a potent ideological platform as she presented a factual, highly political evaluation of a vast history.

Despite Shub's ideological manipulation of film material, *The Fall of the Romanov Dynasty* remains a valuable document in its observation and preservation of time and place. The specificity of temporality and location inherent within the newsreel itself enabled her to present factual sociopolitical cinema. Shub believed with conviction that by working with unadulterated newsreel, she would be able to verify the genuine nature of her nonfiction film. In addition, she emphasizes that 'the position itself (that is, the relationship towards the showing of current facts) must be goal-oriented, class directed and aligned with Party ideals'.[11]

The Fall of the Romanov Dynasty: The Transformation of the Raw Material

The first step in this process was Shub's search for a substantial body of cinematic proof to establish her historical thesis. Her research methodology, while commonplace in the documentary filmmaking process of today, was a major breakthrough in the cinema of the 1920s. Shub's preliminary groundwork for *The Fall of the Romanov Dynasty* was indeed a challenging task. Depicting her as a 'devoted supporter of newsreels', Sergei Yutkevich describes Shub's preparatory investigations: 'Using a new method of montage in documentary film . . . it was necessary to work not only on cinematic problems but also to do historical research. This required not only montage skills but also intuition, the patience of an archivist, a historian and a collector of facts.'[12]

Yet, Shub's path in the prelude to her groundbreaking work was fraught with difficulties as she was to record in her memoirs. Aside from her aspiration to educate her spectators in the cultural reception of her newly emergent compilation genre, firstly there was an immense struggle ahead for her: the pursuit of the actual raw material in order to construct *The Fall of the Romanov Dynasty*.¹³ As she relates:

> At the end of August 1926, I was assigned to make a . . . film for the tenth anniversary of the February Revolution. Having decided the purpose of the work and the method by which it would be achieved, I disappeared in search of material. 'Discovering' material became a sport almost verging on mania. There was no film library either in the Leningrad [Film] Factory or in Moscow. The most valuable historic material lay unaccounted for. In secret places lay heaps of unnumbered boxes, and what was inside nobody knew.¹⁴

Searching in Leningrad, she 'found films in basements, in places so horribly humid that the emulsion was trickling down from them. And these were documents of great historical importance.'¹⁵ Not only was the footage in a state of decay but the cans of film were unmarked and the scene was one of neglect and disorder. In this environment of confusion 'lay boxes of negatives and random prints, and no one knew how they had got there'.¹⁶

Recording this incident in even greater detail, Shub declares that she was shocked to discover that

> All the valuable negatives and positives of wartime and pre-revolutionary newsreels were kept in a damp cellar on Sergievsky Street. The cans were coated with rust. In many places the dampness had caused the emulsion to come away from the celluloid base. Many shots that appeared on the lists had disappeared altogether.¹⁷

Added to the difficulties of actually locating these dilapidated reels in the first instance, it is quite apparent that Shub's task in assembling *The Fall of the Romanov Dynasty* was technically of the utmost challenge. This was due to the physical nature of her raw material. Variations in film speed aside, Graham Roberts outlines how there were 'differences in style and quality of filming, different formats of film stock and differences in emulsion quality, few sequences would have been of any great length'.¹⁸ It was a testament to Shub's perseverance and skill that from this unlabelled jigsaw, she was to construct her flowing trilogy. For Shub: 'the conviction that this premise was right, that only authentic, non-scripted cinematic documents could and should represent the past and our times, helped to overcome all the difficulties faced.'¹⁹

Understandably, as a result of this experience, Shub became a passionate advocate in her campaign for the establishment of film archives. She stressed the vital need for such documentation: 'reality demands the organization of a non-acted cinema library. The [film] factory must contain a scientific and technical film library.'[20] Shub's explorations in Leningrad had been frustrating, laborious and demanding, but despite these complications, they bore fruit due to her dedication and ability. 'For two months' she had pored over '60,000 metres of film and selected 5,200 metres. Of this, 1,500 metres were included in [her] film'. In addition, she 'photographed a long array of historical documents, newspapers and other objects and performed the laboratory processing of many sequences'.[21] This was Shub's physical act of objectifying information by using a camera to record genuine texts such as letters and edicts written by Nicholas II. These images became, for example, a frame filled solely by his signature or newspaper headlines in the press of the day. This was consistent with Shub's Constructivist methodology and that of nonfiction film.

In her use of facts through tangible documentation, Shub was striving to instruct the audience and conserve the history of her era simultaneously. This was a filmic representation of collected specimens evoking past lives and times. Where once these items would have been preserved and displayed as exhibits or under a glass case in a museum, now the technology of cinema could add a new dimension and, indeed, a far greater audience. From these artefacts Shub created a living archive: *The Fall of the Romanov Dynasty*. Miraculously, while Shub was rummaging through, unravelling, repairing and reconstructing these disconnected and fragile prints, a discovery of some significance was unearthed. As previously referred to, Shub came into the possession of films belonging to the imperial family, which were then utilized in *The Fall of the Romanov Dynasty*. Shub related with some degree of satisfaction that 'The chronicles of the tsar had been thrown into a damp basement and had never been considered by anyone before'.[22] Accordingly, as a result of this, Shub was later to recall in more detail that 'These films of the Tsar [and his family] were quite devoid of any real meaning. But my task was to select the material that I could transform, making it accusatory.'[23] Conversing with Mayakovsky regarding this specific footage, Shub recounts with gratification that he informed her: 'you processed all the material very well – exceptionally well because you transformed material that was in essence anti-revolutionary, the tsarist film, into a manifesto for the Revolution.'[24]

Significantly, Shub used approximately one sixteenth of the material she had uncovered in Leningrad. Jay Leyda observes that 'more sensitively than Vertov and more carefully than any newspaper editor in the world, Esther [*sic*] Shub examined the . . . newsreels frame by frame, finding the implications and connectives in each shot that only a skilled editor is trained to do'.²⁵ Additionally, in this disorganized environment in Leningrad, nothing was catalogued or labelled so, as Shub remembers it: 'The incomplete negatives that I was able to acquire were thoroughly studied. I had to determine the year of filming. At times, I would be able to assemble a whole episode whose pieces had been scattered around in different locations'.²⁶ This acute degree of attentive analysis and focus on detail makes *The Fall of the Romanov Dynasty* highly effective.

Hence, Shub wished to contribute to Soviet society by showing on screen the reality of her world. As she reiterated: 'in a genuine, business like way, the workers of non-acted film want to take part in a rigorous construction of our days'.²⁷ Moreover, Shub was able, 'in spite of the known limitations of the photographed events and facts, to link the meanings of the material so that it evoked the pre-revolutionary material and the February Days'.²⁸ As has been indicated, the success of her first compilation feature film was even more praiseworthy, given the paucity and inferior quality of the relevant footage available. The Bolshevik utopian dream thus fused with Shub's utilitarian Constructivist vision.

The Archive and Issues of Authorship

Through the production of *The Fall of the Romanov Dynasty* Shub single-handedly endeavoured to alter public perceptions of nonfiction film in order to bring to it much needed acclaim and approbation. Undeniably, unlike the popular acted dramas of fiction film, nonfiction film was permanently under-subsidized and inadequately equipped. Whereas the former, due to its sheer entertainment value, brought wealth to the box office, the latter was not deemed profitable. *The Fall of the Romanov Dynasty*, however, was to set a new standard, and the reception from audiences was a positive one, with queues outside the Moscow cinemas showing Shub's film.²⁹ Even though *The Fall of the Romanov Dynasty* brought prestige to both nonfiction film and Shub's Constructivist compilation genre, the question remained as to whether nonfiction film could ever hope to successfully compete against the overwhelming popularity of fiction film. In her article 'As a Reminder' [V poriadke napominaniya], written in 1933, optimistically it was Shub's belief that:

> The only thing needed is the creative skill to select and film the authentic events of our life and the authentic, rather than the fictional heroes. We need to learn

to show their thoughts and feelings, together with the selected material and selected episodes from our reality, in an interconnected way, so that the whole becomes a unit of dramatically developed action. The well-known similarities in the approaches of acted and non-acted film must not confuse us when it comes to recognising the fundamental differences between them.[30]

There were not only issues of rivalry between nonfiction and fiction film to consider but also something far more fundamental to the actual structural foundation of Shub's compilation style. With her trilogy, she had subverted traditional assessments of cinematic authorship though her Constructivist utilization of a library of ready-made images. In his assessment of this aspect of Shub's nonfiction film, Martin Stollery states that she should be 'the acknowledged model of the author as producer in the late 1920s'.[31] Unfortunately, Sovkino did not have the foresight to recognize this. At Sovkino, Shub's work had been superficially interpreted and misunderstood by Ilya Trainin and his associates. They simplistically viewed the compilation film as the work of others rather than the heralding of a new and far-reaching genre. Consequently, Sovkino's administrative and financial policymakers attempted to dismiss the significance of Shub's innovative conceptual contribution.

In an explosive outburst at a public debate, an indignant Mayakovsky had vociferously defended Shub. He had angrily demanded an explanation:

> People point to Eisenstein and to Shub. There's no doubt that these directors are the pride of our cinema: they became this in spite of Sovkino. . . . People talk about Shub's victory. She is an artist because behind her cinematographic lens lies a totally different principle: the montage of real shots without a hint of the slightest preliminary re-shooting. What on earth is Sovkino up to? It refuses Shub royalties. You just filmed bits and pieces – anybody can do that![32]

Understandably, Mayakovsky was outraged at Sovkino's narrow and rigid focus, stating that they had 'never been able to appreciate the importance of the newsreel and do not appreciate it even now'.[33] After his open berating of Sovkino, the organization was forced to reconsider its policy and give Shub full credit as author–producer of *The Fall of the Romanov Dynasty*. Moreover, Mayakovsky not only publicly defended Shub and her film, but after its release he arranged a personal celebration in her honour at his home in Hendrikov Lane. Gathered there were the other key luminaries of LEF, such as Shklovsky, Brik and Tretiakov, who, like Mayakovsky, believed that nonfiction film was the way forward. Shub proudly recorded that 'they spoke like comrades about how

Figure 17 The original poster for *The Fall of the Romanov Dynasty* 1927, *In Close-up*.

my film reinforced the importance of the newsreel'.³⁴ She also observed that Mayakovsky not only 'believed that the newsreel was the most important form of cinematography and, that the number being filmed was abysmally low' but that, also like a newspaper, it 'dealt with real things and facts'.³⁵ Shub acknowledged Mayakovsky's encouragement and was deeply appreciative of his support. With gratitude she recalled in her own words:

> Not only did he talk, but he also fought. I felt extremely supported by Mayakovsky's opinion of my three films – *The Fall of the Romanov Dynasty*, *The Great Way* and *The Russia of Nicholas II and Leo Tolstoy*. Not only did he discuss them with me in comradely conversations, but he also appeared before the public and fought with the leadership of Sovkino for my place in cinematography.³⁶

What is more, the success of *The Fall of the Romanov Dynasty* with the avant-garde and the educated Party faithful, together with Sovkino's change of heart, paved the path ahead for Shub (Figure 17). She attributed permission by the authorities to commence the second part of her trilogy, *The Great Way*, to the following salient factors:

> I was aided in the first instance by . . . my film début, *The Fall of the Romanov Dynasty* . . . Vladimir Mayakovsky and Sergei Eisenstein were instrumental in securing adequate studio facilities and assistance [for me]. Also, I was finally granted the right to be considered the author of the film *The Fall of the Romanov*

Dynasty, received the title of 'director' and was given the opportunity to film – or rather do preliminary filming – for my next work.[37]

Shub held no false illusions about her objectives in film. Instead of developing her filmic creativity, as was illustrated by her contribution to *Wings of a Serf*, Shub privileged 'the element of mastery' over Platonic concepts of divine inspiration.[38] In 'We Do Not Deny the Element of Mastery' [My ne otritsaem element masterstva], written in 1927, she stated categorically that filmmaking was 'all a matter of technique'.[39] Shub's sentiments reaffirm the statement by the critic and Constructivist supporter Boris Kushner: 'art – this is simply work: knowledge, craft, skill.'[40] There was no mystery to this new art of cinema: for Shub and her documented facts, the fundamental concern was the 'aims and methods' of nonfiction film. Her objective was to present a mirror of her milieu through 'contemporary people, contemporary events' and by filming daily life to 'preserve our epoch for a future generation'.[41]

The notion of technology overriding art epitomized Shub's Constructivist beliefs. Once the script was complete and 'the gathering of raw material' was accomplished, as in *The Fall of the Romanov Dynasty*, Shub believed that what was necessary were the 'technical opportunities' such as 'good lighting equipment'.[42] Her article, written in the third-person plural, accentuates Shub's collective standpoint. By extension, Shub asserted also that documentary was the only means by which filmmakers could offer an echo of their times:

> It is necessary to understand that every piece of newsreel that is shot now is and should be assessed as a document for the future. Consciousness of this fact must determine meaning and content of what is selected for filming, its shape, montage plans and dates recorded. Without such materials from our time, the future will not be able to comprehend and understand its present.[43]

For Shub, the cataloguing and conservation of newsreels for future generations of filmmakers and their audiences became an enterprise of paramount importance. In order to safeguard the compilation, Shub assisted in the creation of a permanent warehouse for the preservation of nonfiction film: a film library that could be accessed both in the present and in the years to come. Therefore, she showed regard for the work of others most conscientiously. For instance, as Jay Leyda relates:

> When Shub began this work [her compilation trilogy] there were no rules for the physical use of old film materials . . . but Shub's orderly mind evolved its

own rules: she never cut a piece of original film, positive or negative, and never employed an original piece – her first move was to make duplicate negatives of every metre she considered using. Later editors were not so scrupulous . . . so that there are no complete negatives today of Shub's films.[44]

Ironically, in light of Shub's punctilious attitude, *The Fall of the Romanov Dynasty* eventually was to become an archive itself, both in Russia and in the West, as segments from it were cut up and inserted into other films.[45] Yet, the archive and its purpose led to other challenges.

While films such as *October* could be adjudicated to Eisenstein, establishing authorship was not as straightforward with *The Fall of the Romanov Dynasty* because Shub had dissolved into her work. She had introduced a film genre that by its very composition, fundamental structure and function excluded the signature of the filmmaker. Was it the archive itself as Mikhail Yampolsky, the Soviet film scholar and cultural theorist, has asked that could claim authorship for Shub's work?[46] There were restrictions of form imposed by the dominating force of the archive not only as a repository of facts but also as the potently defining controller of the compilation genre. Yampolsky, quoting Kuleshov, perceptively pinpointed the precariously dominant role of the archive itself as the underlying producer of nonfiction film. The concept of a 'reality at second hand', this alternating screen simultaneously both past and present, was composed of the camerawork of others and then reassembled by Shub. Newsreel footage once viewed during an earlier era, as up to the minute reporting was being reselected, brought to life and reused in Shub's reconstructed compilations. The characteristics of this second-hand film denoted quite clearly that it was not the individual artist but the raw archival fragments themselves that gave rise to the thematic structure of the film.[47] The archive itself dictated the subject matter. Shub substantiated this when she described her investigative methods for *The Fall of the Romanov Dynasty*: 'the theme stemmed organically from the material. The study of the compiled material made it possible to clearly establish the theme . . . [together] the theme and the material also determined the form of the piece.'[48]

In the opinion of the LEF community, Shub's archival renditions of reality (reconstituted from documents of the past) were to be privileged over an engagement with the present. Mystifying though it may appear, her compilations, primarily sourced from old newsreel footage, were preferred by them to the immediacy of Vertov's active pursuit of 'life caught unawares' [zhizn vrasplokh].

To the followers of LEF, the indisputable authenticity of the contents of the archive, as utilized by Shub in *The Fall of the Romanov Dynasty*, seemed far more real than Vertov's imaginative impressions of the here and now. The archive was a highly respectable site for the resurrection of reality. Archival images screened previously as genuine up to the moment current events now were revived by Shub to be re-presented as chronicles documenting the history of epochs that had passed. Hence, the raw material recycled from the archive could give fresh meaning and insight into social, political and historical milestones depicting the revolutionary struggles resulting in the birth of the Soviet state. The reality portrayed by Shub's nonfiction film, compiled though it was from the films of newsreel camera operators from a bygone age, was perceived by LEF as having a greater veracity than Vertov's creative interpretation of nonfiction film in which he captured life in the present.

For Kuleshov, *The Fall of the Romanov Dynasty* transcended the doubts held by Sovkino regarding authorship of this work together with the image of Shub as a glorified film librarian. In his view: 'Shub, who made *The Fall of the Romanov Dynasty*, has not only produced a magnificent film in terms of montage and content, but she has also created a new stage in the development of the nonfiction film.'[49] Shub was indeed the ultimate example of the role of the author as producer, and this was also the appraisal of LEF regarding Shub's noteworthy contribution to nonfiction film.

The Problem of the Audience: The Dilemma for Nonfiction Film

In 'filming... genuine slices from life', *The Fall of the Romanov Dynasty* depicted for Shub 'real history in cinematographic form'. It was 'a chronicle of our country from 1912 to 1917'.[50] Although Shub never explained the relevance for selecting 1912 as the starting point for this film, it is interesting to note that 1912 saw the establishment of the newspaper *Pravda* meaning 'Truth' and the formation of the Fourth (and final) Duma. This is pertinent to Shub's subject matter, because both events may be seen as precursors of the Revolution. Indeed, it is the symbolism within the founding of a daily news outlet called 'truth' that allies itself so appositely to Shub's film practice: *Pravda*'s truth on paper is transferred into Shub's truth on celluloid. The year 1912 also celebrated the centenary of the decimation of Napoleon's mighty armies in his disastrous Russian campaign.

Apart from the obvious similarities between Napoleon and the last of the Romanov Tsars, as failing autocrats and oppressors of the Russian people, there is also the parallel between subjugation and a call to arms.

Of equal symbolic significance is the year with which Shub begins her historical chronicle. In the first part of her trilogy, *The Russia of Nicholas II and Leo Tolstoy*, Shub covers the period just prior to that of *The Fall of the Romanov Dynasty*, that is, the years from 1897 to 1912.[51] The year 1897 is of note because this was when Tolstoy published his book *What Is Art?* in which he composed a refrain that was to be used over and over again by Boris Shumiatsky the head of the Soviet film industry in the 1930s: 'Great works of art are only great because they are accessible and comprehensible to everyone.'[52] Similarly, Shub's objective was to make visual histories for a general audience through intelligible documentary films that were both 'accessible and comprehensible' to the masses. Clearly, as an artist, she aimed to illustrate graphically the ideological foundation of her filmic dialectic through nonfiction film. As Shub was to affirm, her 'intention was not only to show facts, but to evaluate them from the point of view of the class that achieved victory in the battles of the Revolution. Hence, a film mainly put together from counter-revolutionary material became revolutionary, an instrument of agitation.'[53] Therefore, nonfiction film gave Shub an opportunity to pay homage to the revolutionaries and workers who brought about the fall of the Romanovs, and to give reality and pictorial clarity to their world through authentic footage.

However, as discussed in the previous chapter, the relationship between Shub's new film genre and her audience was a problematical one. In fact, *The Fall of the Romanov Dynasty* would have absorbed only the most dedicated of viewers, such as the members of LEF and the avant-garde arts community (Mayakovsky, Brik and Shklovsky, as well as the Constructivists Gan, Stepanova and Rodchenko, amongst others). Even though Shub stated naively: 'I make my films for a mass audience', *The Fall of the Romanov Dynasty* was a history lecture devoid of laughter, drama, romance or light-hearted entertainment.[54] Despite these factors, Shub believed in her role as a social, historical and ideological commentator, an educator of the Soviet working classes through the popular medium of film. In this sense, the assessment of Shub's film by the celebrated documentarist Roman Karmen (who filmed the brilliant footage that Shub was to use in her film *Spain* in the following decade) was an affirmation of this:

> [The] *Fall of the Romanov Dynasty* . . . was a vivid and successful attempt to convert some scrappy material . . . into a moving epic, giving a clear and brilliant

picture of the epoch. In this film . . . Shub went beyond the borders of Czarist Russia to show the whole capitalist world and the motive forces of the Russian Revolution . . . [her trilogy] had great success with mass audiences.[55]

Furthermore, the historians Valeriya Selunskaya and Maria Zezina referring to both *The Fall of the Romanov Dynasty* and *The Great Way* argue that 'Shub's films . . . represent an interesting example of her own interpretation of historical newsreel . . . we see clearly the role of the author as historian making sense of and interpreting a historical document'.[56] Cinematically demonstrating the antagonism between the classes, Shub's message for the mass audience is unmistakable: *The Fall of the Romanov Dynasty* depicts the economic conditions that Marx foresaw as the driving factors for social reform. When conditions become intolerable, the proletariat inevitably unite and become a positive force for change. In accordance with Marxist doctrine where the working collective was articulated as the focus, in *The Fall of the Romanov Dynasty* the attention also centres on the will of the people and their power to transform their world. In addition, Shub saw her role in this experimental field of filmmaking as a battle. Just as the proletariat had struggled through labour to create their new socialist homeland, equally Shub fought as she endeavoured to give a universal voice to her Constructivist avant-garde genre. As she elucidated: 'each of my compilation films was also a form of agitation for the new concept of documentary cinema, a statement about non-acted film as the most important cinematic form of the present day'.[57]

Hence, Shub's stance towards her agitational nonfiction film is reinforced by her practice. Significantly, with her use of long takes Shub's audience had the time to consider and evaluate the meaning of each sequence. As she herself emphasized it, her 'focus on the facts' was 'an emphasis not only on showing the facts, but also on making people examine them, keep them in mind'.[58] Kuleshov reiterated this aspect of audience reception in an essay on Soviet nonfiction film, where he observed that 'filmed events . . . must be shown in such a way that we can examine them properly'.[59] Shub's emphasis on the device of the long take distinguished her from Vertov's rapid cutting, with Kuleshov complaining that, as in all Vertov's work, 'the best bits are too short – you don't have time to examine them'.[60] Also, the 'examination' of Shub's film by an audience also served to maintain a certain emotional distance between them and the material on the screen, in what was essentially a rational and measured response to the footage. Thus, for Yampolsky, 'the length of the edited sequence became one of the main formal achievements of Shub'.⁶¹ This is noteworthy because Shub's use of long takes as a marker of enhanced realism in nonfiction film, together with her Constructivist methodology, helped establish the foundation for the debates on documentary truth. This would be apparent decades into the future in *cinéma vérité* and direct cinema. Speaking expressly of *The Fall of the Romanov Dynasty*, Yampolsky explains:

> The film was greeted enthusiastically as a significant landmark and, according to some scholars, heralded the 'second period' in the history of the Soviet documentary cinema. Almost immediately it became the ideal model for documentary film, a standard of judgement for criticism to be directed against the previous phase, dominated by Dziga Vertov.⁶²

Nevertheless, Shub's growing status as a filmmaker brought with it more responsibility towards her viewing public. The issue of spectatorship had to be addressed, and this made Shub aware of the problems associated with the cultural reception of nonfiction film. Writing in 1929 in 'And Again – The Newsreel' about the making of *The Russia of Nicholas II and Leo Tolstoy*, she speaks directly to a prospective audience about film reception. Appealing to the viewer, Shub elucidates:

> I have something to ask of the comrades that are going to watch this film. You already bring with you a certain convention when you watch an acted film there is such a thing as the spectator's culture. Unfortunately, this culture does not yet exist for nonfiction film. The audience is not to blame for this. We are to blame. We have very few non-acted films, as we have just started to work. Our efforts need to be considered as scholarly. We don't have the traditions, conventions or the possibilities that exist in staged cinema. Our work needs to be viewed in a different way. Unlike what is received in acted films, there is no plot [syuzhet], no story [fabula]⁶³ in what we do; the material works in a totally different way: on documentary, on authenticity. Acted cinema appeals primarily to the audience's emotions, whereas we appeal to their intellect.⁶⁴

This insight into Shub's cinematic *raison d'être* clearly delineates the desired audience response to nonfiction film. As she assesses it, this is a 'scholarly' genre that asks the spectator to be ruled by their head rather than their heart. In so far as nonfiction film is to be illuminated by the documents of reality and dominated by factography, by its very instructive nature, Shub's cinema asks much of her viewers. In these works there is a major shift in terms of expectations of the audience's contribution: paradoxically, the public must be well versed before they enter the auditorium in order to be further educated by the film.

Consequently, they need to contemplate the weighty messages permeating the film, after its screening as well. As Shub asserts: 'our work must be viewed with the introspection of an intellectual not an emotional kind. Only this will generate a possibility to appreciate the film as it should be viewed.'[65] Thus, Shub's audience must be fully engaged rather than merely waiting to be entertained. Her nonfiction film was a visual lecture, pictorially presenting the events creating and governing their society. Informative and absorbing though Shub's films may have been, they required concentration and serious consideration: the focus and participation of a thinking viewer.

However, only a small and devoted proportion of the cinema public was willing to sacrifice comedy, glamour and acted fiction for Shub's documentaries. Sadly, for her, what the average Soviet moviegoer wanted was Charlie Chaplin, Mary Pickford and Douglas Fairbanks, Harry Piel or Max Linder. In fact, Denise Youngblood shares with us an unintentionally amusing letter sent by a young movie fan to the company that published *Soviet Screen* [Sovetsky ekran]. This moviegoer makes her feelings on the situation abundantly clear:

> It's boring, comrade editor, in a country busy with the replacement of the plough with the tractor, where peasants ... run the government, where lovers of the electric light bulb don't understand the tales of Baghdad. It's boring and I'm tired of life. Life has become loathsome. I want to forget myself. I want romance. For that reason I love Harry [Piel] and Douglas [Fairbanks] and Conrad [Veidt].[66]

The Fall of the Romanov Dynasty could never hope to compete with a need for such diverting fantasy. On the contrary, Shub demanded that her audiences remembered and reflected on the great socialist upheaval. While for the modern viewer such rhetoric can be construed as propaganda, in its day *The Fall of the Romanov Dynasty* was heralded by the avant-garde as an uplifting, patriotic and inspiring testament to the power of the people. Shub's film was couched in the language of her age and expressed the sentiments of the Soviet Union's political vanguard. As such, it was an attempt to convince an audience of the historical legitimacy of socialist rule.

To 'drink from the river named Fact': Shub on Nonfiction Film and Historical Truth[67]

Therefore, as a Constructivist, essential to Shub's approach to filmmaking was the use of factography. According to her in *The Fall of the Romanov Dynasty*:

> the realization that viewers are agitated by real environments, real people and events, presented in historical succession and in the right sequence, made the film not only a means of agitation and propaganda, but also emotionally rousing . . . there is not a more effective force than the force of a fact, presented . . . with a clear purpose of vision.[68]

Nonfiction film gave authority to Shub's work, and she presented it as a genre that sought to reveal historical and political fact. This premise was based on the notion of the inherent capacity of non-acted film to expose, without mediation, the truth of historical events. People were expected to believe the evidence presented by Shub simply because the proof was there on the screen. However questionable this concept may appear to us today, for Shub and her audience there were valid reasons to believe in an immediate connection between non-acted filmic documentation and historical reality. For example, Shub claimed that Sovkino had expressed concern that *The Russia of Nicholas II and Leo Tolstoy* 'would canonize Tolstoy'. However, when Shub talked to his daughter, Alexandra Tolstaya, she received an altogether different perspective. Tolstaya informed Shub that she was ashamed to admit that 'when she watched the film, she realized that Lev Nikolaevich [Tolstoy] was as much of a landlord as the others'.[69] This awareness made Tolstaya uncomfortable about screening Shub's film at Yasnaya Polyana (her father's sprawling estate) and destroying a myth. Shub observed triumphantly that

> the film does not lie, it speaks for itself . . . the persuasion of authentic cinematographic material. . . . Look at how elegantly Tolstoy wears his vest, or his gesture when he drinks water. It is a lordly gesture. And those walks . . . It's important to watch this film very attentively. Tolstoy saws for a while, then calmly walks away and a worker stays behind to continue sawing. How could this film not be persuasive?[70]

Furthermore, Shub goes on to comment that she 'spoke with the old land workers. They don't talk about Tolstoy or those times with much enthusiasm at all'.[71] Thus, *The Russia of Nicholas II and Leo Tolstoy* was a significant reminder of the power of newsreel footage in revealing historical truth, as it gave audiences an intriguing portrayal that was far from the dominant romanticized version of the revered writer as a man of the people.[72] Shub's comments about her representation of Tolstoy in *My Life – Cinematography* described in detail how her selection of genuine footage revealed lesser-known traits of Tolstoy, not hitherto available for public consumption. She had found compiling this aspect of the film extremely challenging because as she was aware

> Tolstoy's personality was extremely complex and contradictory and there was very little material recorded on film. . . . There was only eighty metres of film shot of Tolstoy . . . because of course using this limited amount of material, I could not give a complete assessment of Tolstoy's religious and philosophical theory . . . I attempted to use non-acted material to show not a collective but an individual and to evaluate Tolstoy's general political leanings.[73]

Openly divulging these previously unexplored facets of Tolstoy's character, Shub asked rhetorically: 'how could this film not be construed as convincing?'[74] She had presented her audience with an entirely fresh and fascinating perception of the famed Leo Tolstoy. In addition, 'the persuasiveness of authentic, non-staged material realistically reflects the spirit of the period and shows where and in what environment Tolstoy's last years were spent. This material, in and by itself, expressively illustrates . . . Tolstoy's complete isolation.'[75] For Shub, and for Brik, Shklovsky, Mayakovsky and other members of the avant-garde, this was the undoubted power of nonfiction film. For them, this attribute was the unique quality of documentary and the characteristic that placed it above fiction film. It was the ability of unstaged nonfiction footage, in the form of archival film, to place documented reality in front of the viewer. Hence, it was the genuine evidence provided by newsreels highlighting prominent political, historical (and, in this case, literary figures) intertwined with past events relevant to the emerging nation, that breathed life into Shub's factual compilations. Consequently, Jay Leyda asserted that 'Shub . . . found her basic material – and her chief inspiration – in the idea of shaping old newsreels to show history – alive and true – to Soviet audiences'.[76] Thus, from simple raw footage Shub constructed a credible compilation of her society, its key personalities and its history.

Paradoxically, in her quest for historical truth Shub always meticulously prepared shooting scripts. This is evidenced by her later and extremely detailed preparatory written work on her unrealized film *Women* in 1933 to 1934.

However, this was despite the fact that she was aghast at the concept of and contrivance associated with acting out real events:

> We are told... Why not film actors, write scripts, play out life?... We find actors sweating copiously in an attempt to connect the authentic fact with the staged fact. The result is a total fiasco. In juxtaposition with the facts, the falseness of the play is even more evident, and the viewer even stops believing in the facts.[77]

While, admittedly, Shub used a scripted plan to map out and construct the framework of her trilogy, her compilations continued to be reconstructions of newsreel footage with additional camera work, never including any fictional dramatizations. The conscientious pre-scripting and direction that she proposed for *Women* in the 1930s, however, was atypical. It represented a distinct departure away from Shub's earlier pure nonfiction film form and indeed all her subsequent major films in the 1930s from *Today* to *Spain*. Nevertheless, it must be noted that in 1929, when Shub wrote her analysis on non-acted film, she was still committed to the most stringent principles of nonfiction film.[78]

The overriding element of pretence, the obvious melding of fiction with a modicum of fact, diluted the power of a work considerably in Shub's eyes. For example, as discussed earlier, Shub found Eisenstein's method in *October* deeply concerning and her remedy for this impasse was straightforward: 'this work cries out: film something more organized, film a newsreel, film events, facts, people who are active in life and not acting life.'[79] For her, authenticity was the key to the successful filmic illustration of real events. Shub firmly believed in the purity and simplicity of the unadorned newsreel, an actorless, unstaged recording of the shaping of her epoch. Unlike acted fiction film, she perceived her historical documents as authentic and worthy of preservation. 'Non-acted film', as Shub declared, 'survives; it is interesting because it is a small fragment of the life that has really passed.'[80] In accordance with this statement, Shub refused to stage a dramatized film shoot in an attempt to enhance reality.

Nonetheless, in Shub's era, there were examples of film where, unlike Eisenstein's staged re-enactments, the re-creation of a fact could add to the realism of a film. For example, in 1932 Luis Buñuel made a bleak and disturbing documentary *Land Without Bread* [Las Hurdes: Tierra Sin Pan] about the hopelessness of the poverty-stricken inhabitants of the Las Hurdes region in Spain. Buñuel himself stated that 'we were trying to show an image of life among the Hurdanos and we had to show everything'.[81] Significantly, Buñuel's recording of a reality filled with squalor and despair needed to be made more real. Unlike Shub, who in her trilogy (even when there was a genuine scarcity of material) would never fabricate an event, Buñuel had no qualms about shooting a goat so that it could be realistically seen plunging off a cliff. The common denominator between Shub and Buñuel is that they both attempted to demonstrate authenticity, while differing in their film theory and praxis. Buñuel reconstructed an occurrence (described to him by the villagers) by recreating it in front of the camera, whereas Shub re-presented genuine events, which had been recorded on newsreel as they happened.

However, the staging of Buñuel's falling goat differed radically from the intent behind Eisenstein's white horse plunging from the bridge in *October*. Eisenstein's motivation for his dramatic and highly effective fictitious mise en scène was symbolism. On the contrary, Buñuel's orchestration of the incident in *Land Without Bread* was staged to heighten authenticity. Buñuel simply admitted, 'since we couldn't wait for the event to happen, I provoked it by firing a revolver'.[82] Ironically, his purpose was not only 'to show an image of life' but also to add further to the stark realism of his thought-provoking documentary. Yet, in *The Fall of the Romanov Dynasty* Shub, unlike Buñuel, does not seek to visually accentuate reality. Instead, she aims to present her audience with an analysis of class relations through the use of newsreel documents (and additionally, the Tsar and Tsarina's professionally filmed family footage). In order to achieve this, Shub highlighted the struggle against Romanov imperial oppression and this, in turn, glorified the new socialist state. In this task she was motivated by the potential of newsreel and also the further promise that nonfiction film had to offer. There was 'an intense desire to record on film our heroic reality, the new social events . . . the aggressive participation of the masses in the fight against their enemies . . . to do this not through scripted acting, but through the filming of fragments from real life'.[83]

In order to fulfil these objectives for this crucial expression of USSR history and culture, and despite Soviet filmmakers 'not having in their hands all the technical means that already existed in the West', Shub did not see the film apparatus as an intrusion upon or impediment to the 'normal behaviour' of people being filmed in everyday situations.[84] In Shub's opinion, in her essay 'Non-acted Film' [Neigrovaya filma] of 1929, they inadvertently reveal themselves despite the fact that 'they are "acting"' because 'each of their "poses" is a real characteristic of their personality'.[85] Shub elaborates on this further:

> in the process of working on my films, I have made a conscious decision not to edit out those moments in which a person, upon seeing the cinema equipment,

prepares to be filmed. In this way I have shown . . . Kerensky in *The Fall of the Romanov Dynasty* . . . these pieces will convince anyone. In them, people are not 'acting' they are not pretending to be something that they are not. On the contrary, when preparing for filming, people show with every movement of their body, sometimes with an almost imperceptible smile, sometimes with statuesque immobility, that they are ready to give an accurate cinematic expression of themselves.[86]

Like Shub's use of the long take, the above deliberations on the use of the camera to document 'film-truth' proffers yet another example of Shub's anticipation of the principles and motivations of *cinéma vérité* and direct cinema in the 1950s and 1960s.

Hence, for Shub, cinema was primarily a method of accumulating and conserving the authentic historical facts of her era through newsreel. Her nonfiction compilation was the epitome of what Mikhail Yampolsky had labelled as 'reality at second hand' and 'the dominance of the raw material'.[87] As Yampolsky asserts, 'With the appearance of *The Fall of the Romanov Dynasty*, Shub dotted all the i's; the period of canonisation of "long sequence" montage had begun.'[88] This was a triumph, however short-lived, for Shub, nonfiction film and Constructivist art.

Shub's 'Our Way' [Nash put] 1937, was a re-evaluation by her of her craft. When the success of *The Fall of the Romanov Dynasty* and the Constructivist movement were distant memories, Shub pondered:

> What were the main mistakes of documentary film workers? . . . The first and most important mistake was in our setting up non-acted film in direct confrontation with all acted film . . . Is it possible for non-acted films to have expressive themes, their own emotionally charged plot, their own heroes, and a dramaturgy, a mystique. . . . Can those films portray our life not in a schematic way but deeply and truthfully, in all its diversity, with all its complexities and contradictions? I am firmly convinced that they can. A myriad of documentary films have proved this.[89]

As can be discerned in these contemplative statements by Shub, she continued to promote the importance of nonfiction film as a valuable record of life in the Soviet Union. The difference now was her admission that the relentless rivalry between non-acted film and acted film had been a futile exercise. Significantly, even towards the end of her career, Shub believed enthusiastically in the worth and potential of nonfiction film; not only as a genre that was as stimulating and interesting as fiction film but also, unrealistically, as a mirror of her society. Regrettably in the Stalinist period it was dangerous to hold up a true reflection of Soviet life.

The Function of Authentic Material: Shub at the Nucleus of Early Nonfiction Film

In her article 'The Film about Tolstoy' [Filma o Tolstom] in 1929, Shub reiterates her conviction that 'the persuasiveness' of the archival footage is 'dictated to me by the material itself and I want to bring it to the Soviet viewer'.[90] Shub's methodology, the meticulous reconstruction of newsreels from the archive, ready-made material employed in *The Fall of the Romanov Dynasty*, was seen by LEF as a blueprint for nonfiction film. After she had completed her compilation trilogy, the preparation for her subsequent documentaries was just as systematic. Likewise, as a Constructivist, Shub had definite views on groundwork:

> the role of the author-organizer is different from the role of the director of acted films. Intricate scripts and director's scene lists, which are not necessary in non-acted films . . . are replaced with a written plan that must include an exact formulation of the objectives of the piece, a clear indication of the filming themes prescribed by the author. . . . In this way, the author of a non-acted film is also a sui generis script writer. . . . Such reconnaissance work is unavoidable. It affords the possibility to develop a concrete plan and, as unexpected issues arise during filming, it allows us to assess the changing situations immediately and to proceed further within the given framework of the plan.[91]

Osip Brik concurred with Shub's assessment for this necessary procedure in film development, with its need for careful scheduling and planning. For that reason he vehemently disagreed with Vertov, who had repeatedly expressed his disdain for the scripted plan in non-acted film. In fact, making a public speech on *The Eleventh Year* [Odinnadtsatyi, 1928], Vertov himself was to declare with his customary bravado that 'like all the Cine-Eye films, it was made without a script'.[92] In confirmation of this, Shub made the following observation about Vertov's Cine-Eye collective [Kinoki], consisting of Vertov, his editor Elizaveta Svilova and his cameraman Mikhail Kaufman. Shub claimed that they 'denied the need for preliminary work on filming or a script, considering that this was only necessary in acted cinema'.[93] For Osip Brik, lack of script in nonfiction film was equated with lack of meaning. Using Shub as a point of comparison with Vertov and the former as worthy of emulation, Brik noted that 'Shub's film *The Fall of the Romanov Dynasty*, which is composed of old film sequences, produces a much more coherent impression because its thematic and montage plan has been carefully devised'.[94] Shub's conscientious mapping and shooting schedules found favour with Brik for whom Shub's praxis constituted the ideal method for presenting reality in nonfiction film.

Moreover, LEF believed that not only was art for art's sake an irrelevance, but that it overshadowed and negated what should be the primary objective of a film depicting the events of 1917: historical authenticity. Speaking on behalf of LEF, Brik makes their position plain:

> Eisenstein was commissioned to make a film celebrating the tenth anniversary of October. For those of us in Lef this is a task that can be executed in only one way: by a montage of documentary shots. That is what Esfir Shub did in her films *The Great Way* and *The Fall of the Romanov Dynasty*. We in Lef think that the October Revolution is such a major historical fact that any playing with this fact is unthinkable.[95]

As a result, Shub's particular style of nonfiction film was for Brik the only possible cinematic representation by which the true facts of the events, which precipitated the Bolshevik uprising, could be successfully embodied. In line with the Constructivists and in particular Shub, LEF maintained that 'the main consideration in cinema art is the raw material'.[96] On the contrary, Eisenstein was not interested in 'the raw material' nor did he want Shub's 'montage of documents' and recording of the facts. As he claimed: 'for me, the Revolution was not only historical but had to be continually reinvented.'[97] Viktor Shklovsky gives us an example of Eisenstein's imaginative atmospheric 'reinvention' by wryly describing a specific mise en scène in *October*. 'The October Revolution did not take place in incessant rain: was it worth hosing down the Palace Square and Alexander's Column? Because of this water and the millions of lights the crowds look as if they have been greased with machine oil.'[98] Brik, Mayakovsky and Shklovsky agreed, as did the critic Viktor Pertsov.[99] For them Shub represented fact, authenticity and true Soviet documentary.

Like Mayakovsky and Brik, the film journal *Soviet Screen* commended the achievements of both *The Fall of the Romanov Dynasty* and, its sequel in the trilogy, *The Great Way*. It believed that the popularity of these two works signalled that audiences wanted more nonfiction film. As *Soviet Screen* declared somewhat naively but nevertheless with gusto: 'the success of *The Fall of the Romanov Dynasty* and *The Great Way* revealed that the spectator needs non-acted film.'[100] *The Fall of the Romanov Dynasty* was to set a new standard, and the reception from audiences was a positive one, with queues at the Moscow cinema screenings. However, the film scholar Graham Roberts considers that this success must be partially tempered by the observation that 'This may well be an exaggeration of the level of distribution offered to the film'.[101]

Nevertheless, like *Soviet Screen*, Shklovsky was also hopeful as he highlighted Shub's successful struggle to bring nonfiction film to the fore, albeit temporarily:

> It is difficult for our comrades who work on factual films to find work. ... People say their films are uninteresting. [But look at], the box-office success of *The Fall of the Romanov Dynasty*, which for five thousand roubles is overtaking *The Decembrists*, a film that cost so much that the figures are approximate. Even box-office considerations do not rule out factual films.[102]

Yet as has been revealed earlier in this chapter, box-office receipts aside, Shub's trilogy, which members of LEF such as Mayakovsky, Pertsov, Brik and Shklovsky enthused over, ultimately appealed only to the avant-garde and intelligentsia. In discussing the differences between nonfiction and fiction film, Shklovsky claimed that at the core of the issue lay 'the priority of the material' and that this is where the emphasis should lie.[103] Shub's filmic essence was indeed the untapped newsreel material, and this was embedded within the texture of her ideologically based nonfiction film. For example, as illustrated in the previous chapter, her intertitles often enhanced her images, framing them in meaningful communicative structures. In *The Fall of the Romanov Dynasty* Shub systematically presented the text followed by the moving picture. This coupling of two readable signs, instructing by the word followed by a visual cue, was reversed in *October*, which showed the drama unfolding and then the intertitle.

For Viktor Pertsov: 'the intertitle establishes our attitude to the frame.'[104] Shub gives us factual language (an intertitle) before reinforcing it with authentic cinematic proof from her archival fragments. By using this didactic device, Shub was always preparing her audience for what was about to unfold. Shklovsky reinforced this notion: 'the intertitle alters the shot ... indicates a way of looking at the shot, it unravels it all over again and once more links individual and widely separated shots'.[105] Consequently, intertitles 'that produce a new and different consciousness of the shot are good' because they 'change the shot'.[106] Furthermore, Pertsov stressed how Shub's use of political agitation through the medium of film defined the fundamental nature of nonfiction film. For Pertsov, *The Fall of the Romanov Dynasty* and *The Great Way* 'represent genuine agitational journalism expressed in cinematic language. The authentic . . . impact of these films derives from the real facts which comprise the films' structure.'[107]

Nevertheless, some facts were more real than others, as was evidenced by Vertov's blatant staging of scenes in *A Sixth Part of the World* [Shestaya chast mira, 1926], where his cinema truth was proven to be fiction. Vertov was too experimental, individualistic and focused on creativity for Constructivism (and in fact for documentary reportage). He was valiantly trying to straddle the impossible divide between authenticity and sheer artistry. The critic Ippolit Sokolov denigrated Vertov's film by harshly criticizing what he claimed was *A Sixth Part of the World*'s: 'confusion . . . of the methods of artistic and scientific cinematography [where] *factual material is changed into artistic material* [producing a] *deformation of facts*.'[108]

Unfortunately for Vertov, the castigation of his methods was only to escalate.[109] Whereas Shub manipulated her raw material through the medium of ideological montage, she did not confuse art with documentation. For Shub it was imperative that factography always predominated. In glaring contrast, Vertov had subverted this principle by purporting to screen the truth (and shouting it from the rooftops), and then had fabricated and altered these facts by staging and filming dramatized moments. While Shub did not negate the splendour of Vertov's images, she sought to preserve the strictest of guidelines where her film facts and montage were concerned. Although both were adherents of nonfiction film, Vertov concentrated on aesthetics, while Shub focused on the representation of evidence. Additionally, Pertsov stated that 'montage is an active method of analysis and synthesis' thus enabling a 'juxtaposing of the shots within a given theme'. This gave the editor the potential to 'add [a] personal voice to the chosen facts.'[110] *The Fall of the Romanov Dynasty* exemplified Pertsov's assertions, as well as his conclusion that 'to edit facts means to analyse and synthesise, not to catalogue them'.[111]

Indeed, Shub was undeniably an authority when it came to definitions of nonfiction film. Her raw material was constituted into a storehouse of newsreel facts that were systematically classified, cut and then reassembled ideologically into a synthetic fusion. However, this documentary vision was being hampered by the lack of available newsreel. The uphill battle to showcase compilation documentary was compounded by the lack of stored footage, as there were as yet no depositories to catalogue and preserve newsreels. In

1927, Shklovsky aired his concerns, publishing an article in June of that year, before Shub had commenced her ardent campaign for nonfiction film archives. Shklovsky complained that 'now we almost completely fail to shoot facts. Our cinema is repudiating what it is: photography. We are not filming the heroic struggle . . . factories that are being built, people as they walk along the street.'[112] This was precisely what Shub had given us glimpses of in *The Fall of the Romanov Dynasty*.

Alas, Shub knew only too well about the paucity of photographic records for both key events and everyday life. As Shklovsky lamented, when filmmakers did go out on a shoot to capture reality, the crew 'sets out in the old way in search of something beautiful'.[113] This comment is probably a reference to the artistic liberties that Vertov and Mikhail Kaufman invariably took in order to demonstrate and emphasize the reality of their supposed 'life caught unawares'. Unlike Vertov, however, Shub attempted to evaluate and present the historical truth of her time without searching for 'something beautiful'. Distinct from Eisenstein in *October*, Shub was content to allow the visually represented historical events of the rise of the Soviet state to be revealed through the unassuming newsreel. Waving the flag for Shub's non-acted films, Shklovsky warned that 'the failure to appreciate the significance of the document, the absence of a feeling of responsibility towards the audience. These are pointless unheroic mistakes.'[114]

No one could accuse Shub of these 'mistakes'. As Leyda so succinctly substantiates in relation to the groundbreaking path of Shub and 'the significance of the document': 'newsreels that had been filmed with as little thought of permanent value as is put into a daily newspaper were to be given by Shub the dramatic shape of historical chronicles.'[115] Shub's revival of forgotten footage, and its often ironic representation in her trilogy, elevated her work to a higher dimension.

Additionally, in Shub's essay 'And Again – The Newsreel' in 1929, on *The Russia of Nicholas II and Leo Tolstoy*, it seems clear that her text relates just as pertinently to *The Fall of the Romanov Dynasty*, *The Great Way* and *Today*. Although sadly a complete copy of Shub's film on Tolstoy's world has disappeared, her objectives endure through her surviving films. With reference to all three parts of her compilation trilogy, Shub believed that by 'organizing the cinematographic construction of the theme exclusively on the basis of non-acted, newsreel material . . . that the authentic events and occurrences, afford the possibility (with the right montage) of showing an era and the real characteristics of the people that took part in it'.[116]

The raw fabric of her craft, the archival newsreel footage itself, was the material that guided Shub in her filmic construction. In *The Fall of the Romanov Dynasty* she assembled these unrelated images very specifically and analytically, giving them form and meaning through her tightly scripted ideological montage. This is early documentary at its finest: Shub's nonfiction film exemplifying the core of Constructivist art.

Summarizing Shub's achievements, Sergei Yutkevich described the significance of *The Fall of the Romanov Dynasty* for the annals of global cinematic history:

> Archival footage used in this film, for the first time in the history of world cinema, was not merely pasted together in a simple logical sequence. Shots were compared and contrasted to reflect the thoughts of the artist. The distinctive creative approach of the author was revealed in this film with full clarity and power.[117]

Yutkevich was giving Shub the credit she deserved for introducing her Constructivist compilation feature film to the screen. Shub was presenting an entirely new genre form, which would become accepted and absorbed worldwide by mainstream documentary cinema. In the opening titles of *The Fall of the Romanov Dynasty* we have the coining of a specific expression to describe this category of cinema: 'a montage of film documents'. This apt defining phrase, which as Shub states was used 'for the first time' by her and no other, encapsulates the quintessential structure of her compilation genre.[118] Shub connected historical, social and political markers with insertions of contradictory and complementary newsreel images in her filmic juxtaposition through the use of ideological montage. She believed that the 'montage of a documentary film must be simple and meaningful. The viewer must be allowed the time not only to see the people and the events properly, but to remember them as well.'[119] The work was to be assembled with the maximum of perspicuity and with lengthy takes so that the audience could easily read its themes and immerse themselves in its ideology.

Accordingly, Shub wanted her films to be conduits of information, not 'purveyors of cheap effects'.[120] It was, therefore, with the utmost satisfaction that Shub commented in 1929: 'non-acted cinema has become a reality . . . even in conditions of total inequality of opportunity'.[121] Furthermore, as Shub explained: 'newsreel material is beginning to be commonplace . . . these days there are almost no acted films without documentary episodes.'[122] Significantly, due to Shub's endeavour, not only was nonfiction film exerting a stronger presence since the release of *The Fall of the Romanov Dynasty*, but fiction film was also adding to its repertoire by inserting archival newsreel segments. One could therefore point to the considerable influence and contribution of Shub through her mouthpiece *The Fall of the Romanov Dynasty*. Her first work in this new Constructivist version of the compilation gave the nonfiction film greater prominence and a newly found respectability.

As she stated: 'I treated the success of *The Fall of the Romanov Dynasty* as the success of a school and a method.'[123] Ever the modest socialist worker, Shub always acknowledged the contribution of her technical crew, with glory attached to her film being attributed to the philosophy of Constructivism and nonfiction film (that is, the 'school' and the 'method') rather than to herself.

Consequently, two years after Shub commenced her labours on *The Fall of the Romanov Dynasty* she was to conclude that 'a few results have been achieved. The film libraries of Moscow and Leningrad have begun to gather and systemise the material thoroughly'. Thanks to Shub's exertions, the status of nonfiction film had been elevated beyond the 'standard filming of May and October festivities, parades and sporting events'.[124] Shub had given non-acted film a powerful added dimension as she translated newsreels of isolated events, reconstructing them into a meaningful and panoramic message.

Nonfiction Film and the Troubling Facts

As identified previously, Shub typified the cinematic ideals of LEF. Mayakovsky, Brik and Shklovsky perceived nonfiction film as morally and ideologically superior to fiction film, and this accounts for their support of Shub as the leading exponent of Constructivist documentary.

The theoretical texts of Mayakovsky and Walter Benjamin had impinged upon and were reflected in Shub's nonfiction film. These theorizations of art and cinema, together with political doctrine, melded within Shub's Constructivist work and translated into her methodology and praxis. Indeed, Shub's *The Fall of the Romanov Dynasty* is a prime example of the shift away from an elitist, irreplaceable and original artwork to a machine-made reproduction accessible to everybody. Benjamin discussed this new stance in his classic essay 'The Work of Art in the Age of Mechanical Reproduction', where he charted the dramatic effects of technology on the traditions of art. He defined *aura* as an element that was being lost forever in the transition from priceless art to the multiple facsimiles made by a machine. *Aura* was the unique essence inherent within a traditional work of art (and nature), which exuded a distinctive quality or presence. For Benjamin, this magical emanation was absent from the mass reproduction of an image through photography or film. The substitution of a reproduced artwork, which could be replicated to infinity, had destroyed its *aura*, its uniqueness.[125] Furthermore, he astutely differentiated between what is seen by the naked eye and what the camera's eye is able to visually manipulate in the print media or newsreel.[126] For Benjamin 'photographs become standard evidence for historical occurrences, and acquire a hidden political significance... captions have become obligatory ... the directives which the captions give to those looking ... soon become more explicit and more imperative in the film where the meaning of each single picture appears to be prescribed by the sequence of all preceding ones'.[127]

Similarly, in *The Fall of the Romanov Dynasty*, Shub guides the viewer in a highly specific direction. While nonfiction film may seek authenticity and realism, it is nevertheless based on point of view and is biased, as is contemporary documentary. Through her montage Shub builds a progression of painstakingly assembled newsreel footage, in order to form her thesis. Thus, in the context of the film's historical construction, there can only be one outcome arising from the forced abdication of the Tsar: an inevitable revolution and Lenin's ascendancy to power. Significantly, Walter Benjamin quotes Georges Duhamel (the French novelist and playwright) who, commenting about the power of film in 1930, states: 'I can no longer think what I want to think. My thoughts have been replaced by moving images.'[128] Correspondingly, Shub's film appears to do the thinking for her audience as it controls and reinforces the narrative that the regime needs the population to absorb and remember as historical truth. Shub's film destroys the idea of the individual artist and the *aura* of a matchless work of art, while simultaneously creating propaganda for the state. In Shub's film the *aura* of a work of art is a forgotten relic of the past, superseded by easily reproducible multiple copies that are produced by the machines of modernity.

Correspondingly, Mayakovsky had eagerly embraced both the new technology of cinema and the melding of politics and art, long before the advent of Shub's compilation genre and Walter Benjamin's theoretical texts. As far back as July 1913, Mayakovsky had published a journal article in which he outlined his 'investigation of the relationships between art and life'.[129] 'Art into life' was to become the catch cry of Shub and the Constructivists eight years later. The seeds of Constructivism were being sown not only through the art of Malevich and Tatlin but also through Mayakovsky's questioning mind. In his analysis Mayakovsky also explored, as Constructivism would do, the significance of the role of the artist in society. He asked: 'in what circumstances does... work cease to be individually necessary and become socially useful?'[130] The Constructivist movement would answer this question with its emphasis on utilitarian production art and their call for the death of easel painting.

Noteworthy, therefore, had been the confrontation between photography and painting in the nineteenth century that swept into the cultural clashes of the avant-garde in early twentieth century pre-revolutionary Russia and continued until the end of the 1920s. Hence, in the words of the French poet Charles Baudelaire in the mid-nineteenth century, photography was 'a cheap method of disseminating a loathing for history and for painting'.[131] The result of this threatening new force of technology was that 'art further diminished its self-respect by bowing down before external reality'.[132] Baudelaire's notion of the alienating nature of the photographic document (what he perceived as a technological science, rather than art), which could be mechanically reproduced, hid a far graver concern: the destruction of traditional art forms.

In the early years of Soviet rule, these controversies had concerned themselves with both the death of art and the ensuing conflict between nonfiction film and fiction film. They translated themselves into the disunity and filmic rift between those like Shub, who aimed at the capturing of a real image (in nonfiction film), and those like Eisenstein, whose objective lay in the creation of an imaginary image (in fiction film). In essence, it was the contest between the Shubian 'photographers' of nonfiction film versus the Eisensteinian 'painters' of fiction film.

The disputes regarding the imitative nature of art and its representation were to be unravelled and deconstructed to the point of no return by the Soviet avant-garde. Their contemptuous dismissal of easel painting and the traditions of art (and their experimentation into abstraction) took them to a creative implosion. Just as the classical traditions of painting, sculpture, literature, music and theatre re-emerged triumphant at the end of the 1920s in the Soviet Union, so did their counterpart in film: fiction film. Baudelaire's horror of photography (and its base depiction of 'external reality'), its potential for wreaking havoc with creativity and fantasy was the nineteenth-century equivalent to the late 1920s struggle between nonfiction and fiction film. Documentary reality was to be overpowered by the need for make-believe and uncomplicated entertainment. This was to be Shub's Achilles heel.

She successfully used the actuality of newsreels not only to reflect an era but also to create an assessment of her times. Ultimately, Shub's very triumph would prove to be her undoing, as her depiction of historical facts in black and white would become increasingly incompatible with Stalin's manufactured vision for and of Soviet Russia.

Nonfiction film was able to produce a genuine picture of the external face of the country through topical newsreels of its people and their everyday mores. Portrayal of an interior world – that is, the private concerns, dreams and hopes of its citizens, the underlying heart of the Soviet Union – was another matter entirely. Similarly, events of the recent past would eventually need to be distorted and altered accordingly. At the All-Union Creative Conference of Workers in Soviet Cinema held in Moscow in January 1935, a courageous Kuleshov publicly stated that 'life will be merciless towards those who cannot walk in step with the Party. These people – possibly even particular talented individuals – will be eradicated from Soviet cinema.' Using his own bitter experience as a point of reference, Kuleshov issued the following warning: 'Furthermore, the absence of a Party friend, a favourite guide, during production inevitably leads to failure.'[133]

It signalled the demise of the individual in every genre of experimental art, as all was to be sublimated to the edicts of the state. Echoing Kuleshov's statements, the film historian Peter Kenez has asserted, when referencing film censorship, that during the Stalinist era, 'Artists did not submit their films to a body of censors. The state was the producer . . . Political institutions were involved in . . . the envisaged product.'[134] At the time, confirming this reluctant allegiance, Kuleshov had admitted that 'it is a basic fact that art must be Party art.'[135] Correspondingly, R. C. Williams's concise evaluation was that 'The Russian avant-garde perished at the hands of the revolutionary army it claimed to lead into battle' because it 'antagonized both the old society it helped attack and the new society it helped legitimize.'[136] Subsequently, as the 1930s progressed, the transferring of the truths of Shub's era onto the screen through the genre of nonfiction film was deemed too difficult ideologically.

Apart from the unachievable restrictions being imposed upon nonfiction film from the early 1930s onward, admittedly, there was also a distinct lack of sheer entertainment value in Shub's chosen genre. How could it possibly hope to compete with the lauded masterpiece *Chapayev* [Chapaev, 1934]: a work of acted narrative cinema much loved by audiences, critics and Stalin alike? From the end of the 1920s, the avant-garde was slowly to make itself redundant.

Ever the optimist, Shub declared her objectives in 1928, the year after the release of *The Fall of the Romanov Dynasty*: 'my long term work path is to make films using the authentic material of today, with people behaving like themselves in their daily struggle for a new life.'[137] Yet again, these filmic aspirations connect Shub with avant-garde movements years later such as *cinema vérité* and direct cinema. Shub's objective of authenticity through nonfiction film was to find itself at odds with the acutely conservative academicism of Socialist Realism. In 1932, the film journal *Proletarian Cinema* [Proletarskoe kino] proclaimed its mission stridently. It promoted the final assault on 'formalism' and the necessary destruction of nonfiction film. In its editorial it openly attacked 'notorious documentarism' as 'illiterate, presumptuous and excessively pretentious "theory"'.[138] It added that their journal 'hopes that the struggle against documentarism will be supported by all those comrades fighting for proletarian cinema.'[139] Even more concerning was the pronouncement that 'we have set ourselves the task of destroying it [documentary] completely.'[140] Shub had been warned.

Undoubtedly, experimental montage had been the badge of originality worn by the members of Soviet revolutionary cinema. By the close of the 1920s, the avant-garde were forced to comply with more traditional modes of filmic representation. Innovation and experimentation were soon to be blatantly pilloried as 'leftist' and 'formalist'. Montage as practised by Shub and Eisenstein began to die a predictable and painful death. Shub's ideological montage and Eisenstein's montage of attractions and intellectual montage had served their purpose, as had LEF and the vanguard in the arts. Kuleshov's days as a leading filmmaker were well and truly over. After the brilliance of *Man with a Movie Camera*, Vertov was beginning his walk in the wilderness. Eisenstein had temporarily escaped to Europe and the United States of America. With his suicide in 1930, Mayakovsky had made the most tragic of exits from the avant-garde. Meanwhile, Shub's career direction was uncertain.

Thus, I have contended that *The Fall of the Romanov Dynasty* exemplifies the struggle of nonfiction film in the context of the tensions between historical reality and state propaganda. Furthermore, Shub's compilation was more than just an exercise in political pamphleteering, created in an environment that would become increasingly fraught with deprivation and persecution. On the contrary, made from historical documents in the shape of raw newsreel, *The Fall of the Romanov Dynasty* presents a unique visual commentary on the lives of a people on the brink of a new socialist world. Finally, *The Fall of the Romanov*

Dynasty situates Shub at the heart of the Constructivist movement and the Soviet avant-garde. Shub's film heralds the formation of new vocabularies regarding the nature of art and the notions of authenticity and truth, in both nonfiction film and in the genre of modern documentary film.

It has been argued that *The Fall of the Romanov Dynasty* was more than nonfiction film as ideological Party propaganda, because it extols, as Shub did, the melding of Constructivist art and technology into the fabric of socialist society. The subsequent chapters on *The Great Way*, *Today*, *K.Sh.E.* and *Spain* follow the shift from the utopian dreams of Shub and the avant-garde to the conflicting issues of fact and truth in the nonfiction film of the Stalinist regime.

5

Only Newsreels: Shub's Triumphant Way Ahead

For Bill Nichols, 'In documentary, an event recounted is history reclaimed. Qualification and subjectivity infrequently intrude as complicating factors.'[1] Despite the problematic issues regarding an objective focus and representation of, in this specific case, Soviet-era historiography, 'it contributes to the formation of popular memory'.[2]

More specifically, and decades earlier, in 1929, 'And Again – the Newsreel', Shub had remarked that 'We are deeply persuaded that only newsreel, only live material can adequately reflect the great era in which we live.'[3] With this firmly in mind, she turned her attention to the final film in her triptych.

A chronologically compiled historical commentary, *The Great Way* is a sequel to *The Fall of the Romanov Dynasty*. It documents the decade from the October Revolution in 1917 to the year 1927 and is the third chapter in Shub's trilogy. Soviet audiences, who had seen *The Fall of the Romanov Dynasty* during the previous months, could now be further instructed on more recent events in their history through the construction of Shub's continuing utopian socialist chronicle. *The Great Way* serves to crystallize the prevailing narrative of the day. As Bill Nichols perceives it:

> Narrative allows documentary to endow occurrences with the significance of historical events. . . . [It] facilitates the representation of historical time [and] supplies techniques by which to introduce the moralizing perspective or social belief of an author and a structure of closure whereby . . . resolution gives an imprimatur of conclusiveness to the arguments, perspectives and conclusions advanced by the film.[4]

Once again, Shub is an agitational constructor of proletarian art in her commitment to the aims and ideals of utilitarian Constructivist theory. *The Fall of the Romanov Dynasty* had concluded with the February Revolution of 1917. With *The Great Way*, Shub extends her thematic methodology as she endeavours to further raise the political consciousness of her audience. It is a diachronically assembled observation of events highlighting and glorifying the October Revolution and the period that followed. Shub's audiences are fully aware of the ideological struggles of the past decade, not only because they have viewed them in *The Fall of the Romanov Dynasty* prior to this but also because they have lived and experienced them. Significantly, *The Great Way* serves to clarify and reinforce this prevailing Soviet commentary, and thereby it aids in extending the sociopolitical awareness of the populace.

However, differing from *The Fall of the Romanov Dynasty* which was constructed almost solely of archival material, in *The Great Way* Shub not only uses found newsreel footage but also, in her role as filmmaker, creates substantial reels of documentary film herself. By doing so, she adds to the existing archives.[5] This was borne of necessity, as there were challenges due to the paucity of footage relating to that period. For Shub frustratingly:

> Newsreels were shot without much plan and quickly put aside with little comprehension of their historic value, which of course increased with each passing year. Even worse is their change of tone after the Civil War; suddenly the concentration was on parades, meetings, arrivals, departures, delegates and such – almost no record was kept of how we transformed the country.[6]

Accordingly, in her memoirs, writing about her preparation for the making of *The Great Way*, in her essay on 'Vladimir Mayakovsky', Shub informs her readers:

> Here I am at the camera's lens. I film delegations of foreign workers, industrial colleges . . . the factories of Moscow, collective farms . . . the Lenin Institute, day nurseries, working camps for children, the everyday life and socialist education of the Red Army, the Don region, an agricultural machine factory in Rostov-on-Don . . . Volkhov's electrical plant, the tractor and train sections of the Putilovsky factory . . . the historical places connected with the Great October Revolution and with the name of Vladimir Ilich Lenin.[7]

Furthermore, Shub remarks that during pre-production, 'In addition, documentary film of current events in Europe and America were purchased for me.'[8] Cinematically and factographically, *The Great Way* can be viewed as 'an instrument for the class education of the proletariat.'[9] The intertitles are not as acerbic and ironic as those to be found in *The Fall of the Romanov Dynasty* although there is the occasional bitingly witty observation such as the breakfast between the Georgians and the French together with the startling satire of the introduction.

Nevertheless, Denise Youngblood concludes that, in comparison with *The Fall of the Romanov Dynasty*, 'Shub's tenth anniversary documentary *The Great Way* . . . was not as successful, lacking the inherent drama of the decline of a world and a revolution in the making . . . much of it is visually boring with excessively long titles, several quoting from Communist International reports'.[10] Her argument is persuasive, and the observation regarding some of the dull textual overload and excessive flag-waving cannot be denied. Sections of *The Great Way* can be viewed as tedious agitprop, although this is a feature of Soviet documentaries of this era. On the other hand, despite Youngblood's summation regarding the prolixity of some of the intertitles and documents, Shub's film does stand the test of time. It shines as a Constructivist and propagandist meditation showcasing the country as it takes its initial steps on the path towards a socialist state. Notwithstanding Youngblood's unfavourable comparison with *The Fall of the Romanov Dynasty*, *The Great Way*'s footage speaks for itself with clarity as Shub continues to target elitism through the institutions of the recent past. These bastions of privilege first seen in *The Fall of the Romanov Dynasty* are the church, the Romanovs and the bourgeoisie.

Hence, on closer examination, there are admirable and memorable elements of *The Great Way* that deserve further scrutiny. As I have stated previously in a journal article, *The Fall of the Romanov Dynasty* was to set a benchmark for Constructivist compilation film.[11] Although *The Great Way* does not reach such dizzy heights, the film has much to recommend it, as Shub paints an image of their history following the Revolution. Viktor Shklovsky's musings are apposite here: 'Art always and only deals with life. What do we do in life? We resuscitate art . . . what is art's great achievement? Life. A life that can be seen.'[12]

Scorning the Old Order: Promoting the New Leninist Future

Shub's irreverent opening frame is both audacious and amusing. The introductory shot in *The Great Way* is of the rear end of a stocky horse in graphic close-up. Admittedly, it is a sculpture, but then the camera pans back and all is revealed. It is Pavel Trubetskoi's monument to Tsar Alexander III, a bronze equestrian statue standing in a square in St Petersburg.[13] However, rather than being suitably regal and commanding, Alexander III is depicted as a squat, portly and lumpen figure on a less than majestic beast. As a filmic introduction, Shub's comic and outrageous image was verging on the scandalous. It is one of the few instances in

The Great Way where Shub demonstrates some of the thought-provoking irony that had been prevalent in *The Fall of the Romanov Dynasty*.

In this specific instance, Shub's visual subversion of the familiar relates to Shklovsky's formalist principle of 'defamiliarization'.[14] Using this element, she takes something mundane and encourages her audience to perceive it afresh. Added to this is the blatant ridiculing of the Romanov monarchy rather than genuflecting to it and lamenting its passing. This is consistent with Shub's polemic in *The Fall of the Romanov Dynasty*. It serves to reinforce her discourse as she introduces her audience to the continuing chapters of the conflicts that celebrate their liberation from the yoke of monarchical tyranny. In place of the crown is the promise of a new unshackled world infused with the reforming ideals of socialism.

Why does Shub specifically target Alexander III as an object of ridicule rather than his ineffectual son, the recently toppled Nicholas II? Is this thematic nexus acknowledging Lenin and the centuries-old autocratic rule he obliterated? Lenin was celebrated as victorious in the closing stages of *The Fall of the Romanov Dynasty* with the final triumphant shots of the film devoted to him. Not only this but there is a significant association between the sculpture of the tyrannical Tsar Alexander III and Lenin, connecting the finale of *The Fall of the Romanov Dynasty* with the introductory images of its sequel.

The linking subtext concerns one of Lenin's brothers (and Lenin's 'childhood hero'), the revolutionary socialist Alexander Ulianov.[15] A member of the 'People's Will' [Narodnaya Volya], Ulianov was implicated for his role in a failed conspiracy to murder Alexander III in 1887. According to Victor Sebestyen, Lenin's 'thirst for revenge after his elder brother was executed for an assassination plot against the Tsar motivated Lenin as powerfully as did his belief in Marx's theory of surplus value'.[16] If this observation is accurate, Shub's representation is a potent symbol of power and retribution.

Although some of the images that follow the literal felling of a despotic tsar had been seen in *The Fall of the Romanov Dynasty*, Shub deliberately uses cinematic repetition for emphasis. In *The Great Way*, she reinforces the collapse of centuries of Romanov rule in the sequence after her mockery of Alexander III. After the symbolically laden shots of his monument, and the accentuated disdain, comes fact. Now we view the fragments of royal statuary that have not survived and are scattered unceremoniously on the ground. Shub showed some of these visuals in *The Fall of the Romanov Dynasty*. These are fallen relics of the past, trappings of the former glory of the Romanov Tsars. These shrines, paying homage to a royal ruling class, have so little worth that the final frames of this mise en scène are of an infant unaware of their historical significance. These discarded vestiges of supreme power, transformed into nothing more than crumbling ruins, have become a little child's playground. Thus, apart from Shub's graphic and emblematic strand joining the end of *The Fall of the Romanov Dynasty* with the beginning of *The Great Way*, her considered act of deriding a monarch is a potent ideological motif. It is a cinematic cue relating to the Soviet struggle towards nationhood in the narrative to come.

In addition, the continuing link with Lenin is noteworthy. From the joyous shots of Lenin at the close of *The Fall of the Romanov Dynasty* to the threads of personal grief and revenge that bind him to Alexander III, Shub accentuates Lenin's presence and authority further in *The Great Way*. In this documentary, both in life and in death, Lenin occupies more footage than any other individual. Stalin's presence in *The Great Way* is limited to a few shots during Lenin's funeral, and he is not seen centre stage during Shub's documenting of this decade. The attention given to Lenin's funeral alone is of significance.

As Shub presents her historical pageant chronologically, long before we are taken to the spectacle of Lenin's funeral, the next step along this great road is where Shub directs us to the latter stages of 1917 and 'the October Revolution where the victorious masses rose up united'. The images to accompany this

Figure 18 Barrel of a ship's cannon: 'workers and peasants become the Red Fleet' in *The Great Way*.

text are of people demonstrating in their thousands, holding banners and marching through the streets of Petrograd. She continues: 'Workers and peasants become the Red Army. Workers and peasants become the Red Fleet' (Figure 18).

The army parade with military precision and is followed by an equally impressive formation display from the navy. There are Alexander Rodchenko-inspired shadows falling on this photographic display of martial potency. This is accompanied by an aerial shot of the tops of the sailors' hats, which gives a moment of visual patterned splendour.

From the Darkness of Capitalist Privilege to the Shining Torch of Socialist Egalitarianism

In contrast to this glorification of the nascent USSR, Shub's next intertitle is 'Over the heads of the rulers of the capitalist world'. Instantly, we are introduced to well-dressed bourgeois foreigners, self-important dignitaries and politicians. Their parading closely mirrors a tableau in *The Fall of the Romanov Dynasty*, where Tsar Nicholas II and his Tsarina, Alexandra, march solemnly, followed by a lengthy line of haughty aristocrats, in a patronizing nod to the plebeians during the Romanov tercentenary celebrations. Through this visual relationship, Shub is accentuating the fact that both parades, one at the end of Romanov rule and the other in the capitalist world, speak of unfettered privilege.

In *The Great Way*, the upper classes in their finery are soon replaced by a shot of an almost unrecognizable Mussolini in elegant civilian garb. Presumably, this was filmed before the formation of the Italian Fascist Party in 1919. Additionally, we glimpse Raymond Poincaré, the President of France from 1913 to 1920, also featured by Shub in *The Fall of the Romanov Dynasty*. Despite being right wing, Poincaré had journeyed to Russia during 1914 in order to maintain an existing alliance against Germany. After the entrance of Poincaré, the French Prime Minister Aristide Briand and the British Foreign Minister Austen Chamberlain appear smiling broadly for the camera.[17] This footage would have been taken in either Locarno or London in 1925.

Adding to Shub's prominent public figures, Marshal Josef Pilsudski is the next face on the screen. Unlike the previous images of Poincaré, Mussolini, Briand

and Chamberlain, he is the first dignitary to be shown with specific focus in a striking close-up. It is an imposing portrait of the high-ranking soldier. According to the historian Terry Martin in his work *The Affirmative Action Empire: Nations and Nationalism in the Soviet Union*, Pilsudski was a politician with fascist leanings.[18] Nevertheless, he was 'recognized by most Poles as the greatest Polish statesman of the twentieth century'.[19] His appearance is notable because Pilsudski's foreign policies were troublesome for Stalin, and there were fears of civil unrest and conflict.

> Pilsudski's *coup d'état* in Poland in May 1926 was, after some initial confusion, soon interpreted as the first step in an imminent attack by world imperialism on the Soviet Union. Pilsudski's well-publicized domestic policy initiatives to improve relations with Poland's Ukrainian and Belorussian populations further alarmed the Soviet leadership.[20]

We move from the 'rulers of the capitalist world' in which Shub includes Pilsudski, currently a member of the establishment. She places him firmly in the enemy camp despite his historical connection with Alexander Ulianov.[21] Now the linking caption appears. 'Over their heads, the worldwide revolutionary proletariat demonstrate their international solidarity.' This is accompanied by large political gatherings of communists marching en masse in Germany and then their downtrodden and exploited brothers and sisters on the streets of Mexico and China. These scenes are interspersed with Soviet crowds parading as they proudly carry a multitude of banners. The spectacles are further interspersed with socialist bands of drummers and processions of flag-bearing supporters. As Shub's adjoining intertitle declares:

> Under the red banner they swear allegiance
> They pledge together with the workers of the Soviet Republic
> To follow their leader Lenin to a world-wide October

Bright-eyed Young Pioneers in their distinctive crisp white shirts and red kerchiefs, holding flags, sing earnestly but joyously. Here is their leader! Lenin speaks. Massive crowds respond with zeal. The cheering multitude begins to spontaneously wave their hats in the air in this rousing exhibition of cinematic propaganda. Lenin's words appear on the screen. At this moment, Shub proceeds to give her audience a summary of the facts, reinforcing the significance of these events and the following text appears on the screen:

> The year is 1917. Russia was the first country in the world where workers and peasants took power into their own hands, in the factories and on the land.

The lesson continues with a focus on the October Revolution. Accordingly, there is an image of the Smolnyi Institute, and we are informed that the Institute is now:

> the headquarters of the proletarian revolution. On that October day, the Bolshevik Central Committee, the Petrograd Soviet and the Military Revolutionary Committee were gathered at the Smolnyi.

As Osip Brik was to declare in reference to documentary methodology, 'newsreel requires only the extremely careful and attentive presentation of the fact, playing it through to the end and linking it with other pieces through . . . a subtle semantic link . . . every individual piece is comprehensible and finished in itself'.[22] Brik cited *The Fall of the Romanov Dynasty*, which he deemed an 'exemplary' illustration of this theoretical approach. It can also be readily applied to *The Great Way* where each filmic paragraph serves as a motif threaded through the fabric of Shub's historical commentary. *The Great Way* is evidently a model that is highly relevant to Brik's assertions about newsreel. In fact, Brik championed Shub's 'montage of documentary events' in both these films.[23]

There are sailors marching in thick snowdrifts. Then the action temporarily moves back to the Smolnyi and the changing of the armed guard. From the soldiers we return to the sailors who are now trudging through deep snow towards the battle cruiser Aurora, moored on the Neva. Shub recounts that the Aurora 'having joined the uprising, bombarded the Winter Palace'. Her pictorial evidence of the shelled Winter Palace shows rubble and masonry outside the Palace's perimeter, but the damage to the facade does not appear extensive. Nonetheless, the level of destruction is not Shub's focus. Rather, just as with the fallen and smashed Romanov monuments earlier, she is alerting her audience to the physical erasure of this former royal dynasty's excess and privilege. With more subtlety, this is a reminder of the failure of the Provisional Government that followed the monarchy, as their members now cower in the besieged Winter Palace during the victorious Bolshevik days of October 1917.

From Nicholas II to Kerensky and the Provisional Government's failed attempt at liberalism, replacing Romanov rule, we see the new order. Lenin speaks. This is followed by clear images of some of the leading figures of the day such as a relaxed and smiling Anatoly Lunacharsky, the People's Commissar for

Enlightenment and Nikolai Krylenko, an Old Bolshevik who was instrumental in creating the USSR Constitution and later presided over the Stalinist Show Trials as a ruthless Chief Prosecutor.[24] Next is Vladimir Antonov-Ovseenko, one of the instigators of the symbolic storming of the Winter Palace, and, finally, the brilliant Yakov Sverdlov, who possessed an encyclopaedic knowledge of the workings of the Party. These are some of the men heralding a new dawn as they devise fresh policies for the emerging revolutionary state.

Political statements literally fly through the streets as pamphlets are thrown from a train and flutter through the air. The anarchist Vera Figner appears on the screen. This indomitable political figure is standing on the back of a truck, enthusiastically shouting slogans in scenes reminiscent of her similarly filmed segment in *The Fall of the Romanov Dynasty*.[25]

The Peace Treaty of Brest-Litovsk

A fresh scenario is introduced with the first intertitle declaring that 'The masses demanded', and this leads to a frame displaying an edict from Lenin. It urges peace. Consequently, we are taken to the site of the action during the latter stages of World War I. This is presumably in early December 1917 when Germany agreed to negotiate an armistice with Lenin's newly formed Soviet Russia prior to peace talks. German soldiers climb out of their trenches and clamber over barbed wire at the front. We see Russian troops fraternizing with their German foe in a jovial fashion. The film scholar Graham Roberts considers this section to be 'bogus', and although this war footage seems slightly contrived, it is highly possible that the Germans filmed this scenario, as it appears to be shot from behind enemy lines.[26] It is difficult to ascertain if there is a lack of authenticity as Roberts suggests. Is it a staged representation? If this is so, it is inexplicable because Shub's creed is centred on non-staged events without any actors. Why would she compromise her ideological stance for an Eisensteinian moment of dramatized action? It could easily be genuine because to our eyes in the twenty-first century accustomed to cutting-edge cinema, so many documentaries from this era appear contrived. From scenes at the front, we are notified that

> Seeking to establish a pause in the fighting, the Soviet Government instigated international talks at Brest-Litovsk.

An official document appears on the screen bearing Kaiser Wilhelm II's emblem, official seal and signature. We can surmise that this is an original manuscript from the Treaty of Brest-Litovsk. In March 1918 the Bolsheviks and the Central Powers signed the accord. It laid down excessively punitive terms for Soviet Russia. She was forced to surrender a massive swathe of her territories including Ukraine, the Baltic States, the Caucasus and Poland.[27] The Russian delegation was spearheaded by Trotsky, and yet, there is no reference to him by Shub in either image or text. Instead, there are merely some blurred shots of Austro-Hungarian dignitaries. Was the erasure of Trotsky's key role in the negotiations ignored by Shub in order to appease the Party? Yet, unlike Eisenstein who had to comply with orders from Stalin himself to remove all glowing references to Trotsky from *October* before it was released for screening in March 1928, Shub makes the 'error' of boldly including footage of Trotsky in a later reel of her film.[28] She recorded the implications of the conditions imposed at Brest-Litovsk and the bitter reality was evident in her next statement:

> Ukraine came under the power of Romanov Imperialism. On March 16 1918 the warmongers entered Kiev.

The armies of the Germans and the Austro-Hungarians had temporarily weakened the Red Army, forcing them to retreat from the Ukrainian capital. Here Shub expertly utilizes enemy archival material, and we watch as, filled with self-importance, victorious German soldiers parade in the heart of Kiev. To accentuate the punishing consequences of the Treaty, we are taken to Vladivostok in April where the occupying forces are not the Germans but the Japanese. In Vladivostok Shub states: 'They met with the friendly "liberators."' This is followed by lengthy parades of Cossacks and Kadets, high school students and primary school children.

Next we see the pro-monarchist General Mikhail K. Diterikhs, and thus, Shub's earlier reference to the Romanov Dynasty and Ukraine becomes clarified. Diterikhs was a supporter of the Tsar and was the military leader of the Whites in the Russian Civil War. Shub would have viewed him as a traitor to the cause.

The authoritative declaration 'Menshevik leaders of democratic Georgia a united front with the French military' is followed by two words: 'Our Zhordania'. Here Shub is using heavy-handed satire as she refers acerbically to Noe Zhordania, a Georgian journalist and revolutionary socialist. Although in the early twentieth century his 'was the dominant voice among Georgia's Marxists', he became the founder of the Menshevik movement in Georgia.[29] Zhordania then became critical of Lenin's stance on recruiting peasantry to the cause.[30] A clash of Marxist interpretation between Zhordania and Lenin regarding the role of the peasantry versus the working proletariat also stretched to the opposing strategies of Stalin.

To reinforce Shub's sarcasm, there is 'A friendly breakfast' where the 'collaborators', the Georgian Menshevik dignitaries, are filmed in a carefree and jovial mood entertaining ambassadors of the French military (the French being enemies of the Soviet Union during this period). The Georgian hosts and their French counterparts drink vodka and feast from a table laden with delectable comestibles at a time of rations, famine and dire food shortages in other regions of the Soviet Union. Again, Shub deploys footage filmed by opposing forces to construct a conflicting and scathing evaluation. To add to Shub's filmic critique, this is followed by a cavalcade of high-ranking commanders of the White Army: the anti-Bolshevik Tsarist Generals Kaledin, Yudenich, Kornilov and Admiral Kolchak.

Discussing nonfiction film, Lev Kuleshov was to remark that 'Newsreel is the demonstration of filmed events. The events must be shown in such a way that we can examine them properly.'[31] True to her Constructivist methodology Shub continually instructs her viewers, in the instances stated, by employing the device of irony through the use of ideological sequential frames.

Shub alerts us to the abdication of Kaiser Wilhelm II in November 1918. We read on the screen that 'The first murmurings of an October Revolution outside of Russia was happening in Germany'. As Wilhelm's reign turns to tatters, we are shown the statue of a lion, emblematic of the monarchy and then revolutionaries tearing down the German Imperial flag. Shub boldly crosses out the Kaiser's signature on the screen, effectively erasing his power.

We now go backwards in time to March of that same year for the Treaty of Brest-Litovsk as viewers are reminded that 'Representatives of the defeated nations met the victors at Versailles'. Fast-forward to the following year and the Treaty of Versailles in 1919 where, as Shub instructs us, 'The victors divided the spoils of war by a peace treaty'. Amongst them are the French statesmen Foch, Poincaré, Clemenceau and Joffre. More significantly for Shub and her political argument, there is celebration and a lengthy segment showing French bourgeois self-indulgence as these individuals are filmed in a street parade. They ride through the streets on floats wearing lavish fancy-dress costumes, and Shub comments scathingly: 'They rejoiced.'

Enlightenment: Lenin the Saviour

In contrast to this Western excess, Shub tells us that freed from 'the capitalist yoke, the country of the Soviets illuminates the darkness for the oppressed'. Soviet children march in unison. The next title informs us of 'The Second Congress of the Comintern from 19 July to 7 August 1920'. Shub quotes Lenin: 'a new era begins in world history. Mankind overthrows the last form of slavery.'

The next shots are of coffins, burials and sorrow. It is the funeral of twenty-six commissars from Baku who had 'fallen at the hands of English invaders'. More misery follows as the masses travel from the countryside flooding the cities in search of employment. On Kuznetsky Bridge, the realm of the bourgeoisie, all the exclusive shops are empty. There are bombed-out buildings.

Desperate people sell almost worthless personal items. Pitiful children shiver with cold in the icy temperatures. A skeletal horse lies in the street unable to get up. 'There were not enough provisions (food)' is presented on the screen. To illustrate the gravity of this issue, in the next shot, a hand appears clutching five pieces of black bread and then it becomes merely a single slice. It's a potent symbol of Lenin's decree for food rationing. Naturally, this statement is not emphasized further by Shub as it would have implied criticism and blame for the famine on the government. Tragically, in the Soviet Union, 'It has been estimated that in the years 1918 to 1920 over seven million people died of starvation.'[32] Added to this appalling devastation of human life, there was disastrous hyperinflation, and Shub makes the understatement that 'money had depreciated'. As if the situation could not be more calamitous, conflagrations appear before our eyes as 'the Whites burned and destroyed'. Massive explosions and wholesale destruction by these anti-government forces fill the screen. It is 1919.

Amidst this chaos and destabilization, Lenin appeals to the population to 'volunteer' for unpaid weekend work [subbotniki]. Massive crowds of rapturous followers gather to listen to Lenin's address as he extols the virtues of unpaid labour for the good of the Party. This spirit of Bolshevik unity is accentuated and reinforced by Shub's didacticism: 'Under the leadership of the Communist Party they toiled victoriously in this heroic struggle.' To give an inspiring example, to illustrate this, we are presented with a hero from the Civil War, the legendary divisional commander Vasily Chapaev.[33] We see rare authentic footage of him. He was the eponymous leading character of Dmitry Furmanov's novel. The book was adapted into a highly acclaimed Socialist-Realist film, bearing Chapaev's name.

From a hero of the Civil War to the founder of the Red Army, in which Chapaev fought, the Soviet War Advisor Trotsky arrives at the front. He meets, as is written in an intertitle, the 'very oldest and the youngest'. This segment concludes with the emphasis on the ushering in of a new dawn where the socialist youth seen greeting Trotsky are zealously upholding the doctrines of Lenin.

In the next reel, continuing with the theme of the Red Army and the struggles of the Civil War, Shub's subsequent footage shows the Bolshevik military hero Mikhail Frunze. Shub comments on Frunze's victory against the Whites. We are informed that the Red Army reached Kiev in February of 1919. Furthermore, in April, they arrived in Odessa. Finally, in this bitter and long fought campaign, the Red Army had entered Vladivostok in October 1922. Shub now narrates that 'Having been victorious in the Civil War, the workers moved to the offensive on the economic front'.

As Shub recounts, 'Together they moved forward under the guidance of Lenin'. Productive industry and agriculture are featured. Not only are there factories aplenty, their chimneys belching forth smoke but also the more rudimentary turning of the windmills and finally women winnowing grain. This is followed by the simple words 'Vladimir Ilich' and then there is ample film of Lenin. To reveal a more personal and human side of their great leader, the audience is privileged to view rare footage of Lenin affectionately stroking his pet cat. We see him in an interior setting conversing in an animated fashion to someone off-camera. There are shots of Lenin speaking to ordinary people in the street and him in a stationary car chatting with the masses (Figures 19, 20 and 21).

Thanks to Lenin's leadership, the shops are no longer empty. Their display windows are filled with merchandise. People are shopping. A man tries on a leather coat. Workers attach rivets and paint a brand new train. There is an unending supply of currency, and this is emphasized by the insertion of a sea of glistening coins spilling onto the screen. Instead of the devalued rouble, there is now economic stability and the country is thriving.

Figure 19 The personal touch: Lenin in Gorki with Nadezhda Krupskaya, 1922 in *The Great Way*.

Figure 20 Lenin in conversation: filmed in his office at the Kremlin, 1921 in *The Great Way*.

Figure 21 Lenin appears in the official car, surrounded by supporters in *The Great Way*.

His Light Will Not Be Extinguished: Lenin's Legacy Remains Undimmed

That was the good news. In this flourishing environment, 'The year is 1924' is flashed onto the screen. After Shub has catalogued these numerous achievements, attributed to Lenin, comes the shocking newspaper headline that announces the death of their esteemed leader. Lenin died on the evening of 21 January 1924 in his dacha in Gorki. From this location, the next morning, Lenin's body was transported to Moscow. A frame is filled with the Red Flag flapping in the bitter icy wind of a bleak and wintry January day. Groups of mourners plod through heavy snowfalls battling against impossible weather. Helmeted soldiers stamp their feet as they stand outside trying to warm themselves near ineffectual bonfires. Each day until the funeral is over, hundreds and thousands of women, men, children, workers, peasants and Party officials brave the freezing temperatures to queue in the street before entering the Hall of Columns within the House of Trade Unions. There are interior shots of a never-ending stream of citizens coming to pay their last respects to the founder of the socialist regime. Just as in the section on Trotsky, Shub shows 'The Old Guard' again. She contrasts this intertitle, and accompanying images, with the future as young schoolchildren are brought into view, some accompanied by their teachers, filing past Lenin lying in state.

Trotsky is conspicuous by his absence as he was in the Caucasus recuperating from a bout of ill-health. There are many conflicting reports as to the significance of his non-appearance, including one that Stalin deliberately gave Trotsky the incorrect date for the funeral, in order to prevent his attendance.[34] If there is any veracity to this rumour, it is understandable due to the power play left by the vacuum of Lenin's death together with Lenin's close association with Trotsky.

Also, there are close-up shots of a numb and dazed Nadezhda Krupskaya standing close to her husband's bier. On 29 January, two days after the funeral, she was to make the following request of the Party: 'Do not let your grief for Ilyich [sic] spend itself in an outward veneration of his person. Do not build monuments and memorials to him, palaces in his name. Do not organize splendid celebrations in his memory. In his life he attached little importance to these things.'[35] Krupskaya's entreaty was to fall upon deaf ears.

From the Hall of Columns, on 27 January, leading Party members acting as pallbearers, including Nikolai Bukharin, Lev Kamenev, Grigory Zinoviev, Stalin and Vyacheslav Molotov, carry Lenin's body to the temporary mausoleum in Red Square, close to the Kremlin Wall. Suddenly, Stalin comes into full view. He walks behind Lenin's coffin and is then seen in the lower centre of the shot.

In the Kremlin, overlooking Red Square, the camera pans to the Spasskaya Tower. On the afternoon of the funeral, its clock, the Kremlin Chimes, is flashed onto the screen on two separate occasions. The clock face shows the time as four o'clock. This is followed by the thunderous noise of simultaneous volleys of shots ringing out on land and at sea, the blowing of factory sirens and the piercing whistles of steam trains. Lenin is laid to rest. His funeral alone is the longest segment in the entire narrative of *The Great Way* and occupies almost six minutes of the film.

The next statement attempts to reassure Shub's audience. 'Lenin is dead but the cause of Lenin lives on!' After paying homage to him, there is a brief segment showing the wheels of industry. They turn regardless of the death of Lenin because time does not stand still and his work continues. Moreover, to emphasize his overarching significance, there are a far greater number of film frames devoted to Lenin in *The Great Way* than to any other historical personage of this era.

The next moment, we have a radical contrast with one word 'There'. The bustling metropolis of capitalist New York, and more specifically Wall Street, appears. 'Where the uncrowned kings [are] Rockefeller: King of the Stock Exchange' and 'Ford: King of the Automobile Industry'. Here, we are whizzed off to another capitalist stronghold, the Bourse in Paris. A close-up of a sinister chimera high up on Notre Dame symbolizing religion is intercut with shots of stockbrokers massing on the steps outside the Bourse and frenetic footage of speeding vehicles. Shub seems to suggest that money is the new religion of the capitalist world where they bow to and worship mammon. Whether this is Shub's intention or not, this footage is used as further proof of the excesses of the West. Shots of the Parisian slums nearby follow the images of privilege. Accentuating her point the text 'In the colonies' corresponds with documentary of primitive villages. Shots of exploitation: slave labour as men cut sugar cane on plantations and mothers toil in the sun with babies strapped to their backs. We are taken from one form of abuse to another.

'Whenever the working masses declare their needs . . . they go on strike.' Accordingly, Shub shows us industrial action in America. The factories are shut. There is civil unrest. Mounted armed police appear in the streets. Arrests follow. From here, we are shown a prison and prisoners 'exercising', walking aimlessly around a compound. 'Let us remember! The protests of the millions' but 'they could not save Sacco and Vanzetti who were executed by the electric chair'.

Highlighting the frivolous and soulless nature of materialism in the United States, Shub goes from the senseless electrocution of the two anarchists Sacco and Vanzetti, who many believed were innocent, to the endless electric billboards and flashing neon signs advertising the decadent pleasures of nightlife and rampant consumerism. There is a merry-go-round of champagne bottles on an assembly line as the whirl of Western life spins faster and faster out of control.

Shub now compares the debauchery of capitalist America with the restraint and industrious nature of her homeland fighting for the values bequeathed by Lenin where 'we are prepared to confront ... let us prepare ourselves'. Battleships and Soviet naval destroyers proudly display their might. Soldiers drill. Tanks advance. As Shub describes it, 'The USSR is the very first country in the world where workers and peasants have victoriously built a socialist state.'

In the following intertitle, Shub explains that 'In spite of repression from all over the capitalist world, delegations of foreign workers are drawn to Moscow ... to convey brotherly support ... to the working masses of the Soviet lands'. These eager newcomers are welcomed at the railway station with placards and banners both in German and Russian, which simply say, 'Workers of the World Unite!'

At the conclusion of Lenin's funeral there was a frame filled with the word 'LENIN' carved into his makeshift wooden mausoleum. In this current segment of the film, we see his name written again. Only this time Lenin is shown as part of the new age of technology, and his name is illuminated by a myriad of light bulbs. Even though it lacks the sophistication and superior technology of the neon billboards in the United States, Shub stresses that Lenin's power and ideals continue to blaze as a shining beacon pointing the way forward as part of the USSR's modern expansion. The presence of Lenin permeates *The Great Way* (Figure 22).

Returning to the 'delegations of foreign workers' referred to earlier, we are informed that these 'foreign comrades personally see how we are rebuilding'. We've seen the might of the Soviet Union militarily, and now Shub highlights its industrial strength. Consequently, we are taken to a hydroelectric power plant and the construction of a dam.

From rebuilding the nation's infrastructure, there is the equally vital matter of education. The camera's focus is now on a printing works where they produce textbooks and newspapers in order to educate the societies of this vast realm. Now to be more specific, we see a teacher with a blackboard and

Figure 22 Lenin's name is in lights in *The Great Way*.

chalk instructing her students. We are made aware of the multi-ethnicity of the Soviet Union as Shub presents us with different nationalities living in the vast territories of the USSR. Communities in these far-flung regions are being taught to read and write.

Added to the importance of education and the wonders of hydroelectricity, there are modern blocks of Soviet housing developments springing up as accommodation for the workers. Not only this but vats of steaming food are produced and delivered to communal dining rooms within these complexes. We are taken to kitchens where there is catering on a massive industrial scale. Here are the latest innovations such as colossal mechanized potato peelers and gigantic commercial dishwashing machines. These scenes of achievement are imbued with the pride of progress.

Likewise, there are advances in agriculture. There is a display of harvesters and tractors built in the Soviet Union with workers marvelling at this latest technological achievement. The emphasis is on abundance, and there are shots of numerous dairy herds.

Shub announces the appearance of Mikhail Kalinin as he travels to a Soviet village where electricity has recently been installed. He chats with the peasants privileged enough to have access to this miracle of modern innovation. It is, as Shub proclaims, 'the Electrification of the Countryside'. This is another example of the patriotic catalogue of triumphs and places emphasis on national glory. Shub has proved to her audience that the sacrifices of revolution have yielded success. Her film has achieved this objective by giving audiences tangible examples of what had been accomplished from 1917 to 1927.

After itemizing all the advances in the motherland, the text on the screen reads: 'and the Young Leninists'. Next, the word 'Strong' is flashed before the audience's eyes, and they see a display of gymnastics and calisthenics performed by members of the Komsomol en masse. The precision and scale of this spectacle is a modest forerunner to the lavishly produced propaganda films of Leni Riefenstahl in the middle of the 1930s.

The next caption on the screen is 'Brisk' as these youth brimming with vitality march towards us. There are bronzed, bare-chested young men accompanied by young girls attired in shorts. 'Hooray for change! They vow to finish the work of their fathers.' They wave and sing as they march hopefully into a bright and glorious future of prosperity and harmony. This continues Shub's recurring motif about the Old Guard giving way to the younger generation to fulfil Lenin's legacy. Thus, Shub's text concludes with: 'And on this great way, following the testament of Ilich, we are building a new world order for us!'

The closing shot is of the emblem of the USSR, a potent symbol of pride and progress. *The Great Way* starts with a representation of the repressive past, the autocracy of the Tsars. It ends with the coat of arms of the Soviet Union, ironically an insignia of increasing totalitarianism under the reign of the current regime.

In Shub's eyes, in *The Great Way*, the authenticity of the material was paramount in the documentation of the history of the Revolution and Lenin's ascendancy to power. This was reinforced by the public reception of her film, and according to her, it 'was evaluated positively by the Party and the Soviet press, as well as by many foreign comrades'.[36] To confirm this, Shub was witness to the community's response during an evening screening of *The Great Way*, after a Party Conference. 'The audience showed a lively reaction to the film, which resurrected for the screen the different stages of the proletariat's heroic struggle that led to its victory.' Not only this but the viewers 'reacted with particular enthusiasm to the cinematographic portraits of the great Lenin, especially to those that were shown for the first time in my film'.[37]

Reflecting and adding emphasis to the ideological underpinnings of *The Fall of the Romanov Dynasty*, similarly, *The Great Way* was the personification of Shub's Constructivist principles. Consequently, it, in turn, set a standard for the continuing expression of her aims and objectives for the compilation genre with its nonfiction narrative: as it underscored the political, historical and social mileposts on the great road forward.

6

Shub's Final Silent Documentary: *Today*

The Fall of the Romanov Dynasty and *The Great Way* had both reinforced the class struggle: the triumphant overthrow of the Romanovs versus the October Revolution and the victories of the Bolsheviks. In *Today* [Segodnya, 1930] Shub extends these thematic elements and, furthermore, presents the impressive progress being made in modernizing her country. Ideologically driven, *Today* was Shub's last silent compilation, and she delineates it as follows. 'What is *Today*? It is a political film made of concrete material from our reality.'[1] This was Shub's defining statement after the release of *Today* in November 1930. Encapsulating her prime objectives, this declaration was part of a short essay 'On the Film "Today"' [O filme 'Segodnya'], written by her in defence of her documentary.

The Righteousness of the Socialist USSR as Opposed to the Depravity of the Capitalist United States

Added to her assertion above, *Today*'s narrative and thematic structure can be summarized by examining an essay that Vsevolod Pudovkin and Shub, as the leading signatories, together with others, published in *Proletarian Cinema* [Proletarskoe kino]. This was a journal acknowledged as a publication promoting Socialist Realism. Of necessity, Pudovkin and Shub's article was infused with a steadfast adherence to Party slogans. Seemingly desperate to conform, they contended that

> The entire capitalist world is undergoing a severe economic crisis. The contradictions are constantly widening between the world's two social systems – the socialist system that is moving upwards and achieving vast success in its economic development and the capitalist system that is moving into decline, rotting, bringing with it the suffering, tears and misery of millions of workers.[2]

This Marxist proclamation is integral to Shub's argument, as is evidenced by the filmic preface to *Today*. She opens her work with a quote on the screen attributed to Vyacheslav Molotov, at that time a member of Stalin's inner circle. Molotov's words carry authority and reinforce Shub's thesis as he lays emphasis on the essential and radical contrast between the 'two worlds'. Succinctly, he labels them as 'socialism under construction' and 'capitalism doomed to destruction' as they 'stand against each other'. Shub will focus on pitting these two polar opposites in conflict with one another, throughout her compilation. Molotov's pronouncement is not only a concise synopsis of *Today* but it also leaves the viewer in little doubt of the visual and textual discourse about to be unfurled under the banner of the USSR.

Cinematically, Shub emphasizes continuously the Soviet Union as a shining beacon lighting the path forward for the diligent and faithful proletariat of the socialist world. As expected, this is in glaring opposition to the decadence and worthless ways of the capitalist West with its exploitation of downtrodden workers. It is a persuasive, albeit well-worn, political narrative familiar to all Soviet cinema attendees of the era. Indeed, Shub had used this same evaluation in a section of *The Great Way* where she'd shown evidence of the inequalities in the class system of Western society, with specific reference to the United States, while differentiating this foreign way of life from that of the brave new world of the Soviet Union. The latter was a domain that brought hope and enlightenment to all the downtrodden workers throughout the globe. By extension, Shub's commentary supports the Stalinist mythology relating to the initial Five Year Plan and the triumphant success of the proletariat all working together harmoniously in order to deliver it in four years. Naturally, no mention is permitted of the widespread famine and abject misery caused by the brutal crushing of the kulaks. Only the rationalization, along Party lines, for the decimation of the kulaks is allowed in Shub's narrative. Instead, *Today* showcases the technological advancements in both agriculture and industry in the USSR. In fact, in Shub and Pudovkin's journal article in *Proletarian Cinema*, they made a commitment to 'actively participate in completing the Five Year Plan in four years, of constructing a classless society, of strengthening the defence capability of the Soviet state against any encroachment by imperialism'.[3] This text translates into the crux of this film's rallying cry.

As a consequence of this ideological pledge, it was understood to be the patriotic duty of all inhabitants of the Soviet Union to guard the principles of socialism from hostile outside forces – namely, the dangers and corrupting influences of capitalism. The populace must be ready at all times to defend the Stalinist regime against imperialist aggression. This doctrine, further reinforced by Molotov's sermon, encapsulates Shub's cinematic discourse. However, in spite of the didacticism that permeates *Today*, the work has occasional glimpses of humour and satire and beauty. They filter through Shub's chronicle and bring light relief to the serious theories contained therein.

The simplicity of the visual introduction of the film takes us 'from the snows of the North' to the present day. The opening images are close-ups of an icebreaker followed by a mid-shot of the frozen wastes of Karelia in the northwest corner of the empire. The latter and surprisingly poetic scene is of a crisp icy-white landscape punctuated by contrasting dark and denuded spindly pine trees. Their boughs are powdered with snow. Reindeers enter the frame pulling pine logs from the forest past rustic wooden cottages. The next beasts of burden are Bactrian camels, but they are contrasted with the new, the modern and the present day. From the undeveloped North, Shub moves to an intertitle noting that 'where today there are . . .' and we see up-to-date modes of transport as a convoy of trucks and a car drive through ice-cleared roads. This symbol of progress is compared with more scenes of reindeers pulling supplies in the time-honoured tradition of a bygone era. Once again, Shub uses the juxtaposition of imagery as a persuasive tool supporting her debate, a device that had proved so successful in both *The Fall of the Romanov Dynasty* and *The Great Way*.

Remaining in Karelia, the following frame showcases the majestic 'wild Kivach Waterfall'. The banks of either side are dotted with the ever-present pine trees of this region. In the next frame, tree trunks float down the Suna River adjoining the falls. Directly following this, the camera revisits the rushing power of the Kivach. Trees are being felled. More fast-flowing swirling eddies and logs are tumbling over and into the waterfall. The cross-cutting of these images, skilfully edited by Shub, gives added movement and rapidity to the mise en scène. Where is this leading? Shub will reveal all as she melds these segments relating to the harnessing of Mother Nature with modern advancement. But first, we are once again transported back to the primitive way of life: the 'ancient villages of the past'. Shub elaborates further on earlier footage that we'd seen of traditional peasant housing by a display of patterned timbered architecture. There are some grand dwellings of three storeys in height with ornate balconies and decorative folk carving adorning their facades; other more modest homes sport ornamentation under their eaves. There is a wooden Russian Orthodox Church with onion domes.

Two young women carry cumbersome pails of water, attached to heavy wooden yokes. They climb steps leading into their doorway entrance. In another instance of this simple and outmoded form of existence, a handsome girl on horseback is shown in close-up. The camera pans back to reveal that her horse is dragging a sled, laden with sacks. A man walks beside a horse-drawn cart containing hay. There are no trucks to assist them with their heavy loads. A woman stands holding a pitchfork with a sheaf of oats or barley attached. She passes bundle after bundle over her head to a man balancing on a vertical structure with horizontal wooden slats. Without any form of machinery, he laboriously affixes each of the sheaves between the planks, leaving them to dry in the sun. The whole structure eventually fills with an abundant cereal crop. These idyllic images of a seemingly slow and bucolic way of life do not belong in today's world. Instead, they are an idealized representation of the cycle of perpetual labour together with the traditions of the past: a romanticized tableau of the daily life of the peasantry prior to collectivization.

The Simple Life of the Non-mechanized Past and the Startling Technology of the Present

From these humble modes of life, Shub now introduces us to 'today in Karelia' where 'Kondopozhsky kombinat built . . . .' The camera leads the eye to an impressive modern marvel: a hydroelectric power station. The next frames are of a massive paper mill, which, of course, uses vast quantities of water, trees and electricity in order to manufacture the finished product. These stages of assembly join fluidly with the past shots of forests being chopped down into logs, sailing down the Suna River. These pines have been earmarked for use as paper pulp. Inside the paper mill, Shub photographs the rollers using an aerial shot, a side view, and then the torrents of water used in the processing. At last! The pristine paper is being turned on gargantuan rollers and then hoisted onto countless carriages on a train. The last shot takes us back to the natural world – a glazed canal of stillness bordered by trees.

The geography alters radically as we travel southwards. Oxen carry supplies. Behind them walks a peasant woman. Women and men on horseback trotting at a leisurely pace follow. Their horses transport packs of provisions. One man nonchalantly smokes a pipe as he rides by with dogs and a foal at his heels. These animals are integral to the survival of what appears to be a nomadic group. Rather than an onion dome, a minaret is glimpsed amongst the trees.

The camera pans across 'tea plantations and state farms of Chakvi'. Tea is grown on the slopes of this hilly region of Georgia. Women pick the leaves with secateurs unlike the cultivators in India, Ceylon/Sri Lanka and Japan where they're traditionally harvested by the use of nimble fingers, with not an implement in sight. Men and women harvest tangerines and fill large baskets with this delectable citrus fruit. From the profusion of agriculture, we visit the city of Baku, the capital of Azerbaijan, and dilapidated housing. Two men walk past the camera and one self-consciously glances into the lens. Three women, with heads covered, sit by a stone wall with a child. Then the shot moves to a woman walking along wearing a burqa; only her hand is fully discernible. In a sunlit alley, another Muslim woman hurries past the camera. Children play and fight in the restricted quarters of this community. A woman squeezes through a narrow doorway.

In another scenario entirely, the audience is shown the delights of male bathhouse rituals. The first man is covered in a sea of foam while a semi-naked plump attendant solemnly squeezes soapsuds from a sponge over the prone figure. The next client is seated and has what appears to be an early form of physiotherapy or osteopathy administered to his skeletal frame. The practitioner stands on this unfortunate individual and torturously manipulates various parts of his body. Serious work this might be, but it clearly shows Shub's sense of playfulness, as it is immensely humorous to observe. The camera then pans to a more pleasurable experience as a fat moustachioed gentleman is gently massaged while being covered in bubbles and froth. It appears that there are no bathhouses for women in order for them to fritter away the hours, thereby enjoying such a leisurely and luxurious pastime.

Instead, a graceful woman, fully covered with her face just visible, walks next to what appears to be an open drain. Burqa-clad women walk in the shadows. These images appear claustrophobic (Figures 23 and 24). Despite the otherworldliness of these hemmed-in individuals, Shub's intertitles now confirm that, in contrast to this old and therefore primitive way of life, 'a new proletariat grows up in Baku'.

Gleaming white, Soviet-style modern apartment blocks (albeit identical and soulless) come into focus. A woman, with two small children, walks along a pristine pathway past the bland buildings. A man on a bike is seen cycling past electric power poles on another spacious streetscape. This is progress! Amusingly, a man near the kerb waves to the camera as another newly constructed, and equally antiseptic, housing complex is proudly featured. The visual disparity

Figure 23 Veiled in sunlight and shadow in *Today*.

Figure 24 Another veil – the same time but another place: the USA in *Today*.

with the previous scene of, what appeared to be, suppression, bleakness and backwardness could not be more marked.

In order to reinforce her message of the transition from 'yesterday' to 'today', Shub has a primitive horse and cart of yesteryear travel through the iron gates of the contemporary dwellings built for the proletariat of today.

In comparison with earlier documentation of Muslim children in their stifling environment, we are now shown robust, smiling, well-dressed children playing in large open spaces. These Soviet girls and boys of today are the leaders of tomorrow. A little girl in the foreground, wearing her best bonnet, skips for the camera. Other faces appear. A blond boy in a cap and a smiling youngster in her white scarf are followed by the first child still using her skipping rope. Unselfconsciously and enthusiastically, she 'performs' again. In contrast, there is an enchanting shot of another little girl as she shyly looks away from the shot. A tram moves smoothly by a car parked on the street, signifying signs of growing affluence and progress with the coming of modernity to the city (Figures 25 and 26).

Figure 25 A Soviet girl smiles, happy in her new environment in *Today*.

Figure 26 One of her playmates, in the same apartment complex, shyly averts her gaze from the camera in *Today*.

Several years before the making of *Today*, Shub in a symposium on Soviet documentary had advocated for the crucial importance of preserving this film form. Writing in her accompanying article of 1927, titled 'We Do Not Deny the Element of Mastery', she considered that 'when you see a nonfiction film, it survives because it is a small fragment of genuine life which has now passed'.[4] Every visual element of *Today* attests to this principle of Shub's cinematic philosophy. At this same symposium, Sergei Tretiakov, although referencing *The Fall of the Romanov Dynasty*, believed that 'Thanks to the work of Shub, tiny individual pieces of everyday experience . . . become . . . magnificent material for synoptic, historical and kino-articles that are illuminated by polemical fire and genuine enthusiasm'.[5] His commentary is just as pertinent to Shub's structural working of *Today*.

This is a documentary filled with 'individual pieces of everyday experience'. From footage portraying robust proletarian children at play, we view their fathers at work. Today, as Shub writes across the screen, 'there is a socialist offensive on a new front . . . a huge effort of will and muscle'. A banner with 'In Four Years' emblazoned across it refers to the superhuman effort required in aiming to complete the Five Year Plan a full twelve months sooner than scheduled (as referred to in Pudovkin and Shub's journal article and constantly re-emphasized).

Hence, the next cinematic frames that appear are of industrial might – specifically steel production. The blast furnaces belch forth plumes of black smoke, breathing life into the chimneys of industry. This is a steel mill where they are smelting and moulding metal for railway lines. Just as in factory production, workers labour ceaselessly in unison, laying the railway tracks. Shub is commenting on Soviet construction projects in which every phase is attributed to the collective. Everything is conceived, made and built by many, not by one individual. All is for the glory of the socialist state.

'The enthusiasm of socialist competition' appears on the screen. The flag with the hammer and sickle is accompanied by gathering crowds of women and men, from every corner of the Soviet republic. They are seen waving placards. A speaker is reading from a paper he holds in his hand. Miners bearing their lamps are part of the throng. Workers sign documents, not with a cross but confidently write their own names to signify the success of literacy programmes throughout the land.

A squadron of tractors lines up to enter the competition, with the spectators cheering the drivers standing by their vehicles in readiness (Figure 27). Brimming with health, a handsome young man in goggles and a cap is filmed in

Figure 27 Let the tractor race begin! *Today.*

close-up. He raises his hand to start the tractor race. People watch the spectacle unfold. A man carries his chubby infant daughter. A stunning young woman, epitomizing the wholesome young Soviet pioneer, comes into the shot on the right of the frame (Figure 28).

A parade of scythes fills the sky in an image of sheer loveliness. It is a bucolic image worthy of the films of the Ukrainian director Alexander Dovzhenko, who was known for his visual lyricism. The workers also carry branches with leaves. It heralds the coming of the harvest (Figure 29).

From peasants and their sickles we move to delegates, a gathering of suited men. They appear in a conference meeting hall. There is a prominent image of Lenin in the background. Lenin again is lit against the darkness of the room. By bringing this representation of him into focus, Shub again reintroduces the motif of light and dark in relation to Lenin. He lives on. This effective thematic strand links *Today* with *The Great Way*. This is followed by a differing focus altogether: the Soviet peasantry in the early 1930s.

'This winter . . . a socialist offensive of the working class' is the intertitle. On a wintry day, befitting the subject matter, a spokesman stands on a podium. He addresses a massive crowd of predominantly women. They hold banners. Visually connected to this scene is another text, which is explosive: 'Close ranks!' 'Rural Bolshevik activists killed by kulaks!' 'Eliminate the kulaks as a class!' In her book *Red Famine: Stalin's War on Ukraine* Anne Applebaum reveals

Figure 28 The unselfconscious beauty of a young Soviet woman is shown to perfection in *Today*.

In just a few short months during the winter of 1929–30 the Soviet state carried out a second revolution in the countryside, for many more profound and more shocking than the original Bolshevik revolution itself. All across the USSR, local leaders, successful farmers, priests and village elders were deposed, expropriated, arrested or deported. Entire village populations were forced to give up their land, their livestock, and sometimes their homes in order to join collective farms. Churches were destroyed, icons smashed and bells broken.[6]

Footage of shattered church bells, referred to by Applebaum, will be seen in this next segment of Shub's film. The spokesman at the rally now comforts a woman who has joined him on the platform. A vast throng of participants are there to farewell the dead. In keeping with the state-sponsored policy to promote atheism, a bell falls from a church steeple and smashes to smithereens on the ground. Applebaum confirms, 'Religious repression in the USSR began in 1917 . . . but in the Ukraine it reached its . . . height during collectivization.'[7]

There are two open coffins on the cold earth. Grieving women kiss one of the bodies. A man kisses the other inert form. Another church bell crashes

Figure 29 The Reapers in *Today*.

into the dirt. More women pay their respects. A man openly weeps, holding a handkerchief to his face. A fine-looking young male in the foreground stares directly into the camera lens and then turns his attention to a female. Distressed women surround one of the coffins. A banner slowly covers the screen. There is a close-up shot of one of the dead Bolshevik heroes. His head, although bandaged, appears to be surrounded by a laurel wreath. To the left of the camera, a suited official stands solemnly behind the mourners.

From talk of 'the continuous collectivization of districts' and 'liquidating the kulaks', Shub turns her attention to the 'genuine' Soviet peasantry and their supporters. This time-old tradition of rural life is about to be destroyed by the horrors of collectivization, but only the most positive outcomes must be shown on film.

Nonetheless, this is before the famine of 1932 to 1933, and farmers prepare the soil for sewing. Peasants with a horse make furrows. Cattle plough the soil. There is a close-up shot of the clods of earth being rhythmically turned over, followed by horses pulling a harrow. Oxen drag a chain attached to another plough. These methods are laborious and slow and old-fashioned. That was the case in the antiquated chapters of yesteryear, but today is a dramatically different story. In fact, today is the dawning of a new age. Help is at hand! Here comes the tractor brigade!

Men proudly walk the land followed by a procession of tractors bearing banners. Peasants stand admiringly as the tractors cultivate the land more efficiently, speedily and with far less effort than the old ways with horses and oxen. A long shot, and then a close-up of a man on the mudguard of a tractor beside the driver, comes into view. The marvels of modern mechanization are shown in extreme close-up as a tractor pulls three ploughs simultaneously in a convoy of machines. Weeks of work can now be accomplished within a matter of days. A beaming peasant from the steppes uses his collective's tractor and prepares their land for the sowing of crops.

Yesterday and Today: Shub's Cinematic Actuality

These scenes of Shub's are exactly what the film scholar Sergei Drobashenko was accentuating and referring to when he published his essay on Soviet nonfiction film covering the years 1917 to 1940. In part, he was investigating and giving evidence to support his views on authenticity and the documentary. Therefore, his focus was on 'the relationships between film and reality . . . treating a documentary picture as part of the historical evidence'.[8] As Shub had asserted when writing about *Today*, 'this film was made from the material of real facts, real events and occurrences'.[9] She succeeds in reflecting and fulfilling Drobashenko's objectives. Thus, Shub documents in great detail the life of those who build the nation either by farming the land or working in factories to produce and manufacture machinery, or constructing hydroelectric stations.

From the working of arable farming land with the introduction of tractors, Shub transfers her attention to industrial sites. 'We plan major great works for the socialist Five Year Plan.' Excavating explosions blast into rocks near the waterside. Buckets of concrete are transported by train and are lifted off by a crane. This leads to a filmic symphony of cranes in an abstract display worthy of Liubov Popova's Constructivist art (Figure 30).

From the cranes, we fast-forward to work proceeding on a dam. Thanks to advancements in Soviet technology, today there is a hive of productivity. Shub

Figure 30 Constructivist imagery and the poetry of the crane in *Today*.

presents a detailed visual study of the stages in the building of a hydroelectric dam. Tree trunk logs are brought in, a plethora of additional concrete containers are emptied. There are images of a man on a crane, close-ups of pistons pumping, cogs turning, men pouring concrete into moulds and more explosions shattering the air as the landscape is blasted. Shub's rhythmic editing is extremely effective as it serves to mimic and give emphasis to the pulsating physicality and industriousness of all those involved in this crucial venture. It is aiding in the overall prosperity of the country. The obvious subtext is look how far we've advanced under Stalin's rule!

Shub now turns her focus to nature and rural dwellers. 'In May, the desert came alive.' A caravan wends its way through a mountain pass followed by a herd of camels. On horseback and carrying banners, nomads traverse the land. Travelling in their hundreds over such a vast territory, they cross rivers and eventually reach a railway line. It is no ordinary railroad, but as Shub instructs us in an intertitle, this is part of the construction of the Turksib Railway. This gargantuan project, stretching from Turkestan to Siberia, was completed as part of the First Five Year Plan in April 1930.

A train is visible in the background. In the blazing sun, bare-chested men labour on the tracks. Now we discover the reason for the transportation of logs in the previous sequence. The timber has been cut as sleepers to build the Turksib railroad. There is more spiking of the rails by the labourers. Not only this but there had been earlier footage of railway lines being manufactured in a steel mill. Are these the self-same tracks that we see being affixed at this point in the film?

Shub cuts to a teeming gathering of onlookers, followed by dignitaries on a platform. Are the VIPs there to officially open this section of the railway line? Shub documents an appealing array of portraits of the young and the old. There are remarkable profile shots of two Kazakh men, wearing Astrakhan hats, and of Kazakh women with ornate headdresses, one with a child. They sit patiently on horseback. This display of multiculturalism shows the diversity of the population of the USSR. After this interlude, the camera returns to the laying of the railway line. The crowds watch in apparent fascination as workers bolt the tracks together in a show of muscle and intense activity. Here is the train! The people wave their hats in the air in a sign of solidarity and celebration! Those who have laboured on this project embrace one another or shake hands with great vigour. There are scenes of jubilation as the last track is laid. Workers are thrown aloft. This is the Soviet Union of today, working for the common good of the nation.

At long last the train passes by with close-up shots as it runs smoothly over the newly laid railway line. The shadow of this mighty and efficient means of transport races past the people from the far-flung territories who have travelled far and wide to experience this marvellous event of Soviet progress. Shub emphasizes, yet again, how the old life has been supplanted by the new.

There are more close-up shots of the waving throng, including one of another handsome Soviet youth, a symbol of the new heroic breed. His face is flashed on the screen and repeated twice more in the crowd scenes, for maximum effect, as he smiles radiantly on this joyful occasion. The train carriages hurtle by carrying banners emblazoned with many languages. Shub seems to be reinforcing the viewpoint that they are all united under one flag: the hammer and sickle. They may belong to different national groups, but there is strength in heterogeneity, and just as significantly, they are all loyal members of the Soviet Union (Figure 31).

With great clarity, Shub has presented the attributes of her socialist homeland and its inhabitants in the most glowing of terms. She now turns her attention towards the country that personifies capitalism, the United States of America.

Figure 31 A trio of comrades in *Today*.

Greed, Excess and Exploitation in the Capitalist West

A dirigible flies over New York with a gondola hanging underneath the airship. This will be visually described in a further sequence. In the harbour below, the Statue of Liberty is being cleansed of air-borne pollutants. On harnesses, three men scrub the tabula ansata held firmly in the statue's hands. The camera lingers on the date of the Declaration of Independence, using Roman numerals, in prominent relief on the metal background of the tablet. Additionally, the perilous work of these industrious workers includes scrubbing the grime from the Statue of Liberty's fingers, her face and her spiked crown. Ingrained dirt has encased this symbol of freedom. Is this symbolic? The audience is left to draw their own conclusions before being bombarded with visions of this other world.

It is 1929. On board a boat, the visiting Prime Minister of Great Britain Ramsay MacDonald in a top hat shares a joke with the American President Herbert Hoover. After this shot of two 'leaders of the free world', we read the words 'Skyscrapers in prosperous America'. An airship hovers over New York. The city skyline is peppered with towering high-rise architecture. Down below is a bustling metropolis. Millions of cars clog the streets. There are masses of well-dressed people. It is a city of great affluence, and tellingly, there is nothing to compare with it in the Soviet Union.

In the United States, the display of empty vanity and wealth is staggering. A lady holds a make-up compact in her hand and presses a powder puff onto her face. Women try on fine evening gowns over their silk lingerie. Bracelets are affixed. Another woman in a strapless party dress wears a diamond headpiece and a diamond pendant with a massive square-cut stone in the centre. On her finger she has an ostentatious ring bearing a huge precious gem. The level of opulence is astounding.

As if this wasn't enough, we see a young woman applying her make-up using the reflection of a shop window. Cars speed by also mirrored in the storefront. Also in this streetscape, beautifully attired women saunter by. We are now taken into a hairdressing salon as a row of bored-looking women sit under hairdryers reading magazines.

In the foreground, a manicurist attends to a woman's nails. In an almost futuristic science-fiction shot, a suited male hairstylist attends to a woman's hair. Her locks are attached to a fantastical towering electrical contraption. Is this cumbersome machine an early prototype of a portable handheld electric curling tong? There is a close-up of this femme fatale, followed by even more extremes of self-indulgence. A woman sporting a ridiculous hat, which appears to have a fruit bowl on its side attached to her bonnet, powders her face. These well-heeled women are seduced by extravagant jewellery, up to the minute fashions in clothes, and they also squander their money on visiting beauty parlours. Their vacuous lives, focusing on material acquisitions, are devoid of purpose. These idle rich symbolize the ultimate in an existence centred upon empty gratification. Hence, Shub is listing the objectionable habits of the wealthy classes in a capitalist society.

Affluent ladies in the latest attire, wearing cloche hats and furs, stroll towards an outdoor café. They laugh, smoke cigarettes and idly drink cocktails while a maid on a ladder cleans windows. It is a shocking indictment of societal injustice with Shub commenting on the class system, as she emphasizes the divide between privilege and struggle. This is the purpose of the footage showing servants and those who they serve. Shub is repeating a well-worn leitmotif. She had presented this dichotomy of hierarchy previously on many occasions in *The Fall of the Romanov Dynasty*. In that film, Shub had distinguished between the downtrodden peasants versus their masters prior to the Revolution. There was a scene where servants stood and waited in attendance on wealthy landowners, the Governor of Kaluga and his wife, as they savoured the ritual of afternoon tea.

In *Today*, there is another comment on class. We are introduced to an additional group of the oppressed that serve the rich in restaurants. They are a team of wine waiters, each carrying a tray of drinks. Following this image, they race against one another carefully balancing these tools of their trade, aiming not to spill a drop as the glasses wobble. It is sheer frivolity and an amusement for their masters. The waiters run towards the finishing line. A man in a position of power congratulates the winner of this meaningless event (which can be contrasted with the 'worthy' tractor race in the USSR).

The frivolity of these pastimes is sharply contrasted with a view of tradesmen labouring high above New York. They are precariously balanced on steel girders as they carry out their death-defying work. To accentuate the height factor, there is a dizzying shot of the cars far below. They appear minuscule. Shub's inference is that these men risk their lives to earn a wage and are exploited by the greed of their wealthy employers. To emphasize her point, Shub takes us back to the dirigible. Firstly, we see the pilot steering the airship. A fellow crewman joins him. Meanwhile, inside, in another part of the gondola is a restaurant filled with prosperous-looking gentlemen. They represent the bosses engaged in the exploitation of the workers. Some of the latter are perched dangerously while working on the tops of skyscrapers overlooking the city. Revisiting the dirigible, we watch as the chef in his white uniform serves his bourgeois customers by carving succulent roasted meat for them. The consumers eat and drink their fill. In graphic contrast, one of the workers is hazardously balanced on a girder, without a safety harness, hundreds of feet above the bustling metropolis. He swigs milk from a bottle. There is no champagne or gourmet food for him, only the basic staples of life.

No one but the proletariat appear to be labouring. Everyone else in New York is shown at leisure: dining on extravagant foodstuffs and drinking alcohol or being pampered at the beauty parlour or socializing by meeting friends. They also indulge in ballroom dancing, as we watch a performance that is taking place on a balcony roof of a skyscraper. A woman in a glamorous dress and her partner, in a dark suit and bow tie, show off their elegant footwork to an admiring crowd. Another couple appear and dance.

As Bill Nichols propounds, 'Documentary points us towards . . . the truth' as 'we prepare ourselves not to comprehend a story but to grasp an argument'.[10] Within her narrative Shub constructs her paradigmatic framework in order to inform her logic. It is unambiguous. Her censorious cataloguing of the discriminatory practices and shocking overindulgence to be found in the West is clear for all to grasp. Using a Marxist interpretation, she presents with lucidity the economic circumstances, social injustices and inequality present in a capitalist world. Shub's depiction of the worthless West is compared with the worthy Soviet Union. She uses a myriad of examples that examine the excesses and indolence of the profligate capitalists in America and continually cuts them with the contrasting behaviours of the industrious citizens in the Soviet Union. Shub's model is based on what Nichols refers to as 'evidentiary editing' where 'gaps and leaps in space and time' . . . 'are joined together to give the impression of one continuous argument that can draw on disparate elements of the historical world for evidence'.[11]

From the rooftop space of a very high building with stylish performers, now there is another form of dance entirely. As Shub informs her audience: 'They go to church on St. Vitus's Day.' There is a never-ending queue of churchgoers, with a knee-deep throng of onlookers lining the path. The faithful attend a service to pay homage to the martyr, Saint Vitus. The parishioners bob up and down as they reach the entrance to their house of worship.

Following these rituals of the dancing congregation on their feast day, at the waterfront, there is an amazing feat of skill, balance and strength. On a platform, a couple perform on roller skates. The man whizzes his partner around in a circle at the most dizzying of speeds. Is there no end to such superficiality of purpose? Again, like the waiters' race, this roller skate extravaganza is yet another example of the ludicrous pastimes in a decadent capitalist society as they waste their time in meaningless pursuits.

As if Shub's examples couldn't become any more preposterous, we have an extraordinary underwater wedding. There is more absurdity to follow as bizarre giant balloons in the shape of animals float above the street followed by a procession of larger than life figures with disturbing satirical masks parading along the road. It is reminiscent of the meaningless floats and giant figures Shub documented in *The Great Way* where the Treaty of Versailles led to carnival gaiety on the streets of France.

Subsequently, Shub comments scathingly, and with understatement, that 'life is full of entertainment' and the cinema audience is whizzed off to Coney Island. Shub seems to be confirming her socialist belief that there is too much leisure time and not enough labour. Adults continue their seemingly endless spare-time activities at the fairground and ride on the Big Dipper and other amusements. There is a close-up shot of a glamorous woman wearing an extraordinary hat. It is extravagant in design and has a satin-trimmed veil attached. We return to the sensations of Coney Island and all the fun of the fair. Furthermore, additional trivial pursuits are featured. On a circuit, racing cars speed by. There is entertainment for the gentry, as men appear in top hats and morning suits. Competitive cyclists flash around a velodrome, athletes sprint to the finish line and one manages to wave at the camera as he races past. Borzois jump over a fence. A motorcyclist performs stunts. Cavalry gallop on and this scene is merged with a shot of a steeplechase. A horse and its rider fall awkwardly bringing down another animal as the rest of the field charge past. Shub cuts back to the mounted soldiers and then to subsequent shots of the steeplechase. The bourgeoisie applaud the exhausted winner of this gruelling equestrian race.

From a life that is 'full of entertainment', Shub writes in the next intertitle that it is also a 'life full of events'. A man dials the telephonists at the exchange. Another phone is answered. It is an emergency. The fire brigade sound their sirens as they speed excessively and swerve through the busy streets jammed with automobiles. Shub temporarily blurs her footage to emphasize the swiftness of the action. Haste is of the essence and a fireman steers a fire engine with great dexterity. This is intercut with scenes of life on a busy street. Cars are seen flashing by at an alarming rate, but the racing fire engine hurtles past even faster.

A tickertape machine, a keyboard, a typesetting machine are filmed. Newspapers are being churned out at breathtaking speed on a roller. This form of mechanization is more advanced than its Soviet counterpart. We see a stack of newspapers ready for distribution. To avoid the chance of a Soviet audience being impressed with this technological sophistication, Shub's next intertitle reads: 'A world of exploitation and oppression.' In the United States, there is an assembly line where they are building engines. It could be a Ford plant. We are taken to an industrial scene with thick choking smoke and scrap metal being readied for smelting. This scenario is repeated over and over again. Money pours onto the screen – more and greater wealth to line capitalist pockets. Bank notes of higher denominations swamp the frame as we see the tsars of the business world in their formal evening attire. More bank notes, more skyscrapers, including aerial shots, masses of American dollar bills and other currencies provide Shub with her evidence. Now there is a production line manufacturing car radiators for 'capitalist profits'. Shub observation is summarized: 'people are machines'. The workers, who fund the lavish lifestyles of their bosses, are merely a part of the mechanism of production. Men on the assembly line hammer metal. After drilling and setting explosives into the rock, miners extract ore. All these manual labourers are driven by necessity to provide a basic level of subsistence for them and their dependants.

Now we are introduced to another area of industry: the seascape of a thriving port. Sacks are being swung by a worker operating a crane and are moved over the water and onto a boat. Coal is being loaded onto barges. Well-to-do businessmen in suits and hats watch their cargo being unloaded. Shub's thesis is irrefutable. While the wealthy bourgeoisie fritter away their time in idleness, they are propped up by the might of the proletariat. They are the blue-collar workers. The firemen, the labourers on the New York skyscrapers, the factory workers, the miners and the dockworkers, are all shown at their daily grind. They are responsible for a thriving economy. However, these manual labourers do not receive the profits of their labour and, instead, survive on a basic wage. It is the working class who keep the wheels of the city turning.

From the misery of the American proletariat, a new topic is introduced: the defence of the Soviet Union against the capitalist aggressors in the belligerent West. Shub makes pointed reference to the United States' defence policies with the intertitle 'Under the flag of maritime disarmament'; skilled workers build a destroyer. Shub then cuts to a shot of this vessel being launched. Women of means appear in their fine apparel carrying enormous bouquets of flowers. A bishop blesses the vessel as it moves down the slipway. An altar boy holds the holy water in a bowl. A woman in an extravagant fur anoints the vessel with champagne. The bishop applies holy water with relish.

Shub continues her new topic of criticism regarding the build-up of the military in the West. From the navy and the launching of a warship, she moves on to the armed forces. As Shub's intertitle phrases it 'under the cover of talk about reducing the army...' not everything is as it seems. This is confirmed when aeroplanes appear and bombs fill the air. Anti-aircraft weapons are discharged in military exercises. In further practice manoeuvres, huge anti-aircraft cannons fire, exploding into the sky. A large cannon is tested, filling the atmosphere with smoke. Soldiers scatter and run for cover as a plane flies overhead. The tanks roll, perhaps purchased from the French, crushing all vegetation in their path. British tanks appear. There is far too much tedious footage, but Shub has made her point.

At the United States Military Academy, one of the most prestigious institutions for officer training, cadets parade in their dashing and immaculate uniforms. They drill on a parade ground, perfectly in step. From the cadets' ceremonial dress, Shub turns her attention to far more menacing regalia, one that is synonymous with evil. There are horrifying scenes of the fully robed KKK (Ku Klux Klan) as they advance carrying the Stars and Stripes. From one dangerous and depraved menace to another, Shub follows this with a very short segment in which she refers to the 'terrorist dictatorship of the Nazis'. The footage is too brief, and there is nothing to identify the men who are marching as German National Socialists because there are no swastikas. From mention of murderous Nazis, we view 'Italian fascists led by Mussolini'. In close-up, Mussolini ties colours to a flag, pins a medal onto one of his soldiers and pecks him on both cheeks. The soldier salutes *Il Duce*, who then kisses another decorated and distinguished-looking military man who has a white goatee beard and showy epaulettes. From here it is to 'socialist fascists'. Germans, crowded onto a balcony, watch as paramilitary nationalist organizations, such as The Steel Helmet [Der Stahlhelm], parade below. At a gathering of easily identifiable Nazis, a priest blesses them. This is another indictment of religion.

The next heading is 'the Holy Church'. In a solemn and significant parade, Catholic clergymen walk ahead of Pope Pius XI. Flanked by his cardinals, the Pope is under a canopy carried by his minions. Shub now inserts a parade of delightful waddling penguins as they shuffle along in their feathered finery. After this sacrilegious comparison, Shub returns to the sombre and significant ecclesiastical procession. Again, she intercuts this with another irreverent but highly entertaining reappearance of the delightful penguins, also solemnly swaying as they move along. The church's representatives, dressed in priceless vestments, re-emerge in a never-ending religious pageant awash with riches. This ostentatious display of wealth is a reminder of the show of flamboyant affluence in Shub's *The Fall of the Romanov Dynasty*. Here, there were scenes of the flaunting of privilege and status as the Romanovs and members of the nobility paraded before the plebeians during the tercentenary celebrations for the Romanov Dynasty. Shub's comparison of the Pope and his retinue with a group of penguins illustrates her ability, not for the first time, to use subversive political satire to both shock and amuse her audience.

Remaining with Shub's censure of the church, she documents 'conducting forced baptism of the natives in the colonies'. In Africa, the church spreads its sphere of influence. The people seem ecstatic as they are dipped in the river and blessed during their anointing. Some of them collapse in a trance of spiritual ecstasy and are carried out of the water. Dressed in white, they parade through the streets carrying the Virgin Mary aloft. Choirboys or altar boys follow behind the Blessed Virgin. Some hold a religious banner. Ordinary citizens and then white women, perhaps the wives of missionaries and clergy, are amongst the onlookers.

Shub's narrative is extremely detailed in its investigations of class struggle. The connotation is unmistakable. Her analysis of the repressive institutions of the West together with the similar inequality of colonial rule versus the socialist principles of the Soviet Union is key to Shub's thematic critique. Her doctrinal method illustrates, in the words of Osip Brik, the ability of filmic material to 'reflect reality from a definite point of view'.[12]

'After the suppression of the uprising in the colonies', as Shub's intertitle informs us, soldiers are seen parallel to Africans who wear white robes. The latter lead their horses. 'The native princes meet a Minister of great power.' A brass band plays as Africans on horseback, with some foot soldiers, are seen carrying guns. In pristine uniforms African soldiers with shouldered weapons march past the camera. They appear to be puppets of the colonial power governing their country. A banner exclaiming 'Diagne Vive La Republique' can be seen in the background. The word 'Diagne' refers to Blaise Diagne, a Senegalese-born colonial politician working with the French government.

There is an air of festivity. In the foreground, well-dressed African children wearing jaunty berets play brass instruments. Young native marines with pompoms on their hats bear arms. They are in the pay of the French government. Families look on, and there are close-ups of women in elaborately patterned headwear. A man beats a drum followed by some of his countrymen playing traditional flute-like instruments. The same soldiers, glimpsed in the first shot, stand to attention. They put down their weapons and stand at ease while their brothers-in-arms blow their bugles. Now we see the mysterious 'Minister' mentioned by Shub in the earlier intertitle: 'the French Minister for War, Maginot.' André Maginot and other dignitaries step ashore in West Africa, perhaps Senegal. They are in dazzling white pith helmets and suits. They shake hands with the welcoming party, and one of the Africans greeting them, possibly Diagne, is in formal attire. Bemused Africans look on.

Shub flashes 'Slaves' onto the screen. Tragically, there are naked African children with distended bellies as well as footage of black Africans in military service to the French. Cars are seen outside a colonial building. The Tricoleur flies prominently on the screen as the shot cuts to the parade ground where their colonial masters, dressed in impeccable whites, inspect the troops. Maginot presents gifts to various tribal chieftains.

Now in keeping with the 'Slaves' intertitle of moments before, the audience is told in the text that follows: 'Today. This is Egypt. The whip of the imperialist overseer.' In a quarry in Egypt, colonized by both the French and the British, downtrodden workers are being exploited. Those labouring under the whip include children. In the heat and dust, they slave away. On their shoulders, they cart baskets filled with rubble.

Now we are shown 'the same place in prosperous New York'. From the misery in Egypt, yet again we see the frivolity and excess of the bourgeoisie in Manhattan. There are shots from a train window speeding through the metropolis; prosperity is seen in grand building after building, street after street. Now the camera cuts to a dismal scene in the rain. From luxury we go to squalor and a rubbish-strewn pavement with a police presence in the background. A group of men mill about aimlessly. One looks at the camera. The atmosphere is chaotic. As Shub tells us, these men are unemployed.

Above the streets, trains traverse a railway bridge. From scenes of despair, we revisit prosperous New York. A motorcade passes by. In contrast, destitute hobos are sitting and lying on public benches in the sun. It is a short scene but is filled with a lingering pathos. The message has no need of an intertitle.

There is an image of the White House. An official car, sporting the American flag, leaves the grounds. It is carrying politicians. Within their midst is Herbert Hoover, the thirtieth President of the United States. We glimpse secret service men and photographers walking beside the vehicle. Hoover lifts his hat and smiles for the camera. Again, there is more footage of ragged itinerants, the downtrodden and the homeless. Is the President aware of this abject poverty in his wealthy country? As if in answer to this, Shub's next shots are of people in cars driving by, seemingly oblivious to the expanding tragedy on the streets of New York. Further emphasizing and juxtaposing the haves with the have-nots, Shub writes, 'in vain, proletarians wait in queues at the labour exchange'. The unemployed form a seething mass in front of the building. A well-attired man in a bowler hat, smoking a cigar, walks by this hapless crowd. He looks briefly at this scene of despair and turns his head away. A youth in the queue sadly gazes towards the camera before he joins the hundreds of others filing into the labour exchange.

Unsurprisingly, under such appalling conditions, Shub clarifies the aftermath of such dire circumstances for the lower classes with a call for action. This leads to an intertitle 'the capital of the country today entered into a new revolutionary upsurge'. Signs on a building read 'JOIN THE COMMUNIST PARTY!' and underneath this is a large heading advertising the 'CO-OPERATIVE CAFETERIA'. People wander around as traffic passes by. A further sign appears at the very top of the screen. It is affixed prominently to the facade of *The Daily*

Worker building and states the facts bluntly: 'WORKERS ANSWER: MURDER OF STEVE KATOVIS BY POLICE'. The front page heading of *The Militant*, the Weekly Organ of the Communist League of America, in bold print, is **Police Murder Steve Katovis**. The subheading is 'Communist Worker Shot Down in Cold Blood', and the article goes on to describe how a New York policeman, in a conflict that arose when the police attempted to break up a mass meeting, shot Katovis in the back. The newspaper is dated February 1, 1930. This is extremely topical material for Shub's film.

Shub's *Today* contrasted with Vertov's *The Eleventh Year*

At this juncture, it is interesting to note that Graham Roberts compares *Today* with Vertov's *The Eleventh Year* [Odinnadtsatyi, 1928]. Admittedly, Shub and Vertov are examining similar themes as Roberts has observed, but his statement that 'Shub is dealing with exactly the same material as is seen in *The Eleventh Year*' is perhaps debatable.[13] Vertov's cinematic essay is far less comprehensive in its subject matter than the all-embracing content to be found in Shub's filmic thesis. Shub presents us with an in-depth comparison of the Soviet Union in stark opposition to the capitalist nations as personified by the United States of America (and in addition to this, the Western world's policies of colonization and imperialism). Not only is there a careful international analysis, couched in terms of a Soviet framework, but Shub also presents an assessment of the internal workings of agricultural and industrial progress within the USSR. Whereas, in direct contrast to this, Vertov's narrative is situated solely within the domestic policies of the Soviet socialist state and his focus is on industrialization.

Vertov's work is one of rhythmic creativity, as is evidenced by the choreography and artistry in his journal entry on *The Eleventh Year*. Vertov's script has a musicality and is like a socialist song melding the past with the present. He composes the following atmospheric vision:

> Trumpet blast. Pause. Workers scatter. Horsemen patrol the area of the explosion. A bell is struck. Pause. Slow ringing of other bells. Some toy-like figures are prepared to light the fuses . . . run to shelters. Explosion. And another . . . one on top of another. Stones and dust gush up. Fragments fly far, landing on rails, on cars, on cranes. . . . They reach as far as an opened tomb, where a Scythian has lain for 2,000 years. . . . As if waiting for the explosion. Sky over him. And clouds.[14]

Additionally, in *The Eleventh Year*, there is less moralizing than in *Today*. Apart from his prologue, Vertov has no intertitles for another fifteen minutes or so, whereas Shub's film is awash with informative text. Visually, Vertov's film has a fluidity of composition, an intense lyricism as well as being pictorially experimental. His filmic palette is varied and often inspired in its imaginative use of symbolism. These are principal elements in his film but not in Shub's.

The people of the USSR figure more prominently in *The Eleventh Year* and are more intimately portrayed as individuals than in *Today*, where it is more about the collective. It could be argued that Vertov's more personal approach towards his characters often makes for more engaging cinema. Therefore, there is merit in Graham Roberts's assessment that, for him, 'Vertov's film is more involving', and in conjunction with this, Roberts considers that with 'Vertov one feels like a protagonist; with Shub the feeling is of being a spectator'.[15] This is an interesting observation. However, because Roberts's appraisal, of a Vertovian form of subjectivity versus a Shubian objectivity, is accurate, the latter's viewer is treated to an in-depth history lesson. Shub has a plethora of fascinating facts and details to complement and support her richly wide-ranging documentary. As outlined previously, Shub's and Vertov's styles of nonfiction film came from vastly differing interpretations of the objectives of non-acted cinema and the debates surrounding the role of fact and authenticity in this genre.

Interestingly, the Constructivist critic Vitaly Zhemchuzhnyi considers that *The Eleventh Year* 'as a whole no longer has the character of a "film newsreel"'. Moreover, in his view, 'the method of generalizing newsreel material conceals great dangers . . . nor is the danger excluded of excessive enthusiasm for "beautiful", effective shots and montage combinations.'[16] Zhemchuzhnyi ends his review by heaping praise on Mikhail Kaufman's camerawork by concluding that his 'footage stuns the viewer not only through its technical perfection, not only through its brilliant construction of the shot, but also by its virtuoso inventiveness'.[17] Once again, Vertov is the creative and sometimes dramatic artist, whereas Shub is the Constructivist documentarian.

In illustration of this stance, Shub continues her documentary of facts with newsreel footage of the Communist Party in America. In the 'Communist Party US District 7' slogans appear on a sea of placards: 'Stand by the peasants and workers of the Soviet Union. Fight Against Imperialist War! Defend the Soviet Union!' 'US and other Imperialist Powers are behind the Chinese Government!' The workers arrive en masse and receive pamphlets.

We read that 'The number of political strikes is growing'. The proletariat gather. 'The miners strike in Pennsylvania.' In a baffling scenario, 'Workers picket'. Workers march down a street. Women and men join a picket line, but they look far too well dressed, indeed affluent, when compared with their Soviet counterparts. In pursuit of the workers, two policemen run with truncheons at the ready. These frames of the constabulary look as though they have been plucked straight from a Keystone Cops silent movie (films renowned for their slapstick elements). Following directly on from this, and not in the least amusing, women and their children stand at a railway line waiting for an empty train. Seemingly endless wagons pass by. Some men join the onlookers. Why are they there? It is confusing.

'Against the strike-breakers' is the intertitle. Four men idle around a railway track. The scene cuts to a mine with filled railway trucks in the background. Men in the foreground read newspapers. '. . . By order of the owners . . .' is the intertitle. In support of the workers, a political rally is taking place. There are orators on a platform. In expensive clothes, the well-dressed bosses stand chatting to the police.

A police van arrives followed by a convoy of cops on motorbikes. The camera returns to the bosses and then reverts to the police motorcyclists riding past in droves. There is now an aerial shot of a huge crowd, packed together like sardines in a tin. The protestors carry a multitude of agitational placards. Now more police reinforcements arrive. Shub appears to be repeating the same scenario showing footage of the police as a significant body of power and societal control. It is seen on the screen several times, to provide emphasis of their sheer presence and strength. People start to disperse. Before they can leave the protest, the mounted police and officers on foot attempt to intimidate the crowd. The tension steadily increases. Pamphlets are scattered on the ground where they are trampled underfoot by the police horses. The crowd surges forward although still being controlled by the constabulary. Images of the police appear at the top of the screen. The crowd is in a state of panic. People fall.

'Today American freedom casts a shadow over the Island of Tears.' Shub superimposes a silhouette of the Statue of Liberty over an image of Ellis Island suggesting that the values of liberty are being brutally crushed. She tells us 'Strikers are thrown out of their homes'. We witness the behaviour of the callous lackeys of the capitalist bosses as they toss strikers' possessions out onto the street. A homeless family consisting of a mother and father, with six small children in tow, sit by the roadside amongst their belongings. There are general scenes of grinding poverty, neglect and despair. Destitute children are in rags. A group of wretched children are being fed. A young boy scrubs washing in a tub. Shub uses heartrending shots of children in a world of inequality and deprivation in the richest capitalist country in the West. It is a shameful state of affairs.

Once more, her message is glaringly obvious. There is more of the same to follow with 'proletarians gathered, banners of the Comintern'. There is too much repetitive material, both textual and visual, as yet again impassioned comrades rouse the crowd with their orations. The ethnic diversity of the speakers, including Caucasians, Chinese and other East Asians, points to the universality of the movement. We view even more placards, which encourage the workers to 'Act in Defence of The Fight Against Capital' and 'Act in Defence of the Socialist Fatherland!' These political statements are interspersed with the working class marching in an orderly fashion within a forest of banners that read:

'JOIN THE COMMUNIST PARTY'
'WORK FOR WAGES'
'FIGHT OR STARVE'
'FIGHT WALL STREET'
'FOR A SOVIET REPUBLIC'

They congregate in their thousands outside *The Daily Worker*.

We return to the demonstrators as rain continues to descend. A mounted policeman tears a banner from the hands of a protestor. In the ensuing melee, the police manhandle the demonstrators. Violence erupts as they drag protestors towards the paddy wagon, beating some of them with their truncheons. We see how those arrested are treated roughly. There are wide-angle shots and aerial images of confusion and dispersal that add to the compelling drama. The footage of the crowd scattering gives emphasis to the chaos unfolding before our eyes.

Shub is now being too heavy-handed as she proclaims, 'Protect the USSR'. 'Arm yourself against the imperialist war.' 'Our salvation is in the proletarian dictatorship.' We have had enough slogans, and so Shub moves on to effective imagery as we are taken back to the Island of Tears. However, this time we have a close-up of the Statue of Liberty, and she appears to be weeping as she holds her flame of freedom aloft.

Back in the USSR

From the United States we return to the USSR as Shub proudly presents the Dneprostroi Dam, which will be a major focus of her next film, *K.Sh.E.* The dam is a stimulus to industrialization and modernization and therefore to the economy. Surprisingly, Shub's visual example is more poetic than we have come to expect. Instead, the results of hydroelectric power, with the industrious Soviets working 'day and night', are replaced by shots of a riverbank. Flooded with electric light, almost blindingly so, the reflections illuminate the water. From this unexpected imagery of beauteous abstraction, more suited to Vertov's aesthetics than Shub's, it is back to a dreary factory and more propaganda. A giant lathe cuts through metal. A youthful proletarian is photographed at her workbench while one of her colleagues is seen as she operates a lathe. She explains her progress to a male co-worker who relieves her of her shift (Figure 32). Another girl works intently. A young man uses a large drill. The finished product is a camshaft.

The workers are rewarded for their labours as they are shown participating in leisure time activities in a Palace of Culture. It is a far cry from the liberating joys of Coney Island, but everyone is catered for as we see babies and small children in a crèche. Toddlers go down an indoor slide while children play with blocks and other rudimentary toys. A little boy pulls apart and reassembles a matryoshka doll. Meanwhile, arranged into small groups, their parents play innocuous games such as draughts (American checkers), dominoes and chess.

Figure 32 A diligent factory worker at her daily toil in *Today*.

To the contemporary viewer this appears rather regimented and formal as a means of relaxation, and the obvious comparisons with American culture and leisure are clear to see. Sailors in their uniforms take part in this organized entertainment. Close-ups of various faces show intense concentration. Then they hurry eagerly into the large auditorium for some amusement. Perhaps it will be a fiction film or a suitable staged theatrical drama. But is it? Sadly, the answer is no, as this 'production' is more akin to a dull Party political broadcast. There is not a Western cocktail in sight. Not even an ice cream, a chocolate bar or some popcorn. Officials and military men enter en masse and take their seats. A speaker appears on the podium. The camera reverts to the audience and then returns to the orator. Prominently positioned behind him is a large banner reading, 'Eliminate the kulaks as a class'.

The speaker addresses the multitude. They applaud and then a brand new gleaming tractor is driven onto the stage. On the radiator grille is a sign in numerals indicating that this is the five thousandth tractor off the production line. More applause fills the auditorium. In full, a sign proclaims that '5000 Soviet tractors are a valuable contribution to the industrialization of the country'. Those assembled continue to clap enthusiastically.

Next, on the screen: 'We demonstrate our will to fulfil the Five Year Plan in four years'. There is footage of a large gathering of workers on a bitterly cold night. Rugged up in winter coats, they carry banners. Accompanied by drums, they march in support of this declaration. Fully motivated, they will labour harder and longer in order to achieve this goal. To reinforce this, the text declares: 'We resolutely support the execution of great works in the shortest possible time!'

After this focus on the Five Year Plan, we travel from an evening solidarity march in the Soviet Union to the corresponding nightlife in the capitalist world. Here, neon signs light up billboards, cinemas, theatres and cafés. There is even electrical signage as the screen is lit up with an advertisement for Chevrolet. The amount of electricity utilized in this process of obvious consumerism is extraordinarily wasteful, but it is an evident image of technological progress (and superiority). The next intertitle states: 'behind the glare of advertising lights ...' and we see brightly lit streets crammed with moving vehicles. Cars speed past the flashing signs, which fritter away more electrical power as they advertise SQUIRES DENTAL CREAM and MAXWELL HOUSE COFFEE. Although these are everyday goods in the United States, they would be regarded as luxury items in the Soviet Union of 1930.

Dazzlingly bright lights surround a carousel. Westerners revel in their leisure time enjoying various rides at the fairground: yet another signifier of Western decadence. The comparison can be made between this activity and the worthy Soviet workers spending their free time applauding a tractor as it is driven onto a stage at the Palace of Culture. There are further delights in the nightlife of the West. Automatons come into focus as two naked dolls twirl and then an automated figure in evening dress plays a violin. Shub shows us two Meissen figurines: a woman in elaborate evening dress, her arms in a balletic pose and a man as her partner. Is Shub suggesting that worthless pursuits in the West make the people as empty and devoid of life as these puppet-like figures?

There is more excessive surplus to come. The focus is firstly on a silver platter filled extravagantly with fish in aspic. An elaborate dessert together with a basket of luscious fresh fruit follows this on the menu. Men in evening dress, holding glasses of wine, stand next to a bar. They eat and drink and are definitely merry. A showgirl in a costume drinks champagne. A group of young women in full make-up and fancy dress lift their champagne glasses as they are enveloped in a web of festive paper streamers. The revellers dance. People smoking and drinking at alcohol-laden tables sit and watch the spectacle before them. A band comprising a trombone, a saxophone, a violin and a banjo plays for the uninhibited partygoers.

Dazzling neon stars explode on a building at night forming astonishing patterns. 'Behind the smokescreen of pacifist phrases', the camera pans back, and we see middle and upper-class individuals at a function. Is it a political fundraiser to support the defence industries? Microphones and cameras are set up near the main table. 'Preparing for a new imperialist war' is the next frame. Using an NBC microphone, a politician addresses the distinguished-looking guests who are seated at multiple, white-clothed tables. The magnificent cluster of neon stars reappears as if out of nowhere. They burst and shower their light on the screen and then metamorphose into bombs being detonated. This is cross-cut with the stars again. Canons are fired into the night. This time the beauteous stars are juxtaposed with artillery. This leads to war games. German soldiers on manoeuvres fire machine guns. American soldiers training with fixed bayonets are seen running out of a choking atmosphere into the darkness of the night.

Shub's next intertitle is 'Preparing an attack on the USSR'. Tanks drive through a barrage of explosions. Above a smoke-filled sky, there is a Zeppelin floating through clouds of ash. Now the skies clear, but below it, more explosions ignite clouds of dust smothering and darkening the landscape. Some of the cinematography is quite abstract and Turneresque, and this unexpected artistry gives the viewer relief from the spotlight on what Shub believes is rearmament in the West.

The last intertitles of *Today* are presented in a staccato fashion.

We
On Guard!
Ready
Ready
Ready
With Us
Are Ready
To Protect the USSR
Proletarians of All Countries
We Are Prepared!

'We' refers to a Russian naval destroyer or frigate churning up the ocean as it moves towards the camera. Battleships appear on the screen ploughing through the sea. A close-up of the spray on the water and the crests of the waves is followed by a shot from the bridge looking down onto the bow. It highlights the magnificence and power of the Soviet fleet.

An abstract Constructivist shot, again reminiscent of Liubov Popova or Alexander Rodchenko, is a frame of true aesthetic appeal and power. It is of guns crossing the screen with two funnels in the background belching smoke. Shub lingers on this imagery.

'On Guard!' There are close-ups of both flags with the hammer and sickle and of an armoured vehicle. As the camera pans back, soldiers stand to attention while the flags, seen moments before, flutter with strength in the foreground.

'Ready'. 'Ready'. 'Ready'. From the far-flung regions of the Soviet Union, members of the cavalry stand proudly by their horses. There is a close-up of a soldier's face and then troops en masse. An aerial shot of the military marching forward shows both women and men in the armed forces. Banners are held over the shoulders of workers' militias. Some of these armed forces are extremely young. Everyone is mobilized and prepared. A brass band marches in amongst the troops.

Figure 33 The young look forward to tomorrow with optimism in *Today*.

The smiling face of a young Caucasian boy is shown before the grinning faces of a youth and girl from Kazakhstan. Shub is reinforcing the diversity of the population that comprises the Soviet Union. There are a multiplicity of youthful nationalities documented on film and every face beams for the camera. They are the promise of the future (Figure 33).

'To Protect the USSR' and there is a show of internationalism. German Red Front members march in solidarity. There are workers pledging loyalty to the cause. Their trademark clenched-fist salute is a sign of allegiance to the USSR. 'Proletarians of All Countries' leads to more footage taken in Europe, possibly in Spain, of thousands of women and men singing and shouting slogans. They punch the air with their fists in a salute of comradeship towards their Soviet sisters and brothers. With the closing pronouncement 'We are prepared!' Shub repeats the invigorating mise en scène that we've viewed seconds earlier. The striking symbol of Sovkino brings this saga to a satisfying and rousing conclusion.[18]

Shub has fully adhered to all the tenets of her Constructivist creed as promoted in both *The Fall of the Romanov Dynasty* and *The Great Way*. Graham Roberts considers that in *Today*: 'Shub not only knows how to pace an argument but also when to let her words speak directly without visual distraction. The film as a whole, with its skilful use of others' material and powerful montage to produce telling political points, shows Shub at her best.'[19]

Fighting a Losing Battle against Attack: Shub Defends *Today*

Although in full agreement with Roberts's synopsis, to her detriment and despite Shub presenting a faithful rendition of Stalinist historiography, she was pilloried by Vladimir Sutyrin, a member of the RAPP [Russian Association of Proletarian Writers] secretariat. Shub, together with Vertov, was the most prominent of the 'leftist' documentary film directors, and Sutyrin had made his position clear by his antagonistic attitude towards directors.[20] In the current climate, according to Denise Youngblood, 'the best way to position oneself politically was to attack someone else for alleged political errors'.[21] As she recounts it, 'by the end of 1929, the cultural revolution was in full swing and the cinema industry was approaching the paralysis in production which would characterize the next three years'.[22] Thus, Sutyrin's public criticism of *Today* needs to be seen in this context. Jamie Miller assesses the cultural revolution as 'a form of revolutionary zeal whereby genuine socialism would at last be introduced to replace the relative cultural pluralism of the 1920s. In the cinema industry this involved a struggle against perceived class enemies and "bourgeois" specialists.'[23]

The insoluble struggle regarding the merits of fact versus fiction, documentary as opposed to dramatized film (and the justifications of Constructivist design and photography over the precious gilt-framed oil painting) fuelled and propelled the debates of the artists in the vanguard throughout the 1920s. Their radical stance was allegedly one of the causes of the demise of the avant-garde movement, which also faced increasing state control towards the end of that decade.

In March 1928 the Party Conference on Cinema was a decisive moment in Soviet film, and as Youngblood concludes, 'it marked the end of an era'.[24] Anatoly Lunacharsky, the commissar of Narkompros and Shub's first employer, was publicly attacked at the Conference.[25] Lunacharsky had always judiciously avoided showing favouritism to either the traditional or the iconoclastic factions in Soviet art, theatre, film and literature. Regrettably, by 1928, his balanced approach, celebrating the diversity of creative expression, was deemed unacceptable. In fact, the art historian David Elliott emphasises that 'in the harder political climate of the late 1920s ... such professional neutrality was no longer tenable. In 1929 Lunacharsky resigned from his post and Stalin began to engineer the future development of Soviet culture to satisfy his own ends.'[26] Denise Youngblood confirms this: '1929 not only saw the end of Lunacharsky's role as a policy maker but also the commencement of "the purge of the film industry".[27] She goes on to elaborate: 'It was not until spring 1930 that the purges were in full swing . . . Sovkino disappeared without fanfare.'[28] It was replaced by Soiuzkino, which 'promised that cinema would purge itself of "old bureaucrats" . . . and establish stronger ties with proletarian writers to enable cinema to participate actively in the class struggle'.[29]

Thus, the Party encroached on the autonomy of the creative community and eventually, in the 1930s, took control of Soviet cinema, theatre, art, architecture, music and literature under the aegis of Socialist Realism. The kernel of the destruction of this liberty had been planted some years beforehand as a reaction to the far-reaching and overly zealous dialogues of the Constructivist movement and the avant-garde, which had questioned the very nature of art itself. Ironically, the promotion of these revolutionary notions by the vanguard, including Shub, was in part responsible for the erosion of artistic freedom and the inevitable rise of Stalinist hegemony over the Soviet art world.

Therefore, in spite of Shub's informative and absorbing documentary, a treatise that faithfully adhered to a Stalinist interpretation of the era, a chastened Shub was forced into a public justification of her work when *Today* was severely critiqued by Sutyrin. His attitude to this work is not surprising as Sutyrin was not only a prominent figure in Soiuzkino but also a denouncer of 'formalism'. Shub's film did not fit the mould. The completed version of *Today* was scheduled to be shown at the Party congress but was not released for screening until five months afterwards. This was a situation that Shub judged to be 'wrong and intolerable'.[30] Due to Sutyrin, she was forced to defend her film and its supposed shortcomings (while being simultaneously self-critical) in a journal feature of 1930.

The contents of her article make it a valuable historical document. As a window into the lives of the avant-garde filmmakers of the 1920s, attempting to navigate the perils of the 1930s: it is both an insight into Shub's circumstances and that of her coterie. Not only does it lay emphasis on the commitment she had to her craft but also, more broadly, the struggles that she (Vertov, Eisenstein and others) battled within an increasingly repressive cultural and political environment. Accordingly, a large portion of Shub's written argument is being included here.

> What happened with the film *Today* has to do with simple criticism of this film. *Today*'s viewing at ARRK is extraordinarily important to me personally and it involves great responsibility.[31]

What is *Today*? It is a political film. . . . Anyone may pass negative judgement on it for a whole lot of mistakes that I myself feel and know very well. But they shouldn't attack and badmouth the method that I used. The method has nothing to do with it.[32]

I make my films for a mass audience and that's why I will take and consider all such observations very seriously. . . . The film was made from the material of real facts, real events and real occurrences. Is it possible to consider that these facts are simply shown that they are impersonal pieces of montage, in the words of Comrade Sutyrin? I don't think so. . . . What are shown are not only the facts but also my relationship with them.[33]

Comrade Sutyrin says that the title *Today* isn't right. The film was ready for the Party Congress but it was not released for five months. A documentary film titled *Today* held up for five months! Such a situation is wrong and intolerable. That's a huge period of time. It is very possible that I would construct many scenes in a totally different way, that I would organize the material and the search for it differently.

Why do I leave the title? I think that a film made of factual material doesn't lose its meaning as the years go by. After the title *Today*, I have included an explanation – this is a cinematographic reportage, these are the facts of the year 1930. And if the film is viewed in five, six, ten years then the value of the documents that I was able to gather will be, no doubt, greater.

How easy it is to say now, after five months: 'that's not right, this is not right, this is not like that etc.' There was the possibility of giving these instructions and I would have taken all of it on board. Then we could have corrected everything, and these instructions would not have such a catastrophic effect on the fate of a film that is essentially, useful and politically meaningful.[34]

This heartfelt attempt to justify her work in order to defend it from 'attack' [Shub's word] was part and parcel of what the film scholar Jeremy Hicks deems 'the stifling and hostile atmosphere of the Soviet 1930s.'[35] His reference is aimed at a despairing Vertov, but it is also a situation applicable to Shub and all other artists who were judged as not in step with Party expectations. In the words of Lynne Attwood, 'Like Vertov, Esfir Shub did not find it easy to enter this Stalinist future.' Even though '. . . she moved to contemporary themes and so she began shooting material herself rather than using her old compilation method.'[36]

An obvious criticism that could be levelled at Shub by Sutyrin and other members of RAPP was her highlighting of all the 'bourgeois' activities and luxury products readily available in the United States. It would have inadvertently emphasized the gross inequalities between the world of capitalism and socialism. Thus, even though Shub's intentions were negative and she was damning the Western world for its frivolity and excess, the natural reaction in the USSR from anyone wavering from, or questioning, the socialist creed may have been astonishment and envy at the disparity between the two systems.

In line with this form of temptation, and even worse than Sutyrin's condemnation, was the vitriolic critique that Shub received at the hands of the Leningrad publication *Cinema Front* [Kino-front].[37] They had deemed *Today* as displaying a 'relish and admiration for life in foreign countries' . . . [with] an 'openly bourgeois orientation' and cuttingly dismissed it by adding, 'how this anti-Soviet rubbish got onto the screen is beyond comprehension'.[38]

Yet although *Today* was derided in the early 1930s, decades later, this same work would be praised in the Soviet Union. In the 1960s it would be considered 'one of the sharpest, most political, most topical works of Soviet documentary cinema' in its representation of the United States as a nation of 'scandalous social contradictions, exploitation and slave labour'.[39] Undeniably, Shub's documentary was an in-depth comparative study that set its focus on the strengths of the ever-developing socialism of the day. In order to present this thematic motivation, Shub had enthusiastically promoted her country's victorious First Five Year Plan and starkly contrasted it with the old backward way of life prior to the October Revolution. There was also considerable emphasis placed on the disparity between the politics of the USSR and the United States. Shub displayed the weaknesses, corruption and evils inherent in capitalism. This was in order to differentiate it from the worthiness and industrious nature of the citizens in the Soviet Union, living and working for the benefit of the regime. The savaging that *Today* had received in the press of the day was not surprising. Shub's film was not an insipid document simply toeing the Party line. It was bound to be found wanting.

In spite of Shub's well-founded indignation and despondency at the public and humiliating censure that she'd faced, Graham Roberts concludes his evaluation of *Today* by declaring, 'As a cinematic and propaganda success, *Today* was the last great Soviet silent documentary.'[40] Going even further, and without qualification, I would assert that *Today* was a great Soviet silent documentary. It may not have attained the cinematic accomplishments of *The Fall of the Romanov Dynasty*, but it stands on its own merits, which are considerable. The pacing of the action, the serious didacticism set against segments of humour and irony together with glimpses of cinematic beauty are all elements that make for a highly accomplished historical and political tableau reflecting, documenting and preserving an authentic moment in time.

Be that as it may, Shub was facing an ever more uncertain future due, in part, to the strictures and restrictions imposed by Socialist Realism. Equally alarming were the initial purges in cinema from 1929 to 1936. This proscriptive stance was encapsulated by the rhetoric of the All-Union Creative Conference on Cinematographic Affairs in January 1935.[41]

Denise Youngblood observes that 'Filmmakers were now "in the service of the state", and they received more attention than they desired in the 1930s, as Stalin's interest in film became increasingly obsessive and intrusive, to the point of revising scripts, supervising casting and titling film projects in which he was particularly interested'.[42]

Not only this but Shub's very genre posed enormous issues, not least the danger of presenting a truth, on newsreel, which then might have to be denied and rewritten as a new reality. As Graham Roberts was to consider: 'With Shub, the problem (for the authorities)' lay 'both in her consummate skill and her use of material from the past, a past – or at least its official representation – which was evolving as she worked.'[43] From this time forward, Shub walked a tightrope. Yes, she was a propagandist but not one who was willing to conform to the doctrinal restrictions of Socialist Realism. It was a precarious balancing act between bravery and self-preservation. After her next film, *K.Sh.E.*, Shub was fighting to be heard and was unable to produce anything of distinction until 1939.

7

K.Sh.E.: Shub's Conversion to Sound

As the 1920s drew to a close, the Soviet film industry was in a state of disarray. Chaos aside, Denise Youngblood speaks of a powerful all-pervading 'pessimism . . . even before the purges were in full swing'. Furthermore, in order to clarify this, she records that 'the demands of industrialization had led to the drastic curtailment of imports (both of equipment and movies). Soviet cinema was becoming ever more isolated from the West at the most critical moment in cinema history – the advent of sound.'[1] Accordingly, Jamie Miller asserts that with the introduction of sound, there were basic technical issues to be resolved such as a lack of Soviet film stock and cameras of an acceptable calibre, and hence, there was a reliance on foreign commodities. Added to these complications, in another rudimentary area, it was apparent that 'the industry struggled to produce both the right quantity and quality of sound projectors'.[2]

Yet, the French director and film scholar Alexandre Astruc opined, 'cinema is not an eternal art . . .'; instead, 'its successive faces vanish into the shadows when other ways of thinking rise up, when new techniques make earlier ones marginal'.[3] Astruc's proposition is germane to the Soviet silent film era. In particular, this references the experimental montage theory (and its practical application) created by their vibrant avant-garde in the 1920s, being supplanted by the arrival of sound to the world of cinema.

Notwithstanding the bleak facts regarding the parlous state of the industry (together with the increasingly perilous political climate), Shub embraced this evolution wholeheartedly. This is evidenced in an article written by her in 1929 titled 'The Advent of Sound in Cinema' [K prikhodu zvuka v kinematograf]. In this text she exclaimed with enthusiasm, 'A new invention, sound film, has excited everyone who works in the cinema. . . . For those of us working in non-acted film there is no doubt. We know that the sound film and the radio screen will give the non-acted film a genuine opportunity to become the most perfect instrument of international communication.'[4]

Adding to Shub's acknowledgement of this radical step forward in cinematic practice, and reinforcing the 'evidentiary function' of documentary, Bill Nichols posits that the 'persuasiveness . . . of its representation' was reinforced by its 'sound track'. Moreover, Nichols affirms that this new technological development was a watershed moment and that 'ever since the end of the 1920s documentary filmmaking has relied heavily on sound in all its aspects: spoken commentary, synchronous speech, acoustic effects, and music'.[5]

Transformations in Soviet Documentary: Shub, Vertov, Sound, Touch and Hapticity

Ideological commentary, political assertions and visual acuity apart, the inclusion of sound technology, in this specific instance to Soviet nonfiction film, enhanced and stimulated the overall experiences and perceptions of the receptive cinemagoer. In her exegetic comparative reading of Shub's first sound documentary *K.Sh.E.* (Komsomol Patron of Electrification) [Komsomol-shef elektrifikatsy, 1932] with Vertov's similar debut (made in 1930 but not released until April 1931), *Enthusiasm: the Symphony of the Donbass* [Entuziazm: Simfoniya Donbassa]; Lilya Kaganovsky declares that her critique of Shub and Vertov 'will explore the notion of the haptic as it relates to early Soviet documentary sound cinema'.[6] In light of this, Kaganovsky makes reference to Laura U. Marks's theoretical investigations into filmic hapticity.

In her books, *The Skin of the Film* followed by *Touch*, Laura Marks builds her concept of haptic visuality upon the foundations first laid by Noël Burch and then Gilles Deleuze. The latter defines the haptic attribute in film as being characterized by 'the sense of touch, isolated from its narrative function to create a cinematic space'.[7] Acknowledging Deleuzian scholarship, Marks contends that 'haptic looking' appears to be located 'on the surface . . . not to distinguish form as much as to discern texture'.[8] She gives voice to Vivian Sobchack's contribution to this dialogue whereby 'cinematic perception' is 'synesthetic, an act in which the senses and intellect are not conceived of as separate'.[9]

Laura Marks's haptical sensation privileges touch above all other senses (haptic derived from the Greek *haptikos* meaning the ability to touch or grasp). However, apart from tactility and proprioception, haptics is also a multisensory reaction to the filmic experience. It is therefore a more enhanced means of cinematic engagement, whereby the relationship between the tissue of the unfolding image and the physicality of the spectator also evokes sensations, often subliminally embedded, through the stimulus of memory. According to Marks, this affective instinct is primarily tactile, but the sensory quality of the imagery can likewise activate responses other than touch, those that relate to the auditory or the olfactory (even though she considers them secondary to touch). As a result her focus is not only on the functions of touch but also on the materiality of the body and its interconnectedness to the image on the screen.

By extension, as Lilya Kaganovsky argues, hapticity can include sound. Consequently, she considers that 'Vertov and Shub are interested in the haptic possibilities of a new sound cinema, in what we cannot see, but can sense via hearing and touch'.[10]

A graphic example of Laura Marks's assertions can be illustrated in the opening shot of Shub's film. In a recording studio, a technician feeds filmstrip through a sprocket. His hand is touching the film itself and the tactility, the haptic element, is blatantly apparent. As the reel is threaded, its physicality is akin to a sensory experience. The aware viewer can feel the smooth texture of the celluloid, its essential plasticity.

In contrast, Kaganovsky's intention, with reference to Vertov and Shub, is to highlight 'the way sound gives films a material form, interacting directly with the viewer in a completely new way'.[11] Her argument is compelling as, apart from giving an undeniable richness to a film, sound is multidimensional. Sound has the ability to wrap itself around an audience, engaging and enticing them further into the narrative. Simply put, it heightens the sensory perception of the image thereby adding immensely to the ambience of what is viewed on the screen.

Sound may be pivotal to her documentary, but, for Shub, the word 'electrification' in the title *K.Sh.E.* is a clear indication of the most crucial motif within the diegesis. Shub proudly gives voice to the proletariat in the Soviet Union, specifically the Komsomol, in harmonious counterpoint with the sounds of its technological progress. She announces that, for her, the objective underpinning this documentary 'was . . . to show how the Komsomol worked on the most important areas of electrification'.[12] Hence, Shub's filmic manifesto for Constructivism continues in this ode to the power of electricity and Soviet innovation through collective labour. Even during the opening credits, instead of music, we hear the static crackle of electricity. In line with her theoretical stance, we see a pared-back sans serif Constructivist typeface used for all the text in the titles and credits. These unadorned words are seen on a background of abstract zigzag designs drawn to simulate flashes of unharnessed electricity (such as lightning). We are being given the cue as to what may unfold.

In *K.Sh.E.* Shub offers the viewer a panorama of industrialization in all its glory: the splendour of technology, controlled by the workers, as a means of production and advancement. In 1922 the members of FEKS had loudly proclaimed, 'Let us learn to love the machine!' and *K.Sh.E.*'s visual and auditory document encapsulates their exhortations.[13] Electricity was the key to scientific and industrial development in the USSR.

In the words of Lenin, 'Communism is Soviet power plus the electrification of the whole country.'[14] To this generalization, he added the specific, 'electricity will take the place of God. Let the peasant pray to electricity; he's going to feel the power of the central authorities more than that of heaven'.[15] In my chapter on *The Great Way*, Lenin is shown as playing a role in modernization through the promoting of science and technology, specifically in the form of electrical power. 'Like many Western reformers of the time, Lenin saw electrification as a step toward an ideal society.'[16] Thus, and appositely, there is a highly symbolic frame in *The Great Way*, which displays Lenin's name lit up in sparkling electric bulbs radiating light, and enlightenment, across the screen.

This leitmotif is carried into *K.Sh.E.* where it is used as a spectacle, combining both fact and whimsy. Shub invites the audience to join her at a production line in a factory manufacturing electric light bulbs. Quite unexpectedly, Shub choreographs a charming balletic sequence with this essential item centre stage, as it waltzes smoothly, and rather Disney-like, through the stages of the manufacturing process. Of course, instead of paying homage to the nineteenth-century classical repertoire of Peter Tchaikovsky, in tsarist Russia, the music is a delightful twentieth-century composition by Gavriil Popov. This is the sound of modernity, befitting the new world of socialist endeavours. Thus, rather than the *Waltz of the Flowers*, we are presented with a contemporary dance of the light bulbs. Popov's musical compositions throughout the film (commissioned specifically for *K.Sh.E.*) were impressive enough to warrant a letter of praise to him sent by Eisenstein in which he wrote: 'I've just watched *K.Sh.E.* I heartily congratulate you on your wonderful audio-visual victory with Esfir Shub.'[17] In particular, this quaint performance with twirling bulbs shows the perfect synchronicity of Popov's score with the various processes involved in the production of an electrical light source.

In addition to Popov's melodious arrangements, in her essay 'The Theme of My Speech' [Tema moei rechi], Shub describes how, while shooting *K.Sh.E.*, she was inspired also by the 'absolutely stunning rhythmic work' by the women in this specific factory.[18] She witnessed them labouring with such apparent ease, particularly in the case of Katya Paramonova, a member of the Komsomol and their spokesperson. Furthermore, after observing her, Shub filmed and recorded Paramonova, who is seen talking enthusiastically and at length about the production process. This protracted sequence should have been edited. However, the crux of Paramonova's pontificating, as she addresses the camera, was to proudly announce the fact that the Soviet Union was exceeding the United States in their output of bulbs! Additionally, in describing the conditions in this Soviet production line, according to Shub, 'it is such worthwhile work because they are independent, because there are no clocks and overseers, because they know that they are responsible for the implementation of the scheme.'[19]

As is apparent, the thematic concerns of Shub's film (principally sound and electricity) are foregrounded in every sequence. Accordingly, in *K.Sh.E.* the first sounds we hear are off-camera, in a recording studio, as members of an orchestra tune their musical instruments. This is together with the muffled background noises of them conversing. The audience are watching a process within a process. We view a cameraman as he sets up his equipment. He peers through the lens and adjusts the focus and then wheels his cumbersome apparatus into position. Just as he will film the orchestral performance, Shub, in turn, will film him. A sound engineer works at the controls of the potentiometer adjusting the volume and the frequency distribution. This is an electrical device crucial for the taping of the music. The camera is filming, and the sound is recording simultaneously.

Sergei Drobashenko observes that, in Shub's documentary, apart from the glorification of hydroelectric power:

> there is another subject – the sound cinema itself. K.Sh.E. begins with a parade of cinematographic equipment. The director invites the public to a sound recording studio, displays the possibilities of film technology. And later, the picture is punctuated with shots where one can see the film team at work. This secondary line in the film undoubtedly reflected the film workers' enthusiasm for the new means of expression that appeared with the advent of the soundtrack.[20]

In brief, writing in 1991, Ian Christie asserts that 'Shub's *Komsomol – Patron of Electrification* . . . echoed the Constructivist *faktura*, with its self-referential demonstration of the new sound-film technique.'[21]

In the opening credits it was revealed that in *K.Sh.E.* 'the sound has been recorded on the A. Shorin System'. Two electrical engineers and inventors,

Alexander Shorin and Pavel Tager, were the first to develop sound on film in the USSR.[22] Shub is announcing technological process and progress in the field of audiovisuality. Moreover, this discovery enables an audience to both see the image and hear the appropriate accompanying sound concurrently. These are wondrous developments where the visible merges seamlessly with the invisible. In these intersections we not only have an auditory focus but its visual embodiment. In another first, Shub highlights the theremin – a new musical marvel, producing melody through electricity.

The Soviet Theremin: Sound Waves and Electrical Signals

There is a sculptural close-up of an expressive hand. It belongs to Konstantin Kovalsky. As the camera pulls back, it is revealed that Kovalsky is a thereminist, and we simultaneously see and hear him play the plaintive introductory strains on this hypnotic and somewhat mournful-sounding instrument. The orchestra, seen earlier, accompanies Kovalsky's performance, and, in the background, we can also hear the introduction of a solo tenor voice threaded into the harmony. As though by magic, the music of the theremin seems to have been plucked out of the ether, and this other-worldly quality of such a bizarre instrument adds yet another dimension to the sound itself. As a result, it is no coincidence that Shub has specifically chosen to give prominence to the theremin: a synthesis of electricity and sound.

Not only that but the theremin was the creation of the trailblazing Soviet scientist and inventor Lev Sergeevich Termen (his name anglicized in the West to Leon Theremin). Amongst other achievements such as the first bugging devices and burglar alarms, pioneering work on television in a neck and neck race with John Logie Baird, his biographer the musicologist and composer Albert Glinsky asserts that Theremin 'virtually single-handedly launched the field of electronic music technology'.[23] Significantly, in the early 1920s, Lev's first project for his mentor Professor Abram Ioffe had 'used the human body as an electrical conductor – its ability to store up charges, or the property known as "capacitance". . . . [Theremin] was intrigued by the notion that a person's natural body capitance, when standing near an electrical circuit, could interfere with the capacity of the circuit.'[24]

By extension, there was the body's ability to not only have the capacity to connect in a haptical mode with the image on the screen, through evoking sensations and arousing memories in all their complexities, but also to go beyond this sensory experience. Kovalsky merely uses his hand, not his whole body, in order to obstruct the electromagnetic field. This, in turn, distorts the frequency of the oscillating body. The hand, the instrument of touch and therefore a symbol of the haptic, is able to exert an influence on an electrical circuit and thereby create melodious sound. Electricity is making music, and we are introduced to a mode of electronic perception. Electrical signals in our bodies are transmitted by neurons, and the response to stimuli, nerve impulses, can be aural. Seeing Kovalsky's hand, used as a transmitter of electricity, has an affect on the viewer, in so far as there is an instinctual reaction to this stimulus. This haptic component of heightened consciousness aside, it is apparent why Shub, with her emphasis on sound waves being captured and converted into an electrical signal, would introduce the notes of a theremin into an orchestral recital within a recording studio.

We see another performer contributing to the soundtrack that is being created in the studio. This time it is not a musician but the renowned Georgian actress Nato Vachnadze, credited as one of Shub's assistant directors on *K.Sh.E.* In an essay devoted to Vachnadze, Shub discusses a crucial part of the shooting plan and makes the following statement about the crew's procedures in showcasing sound and its electrical interrelatedness. To this end, they 'filmed the most important achievements in the field of electrical engineering, radio, the first experiments on television' and the laboratories of Professors 'Chernyshev and . . . Ioffe'.[25] Vachnadze is featured in the prelude as a participant in the processes involved in synchronous sound in this new and wondrous medium within filmmaking. All audience members in the Soviet Union would recognize her, and most would be extremely familiar with her arresting face. Vachnadze stands, hand at the ready, waiting for her cue to flick the switch that will start the recording. Her touch activates the apparatus (Figure 34). This segment is interspersed with images of the unilateral variable area of the soundtrack in waveform. That which we cannot see, but only hear, is made visible. We view these representations of the sound itself, and then the introductory chapter of this chronicle comes to an end.

From the relatively high-tech interior of the early 1930s recording studio, the next frame is an exterior shot. The Gothic-inspired Spasskaya Tower within the Kremlin comes into view, and the initial sounds are the chimes emanating from the clock tower. The last time Shub featured the Spasskaya Tower was in *The Great Way* as the bells solemnly tolled the hour on the day of Lenin's funeral. The early Muscovite architecture of this imposing tower, representing the repressive

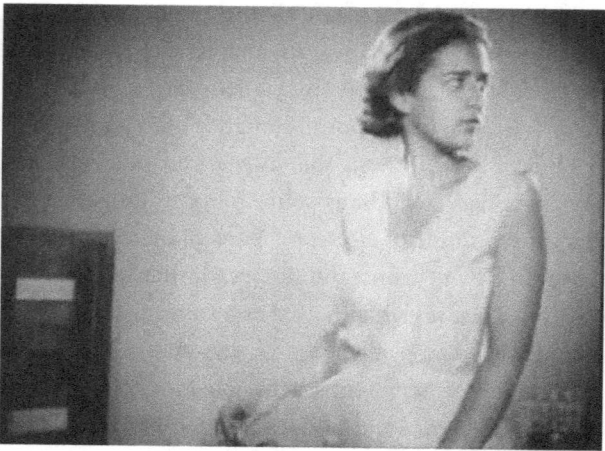

Figure 34 Nato Vachnadze being filmed as she gives the signal in the recording studio in *K.Sh.E.*

imperial past, is now replaced by a shot of Lenin's Tomb. The visual contrast is startling, as the final resting place of Lenin is a sharp-edged Constructivist edifice. Now the red-bricked Spasskaya Tower is relegated to the background. The new regime and the new modern monument to their legendary Lenin have long since replaced the outmoded links with tsardom, as exemplified by the old tower. As the camera pans back, Lenin's red tomb of marble and granite occupies the foreground and then, symbolically, blots out all other buildings. Setting this erasure apart, from another angle, his stone edifice appears to emit a glowing light from the shining surface of its marble. Servicemen congregate in the foreground waiting to pay homage at Lenin's mausoleum. People march with banners. 'Hooray!' they shout in unison.

From the lucidity of the word 'hooray', the scenario that ensues is a cacophony of sound with switchboard operators all talking simultaneously, in a babble of foreign languages, to their respective callers. The quick-fire multilingual conversations are often indistinct, but they act as a symbol of the principles of internationalism. Language transcends borders, as does the voice of socialism. From the buzzing activity of a telephone exchange, a Soviet studio broadcaster announces in English: 'Hello. Hello. This is Moscow calling, from the radio station of the All Union of the Central Committee of the Trade Unions. Workers of the World Unite!' In a studio in Germany, one of their radio presenters mentions Vladimir Ilich Lenin, the Komsomol and the Five Year Plan in a broadcast to his listeners.

Gavriil Popov did not write the music that follows directly after images of the transmissions of political dialogue from the presenters in Moscow and Berlin have been flashed onto the screen. As a thematic extension of the information imparted by these two radio announcers, and remembering that they represent not only socialists in the USSR but also in Germany, Shub introduces us to a serious-faced male baritone. Formally attired in a collar, tie and jacket, he appears in a studio facing a microphone. Accompanied by a pianist, he performs the stirring Anthem of the Comintern [Komintern Lied] composed in 1929 by the composer, and member of the German Communist Party, Hanns Eisler. Shub presents the method of recording, intercut with watching the sound produced visually by the singer. We see his face in close-up, and this up-to-the-minute footage of the procedure is flawless. In *K.Sh.E.*, Shub is underlining, for her audience, the process of Shorin's sound on film system and how this astounding new device produces the desired effect. This is probably the first time that Soviet cinema audiences have both simultaneously heard and seen the Anthem of the Comintern sung live on film. The rousing performance ends. We return to a further discussion of the Five Year Plan as viewers watch and listen to a French radio announcer reinforcing the same opinions on this issue, as had his German counterpart.

From singing and speaking we have an industrial landscape with smoking chimneys. This leads into images of a city at night shimmering in the softened glow of electric lights, and the visuals are complimented by the gentle tones of a hypnotic melody by Popov, heard quietly in the background. In this very short musical interlude, there is a solo accompaniment by Konstantin Kovalsky, playing the theremin, overlaying the tranquil scene. Shub is once again pairing sound waves with electricity. None of these transmitted sounds, whether speech, music or noises of all descriptions, produced for *K.Sh.E.* together with images (in this case, well-lit towns in the late evening) would be possible without the harnessing of electricity and, more precisely, of hydroelectric power (Figure 35).

Hydroelectric Power and the Dnieper Dam Project

Hydroelectricity was a minor theme of both *The Great Way* and *Today*. Hydroelectric power and the electrification of the countryside are featured in the closing episode of *The Great Way*, whereas in *Today*, this subject is re-introduced

Figure 35 Shub filming at the Dneprostroi Dam in *K.Sh.E.*

early in the film and is mentioned briefly during the body of the documentary. Emanating from this focus connecting it to the other two films, in *K.Sh.E.*, Shub takes this subject to the next level. Therefore, hydroelectricity, in tandem with the contribution of the Komsomol to such an endeavour, becomes the principal motif of her first venture into sound.

Accordingly, inside an enormous hangar-sized workshop space, manufacturing turbines for the Dnieper Dam, a Komsomol youth dressed in a leather jacket addresses his comrades. Commenting on this segment of *K.Sh.E.* Sergei Drobashenko notes how

> Shub believes in her material as she takes her camera from one site to another. A young boy who has come from the construction site of the Dnieper Power Station speaks at a factory meeting. He speaks with real ardour, with unaffected passion without choosing his words. The image of this Komsomol leader . . . remarkably corresponds with our idea of the youth of the thirties! His speech was shot in such a way that it did not leave the slightest trace of doubt that this was how it really happened.[26]

With the conclusion of the Komsomol leader's speech, and Shub emphasizing their involvement in this project of modernization and industrialization, we view long shots and close-ups of the turbines. We can sense the might and power of these state-of-the-art machines as one is hoisted slowly into the air with the greatest of care and precision. As an audience there is another form of awareness, a haptic sense of the heaviness of these cold, smooth, steel components, which create mechanical energy. With grinding and grating reverberations and lots of discordant metallic-sounding noise, they are gingerly dragged aloft, conveying their substantial weight. In readiness for their ultimate destination to the Dnieper Hydroelectric Station, the turbines are labelled clearly with the word 'Dneprostroi'.

Within this facility, a young Soviet woman is interpreting the conversation between her and an American consultant on the Dnieper Dam project, to a team of welders. She then relays the American's instructions to her Soviet counterparts by passing on explicit instructions, translated into Russian, to the spokesman for the welders. Finally, she translates into English the welder's response and conveys it to the American in command. It is an assurance to him, in colloquial English: 'alright, we'll do it today.' This is another example of Shub's comment on sound being the ideal 'instrument for international communication', but the amiable cooperation between the socialist and capitalist worlds is not overemphasized.[27] Nor is any credit given to the crucial overall assistance offered by the United States in the building of infrastructure, the providing of consultants, and expert staff on the ground, in order to successfully bring the Dnieper Dam construction to completion. Obviously, this would have meant a loss of face for the Soviet Union generally and Stalin specifically. However, without this invaluable support from the West, this massive undertaking would not have been possible.

Amazingly, though, in *K.Sh.E.* Shub does not include any mention of the involvement of American Hugh Lincoln Cooper in this endeavour. Understandably, not revealed by Shub was the fact that Cooper (who appears close to the denouement of the film as he speaks at the opening of the dam) was the principal consulting civil engineer for the Dnieper Hydroelectric Scheme. Also, Shub neglects to inform us that, for his vital contribution towards the success of this enormous feat, Cooper was awarded the Order of the Red Star.

It must be noted that the Soviet engineer Ivan Gavrilovich Aleksandrov was tasked with leading the project. Although Aleksandrov was a senior advisor to GOELRO [State Commission for the Electrification of Russia], the undertaking would have been impossible without the Americans. The greatest proportion of the expertise for the construction of the dam, highly trained women and men plus machinery, came from the United States. Added to this, on the Dnieper Dam project, 'U.S. firms supplied steel, heavy equipment, turbines and more.' Furthermore, 'International General Electric built five of the nine giant generators needed, the rest were built in Leningrad under American supervision. Moreover, ... about 70 percent of the hydroelectric equipment was American'[28]

Back in the turbine plant, without an American in sight, another Komsomol member, dressed in a woollen cap and coat, speaks earnestly to his fellow workers. We see the camera operator being filmed just as he starts to film the action, emphasizing Shub's process of recording the images and sounds and highlighting the apparatus being used. In turn, the camera films the workers who are now listening to an accordion player performing a folk tune. A sailor in the crowd speaks. The crowd applauds. One of his naval colleagues suddenly begins to dance to the music of the accordionist. The dancer's movements are graceful and professional. Two of his comrades, covered in grime, enter the space. They act with him, to the delight of the crowd, who laugh at their nimble vaudevillian antics and applaud at this slapstick routine. Although the dancing and clowning appear to have been staged for the documentary crew and the workers alike, Shub was adamant that it was a spontaneous recital and not prearranged. Apparently, according to her, she was told that it was not an unusual occurrence for the workers to entertain one another with performances and singing during their short breaks from labour. From leisure time at the factory with music and dance, the camera returns to the work in hand.

Last-minute checks are made on a gargantuan turbine, which dwarfs the mechanics. They inspect the exterior and interior of this massive structure. Other workers look on in pride at this achievement as they, and the cinema audience, hear music approaching. The melody adds to their sense of exhilaration. Comprising mainly of horn players, the band becomes increasingly louder as its members come fully into view. The use of synchronous sound is impeccable. Marching into the space, they weave through the mass of workers, some of whom are sitting on a turbine designated for the Dnieper Dam. The band stops playing, and, in the silence, a meeting commences as its convenor addresses the throng.

All those gathered on the factory floor appear to listen intently to his comments. Then, as if on cue, the horns burst into a rendition of *The Internationale*. The first orator calls upon one of his comrades, who talks to the assembled crowd. With a completely unstaged and unselfconscious gesture, he motions towards a young man who comes forward. Wearing a leather coat, he is introduced as Klimov and he injects some dynamism into the procedure. Thus, Comrade Klimov makes an impression on the listeners as he expresses his point of view with much gesticulating, shaking of his fist and undeniable passion. His closing statement is, 'the Komsomol is the chief of electricity!' Everyone around Klimov appears to be genuinely transfixed by his words. Once again, the band plays *The Internationale* with much fervour. Klimov's parting sentiment is echoed by the initial speaker who concludes the proceedings with the sentence 'the Komsomol is the patron of electrification!' Mercifully, this brings the proceedings to a close after six relentless minutes of repetitious speech making. While a modern audience may think that Shub should have edited this monotonous segment more rigorously (and thus presented her message more succinctly), she had little choice. Shub did what was required of her in the current climate.

From the confines of the turbine plant, we are transported to the open air and the rural landscape of Armenia. An aerial shot of a village then reveals, in close-up, the ruins of a church. Plaintive eastern music gives way to a vista of snow-capped mountains in the distance and sheep and trees in the sunny foreground. An infectiously joyous traditional folk tune is heard as we go from the old way of life, in the sleepy rustic villages with oxen seen pulling a cart, to the new. Not only are there electricity pylons in this glimpse of the countryside in Armenia but also there is a train (Figure 36)! We whizz past houses and through borders of trees on the side of the track, and Gavriil Popov's music intensifies in speed to keep pace with the train's journey. Armenia's Dzoraget Hydroelectric Power Station and the Dnieper Dam were being built simultaneously in 1927. Both were completed and launched five years later in 1932.

Figure 36 A stark Constructivist grid seemingly out of place in the arid countryside of Armenia in *K.Sh.E.*

We don't see any specific evidence of the Armenian dam's construction, but instead, Shub now takes us to Ukraine and the simplicity and yet awe-inspiring majesty of Viktor Vesnin and Nikolai Kolli's Constructivist architectural design: the Dnieper Hydroelectric Station. Thousands of workers have congregated at the dam site. One of them shouts instructions at his colleague in readiness for speakers to take their places.

There are drummers to announce comrades as they make more and more impassioned speeches. We then see long shots and close-ups of women and men in the crowd. The former are not amongst the speakers but are there to listen. The sound of applause rings out loud and clear after each of the many presentations of political dialogue. How much can one audience take of such intense and tiresome oratory? Fortunately, there is a much needed reprieve, and a barefooted child dances for the onlookers. A semicircle of encouraging spectators surrounds him. They clap enthusiastically while he performs to the beat of a drum. It is a welcome interval and seems far more like the simple spontaneity of folk dancing and less like the proficiency of style exhibited by the sailors performing earlier in the turbine hangar.

From the outdoor speechmakers at the dam we go briefly into a studio for a recording of Marietta Shaginyan's voice. Shaginyan is a novelist, poet and social reformer, Moscow born and bred but of Armenian heritage.[29] She speaks directly to camera and articulates with conviction and fluidity. Additionally and knowing all the less-than-ideal technological issues involved, in Shub's film, the sound is of an unexpectedly high standard (Figure 37).

Figure 37 A filmed radio interview with Marietta Shaginyan in *K.Sh.E.*

Marietta Shaginyan wrote a literary work called *Hydrocentral* [Gidrotsentral, 1931]. This production novel is centred upon the Five Year Plan for the building of the Armenian Dzoraget Hydroelectric Power Station. It would explain Shaginyan's valid inclusion in this section of the film, although it seems to be slightly out of sequence. It appears to be an oversight, as it would have been more appropriate and precise of Shub to insert Shaginyan's contribution to *K.Sh.E.* directly after the scenes of Armenia and before the segment on the Dnieper Hydroelectric Station.

Shub's Recordings on Location: A Myriad of Sounds

After this short intermission, we return to the Dnieper and watch the grandeur of the water as it flows effortlessly from the dam, accompanied by Gavriil Popov's symphonic and lyrical treatment. His sounds impeccably mimic this specific visual experience. Popov's sensitive composition enhances the beauty of the imagery, nature in all its glory. Shub treats the shots in an abstract manner, often in extreme close-ups. It creates an intimacy between the audience and the frames on the screen. We see the tranquillity of the pooling liquid, which almost induces a soporific effect, mirrored by the music. In addition, as a contrast, we hear the roar of the water being unleashed. Popov's score adds to the lushness of this sensory experience. The water rushing out of the dam gives the onlooker a feeling of elation. This external stimulus leads to the use, in the sense of Laura Marks's haptic visuality, of our eyes functioning as organs of touch. There is the undeniable sensation of the intense cold to be found in the depths of the icy water and not only this but the feeling of its tremendous power. Additionally, the audience senses fear as we view bird's-eye shots taken by one of Shub's intrepid cameramen. He is winched aloft into position, in an unsafe-looking box-like contraption attached to the end of a massive crane. Precariously hovering, suspended high in the air in this rickety structure, he records the action speedily while in turn being filmed from above. Now the cameraman is gradually lowered over the gushing torrent of rapidly swirling and foaming water being unleashed from the dam. There is yet again the strong sense of the formidable force of nature, and its frosty chill, being harnessed by human ingenuity. The scene prompts a shivering sensation adding to the haptic quality. A piercing siren jolts us out of our freezing watery reverie.

As the siren suggests, Shub's applications of this new advance in film production are endless. Thus, there are a plethora of differing sounds and sound techniques used by Shub such as synchronized sound recording, dubbing, recording in the outdoors and so forth. We hear the pealing of the bells on the Spasskaya Tower, the incessant hubbub of the telephonists at the exchange, orchestral music, the electronic vibrations of the theremin, voices singing, Popov's compositions, the clapping of hands to music and also used in applause, speech making, industrial clatter, muffled chatter, background hum and the sounds of the natural world.

As Shub had observed at this pivotal moment in the history of film: 'For those of us in non-acted cinema the most important thing is to learn to record sound tone, voice, noise, etc. authentically, with the same utmost expressiveness with which we have learned to record authentic, unstaged, real nature.'[30] Shub does indeed introduce authenticity through sound and celebrates this new technology to the maximum, using it organically. Her work is structurally born from the thematic subject matter, together with its corresponding elements, which, in turn, give it a unified form. In fact, Shub confirms this materiality when she writes: 'sound film must not be a mere acoustical illustration ... it must be organic raw material just like the film footage.'[31]

Elucidating further, Shub explains that in *K.Sh.E.* she

> used not only synchronous recording, but documentary sounds, sounds of machines in the factories, the noise of construction, water, crowds, echoes, birdsong, the sounds of a gramophone merging with the sound of water while the American consultants bathe on the banks of the Dnieper and more ... I edited these sounds and synchronous recordings together with the visual imagery.[32]

Following on from this, Sergei Drobashenko makes an observation regarding another dimension of *K.Sh.E.*'s connection to sound, innovation and new methods of filming, by remarking: 'Still here (perhaps unknowingly) Esfir Shub made another artistic discovery. Similar devices (the camera taking in the film team with all their paraphernalia, as if saying "this is all for show") as we know, are not uncommon in films produced today by various directors.'[33]

Although in partial agreement with Drobashenko's opinion, there is little doubt that Shub's cinematic methodology was deliberate and not 'unknowingly' introduced. It must be remembered that this work is a complete departure from her compilations and is not a transformation of old footage, but it is filmed by Shub in the here and now. Thus, it is a precursor of modern observational 'fly on the wall' documentary.

It shows us the process with the audience seeing a camera filming a camera 'where one can see the film team at work'. Not only this but, apart from watching the camera filming the camera crew filming the action, Shub presents us with objects that create sound. We see and hear an electronic theremin, we view the sound engineer as he regulates the controls on the potentiometer, we watch as the filmstrip is threaded ready to receive sound and image synchronously (the optical recording of sound) and we see microphones and loudspeakers. Shub is showing us the varying apparatus that can harness acoustical energy and how, for example, in a microphone, acoustical energy (in the form of sound waves) is converted into electrical energy (the audio signal).[34] Sound and electricity are melded in the next tableau as they promote the new marvel of hydroelectricity.

Leading towards the finale of *K.Sh.E.*, the fruits of everyone's labours are celebrated at the official opening of the Dnieper Hydroelectric Dam. In an orderly fashion, workers in their thousands cross the bridge to the dam. The film shows footage of high-ranking Party officials and other important dignitaries.

The Internationale is played. One of the men saluting as this powerfully emotional anthem is performed is none other than Hugh Lincoln Cooper. He is framed in a close-up. It is a dramatic and impressively angled shot. Journalists belonging to the International Press Corps take notes for their columns while their photographers use small cameras, not on tripods, in order to film stills for their respective newspapers.

The next shot is of Cooper, who comes to stand behind the bank of large microphones. Considering the recording is outdoors, the sound quality is excellent particularly when one is aware of the technical problems besetting this period in Soviet film. Speaking in English, Hugh Lincoln Cooper's address is filled with goodwill and joviality. This is the one segment of *K.Sh.E.* that causes genuine laughter. For that reason, it is worth quoting it in full. Cooper reveals to his audience: 'I had a dream in which I found I could speak perfect Russian. This gave me very great joy but when I awakened this morning, I tried my English on the cook and it was no good.' At this juncture, there is real and unselfconscious hilarity. Cooper and his interpreter, and those officials standing with them at the outsized microphones, are laughing so heartily that there is a brief pause in the proceedings. Cooper ends the general merriment by continuing: 'And therefore, very briefly, I will have to speak to you through an interpreter.' Tellingly, in his summation he reveals that although he 'will never know . . . I hope you will be pleased with his interpretation'. Intriguingly, Cooper's vocal sound, tone, and the information imparted, is purely conversational without a hint of didacticism. He addresses the spectators in a new, informal and refreshing manner as though speaking in confidence to a friend. It is in dramatic contrast to all the other speeches in *K.Sh.E.*, which are saturated with slogans and ideologically focused. Cooper's injection of familiarity into the proceedings instils a feeling of camaraderie and well-being in all those attending to his words. It adds an intimacy to those listening and watching and, more significantly, is a rare moment of complete realism and truth spoken in a seemingly unrehearsed voice. The interpreter then reads Cooper's speech translated into Russian. Shub is emphasizing another mode of communication, after all the propagandist flag-waving of the Komsomol scattered throughout the film. This interchange of ideas from one tongue to another is a new mode of documentary language, provided by an American supporter of their cause. Thus, not only is it a significant step forward in terms of an informal Russian American entente cordiale but it also adds authenticity and light relief to the dense discourse of the Stalinist rhetoric centring on the First Five Year Plan, a key platform of *K.Sh.E.*

This section serves to accentuate Shub's issue with the accuracy of language and the transmission of meaning. Not only is Cooper cheerfully commenting on the hope that his interpreter correctly translates his English speech into Russian but also, in an earlier scene, we've viewed a similar scenario touching on this very subject matter. In the section on turbine production, a young Soviet woman is translating the conversation between the leader of a group of welders and an American supervisor of the works. The welder can only converse in Russian and the American only in English. The interpreter conveys the request from the American, and the welder agrees to comply with what is essentially a demand that the work schedule be completed that day. We've also listened to other languages being spoken by the switchboard operators and the Russian, German and French radio presenters. It is a veritable Tower of Babel but Shub helps her audience to understand the importance of the communicating of ideas and the international dissemination and exchange of information using the latest sound technology of her era.

The documenting of technological innovation and the use of sound waves and electrical signals, the link with Lev Theremin and the 'cosmic resonance' of his electronic musical instrument goes full circle.[35] It is transferred from the prelude of *K.Sh.E.* to its denouement. In the closing segment of the film we see flashing bolts of electricity. Professor Abram Ioffe, Theremin's 'beloved'[36] teacher and supporter, leads Komsomol representatives to watch experiments in, as Shub referred to it, a 'laboratory, of high-voltage transmissions' controlled by scientists.[37] Emphasizing visual continuity through the narrative of the documentary, the group with Ioffe includes the youthful leader wearing a leather jacket, the first Komsomol spokesperson in the film and, in addition, the other Komsomol member who had made a speech while wearing a woollen cap and coat. Not only do these young men symbolize the new generation but also they are essential parts of the whole in the Komsomol collective. As a group they are a united cooperative seen as joint heroes, participating in the rise of the Soviet Union as an industrial leader on the global stage. Shub had revealed that *K.Sh.E.* was made 'to reflect the struggle of the Komsomol in the electrification of the national economy'.[38] Added to this, in the opening credits Shub had used a quote attributed to Lenin: 'A Country Needs Its Heroes' and not only do these comrades in arms appear throughout *K.Sh.E.*, but they are seen in the closing moments of this patriotic film giving hope and optimism for a bright future ahead.

Shub's *K.Sh.E.* and Vertov's *Enthusiasm*

In terms of Shub and Vertov's forays into sound, Graham Roberts, Lilya Kaganovsky and Jeremy Hicks have all compared Vertov's *Enthusiasm* with *K.Sh.E.*[39] Unlike Shub's documentary, which is a cohesive entity with a very clear structural and thematic vision, and each segment flowing into the next, thereby accentuating her argument: Vertov's work appears to be disjointed and somewhat puzzling in its randomness. In his film, there is no visual linking of his early cinematic chapters of pre-revolutionary mayhem with the triumphant post-revolutionary work being undertaken in the Don Basin. In the opening scenes of *Enthusiasm* we see the people of faith, the ardent congregants, worshipping in their church. Vertov couples this with corresponding scenes of the drunk and disorderly staggering around in a state of obvious inebriation. These two scenarios are shot with dreary and unnecessary emphasis. It is excessive. Vertov does not need to be so heavy-handed. His evocation of the old way of life in tsarist times contrasted with modernity and the new Soviet regime is not nearly as effective as Shub's treatment of similar ideological themes. Due to this, Vertov's film seems to lack a well-defined narrative focus. Jeremy Hicks appears to support this assessment and remarks that 'the film does have a narrative that emerges only after repeated viewings'.[40] Unfortunately this would have been of no assistance to a 1930s cinemagoer. Like a modern viewer they might have been perplexed by the film's composition, but it is doubtful that they would go to see *Enthusiasm* twice in order to unravel its structure and experimental use of sound. Added to these impressions, the average audience may have concluded, as did some critics of the day (according to Lilya Kaganovsky), that Vertov's use of sound was cacophonous.[41]

In direct contrast to the problematic issues of narrative and discordant sound, in *Enthusiasm*, the first filmic segments on religion and vodka consumption, as the combined opium of the masses, are pedestrian and overstated. Also in this category is a highly choreographed sequence, later in Vertov's documentary, with a group of male actors dressed in black. The men perform overly dramatic and stylized movements, walking bent double to simulate the miners crouching at the coalface and then the motions of using pickaxes underground. It seems out of place, extremely mannered and inauthentic. Admittedly, the second half of the documentary is clearly directed at enthusiastic toil in the mining of coal in the Don Basin, but the ballet scene is out of place and ineffective.

It may be commendable for its experimental investigation into the new medium of sound, but *Enthusiasm* has none of the exhilaration, bravado, dynamism and intensity of Vertov's dazzling masterpiece, *Man with a Movie Camera* [Chelovek s kinoapparatom, 1929]. Although Graham Roberts commends Vertov by observing, '*Enthusiasm* is striking for its attempts to develop a *use* of sound' (the emphasis is Roberts's), he considers that not only is 'the first half is a repetition of *Cine-Eye* tricks' but also that 'visually the film is rather disappointing. . . . As a representation of contemporary Soviet history it does not have either the grandeur or the emotive power of Shub's work.'[42] Although there is compelling evidence for the former, the latter statement needs to be contested. Visually and aesthetically, *Enthusiasm* is filled with rich imagery. Unfortunately, despite Vertov's urging that in non-acted film, those working in cinema 'should devote all their efforts to preserving the advantages of location shooting in the production of sound documentary', there are some technically unsuccessful results relating to his location filming.[43] There are instances of jarring sound issues due to poor editing choices, which appear to have been made in the studio during post-production. Within his real-world filming, there are two separate occasions when men are speaking, and one added example pertaining to a woman, when their lips are very glaringly out of sync. Was this intentional? If so, it seems affected.

Referring to *K.Sh.E.* Jeremy Hicks identifies that 'there is genuine location sound. Rather sound working as a separate, independent element, often contrasting with the image, as in Vertov's film, Shub respects the integrity of each sound, its real length and relation to the event, and consequently synchronises far more'.[44] This is no reflection on Vertov's sound recording methods but an observation on their differing perspectives and motivations. On the other hand, in spite of some questionable dubbing, Vertov's utilization of industrial noise, the sound of engines, hooters, machinery and the like is most convincing and realistic. It does indeed create a symphonic poem to the Donbass.

In fact, Robert Rosenstone speaks of the crucial input of 'the aural elements', in historical film specifically, and how 'music, dialogue, narration, and sound' itself 'can underscore, question, contradict, intensify or lead away from the image'.[45] Vertov's denouement starts with peasant women working in a field and stopping to join in song. Their so-called attempt at 'singing' is blatantly shrill, and the recording is discordant and indistinct in tonal quality. Knowing of Vertov's strong musicality, this is surprising. After this caterwauling, we see them with other members of the peasantry dancing with gay abandon as though they had not a care in the world. This irksome footage is played for nearly three minutes. Tractors and harvesters in a field of grain, supposedly linked to these workers, fill the screen. Finally, the camera returns to the peasants leaving for home accompanied by cheerful music, and this is followed by the sounds of a stirring marching band playing brass instruments. Thus, Vertov's film ends on a melodic note of harmony and a symphony of contentment.

This is the Party line that has to be adhered to at all times. Be that as it may, why did Vertov end his film on this inconclusive fuzzy note rather than on a summary extolling the virtues and successes of the work in the Donbass as related to the Five Year Plan? Shub's audience would not query the glorification of electricity and its vital centrality to the Five Year Plan in her film because it is a far more palatable form of propaganda than Vertov's forced peasantry jollity. Justifiably, the creation of the magnificent Dnieper Dam was a tangible source of pride (as was the progress of the coal mining industry in the Don Basin), and so the finale with the peasants over-brimming with joy at their labours and bountiful harvest adds little to the thematic flow of Vertov's film.

Disappointingly, despite its imaginative application of sound, *Enthusiasm* is a retrograde step for Vertov. Graham Roberts is correct in that it is not as successful or resolved as *K.Sh.E.* Vertov's message is not delivered with intelligibility, whereas the intention of Shub's documentary is unambiguous after a single viewing. It is an unabashed celebration of the power of electricity, from the introductory sound recording in a studio to the success of the Dnieper Hydroelectric Scheme (and the role of the Komsomol in its implementation). Besides, unless *Enthusiasm* was being screened for a highly educated avant-garde leaning audience, it would have been deemed unpalatable and puzzling for the average attendee. This was in large part due to its esoteric references and motivations. It was not a film for the faint-hearted, and this would prove to be a major stumbling block.

Shub's film, on the other hand, adhered to what Boris Shumiatsky was to refer to several years later in 1935 as 'a cinema for the millions' where films would be 'distinguished by... their "exceptional simplicity"'.[46] Due to the ever worsening of the prevailing political climate, Shub was treading warily, and therefore *K.Sh.E.* was far easier to comprehend than *Enthusiasm*. The film scholar Elena Stishova in her appraisal of Shub's documentary has concluded that *K.Sh.E.*'s 'artistic strength rests both on the mastery of its production and on the film maker's passionate, devoted faith in the ideas and ideals which the film proclaims'.[47] In addition, a specialist in Russian and Soviet cinema studies, Lynne Attwood makes a pertinent observation that Shub's documentary 'provides an interesting illustration of the sexual division of labour . . . in scenes of heavy industry, the workers are all male; when the camera runs along a light-bulb conveyor belt, they are exclusively female'.[48]

Worthy of note, and ironically, although Soviet women are shown occupying the less taxing jobs in *K.Sh.E.*, the Western capitalists seemed to be far more progressive in their attitudes towards the labour force. The Americans had highly trained women in a supervisory capacity working on the Dnieper Dam project. Amongst the engineers and technicians representing General Electric seen during their leisure time, either swimming, sitting on the sand or dancing on the beach to their portable gramophone, are woman employees of the company. In fact, according to Margaret Bourke-White, a photographer sent from the United States to the site of the dam in construction, there were female staff members from the United States 'in charge of the Soviets installing the turbines'.[49]

Like Elena Stishova, Sergei Drobashenko praises the many achievements of *K.Sh.E.* and claims that 'Shub does not gloss over the sharp angles, to beautify reality – she reaches out for facts and views them at close quarters. The author's belief in her materials results in the audience's belief in the authenticity of the film.'[50] He goes on to add, 'These are the qualities that not only make *K.Sh.E.* an outstanding documentary picture but provide tangible opportunities for discussing the cinema and the time, for comparing documentary and fiction films on the same subject.'[51]

Nevertheless, and despite all the excitement and publicity and Drobashenko's pronouncements, the Soviet film industry was ill-equipped to deal with the most rudimentary issues related to the arrival of sound. Crucially, as already mentioned, there were serious issues surrounding the lack of availability of basic sound-film apparatus.[52] Equally concerning was the simple and alarming fact that there were few cinema theatres with the facilities for screening this new cinematic innovation. In reality, according to Peter Kenez, 'in May 1931 there was only a single cinema in the Soviet Union capable of playing sound films. Exactly two years later, out of the 32,000 projectors there were still only 300 capable of producing sound.'[53] Moreover, and an issue that often is not emphasized fully enough, Denise Youngblood underscores the fact that 'the practical effects were enormous, particularly since the coming of sound coincided with the great upheaval of the purges, a dislocation with which no Hollywood studio had to contend'.[54]

The Ever-Increasing Struggle against the Obliteration of Artistic and Political Freedom

Added to this highly unsatisfactory state of affairs in terms of fundamental problems with delivering sound to cinema theatres, and the even more worrying and darkening pall of political oppression, unfortunately nonfiction film was becoming increasingly under fire and its practitioners further isolated. Shub and Vertov were unable to escape the inevitable and vehement public criticism of their work. Shub had already been forced to defend *Today*, her last silent documentary, in print when Comrade Sutyrin savaged it in the press. In light of this, and with reference to *Enthusiasm*, Graham Roberts's conclusions regarding Vertov at this stage of his career are telling: 'Having revealed himself as such a power in the previous decade, Vertov's loss of visual inventiveness is, on a personal level, both sadder and more intriguing and, on a wider level, more indicative of the state of Soviet cinema than any amount of hack-work done in the name of the regime in the 1930s.'[55]

Regrettably, Jeremy Hicks mirrors Roberts's observation and affirms that during 'the stifling and often hostile atmosphere of the Soviet 1930s Vertov became an ever more marginal figure'.[56] Apart from *Three Songs of Lenin* [Tri pesni o Lenine, 1934] being honoured by winning a prize at the Venice Film Festival in 1935, Vertov's fate was clear. Hicks views this conforming film as 'falling short of the standards of Vertov's earlier films, and as a renunciation of everything Vertov previously stood for'.[57] According to Lynne Attwood, due to 'the myth of the Soviet paradise... propagated in the films of the Stalin era', the documentary genre was at a crossroads.[58] In fact, Hicks's evaluation is more definitive than Attwood's. His belief, which is uncompromisingly forthright and profoundly depressing, is that

> the distinction between fiction and fact in this era became increasingly difficult to maintain... this demand for dramatic reworking and entertainment was, effectively, extended to real life. The theatrical effect of the show trials was not only scripted but rehearsed, and we cannot be entirely sure which version was recorded: the rehearsal or the final performance.... Life was a spectacle. Documentary as a distinct category was doomed.[59]

In addition, after having been damned by Sutyrin and *Cinema Front* over her final silent film *Today*, Shub had been given an inkling of what was to come. She was beginning a bitter, protracted, frustrating and disheartening battle, which would now define her filmmaking. This was apparent as she fought in vain for a voice and was denied major projects, particularly her fascinating script for a proposed documentary about women, which had the potential to make her a feminist icon for future generations.[60]

Writing on 'The Purge Years in Film 1929–1934', Denise Youngblood notes that Shub, like Kuleshov and Vertov, was not immune from criticism... and that 'her acclaimed film *The Fall of the Romanov Dynasty* notwithstanding, was added to the growing list of "allies" of formalism'.[61] The web of repression was enclosing the avant-garde of the 1920s, and there seemed little hope of escaping this mesh of creative suffocation.

As referred to earlier and to add insult to injury, in the *Proletarian Cinema* editorial of February 1932, the board mounted a scathing criticism of documentary film, which they labelled 'documentarism'. In it, they attacked 'documentarism' as 'illiterate, presumptuous and excessively pretentious theory' and vowed to obliterate it.[62] They promised that 'the struggle against documentarism' would 'be supported by all those comrades fighting' in favour of 'proletarian cinema'.[63] The documentary was deemed dangerous in its unpredictability. It might show glimpses of the truth. As an illustration of this, in *The Fall of the Romanov Dynasty* and in *The Great Way*, Shub did not give Stalin any prominence as a supposedly commanding figure in the birth and establishment of the Soviet state. History had to be rewritten, and cinema was the perfect medium to fulfil this duty for the regime.

In his book *Stalinist Cinema and the Production of History*, the Soviet film and cultural studies theorist Evgeny Dobrenko writes of cinema under Stalin functioning as a museum: the repository that housed a new alternate 'reality' where history and memory were redefined and manipulated to serve the ideals of the Party. This institution contained the Stalinist representation of a mythological socialist utopian past and present. Thus, as Dobrenko clarifies, it was 'occupied with the ideological constructing – via history – of its own legitimacy and new Soviet identity, it relied on cinema, seeing in this "most important of the arts" the most effective form of propaganda and "organization of the masses", of which Lenin and Stalin spoke. Stalin directly managed Soviet cinematography and devoted an enormous amount of attention to it'.[64]

Regardless of severe systemic problems within the film industry itself in its unpreparedness for sound technology, and its resulting dearth of equipment, together with the waning of documentary filmmaking in the early 1930s (and the daily perils experienced under Stalinism), *K.Sh.E.* is an exceptional document of its era. Elena Stishova commends 'the mass scenes in *K.Sh.E.*' as being 'expertly filmed, especially when one considers that this was a documentary film, a piece of journalism, and not something intended to entertain'.[65] It was to be the final time that Shub was able to hold up a mirror to Soviet society in a celebration of its achievements.

In this repressive climate of accusation, mistrust, renouncing of bourgeois tendencies, political and ideological correctness, Shub was treading a fine line. Yes, *K.Sh.E.* could not be faulted for its adroitness in enthusiastically and inspiringly promoting the Five Year Plan and the advances in science and technology. Indubitably, Shub had fulfilled her brief with aplomb, but was this enough? Unfortunately, despite her triumphant and successful use of early sound techniques and keeping faithfully to the Party script, with the constraints of the regime becoming more and more authoritarian, the future held little promise of creative fulfilment for Shub in the furthering of her film career.

The situation is only too easily discernible in Kuleshov's speech at the All-Union Creative Conference of Workers in Soviet Cinema in 1935. By that juncture, the experimental practices of the avant-garde had long since come to an end. At the Conference, Kuleshov declaimed that 'the director must be, from head to foot, with all his [sic] heart . . . [and] thoughts, a Party man. . . . The most important people are the working class and the most important principle is Party allegiance'.[66] He warned ominously that 'We must all bear this in mind'.[67] Writing 'Our Way' [Nash put] in 1937, Shub substantiates these assertions by Kuleshov. Selecting her words with the utmost care, Shub's re-evaluation is that 'documentary film as a genre of Soviet cinematography is considered a defective genre'.[68] She goes on to relate how from the time of *K.Sh.E.*: 'Throughout these years, I was not given any productions – not that I didn't compete for them, although I must have been competing in the wrong way. I was not able to finish my work about the subway because I was sent to work in Turkey.'[69]

Hence Shub and her comrades were facing an even more uncertain future. For her the intervening years, between *K.Sh.E.* and her documentary about the Spanish Civil War, were times of frustration, unfulfilled dreams and rejections.

Shub's Disillusionment: From *K.Sh.E.* to *Spain* and beyond

For Shub, facts could be verified or potentially criticized for lack of authenticity in every one of her nonfiction films. Lamentably, in the 1930s, facts had the potential to be flagrantly manipulated to suit the purposes of the regime. Stalin and the Soviet Union had to be shown to be victorious in every facet of life.

Graham Roberts gives his bleak assessment of the fate of Shub and all other nonfiction filmmakers of the period.

> At best they could try to keep some integrity for the documentary form (which would bring them violent criticism and/or unemployment) or at worst churn out uninspiring bland product (which perversely would also as often as not be unacceptable).... With Shub, the problem (for the authorities) lies both in her consummate skill and her use of material from the past, a past – or at least its official representation – which was evolving while she worked.[70]

As a result, when she submitted her vigorous thirty-one-page film script titled *Women*, a work that was to be dedicated to a celebration of the rise of Soviet womanhood, Shub was flatly denied funding. Sadly, a powerful voice that would have represented a differing aspect of Shub's creative powers was silenced.

Her article 'I Want to Make a Film About Women' [Khochu delat filmu o zhenshchine] in 1933, which justified and substantiated Shub's objectives, was to fall on deaf ears. Even though she explained clearly and convincingly that it was her:

> deep conviction that an individual hero can also be the theme of an non-acted film. Up until now it seemed like only the actions of the collective, at the time of its organized or spontaneous performances, could be the theme of an non-acted film. I am going to have four heroines. Each of them will have her own biography, her own path in the struggle . . . and at the same time, they will

represent millions of women in our new way of life.... My new documentary work... does not mean that I need to follow the established canons of acted film, nor that I have to use actors to impersonate my characters.[71]

Far from betraying her principles of nonfiction film, Shub was attempting to extend her boundaries and re-evaluate her genre. She realized that the women in this documentary could relate their own unscripted stories by talking directly into the camera and by being filmed as they worked. In addition, Shub was well aware that

> Up until now it was considered that non-acted films lacked the ability to develop events dramatically, or the ability to correctly develop within themselves the plot-like construction of a fiction film ... in my new documentary work [*Women*] I will attempt to build the film thematically ... I take upon myself the challenge of constructing and connecting separate episodes in this way, with the purpose of creating a narrative unity as a developing dramatic action.[72]

Shub's script used pre-revolutionary archival footage of the Russian film star Vera Kholodnaya. Describing her as the 'modern Giaconda', Shub advances a mocking and deliberately exaggerated observation of tsarist fiction film in order to accentuate her point of view.[73] Shub creates a satirical and banal script for this proposed section of her film. In it, she parodies the worst qualities of acted fiction film: a stereotypical female within an unrealistic melodrama. Shub's aim was to portray the transformation of women from passive object and femme fatale prior to the Revolution into the emergent independent Soviet woman in control of her destiny. To this end, by the end of Scene One, we have been introduced to young emancipated women who are dedicated socialists and hold key positions of power on the kolkhoz.[74] In addition, as Shub was to elucidate further:

> I want to make a film about women because this will give me the opportunity to cover the themes of love, birth and death. These themes can be extraordinarily powerful and exciting ... and, at the same time with the help of ... [an] innovative approach, they can showcase the authentic people of our era, of our new developing way of life.[75]

Nevertheless, these women are foregrounded only insofar as they represent the endeavours of all of their sex. As Shub was to argue: 'I want to make a film about women because this theme can demonstrate with singular clarity that only the proletarian revolution, the new conditions of labour and the new social practices can once and for all eliminate "the issue of woman" from the balance of history.'[76]

In the opinion of Soviet film scholar Maya Turovskaya, *Women* 'included the full set of ideals concerning women's equality'.[77] Instead of using actors, they were 'real people whom Shub had sought out for use in the film'.[78] Amongst these was Mildred, an African-American visiting 'the Soviet Union to take part in the real life of Soviet women'.[79] Shub also wanted to examine 'the social problems of the time: prostitution, homelessness amongst orphaned children'.[80] Turovskaya goes on to note that 'Those who want to understand how Soviet women felt about themselves in the early years of the revolution would do well to read the script'.[81]

Despite Shub's persuasive justifications, outlined in her essay, this promising project was never approved for production. Her positioning in the world of cinema may have been vastly different had her meticulous and enthralling film script been accepted. Was it simply too controversial in its subject matter, or was it out of step with the decade? Years ahead of its time, *Women* would have been deemed and celebrated as one of the earliest feminist classics. Its global potential would have brought Shub to international prominence and fame.

The answer to the problem with *Women* may lie with Maya Turovskaya's observations about the period. As she reflected:

> It may seem paradoxical that this film did not appear on the screens. However, Shub had begun the project at the beginning of the 1930s. By then compilative revolutionary cinema was considered dubious and strongly criticized. Films of quite another type were being promoted – commercial mass-culture films with simple plots and simple styles. In this climate, Shub's more intellectual work remained on paper.[82]

Appealing to Stalin, in the closing paragraph of 'I Want to Make a Film About Women', Shub had added the obligatory obsequious content to this essay: 'After the intervention of Comrade Stalin at the kolkhoz congress, after his speech about women working at the kolkhoz, I started to perceive the issue of women as an important, necessary theme in this day and age. This is the best motivation for work and I particularly feel like working right now.'[83] The final sentence is extremely telling.

Shub's life was to become more challenging. Instead, after her documentary of 1932 (her first sound film *K.Sh.E.*) and the rejection of her proposal for *Women*, Shub was even forced to write a desperate journal article in 1934, 'I Want to Work', mentioned earlier, literally pleading for an assignment.[84] In this essay apart from defending herself against a personal attack by a journalist, Comrade Katsman, Shub reiterates her intention to 'create a documentary dedicated to

Soviet Women'.[85] As she explains, her 'application had been approved by the film studio directors. However, shortly after, they received firm recommendations to shoot a drama film on the topic with professional actors involved . . . my idea had become void.'[86]

A demoralized Shub ends her article with a direct reference to Katsman and all those blocking her way. 'I should not have to waste my strength and energy validating my right to work. I don't need polemics. I need work. I want to work!'[87] Dishearteningly, no one appeared to be listening.[88] Maya Turovskaya was right. Shub was simply not marketable because her thought-provoking genre did not fit the approved profile. It was not simple mass entertainment. After the disappointment of *Women*, there were more blows to follow.

Shub's *Moscow Builds the Metro* [Moskva stroit metro, 1934] was filmed but never released for screening. Her film treatment had been provisionally titled *The City Sleeps* [Gorod spit]. In the opening sentence of Shub's script, displaying some of her original literary background, she writes as follows: 'In the night sky the twinkle of a thousand little electric stars from Poklonnaya Hill. The distant shimmering lights of evening Moscow. . . . The distant sounds of the symphony of the evening rush from the screen. In the quiet night, golden pillars on the surface of the Moscow River also reflect the lights of the night.'[89] Atmospheric and beautiful though this rhapsodic description may be, the impressionistic treatment was obvious in Shub's poetic script. Her unexpected ode to Moscow may have been deemed far too abstract, unintelligible to the masses and too fanciful for the powers that be.

Then in 1935, Shub's submission for a proposed documentary, *Land of the Soviets* [Strana sovetov, 1937], was approved. However, when she received the official notification for the undertaking, there were provisos attached with severe restrictions in terms of style, content and distribution. As Graham Roberts reveals in an introductory paragraph: 'Shub recut her 1927 film *The Great Way* . . . for *Land of the Soviets* . . . to rewrite the whole epic of Soviet history',[90] thereby genuflecting to Stalin in order 'to serve his greater glory'.[91] In truth, it was a documentary that (when it was finally released) would be no more than unedifying propaganda.[92]

Land of the Soviets could only be made under the condition that Shub relinquished her status as author and director. Both these positions were to be filled by the powerful Boris Shumiatsky (who was neither a scriptwriter nor a filmmaker). Inexplicable as this might first seem, Jamie Miller has unlocked the key to this conundrum. He has uncovered that Shumiatsky:

reacted to increasing centralization and his own decreasing autonomy by devising an individual defensive strategy to protect his position of power. This involved an attempt to prove his credentials as an ideal Bolshevik leader of Soviet cinema, in the course of which . . . [he] became obsessed with micro-managing the industry. His everyday activities shifted from a broader concern with industry development to checking every film script before production, controlling individuals' movements and writing letters to Stalin and Molotov pleading for funds or approval of some sort.[93]

Land of the Soviets was a panegyric to the Stalinist order and, with Shumiatsky at the helm, it was profoundly problematic to say the least.[94] As Jamie Miller states further: 'Ironically Shumiatsky's almost maniacal obsessiveness regarding 'the desire to defend and protect [the legitimacy of the regime] thus provoked the source of the system's paralysis as well as its chaotic aspects. It helped create elaborate systems of control while simultaneously undermining these principles of organization by taking them to absurd levels.'[95]

Added to this, Shub's project became nothing more than a rehash: a deconstruction and reconstruction of *The Great Way*. Yet Trotsky, who had been featured in this film as a heroic figure, had become a non-person and was erased from the new version. Risibly, due to Shumiatsky's authority, Shub would have no input and no control over *Land of the Soviets*. In reality, as Shub recalled despondently: 'This was considered a method to proscribe me from work. My comrades laughed when they met me. I laughed too, but to speak the truth I did not feel like laughing.'[96] She was not alone.

Jamie Miller puts this into perspective when he concludes that after 1929, censorship 'developed a more draconian character as . . . Stalin himself began to scrutinize scripts and films on a more regular basis'. The Party's objective was 'to remove scripts or films that . . . challenged, questioned or ignored the Soviet view of reality in the 1930s".[97] Then again, the issue is far complex because Miller's investigations point to the fact that 'censorship was often inconsistent and ineffective' and yet it became progressively authoritarian.[98] Adding further to this analysis, Miller considers that

> censorship tended to reflect the defensive mentality of those who made the decisions on whether films could be released. On the one hand this led to an obsession with ideological correctness whereby one institute of censorship would give way to another in the hope that a new body would be more effective in unearthing politically suspect scripts or films. On the other hand,

defensive insecurity obliged the Bolsheviks frequently to denounce popular entertainment . . . as the priorities of politics were increasingly given more value.[99]

After the debacle of *Land of the Soviets*, Shub was awarded the finances for only one major film for the remainder of her career – her production on the Spanish Civil War. After this came a film of possible fascination to the modern viewer. Unfortunately, *Twenty Years of Soviet Cinema* [20 let sovetskogo kino, 1940] has vanished. *Twenty Years of Soviet Cinema* was a documentary that Shub co-scripted and co-directed with the acclaimed filmmaker Vsevolod Pudovkin. Her other films of the 1940s such as *Fascism will be Defeated* [Fashizm budet razbyt] or *The Face of the Enemy* [Litso vraga] in 1941 and *Homeland* [Strana rodnaia, 1942] not only distorted the truth but showed none of Shub's earlier abilities. In these works, catastrophic failures on the world stage and at home were presented as triumphs.

From the beginning of the 1930s onwards, unwilling to compromise and bend sufficiently to the Party line, Shub experienced impediments to the furthering of her career. There was an ever-increasing lack of fulfilment in a creatively stultifying, repressive and disordered system. She persevered. Not prepared to blindly follow the path of Socialist Realism, clinging on to her original cinematic vision, Shub battled against the inconsistencies of confusing political and administrative decision-making.

Through the demoralizing experience of having been denied permission for various film projects, which had the potential to give her a higher profile both at home and abroad, a wiser and self-critical Shub outlines a modified model for documentary:

> Now we don't have to prove that newsreels, both historical and current, are art. However, we still have not learned to film our contemporaries in the new way, even though this is the only method to relieve the monotony of documentaries. The problem of biography in film must be solved very differently. The topic must not just be about the dead and departed, but those living today. A film about . . . a worker, a farmer . . . an artist, must be approached differently. I believe that there will be major discoveries in this area. We must be brave, and then we will be able to clearly express our socialist epoch, see our culture, art, and nature in the new way.[100]

Thus, like many of her comrades, Shub's career was about to flounder. She struggled to find her way after she'd made *Today* in 1930 and *K.Sh.E.* in 1932.

Her career would effectively disintegrate by the end of that decade after the making of *Spain*. Hence, despite the impossible and ever-increasing restrictions placed upon nonfiction film, and therefore Shub's continuing predicament, she made another lasting contribution to film history and the documentary form with her final tour de force, in 1939.

8

Shub's *Spain*: The End of the Line

This chapter seeks to explore Shub's successful preservation of the myths surrounding the Soviet presence in Spain, and Stalin's contribution to the war effort, while simultaneously creating a film of value. *Spain* [Ispaniya 1939], Shub's last major work, is a fitting tribute to her oeuvre in its most evolved manifestation. It is a largely neglected chronicle of the Spanish Civil War. As Antonio Prado asserts, 'the Spanish Civil War was only the second armed conflict to be filmed'. This adds significance to the conservation of Shub's documentary record.[1]

Over a decade prior to this, Shub had set the standard for Constructivist silent nonfiction film with *The Fall of the Romanov Dynasty* and its sequel, *The Great Way*, both released in 1927. This was followed by their noteworthy successor, Shub's final silent documentary, *Today*, in 1930. Yet, with the advent of sound and due to the rapid progress made in film technology, Shub was able to elevate the benchmark for nonfiction film to an even greater degree with the release in 1932 of the clear sounds and fascinating content of *K.Sh.E.* Seven years later *Spain* effectively saw the end of Shub's catalogue of memorable contributions to film history. Furthermore, these five cinematic milestones all stand as an enduring commemoration of class struggle in the early decades of the last century.

Shub's attempt to maintain her original filmic philosophy and retain her creative integrity posed immense challenges to her position as a filmmaker during the Great Terror (which had begun in 1936). Not only were all art forms required to be subservient to Party dogma but, as Jamie Miller records, 'there was an obsession with ideological correctness'.[2]

This aside, just as with *The Fall of the Romanov Dynasty*, *The Great Way*, *Today* and *K.Sh.E.*, in *Spain*, there is nothing staged or fabricated within this up-to-the-minute filming of the Spanish Civil War (1936–9). It is compiled into a gripping documentary. Dexterously, Shub constructed a pictorial saga of historical consequence using current newsreel of the day captured by the renowned Soviet cameraman Roman Karmen[3] and assisted by his colleague

Boris Makaseev, together with a script by Vsevolod Vishnevsky.[4] According to Shub, Vishnevsky, who 'was very interested in documentary . . . believed that artists should be at the forefront of the struggle'.[5] In a letter to Shub, in reference to his career as a writer, Vishnevsky had revealed the following to her. 'As you know, I am increasingly developing issues of cinematic practice and theory. I am interested in the field of interaction between literature and cinema. A new era has arrived, a new phase of cinema: a phase of more active and decisive participation in the whole creative process.'[6]

Vishnevsky's observations aside, the process of *Spain* is markedly different from Shub's experience with her first full-length documentary, *The Fall of the Romanov Dynasty*, where she had reconstructed events from an earlier era (1912–17), not crafting her silent film until the following decade (1926–7). Due to a dearth of archival film of that period, resurrecting the past had been both a challenge of mammoth proportions and an arduous process for Shub.

Conversely, apart from the obvious technological advancements made in the 1930s, Karmen and Makaseev's newsreels (in pristine condition) gave Shub a wealth of contemporaneous material filmed at the scene of the conflict. Their adroit coverage was a catalogue of events that served to exemplify the war. Subsequently, Shub wove these images, at her immediate disposal, into a seamlessly compiled socialist discourse. Yet again, this is the recycling of reality. However, rather than scouring the cellars of Leningrad as she'd been forced to do for *The Fall of the Romanov Dynasty*, holding up a mirror to reflect a previous decade, the material for *Spain* is of the present.

Indubitably, the condition of the celluloid is far superior to *The Fall of the Romanov Dynasty* in terms of its visual quality. Hence, this refinement serves to give *Spain* a heightened sense of instantaneous exposure, adding to a further sense of reality and authenticity. The audience is being plunged into the immediacy of the action, and the images in each filmic frame are crisp and clear. On the contrary, in *The Fall of the Romanov Dynasty* and *The Great Way*, the view is filtered through a slightly grainy haze, giving these two far earlier works much of their legitimacy, charm, and sense of time and place. *Spain* is a template worthy of emulation as a polished example of political commentary at the close of the 1930s.

Shub's *Spain* continues to adhere to her original vision for Constructivist nonfiction film. Yet, despite the methodological strictures that Shub imposes, *Spain* is a richly observational analysis. Shub's documentary spans most of the principal events of the Civil War from all its hopes for victory in 1936 up until the disastrous decimation of the Popular Army at the hands of Francisco Franco in 1939. Furthermore, in *Spain*, Shub continues to uphold the 1920s Soviet Weltanshauung as she moulds her doctrinal armature. It is the justification for the struggle of socialist hegemony against the domination of the power structures inherent in a capitalist culture.

This promulgation, the metanarrative of *Spain*, is indistinguishable from Shub's schema represented, in particular, by *The Fall of the Romanov Dynasty* and *The Great Way* (together with *Today* and *K.Sh.E*). The early Soviet avant-garde's preoccupation (almost to the point of an *idée fixe*) with transforming the dream of a utopian society into reality, through the revolution by the proletariat, is being promoted yet again by Shub in her homage to the valiant battles of the Republican Army against the might of their fascist oppressors. For the citizens of the USSR, this corresponded with continuing political repression. Stalin's rule, together with the abject failure of socialist aspirations in the Soviet Union, is at variance with Shub's somewhat sanguine portrait of a democratically led left-wing government in Republican Spain.

Nevertheless, Shub pursues an ideological vision that is illusory because *Spain* is awash with the victories of the Republican troops rather than their incalculable losses of men and significant defeats at the hands of the enemy. The Republicans were no match for the superior combined forces of Franco and his Nazi German and Fascist Italian allies (with their infinitely superior military weaponry). Consequently, Shub's ardent bias does not permit her to refer to the tragic and ultimately crushing defeat of the Republic.

The Soviet Union and the Spanish Civil War

The public in the USSR had seen the footage from the battlefield superbly shot in close-up and filmed at considerable risk to his personal safety by the intrepid Roman Karmen.[7] Due to his war photography, Shub was provided with an evocative and often graphic visual palette from which to construct her commentary. In fact, Karmen's newsreels served to reinforce the official Comintern standpoint. This underpinned the Republican cause without revealing any of the intrigues taking place in the Kremlin. It was vital for the Soviets to be seen to be offering both moral and practical support to their communist sisters and brothers, in the form of munitions and advisors on the ground, but there were more pressing needs on the home front.

At this time, Stalin was involved in carrying out the purges of the Great Terror. Although they were not singled out, even the cinema workforce (at all levels) did not escape scrutiny: from administrators and technical crew to artists including scriptwriters and actors. The penalties included being sent to a labour camp, imprisoned or executed (the latter being the fate of both the playwright and film theorist Sergei Tretiakov and the administrative head of the Soviet film industry Boris Shumiatsky). As Jamie Miller posits, 'the use of terror, violence and intimidation against personnel from the Soviet film industry' took various forms. NKVD operatives 'would deliberately arrest people during the filming process . . . this created a real sense of fear in the studios that anyone could be victimized'.[8] Although the 'number of arrests and executions escalated', the film community were far from the only targets in the population at large.[9] The Great Terror was primarily a series of show trials which resulted in the arrest and execution of countless 'enemies of the people', including political rivals and Old Bolsheviks. Thus, Stalin was very preoccupied on the domestic front.

Added to this was the harsh reality that according to the historian Stanley Payne, one of the foremost authorities on the Spanish Civil War, 'nothing . . . was more important to Stalin than what he conceived to be geostrategic self-interest'.[10] Accordingly, Payne perceives that for the USSR:

> Support for the Spanish Republic would take a stand against fascism, while public denial and extreme secrecy might avoid alienating Britain and France. Ideology remained important, but Soviet policy sought to combine it with pragmatic policies. If communism became increasingly influential within the Republic, that was all to the good.[11]

In his book *The Spanish Civil War, the Soviet Union, and Communism*, Payne examines the myths about the Spanish Civil War perpetuated until after the fall of the Soviet Union. In light of this, Payne refers to Palmiro Togliatti, who was a prominent Italian communist and their leading delegate to the Comintern. Prior to leaving for Spain in 1937, Togliatti was the author of an essay titled 'Specific Features of the Spanish Revolution'. In this article he outlined his thesis for the establishment in Spain of a left-wing, anti-fascist democracy for the working class. Togliatti's discourse, one that would reflect a Leninist creed adhered to by communists and socialists alike, posited that this republic in Spain was to be a democratic dictatorship of the workers brought about by a 'national revolutionary war'. Moreover, as Payne claims, 'there would be no deviation from this basic doctrine regarding the Spanish revolution of 1936-1939 down to the time of the dissolution of the Soviet Union more than half a century later, and it would still be echoed by Party-line post-Soviet Russian historians even after that.'[12]

The proclamations made by this powerful propaganda machine could explain Shub's bias. No mention was to be made of the annihilation of the Republicans at the hands of Franco's Nationalist forces. The word 'defeat' was not uttered, and yet this utopian concept was just that – an idealized and never realized theoretical construct.

Payne refers to not only Stalin's goals for the region but also the controversies surrounding the vastly inflated prices charged by the Soviets for inferior outdated materiel. In addition, he investigates Soviet motivation, policies and involvement in this conflict. Payne also devotes pages to the betrayal of the Republicans by Stalin with regard to the treacherous Spanish gold bullion swindle perpetrated by him and his henchmen.[13] Consequently, he notes that due to the states' well-developed penchant for falsifying history:

> For years the full extent of Soviet intervention was hidden even from the Soviet public, but by the 1960s it had become a cherished memory for personal memoirs and historical studies, presented as an idealistic struggle against fascism of which all Soviets could be proud. Compared with many other Soviet initiatives around the world, it was long cast as a saga that would always reveal the Soviet Union in a positive light. Soviet historians hid the full motives and activities of Soviet policy, as to some extent Russian historians still do today."[14]

In addition, to substantiate the official Stalinist position, both *Pravda* and *Izvestiya* gave enthusiastic press coverage of the Spanish Civil War from the outset, but, according to Payne's investigations, Soviet newspaper commentary began to be scaled down from October 1937 onwards. This waning could be explained perhaps by the indiscriminate bombing of Guernica in April 1937, followed by the fall of Bilbao in June and Santander in August. These were catastrophes. Showing the crushing defeats of the Popular Army at the hands of their fascist enemies was detrimental to morale not only in Republican Spain but also in the Soviet Union. As the heading of the *Pravda* editorial of August 1936 had boldly proclaimed at the beginning of the conflict: 'Fascism means war; socialism means peace.'[15] *Pravda's* hopeful words were not to bear fruit. There was to be no peace and no socialist society.

In exploring Stalin's duplicitous dealings with his Republican comrades during the Civil War, Payne's research provides an understanding of Shub's somewhat romanticized and partisan position. These idealized sentiments are reinforced in an essay published in English in the journal of *International Literature* in 1939.

> The bourgeoisie, in fear of its impending doom, has betrayed its previous ideals. . . . It is impossible to view the capitalist world without feelings of horror . . . due to 'the growing insolence of fascist aggression'.[16] We want our film . . . to inspire those who are in the very thick of the fight against fascism . . . to bring spirit, courage and confidence . . . where fascism seems . . . invincible.[17]

These are not the words of Shub, although they underscore her objectives in *Spain* to the letter. They are instead the impassioned objectives of Eisenstein in his essay titled 'My Subject is Patriotism'. In it, a contrite, politically chastened and 're-educated' Eisenstein links his apparent devotion to the Communist Party and 'the great Stalinist epoch' in its battle against fascism: with the military victory of Russia's glorious medieval hero Alexander Nevsky fighting the barbaric Livonian Knights in the thirteenth century.[18] Thus, in this text, written in the same year as the release of Shub's *Spain*, similarly, Eisenstein is passionate in his condemnation of fascist aggression and the 'suppression of the independence of . . . blood drenched Spain'. He is adamant that 'Soviet art' must not 'ignore these all-important themes'.[19] While he portrays the terror and carnage wreaked by their foe, Eisenstein shows the courageous Alexander Nevsky, Prince of Novgorod, as the saviour of the Russian people. In Eisenstein's film, released in November 1938, he portrays a historical event filled with both facts and added fictionalized drama. Nevsky and his forces massacre their supposedly invincible enemies during the famed and thrilling Battle on the Ice. On the other hand, Shub must contend with documenting the real world in the present without any added fictional embellishments (such as *October* and *Alexander Nevsky*, dramas based on actual incidents), even though she promotes the Soviet Union's specific ideological position throughout. Of course, both Shub and Eisenstein compromised. They understood the necessity of upholding the message of Communist pride and patriotism, but they were far more than mere propagandists for Stalin and the regime.

Whatever her subject matter, whether it be the thesis outlining the rationale behind the collapse of the repressive sovereignty of the Romanov Tsars over the Russian working classes or the fight decades later by the Republican forces against fascist rule in the Spanish Civil War, Shub never wavers from the nucleus of her argument. Her representation of the image and the text is set firmly on solid ground. There is only one perspective that permeates Shub's documentaries.

It is political and supports socialist principles. Therefore, Shub glorifies Lenin and then Stalin's leadership, together with their policies and their achievements. Hence, every one of her films is seen through the prism of Soviet doctrine, and her unwavering promotion of Leninist and Stalinist ideology permeates them all. The hero is never featured as an individual; rather, the focus is always centred on the collective. Accordingly, *Spain* depicts the struggle of the Spanish workers against the capitalist right-wing Spanish aristocracy together with their ally, the Catholic Church. This is the thematic pattern used by Shub in *The Fall of the Romanov Dynasty*, where the proletariat was pitted against the Russian nobility and the Orthodox Church.

The Image, the Meaning, the Sound: The Continuing Undercurrent of Constructivism

The specificity of Shub's filmic discourse gives rise to a language that constructs a rhetorical dialogue synonymous with her ideological and political stance. This conversation with her viewers affords Shub a synthesis between the image and the didacticism of the text.

In his discourse on cinema and representation, the film theorist Peter Wollen quotes the semiologist Charles Peirce on the indexical nexus between the photographic image and its referent:

> Photographs, especially instantaneous photographs, are very instructive, because we know that in certain respects they are exactly like the objects they represent. But this resemblance is due to the photographs having been produced under such circumstances that they were physically forced to correspond point by point to nature. In that aspect, they belong to the second class of signs, those by physical connection.[20]

In Peirce's semiotic classification system, the second sign in a cognitive world relates to indices. Photography, and by extension cinema, can be viewed indexically as an image or sign connected to its object, which expresses or represents a relationship between an abstract object and its reality in the universe. A photographic image or cinematic frame can signify a connection to that which it refers. Consequently, in this way, Shub takes recent newsreel footage of the Spanish Civil War and juxtaposes signs using images of historical evidence, thereby constructing new meanings that illustrate both a congruity and a familiarity with Soviet ideology.

Nonetheless, *Spain* not only adheres to the elemental principles of Shub's Constructivist philosophy but it is also a more refined realization of this art form than, for example, *The Fall of the Romanov Dynasty*. However, there is little of Shub's ironic juxtaposition and wit, so prevalent in the aforementioned, in her political commentary of *Spain*. *The Fall of the Romanov Dynasty* was an undeniable breakthrough when one charts the early development of documentary history, and it was without doubt a pivotal achievement in nonfiction film.

That aside, it is obvious that *Spain* displays a technical superiority to Shub's first film made over a decade earlier. Also, *Spain* is notable for its aesthetic qualities (together with the precision of its individual frames) and an added richness of depth, the benefit of sound. Aurally, the multi-layering of Vishnevsky's conversational voice-over integrated with the sound effects and the music not only gives emphasis to the allure of the visual image but also adds intensification to the meaning and message of Shub's critique.[21] Accordingly, Shub observed that, in this way, with his use of unadorned commentary, Vishnevsky was 'talking out loud or rather thinking aloud for the audience'.[22] This is the essence of a Constructivist approach. It gives facts and general commentary about this historical event as naturally as possible without the need for embellishment.

Enriching this further was Gavriil Popov's musical direction. Used so effectively in *K.Sh.E.*, in his soundtrack for *Spain*, Popov inserts another dimension – an emotional complexity in which the opening instrumental composition serves successfully to amplify the mood, as the notes soar to reach a crescendo. Indeed, this stirring panoramic theme composed by Popov is imbued with a dramatic colour and thus underscores the political zeal and passion about to unfold. Shub regarded that Popov's music 'played a large part in the design of the script. He took folk melodies as a basis and made excellent use of folk instruments and songs'.[23] Again, in accordance with Constructivism, much of the music is traditional and authentic to the culture of the country.

Despite *Spain* being a serious document of the Spanish Civil War (recording as it does authentic incidents as depicted from the point of view of the Republican side), it is certainly not devoid of ardour and gripping tension in its portrayal of the patriotism and sacrifice of a nation in its battle for democracy. On the contrary, the powerful swell of Popov's introductory melody, in tandem with the opening credits, gives pathos to the text that follows on the screen: 'This film is dedicated to the Spanish people who, surrounded by hostile forces, fought heroically for three years against fascism.' In addition to this, apart from Vishnevsky's controlled use of his spoken material, Shub employs the didacticism of written words on the screen at the commencement of major sequences in the film.

This combination of the rhetorical application of the visual text with the aural message accentuates, supports and augments the additional thematic content of the voice-over narration, thereby inducing the viewer to accept Shub's point of view. Not surprisingly, Shub structured her content in *Spain* in order to present each significant chapter of the Spanish Civil War from a Soviet perspective, and therefore, as referred to earlier, her stance is somewhat distorted.

However, Shub sourced valuable propaganda supporting Franco and the Catholic Church. It was not from Roman Karmen's camera but from Nationalist films obtained through Spanish contacts of Vishnevsky's (he had been in Spain during the conflict). On the rare occasion that Shub uses this Nationalist footage, it is revealed in an overtly negative light and is ingeniously subverted just as she had done with the tsarist material in *The Fall of the Romanov Dynasty*. However, if the contemporary viewer is able to put this problematic subjectivity aside, the work has much to offer. Indeed, Shub's documentary is a handsomely constructed rendition of the Spanish Civil War as seen through the eyes of the democratically elected Popular Front (a coalition of communists, Marxists, socialists and left-wing Republicans). It is pure Constructivist nonfiction film and no less valid than modern documentary, where filmmakers likewise propagate and promote specific political agendas.

In *Spain*, as in other documentaries, there is a fractured storyline comprising of separate observational vignettes that exemplify the overt political message. These are individual chapters adding to and supporting Shub's thesis as she investigates the intricacies of this long and internecine war. It was a challenging project in a multitude of ways. As the historian Michael Seidman states bluntly, 'During the conflict, opposing "isms" – Communism and fascism, anarchism and authoritarianism, republicanism and monarchism, Catholicism and anti-clericalism, democracy and dictatorship – battled each other.'[24]

The Narrative Begins

Shub's filmic introduction turns its gaze towards Galicia in the northwestern corner of the country. This is highly apposite given the support for the Popular

Front in this province. Galicia, with a concentration of struggling peasantry, was a region desperate for change. The Popular Front continued the objectives of Prime Minister Manuel Azaña (1931–3), whose government had initiated major agrarian reform.

Shub's first image is of Mediterranean pines. The distant sound of a set of bagpipes wafts over the treetops. Then a young piper enters, from the left of the frame, playing his Galician *gaita* amongst the hedgerows. With the rustic simplicity of this haunting instrument's sounds embellishing the introductory images, Shub introduces us to the beauty of Galicia, part of the Celtic fringe. As Vishnevsky's voice-over informs the audience: 'Here is the ancient land of Galicia in North West Spain, facing the Atlantic Ocean and the Bay of Biscay.' There are idyllic and painterly reflections in glassy water of a sturdy stone bridge set against hills, followed by shots of lush and fertile land. In a time-honoured tradition, a peasant and his mules rhythmically plough furrows in a vast field. These bucolic scenes are emblematic of peace and harmony and a sense of being at one with the land. The bagpiper reappears on the screen, a handsome figure striding through a cornfield. He personifies the youth and promise of Spain, its folklore and culture. Continuing with his unbroken harmony, he exits to the right of the frame. After culture we come to creed as Shub builds layers of reportage to support her evidence. This is authentic documentation showing the old world before the Civil War.[25]

An architecturally austere stone church dominates the landscape. Close-up shots of a sacred wooden carving and a painted medieval biblical scene hewn out of stone are accompanied by Shub's text, informing us that this is a country filled with 'religious antiques dating back centuries'. This is a reference to the heritage and art of Spanish Catholicism. Although Shub refers to a preponderance of antiques owned by the church in Spain, as yet there is no mention of their embedded historical importance within the society. Nor is there any criticism of the dominance and wealth of the Catholic Church in a country struggling with poverty and genuine hardship.

On the other hand, in *The Fall of the Romanov Dynasty*, the Russian Orthodox Church was the butt of scathing condemnation. Shub applied this denunciation both in her cutting use of images and the accompanying words on the screen, both heavily veiled with irony. This device is not employed in the introductory footage in *Spain*, and yet, as an example, the Bishop of Salamanca's inflammatory sermon in September 1936 would have been a valuable critical tool for Shub's film. As the bishop was to declare, 'the war takes the external form of a civil war but, in reality, it is a Crusade.'[26] This fragment of his address referring to a holy war would have been controversial and effective had it been inserted perhaps into the chapter about Burgos (the official seat of General Franco) showing the Spanish clergy, appearing further on in the film, or alternatively in the section where an armed Nationalist brigade kneel at the feet of a clergyman in order to be blessed.

From religious images, the camera transports us back to the secular world, the common people and their everyday lives. Here, Shub depicts a seemingly joyful segment that illustrates women at their labours. They are rhythmically threshing flax and happily singing in unison as they beat the fibres with wooden paddles. The sound of their melody enhances the scene. Then we observe as an elderly co-worker spins the threads into linen.

After the voices of the flax workers, another industry is documented and painted likewise in an idyllic portrait. The Atlantic is depicted in all its splendour with pounding waves crashing onto the rocks. We hear the haunting sound of sailors singing sea shanties as Shub reveals an enchanting sequence depicting an old woman in black, silhouetted against the ocean. She inspects and mends vast webs of fishing nets. We listen to the mesmerizing sounds of women chanting their compelling and captivating songs. Fishermen in berets march along the shoreline in an unbroken chain carrying their gigantic net like a never-ending sea monster. As they stomp their feet along the wet compacted sand, the hypnotic music is in synchrony with their rhythm. Loading the net onto their fishing vessel, they put out to sea. A life of danger and hardship and toil is portrayed in glowing mode. Where is Shub's critical analysis of the struggles and oppression of the proletariat by both the state and the church?

Instead, we have yet further scenes of exhilaration. Joyous children run to the harbour to see the catch of the day. Fishermen on the boat scoop silvery mackerel out of overflowing vats. Sails unfurled, a boat skims over the still and mirrored pond of the tranquil lagoon. A small girl runs playfully into the garden of a tree-shaded fairy-tale cottage with plump hydrangeas in bloom. Shub is presenting yet more serene, charming and fulfilling scenes of daily life in her study of happy days: before the bloody destruction of the Spanish Civil War changes the landscape forever. It is obvious that Shub is building an image of the country before it is riven with the brutality and appalling bloodshed of war, but there should be a socialist critique, and it is not evident here.

Despite the authenticity of Karmen and Makaseev's footage, Shub is leaving the viewer in some doubt. Life in Spain seems almost too harmonious and normal with an absence of strife and striving. Is this Shub's very point? It appears as though she could be presenting her audience with an accentuation of how peaceful life was in Spain in order to give more shock value when she pounds us with images of slaughter and horror. This would make sense of Shub emphasizing further the rich bounty of Spain before the gathering storm and the chronic food shortages during the Civil War.

Agricultural labourers in fecund orchard groves climb ladders to pick oranges, lemons and almonds from luxuriantly laden trees. These fruit pickers load their capacious woven baskets, spilling over with produce, onto a rickety cart bound for market. These verdant groves of Valencia dissolve into an avenue of palm trees and then a car is seen speeding along the arterial road leading to Madrid.

Now the agrarian countryside gives way to the civilized metropolis at the heart of Spain – its capital, Madrid. The immensely wide streets are bustling with cars and trams. We are introduced to the grandeur of the impressive architecture, and, more specifically, Shub takes us to the Plaza de España. Here is the imposing white marble statue of Spain's famed literary giant Miguel de Cervantes. His monument towers over bronzes of Don Quixote and Sancho Panza. Shub then cuts to shots of an eighteenth-century sculpture of the pagan goddess Cybele. A symbol of mother earth, the giver and sustainer of life, Cybele is seated in her chariot drawn by lions. Shub spends just under a quarter of an hour cataloguing the cornucopia and tranquillity of Spain before plunging her audience into the conflict and nightmare of war.

Shub has paid homage to Spanish literature (and art) with their revered Cervantes immortalized in stone. She has shown us the abundant produce of both rural Spain and the sea, followed by urban images of refinement. Shub now introduces us to the political life of the country as she constructs her thesis.

A plaza in the heart of Madrid is bursting to capacity with a massive throng. From amongst the congregation of Spaniards appears La Pasionaria (Dolores Ibárruri), the mother of Republican Spain. Ibárruri gracefully ascends the steps of the Cortes. Shub informs us that 'La Pasionaria [is the] daughter of a miner, a member of the Spanish Communist Party Central Committee' (Figure 38). Shub has given us Spain as it was immediately prior to the tragedy of the Civil War at the commencement of 1936: a country brimming with hope under the newly elected Popular Front and its promised wide-reaching democratic reforms. However, Shub's language, presented through the speech of La Pasionaria, 'welcomes the successes of the people . . . but also warns of the danger . . . the proletariat demand the arrest of the Fascists Gil-Robles and Franco'. José Maria

Figure 38 *No Pasarán!* 'La Pasionaria' (Dolores Ibárruri) addresses the people in Spain.

Gil-Robles y Quiñones was the leader of CEDA, the most powerful anti-democratic right-wing faction.

Significantly, after mentioning these perils, we are taken from La Pasionaria's words of caution to the slaughter of a bullfight. Firstly there is a single statement: 'For some it was too hard to abandon their bourgeois way of life.' Now Shub reverts to the juxtaposition of word and image to argue her political position. If we consider the overt didacticism of *The Fall of the Romanov Dynasty*, Shub is offering a similar subtext here with her use of ideological montage, a device that has been lacking up to this juncture. Almost the entire sequence is without voice-over or subtitles, as Shub pounds the viewer with her message. She is equating the well-dressed bourgeois spectators (including women in lace mantillas and finery), who enthusiastically watch the savagery, with the fascist carnage to come. To build her argument, Shub presents footage of La Fiesta. We see the spectacle of the bullring with dashing matadors, picadors and an eager audience. Balletic and theatrical heroics of the richly costumed matadors bring to mind their documentation, so vividly expressed in the lively lithographs and paintings of Goya and Picasso. The only sound is festive music as the wounded and exhausted bull is tortured and then finally put out of his misery. After this bloodshed the air is filled with gaiety, and the predominantly male crowd, formally attired and wearing hats, enthusiastically brandish their handkerchiefs. Apart from the war footage soon to come, filled with brutality and destruction,

Shub will give her audience more images of vigorous handkerchief waving later in the film. These latter shots will not be connected to bullfighting, and the gesture will be permeated with an altogether differing meaning. Instead, it will be with reference to the farewell of children being evacuated to protect them from the dangers of the deadly hostilities between Republicans and the Nationalists.

After the savagery at the bullring, the next filmic chapter opens with the seemingly innocuous phrase: 'July 1936: clear skies throughout Spain.' 'Clear skies throughout Spain' is then duplicated shortly afterwards. This emphasis is Shub's method of giving us time to contemplate her specific use of language and what lies ahead. Commencing with the poetic fluttering of white birds swooping over the water, this tranquillity is followed by a shot of a stylish seaside promenade with distinctive wrought-iron railings. Two lovers, arm in arm, saunter down La Rambla in the heart of Barcelona, the capital of Catalonia and a Republican stronghold. As Barcelona is situated on the Mediterranean coastline, we are taken from the heart of the city to the ocean. The camera zooms in on the iron railings to display their elegant patterning at closer quarters. Now, the lens peers through this open filigree, and we observe carefree laughing young boys cavorting and splashing in the shallows of the water.

Shub's editing is perfection, as the shot then moves fluidly towards a lone gull drifting overhead. It skims along the surface of the ocean, and then the following image is of the sky with black birds, visible in the distance. There are no longer any white birds to be seen. Shub is giving her viewers another potent message to absorb. From the white birds to the black birds she brings back, into the frame, the same children smiling and frolicking near the shoreline. The repetition is noteworthy, as she accentuates their playfulness in light of what is to come. Their lives are about to alter irrevocably. This is the calm before the storm. Now, the audience is confronted by a faint shadow in the sky: a silhouette of a black bird, which, on further inspection, could be an aircraft.

Without hesitation, Shub prepares her viewers for an altogether different story. She returns to the seafront. A mother gently pushes a pram, containing two infants, with a small girl walking contentedly by her side. The Art Deco railings dramatically line the backdrop of this domestic scene. As this little family group exits to the left of the frame, a couple of men amble into the shot from the right. Then, at this point, we realize that the black bird is indeed a plane, as it reappears clearly and menacingly. It belongs to the fascist Nationalists, and it releases bombs that explode in the sea. The idyll is broken and in its place is fear and confusion. Birds have metamorphosed into weapons of death, a well-considered and effective device. Shub has presented us with scenes of peaceful, everyday routine for the first fifteen minutes of her film, but now she brings to the screen shots of deadly bombs targeting the city and its population. We have frightening smoke-filled blackened skies and the beginnings of death and devastation. Now Shub displays the casualties of war, with the first images of dead civilians lying in the street. A young man carrying a child in his arms rushes to safety with the child's mother running frantically beside him. They race along the same promenade where, earlier, the woman had strolled leisurely by with her babies in a pram. People are fleeing in terror. As in the modern documentary, the film uses news reportage from a war zone with a polished commentary accompanying images of destruction.

Time elapses. Little boys no longer swim blissfully in the ocean but help to erect barricades by dragging sandbags onto the back of a truck. They also dig up large cobblestones, and afterwards men use them to build defence barriers in the streets. A raggedy group of half a dozen Republicans in civilian clothes march purposefully down the street carrying guns. Shub is noting that the call to arms comes from every quarter. Then another man comes into view: José Diaz Ramos. He speaks directly to the people of Spain. Known simply as Diaz, a politician and trade unionist, he is the General Secretary of the Spanish Communist Party. Diaz is a comrade of La Pasionaria's. He addresses the populace with a passionate exhortation of:

'Forward! Long Live the Republic!'

In the next scene, we survey the might of the enemies of the Republic. The audience is told, 'Berlin and Rome ordered Franco back from Morocco, promising planes, tanks, mercenaries and equipment.' The viewer then sees Franco's Moroccan cavalry and soldiers parading impressively in full regalia. They form part of the contingent of Franco's Spanish Army of Africa comprised of Spanish units garrisoned in Morocco, troops of the Spanish Foreign Legion and local Moroccan cavalry and infantry divisions. Unlike the earlier shot where Shub featured a small band of disorganized Republicans without uniforms, these are professional, experienced and highly trained armed forces. The contrast between the two armies seems vast. Using montage in a dramatic and unmistakeably instructive manner, Shub superimposes a chilling swastika on the screen, layering it over the masses of marching troops in the Nationalist Army (Figure 39).

This highly effective photo collage of images alerts us to the fact that Nazi Germany under Hitler is giving its full support to Franco through not only

Figure 39 Franco's fascist army in *Spain*.

military aid in the form of aeroplanes and weapons but also with expertly drilled troops. Shub's message is transparent.

Directly following this, in counterbalance, Shub inserts the hammer and sickle flying defiantly over Toledo. Soldiers kneel directly beneath this flag in the street with their rifles at the ready. Young Republicans, whom Shub describes as 'urban guerrillas', fire from behind sandbags. The battle is fiercely contested in the streets, and soldiers carry their wounded comrades to safety. Vishnevsky announces: 'HOLD ON BROTHER SPANIARDS . . . YOU ARE NOT ALONE IN YOUR STRUGGLE'[27] Although the Republican forces are initially victorious, due to her political allegiance, Shub neglects to inform us that eventually Toledo is to fall to Franco and his Army of Africa. She manipulates the presentation of historical realism, through the use of authentic footage, in order to amplify a specific ideological position (Figure 40).

Thus, instead of the ultimate defeat in Toledo, in order to reinforce her standpoint, we see the fervour of those supporting the government of the Popular Front. 'We Salute You' and other phrases showing solidarity are inscribed on banners held by enthusiastic crowds lining the docks in their thousands and perched on top of buildings as they welcome flotillas ferrying soldiers towards the wharf at the port of Barcelona.

Figure 40 Yet again, Shub's images speak for themselves in *Spain*.

The International Brigades arrive by ship and train. As Shub informs her viewers, 'the International Brigades comprise of men from twenty-five nations that have come to Spain to fight for democracy and culture. We salute our comrades from the bottom of our hearts.' It is an emotionally intoxicating sequence as a rendition of *The Internationale* is being sung with touching zeal. This rousing anthem accompanies the sounds of cheering Republican supporters on the quayside. Vessels of all shapes and sizes sail proudly into the harbour.

There is a medium close-up of the bow of the supply ship, the *Zyrianin* bearing humanitarian aid to the civilian population. Its name, together with the identifying port of Odessa, is painted prominently on its prow (Figure 41). Shub inserts another close-up shot, and this is of the smiling face of its captain waving to those assembled on the dock. Subsequently, we are presented with yet another image of this Soviet vessel supporting the Republican cause. With this repetition and emphasis, Shub wants to show her audience unequivocally that the Soviet Union under Stalin is providing support to the people of Spain in their struggle against the Nationalist extremists.

Shub cuts to the faces of Dolores Ibárruri and José Diaz Ramos singing *The Internationale* at another time and another place. It is the autumn of 1936, and the location is Madrid. Ibárruri's jubilant countenance and her obvious zest

Figure 41 Supporting the Republican cause: the *Zyrianin*, a Soviet ship docks in Barcelona's harbour in *Spain*.

and vigour contrast radically with the sequence at the end of the film where she is giving an oration in a state of great distress. Shub informs us that at this moment, 'the Spanish communists are rising in Madrid'. This is not referring to what had been the people's successful defence of Madrid in July 1936 against a failed military coup by Franco but the battle for Madrid later that year. Diaz speaks: 'The danger is great. The fascist forces are on the outskirts of Madrid.' We are assured that 'They shall not pass!' *They Shall Not Pass* [No Pasarán] had become the motto of the people and was used by Ibárruri in her famous speech of that name. The crowds cheer.

Sharing the platform with Ibárruri and Diaz is Gustav Regler, the German novelist, socialist and soldier, the commissar of the XII International Brigade. He assures the people of Spain, 'You have the full support of the International Brigades – the Red Front.' The camera pans back to focus on Ibárruri, who encourages the populace to 'Take up arms and fight for your freedom.' As she is to exclaim: 'Long live the Popular Front! Long live the union of all anti-fascists! Long live the Republic of the people! THEY SHALL NOT PASS!' Shub reinforces this ardour-filled segment, complete with Ibárruri's rousing rallying cry, by the following frame. It is a mid-shot of a banner strung across a street, and the sign on it reads in pronounced letters: 'No Pasarán'.

Men are queuing to enlist. Some look like schoolboys. Raw recruits are seen drilling in civilian clothes, and then we see the same group in army uniform.

Shub introduces a portly André Marty, the feared and ferocious Commissar of the International Brigades, sporting his regulation moustache and signature beret. Shub includes wonderful visual renderings of uniformed women fighters, members of the socialist UGT [the General Union of Workers] (Figures 42 and 43). They line up with the men and parade through the streets to the enthusiastic applause of the public. We see the battalions moving out ready to engage with the foe.

Appositely, now Shub shifts the filmic location to the enemy camp: the ancient city of Burgos in Old Castile. It is the headquarters of the military junta established by Franco. Heads of the church in their finery, carrying gold crucifixes rather than guns, walk solemnly in procession accompanied by fittingly sombre music. This menacing refrain is repeated throughout the segment. It is a scenario reminiscent of the parade of the richly gowned church hierarchy at the beginning of *The Fall of the Romanov Dynasty*. In contrast to this flaunting of opulence, monks looking ominous in austere black cowls follow the lavishly attired leaders of the Spanish priesthood. Nonetheless, Franco's pageant of holy men (the historically influential Spanish clergy) is vastly different from the sobering parade of clerics seen at the end of *The Fall of the Romanov Dynasty*. Unlike the ushering in of the reign of Lenin and the banishment of the Russian Orthodox Church from its position of power, the status and authority of the Catholic Church in Spain is not only undiminished by the rise of Franco but its power only increases. It is seen as the 'unifying force among the insurgents'.[28]

Figure 42 A young soldier with the International Brigades in *Spain*.

Figure 43 Her fighting comrade, a member of the socialist UGT [the General Union of Workers], in *Spain*.

Just as she had done previously in *The Fall of the Romanov Dynasty*, here again Shub subverts the original meaning of a filmic sequence belonging to the fascists and gives her audience a new unintended meaning. Similarly, following on from these forbidding images in Burgos, she presents more rhetoric to support her rationale. Waving his crucifix, a church leader in military uniform makes the sign of the cross over the kneeling 'bandits of Navarre' (as Vishnevsky labels them). Shub also characterizes this assembly as 'murderers'. In her eyes, these men from Navarre are nothing more than cut-throats fighting for the destruction of freedom and the Popular Front and, by extension, a democratic Spain. Chillingly, these insurgents hold their rifles as they receive their blessing and are loyal supporters of the church, Franco and fascism. Religion is shown as complicit in its support of the Nationalists. In a similar vein, in *The Fall of the Romanov Dynasty*, Shub had attacked the elitist and immensely wealthy church as being an instrument of the autocratic Tsar Nicholas II rather than a champion of the proletariat. In this film we had seen hapless and exhausted Russian soldiers during World War I being sprinkled with holy water by priests who, like their fellow clergy in Spain, are seemingly impervious to the suffering of the people.

At this moment, Shub returns the focus of her film back onto the capital. Planes fly over Madrid. People in the street are pointing skywards. We hear the sinister droning of the aircraft. Sirens sound. There are the tooting of horns in warning and then the sound of bombs crashing indiscriminately. More sirens signal their alarms. People are running, zigzagging across the impossibly wide streets of Madrid, past solid palm trees and stately buildings. They dash for cover into cramped air-raid shelters filled with young and old – babies, children, their parents and the elderly (Figure 44). Men converse. A mother suckles her infant. A child sleeps seemingly unaware of the danger, while other youngsters look bored or anxious. This is nonfiction film at its finest. No textual observation, either in aural form or through the use of intertitles or subtitles, is deemed necessary. Each frame adds meaning to Shub's developing treatise (Figure 45).

A man receives first aid and we observe his arm being bandaged. A young woman cries. The authentic footage is so immediate: the rising tension of people fleeing the planes bombarding their city is intense. Yet again, there is no need for a voice-over, or any text, and the viewer can sense the panic and terror and tension being built by Shub with such attention to detail. We see whole family groups in the underground shelters. Then the camera returns to the streets. They are deserted. A still calm descends, but this ghostly and sinister atmosphere

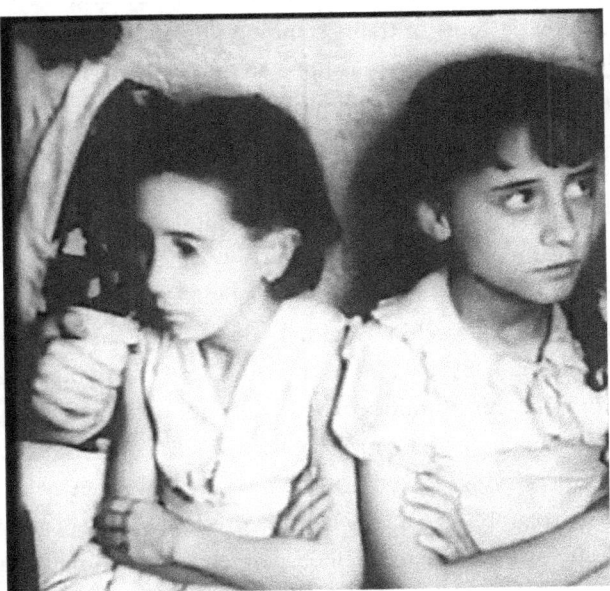

Figure 44 In Madrid, children wait apprehensively in an underground shelter in *Spain*.

Figure 45 Grief and darkness fall on an underground shelter in *Spain*.

evokes dread. After a slight lull, the bombing continues. Shub's focus then falls on dramatically eerie shots of trams standing idle and empty in the sunshine: a masterpiece of evocation. There is not a soul to be seen in this unforgettably hushed silence. The all-pervasive stillness, an absence of presence and presence of absence in this disturbingly eerie streetscape, is one of unsettling beauty. It suggests an artwork worthy of Giorgio de Chirico. Shub's production and sequence of events is faultless, and it is these added and inspired touches of brilliance, such as the almost chilling and deathly quiet of the trams in a deserted Madrid street, which make this film so compelling.

Later in the day, approaching nightfall, Shub shows her viewers buildings that are ablaze and collapsing. We see civilians fleeing from burning apartment blocks. Families, clutching bundles of bedding, pour out into the street to escape the flames. Once again, there is a parallel with *The Fall of the Romanov Dynasty* – there are endless refugees, only this time, the images seem instantaneous. Indeed, they are so graphic that they have the freshness of a current world news bulletin. The city burns while firemen desperately try to extinguish the inferno. Next, we are witness to a shot of a crumbling ruin followed by an explicit and sickening image of a young woman's dead body.

Shub's editing pace rhythmically mimics the action. In a frenzy of activity, frantic volunteers dig a child from the rubble. Ambulance medics rush by with the wounded on stretchers and, sadly, also cover the dead with sheets. There are inert bodies strewn on the ground. The only sounds in this entire segment are that of music and sirens and the noise of bombs. The absence of language adds to the grim reality of the mise en scène. Shub finds no need for the unwanted intrusion of a voice-over, as her message is again unmistakable. Finally, when the narration is reintroduced, we look on in horror. Mothers and children are mortally wounded. Grief-stricken onlookers restrain a distraught mother, as her child lies lifeless on the ground. Thanks to the Popular Army and the International Brigades, the capital has been successfully defended against the might of Franco's forces, but, as Shub has indicated, the vicious fighting has come at an enormous cost to the civilian population.

Then Shub transfers the scene to Diaz and La Pasionaria digging trenches in the bright late winter sun in the fields occupying countryside outside Madrid. They stop only for water. This may be seen as a propaganda photo opportunity on the outskirts of the capital, but they seem to labour as diligently as their co-workers and to be unaware of the camera. There is a parallel here with Shub's earlier footage showing the abiding centuries-old connection of the Spanish people to the earth. We watched as a peasant ploughed a field and then, in a later segment, workers labouring in the citrus and almond groves. The land sustains the population. Earlier, the soil was yielding food in abundance, and now it is providing protection to soldiers taking cover in the trenches.

An evacuation of young children from Madrid takes place. They are loaded onto buses to remove them from harm's way as the fighting continues in the streets. Shub fills her visual commentary with vignettes of humanity in all its aspects.

Alas, as Shub indicates, the coming of springtime brings no solace as the war continues to rage. Cavalry on horseback, followed by tank regiments, traverse through the countryside past fruit trees abundantly heavy with delicate blossom. The trees, in all their glory and affirmation of growth and nature, are at odds with these men and the further destruction of the land that must surely follow. As if to emphasize this dichotomy, seemingly oblivious to all this military traffic, a peasant ploughs his field while the army rides by. Soldiers in trenches with rifles cocked await the next onslaught.

We are introduced to General Enrique Lister, who had triumphed commanding the victorious Republican troops at the Battle of Guadalajara in

March 1937 (where Gustav Regler, seen earlier, was wounded). With Lister is his comrade, the Hungarian communist Máté Zalka who was a leader of one of the International Brigades. We are told in the commentary that Zalka was killed a few weeks after this footage was filmed. 'He died a hero's death'– as Shub poignantly reflects – 'we knew and loved him so well'.[29]

She declares that (together with the resounding defeat of the fascists in Madrid late in 1936) 'The people won their first victories in Guadalajara and in the valley of Jarama. The enemy has been stopped.' This refers to the failure of Franco to sever the crucial lifeline, the Madrid–Valencia highway, thereby isolating Madrid. Nevertheless, despite Shub's reassuring assertions, the Battle of Jarama in February 1937 was a bloodbath and stalemate with massive casualties on both sides. Notwithstanding this, Shub is accurate in her assessment of the Battle of Guadalajara because this proved to be a decisive victory for the Republican forces. However, Shub fails to mention that Guadalajara was their final key triumph in the Civil War.

In counterpoint to this vicious turmoil, incongruously, a shepherd gracefully drives his flock as they meander peacefully through the centre of the city. His sheep compete for space on a wide boulevard with pedestrians, cars and a tram on a busy intersection. It is as though Shub wishes to show us that life goes on regardless, but she also inserts practical information to accompany these images. Vishnevsky's simple but informative statements read: 'The peasants give grain to the army. The peasants give livestock to the army.'

We marvel at the angular and glorious abstract shots as Shub inserts Alexander Rodchenko influenced shadows falling on marching soldiers. Rodchenko's imprint lives on in this tribute to Constructivist photographic art, filmed exquisitely by Karmen (Figure 46). This is followed by disturbing images of children with guns, drilling like the 'toy' soldiers that were seen previously in *The Fall of the Romanov Dynasty*.

Just prior to this segment, there are more images of children helping farmers reap the harvest. Vishnevsky's thought-provoking script reads, 'young people did not lag behind the adults . . . they wanted to be worthy of their fathers'.[30] This scene of involvement where children are filmed providing practical support to the Republicans adds to our memory of earlier shots showing children carrying paving stones and sandbags to form barricades in the streets: their innocent splashing in the sea is gone forever.

After documenting the involvement of the children of Spain in the war effort, Shub shows us industrious women sewing and then ironing innumerable calico

Figure 46 Homage to Rodchenko: his Constructivist graphics live on in *Spain*.

kit packs. They are deftly filling them with tobacco, water bottles and other comforting essentials and then parcelling them with string and attaching labels to send them to soldiers at the front. This is another behind-the-scenes portrait of the people of Spain desperate to contribute to the cause.

Soldiers drive by standing on tanks, being cheered on by the local citizens who wave garlands of flowers. In the meantime, in contrast, Franco takes the fascist salute from the Army of Africa as his troops (soldiers and cavalry) roll by ahead of a convoy of vehicles. Further battles rage with a ferocious intensity and stark realism. Words are not needed. Shub includes no commentary but just accompanying music. In all the battle segments, Shub had bowed to the superior knowledge of Vishnevsky, who'd been part of the Baltic Fleet in the First World War, had participated in the October Revolution and fought in the Civil War.[31] As she recounted in her memoirs, Vishnevsky 'was demanding of himself and of me. We argued a lot before coming to a decision. In combat episodes, I did not argue with him and did only what he instructed.'[32] Not discounting the crucial nature of Karmen's daring camerawork courageously filmed in the thick of the action, Vishnevsky's military advice was extremely beneficial. It gave Shub the opportunity to compile and edit these fragments into the most effective, realistic and transfixing tableau.

Instead of peasants tilling the soil to grow crops, now tanks plough across these workers' deserted and open fields. This is accompanied by more brutal yet remarkable genuine action footage showing both ground and aerial bombardment. The relentless destruction unfolds at a quickening pace before our eyes. The sky is studded with warplanes. Some are shot down and spiral from the heavens, with plumes of black smoke trailing behind them as they plummet towards the earth. Karmen's war newsreels are frightening and sobering due to their unmistakable authenticity. This is true nonfiction film heightening the sense of reality. There is nothing choreographed for the camera. Unlike *The Fall of the Romanov Dynasty* where Shub had to make do with more impersonal and far more limited supplies of vastly inferior quality archival material, in *Spain* we observe soldiers at close quarters firing machine guns, struggling with artillery, racing through streets on foot with their weapons, officers giving the command to fire or men creeping over rough terrain to sneak up upon enemy lines. Karmen's footage is compelling, driving the spectator to the heart of the fighting.

Shub presents us with an overview of not only bitter military engagement but also of the identities supporting the Popular Front (La Pasionaria, Diaz, Regler, Marty and later, Lister and Zalka). Apart from the political figures and those leading the Republican Army, Shub records the youthful faces of those soldiers in close-up as they struggle for liberation against Franco's Nationalists. She produces a sense of familiarization, even one of intimacy, through her depiction of the troops. Welcomed by villagers loyal to the cause, Republican soldiers scrub pro-Hitler graffiti from the walls of a building in the liberated town. During a brief period of respite, the exhausted and grimy troops wash themselves. They cook vats of steaming food. One soldier mends his jacket with a needle and thread. We observe them as they peel and eat citrus fruit, read newspapers or write letters home to loved ones. In these simple everyday tasks, the audience can feel a connection to real individuals. Conversely, Franco and his Army of Africa are depersonalized. They are always seen en masse from a more distant and menacing vantage point, either in a mid or long shot.

At this juncture, Shub pulls her audience firmly back to the Soviet Union inserting an image of a banner with the word 'Chapaev' embroidered across it. Obviously, it belongs to Soviet troops who, in truth, numbered a very small proportion of soldiers fighting against Franco. Nonetheless, Shub's audience in the Soviet Union (as well as being proud of their country's participation in supporting communist factions in Spain) would relate to this reference due to the outstanding popularity and rapturous reception of the film *Chapayev* in their homeland. This allusion to Vasily Chapaev, their admired and decorated military hero, could pertain to the patriotic and selfless sacrifice of the Red Army in their earlier Civil War. Not only this but it could also parallel their battle (against the anti-Bolshevik Whites) with the armed struggle of the Spanish Republicans against the fascists. Additionally, Shub uses this thematic link to emphasize the support given by Stalin and the Soviet people to the cause of the Republicans.

From the patriotic heart of the Soviet Union and the cult of Chapaev, Shub returns her focus firmly back to Spain to give her audience another single intertitle: 'Ebro'. At the Battle of Ebro, the PCE, acronym for the Communist Party of Spain [Partido Comunista de España], fought against Franco's forces. It was a campaign that took place from July to November 1938 and was a major military operation in the Spanish Civil War. We view whole segments of graphic realism that illustrate this long, protracted and bloody skirmish. What Shub neglects to mention is that, disastrously, the Republicans were unable to sustain their early gains in what would become a decisive, brutal and bitter offensive. Although initially in the ascendancy, this slaughter ended in defeat for the Popular Army due to the military superiority of their fascist enemy. Battle-scarred, exhausted men retreat across the River Ebro. Yet the tone of the voice-over is one of enthusiasm with lots of hoorays: 'Death to fascism!' and 'Long live the Republic!'

La Pasionaria comes to rally the troops and give them moral support. Shub simply utters: 'Here is La Pasionaria. We salute our faithful companion!' In every frame, Dolores Ibárruri is presented as an inspiration to her people, whether giving impassioned speeches at political rallies, digging trenches to defend Madrid or visiting soldiers at the front.

Next, Shub informs us 'everything is silent among the ruins of bombed houses in the coastal towns'. In the drizzling rain, displaced persons drag a cart over-laden with their possessions while others have bundles strapped to their backs. At the harbour side in Barcelona, in a much earlier scene, we'd witnessed teeming crowds of joyous Republicans at the beginning of the war welcoming the arrival of the International Brigades. This elation has now turned to grief. Now the viewer watches a scene of heartbreak as mothers and fathers are separated from their weeping children. The latter, carrying pitiful little suitcases and wearing name tags on their coats, are being evacuated by sea. Shub focuses on a small boy crying. As the ocean liner pulls away from the port to safety, all the children are on deck, fluttering their handkerchiefs (like a line of white birds) in farewell. These hankies are waved in sorrow and not with excitement and anticipation as the audience had viewed in the bullfight segment shown near the beginning of Shub's film.

We are party to yet another leave-taking, also evoking deep melancholy, about to occur in Barcelona. As a preliminary sign of what is to follow, Vishnevsky's narration presents the audience with the bleak statistics that 'there were 25,000 soldiers of the International Brigades and 5,000 have lost their lives'. Now we observe a sequence showing a massive withdrawal of the International Brigades striding through the countryside on foot while others travel in vehicle convoys. This is a prelude to the emotionally charged farewell of the much-depleted International Brigades who marched for the last time along the main streets of Barcelona in the middle of November 1938. Leading the procession are girls in Spanish national costumes. La Pasionaria, Diaz and other political dignitaries follow them. There are young women holding bouquets of flowers, and people massed on the streets and leaning over balconies. Everyone waves and applauds the International Brigades, their flags unfurled, as they parade through a sea of ticker tape. They stop only when small children run into the middle of their ranks to embrace their brave champions as they pass by. La Pasionaria pays tribute to them: 'Today many are departing. Thousands remain, shrouded in Spanish earth, never forgotten by the Spanish people.... Long live the heroes of the International Brigades!'

In bitter contrast with the valorous deeds and self-sacrifice of the International Brigades, Segismundo Casado and José Miaja, commanders of the Republican Army, are seen examining a map of Madrid. Shub angrily refers to them as 'Traitors... preparing to inflict a death blow to the Spanish people'. Nevertheless, the casualties and destruction wreaked by the terrifying shelling of their towns and cities, the civilian population has been further demoralized not only by the departure of the International Brigades but also due to the convincing victory of the Nationalists (because of their vastly superior professional troops, aerial might and artillery power). Added to this tragic situation, Spaniards are dying of starvation. In desperation, under these devastating circumstances, Casado, Miaja and others attempted to broker a peace treaty with Franco and the Nationalists. Although Casado and Miaja fought for the Republican cause, now they are viewed as collaborators at best, turncoats at worst. As Vishnevsky angrily remarks in his script, which is shown in bold letters: 'LET THE TRAITORS OPEN THE GATES OF MADRID TO FRANCO'.[33] From this scene of capitulation to the enemy by leaders of the Republican forces, Shub brings us to look at the cost of the conflict as she displays yet again the appalling outcome of war.

We observe, at close quarters, the effect of the hostilities on the civilian population. Entire villages have been reduced to rubble, leading to a never-ending stream of refugees. People carry furniture and bundles of other household goods, and all are bent under the weight of carting their life's possessions on their backs. Mothers, some also holding babies, have enormous packs strapped to their bodies and struggle along with tiny children walking by their side. Somewhat absurdly, a man hurries along the road clutching a single chair. A little boy balances an enormous suitcase on his head. They are all united in a common purpose as they trudge towards the French border crossing, seeking safe haven. Republican soldiers divest themselves of their uniforms and weapons and, having disarmed, are permitted by customs to cross over into France towards an uncertain fate.

A tearful Ibárruri with grief and exhaustion showing clearly on her face gives her final address to the nation with the Spanish flag draped behind her. Shub quotes from Ibárruri's speech:

> They have trampled on our land. . . . Be strong Madrid . . . Listen to the voice of Spain and the cry of her aching heart. This proud and free people will defend their independence and will not bow down before aggression. . . . The Spanish people with weapons in their hands . . . will never be defeated. The people will not surrender. They will never kneel.

Tragically for her Republican comrades, despite having fought so valiantly, they will have no choice in the matter. On 26 January 1939, Barcelona was to surrender to the Nationalists. Two months later, Franco's forces marched into Madrid on 27 March, and he announced his victory on 1 April. The dreams for a democratic Spain were over.

A car seen at the beginning of Shub's documentary, prior to the Civil War, re-enters Madrid. Once more, everything appears to be strangely normal. Now Shub inserts the earlier image of a defiant Cybele and her lion-drawn chariot, but here she is reversing the order of her original sequence. On this occasion, Cybele's sculpture precedes that of the statue of Cervantes rather than coming after it. However, mother earth's lions have been damaged by small arms fire and to emphasize this, Shub focuses on an extreme close-up of the deeply pitted stone to show the aftermath of the hostilities. Fortunately, Cybele herself and the memorial to Cervantes have both survived intact despite the heavy assault inflicted on Madrid. The inference is that culture will not genuflect to the fascist tyrants and that literature and art have lived to tell the tale in spite of all the surrounding devastation.

Once again from Cybele and Cervantes, the camera focus returns to Ibárruri, but on this occasion, she is not alerting the populace to the threat posed by Gil-Robles and Franco. Almost three years have elapsed, and this is her final speech before fleeing into exile. Much admired by the people and a tireless defender of the Spanish proletariat, La Pasionaria represents the mother figure of the Republican movement, the personification of Cybele. On this historic occasion, to emphasize her popularity, Shub adds footage of massive crowds who have gathered to listen to Ibárruri's emotional farewell oration. There are also shots of Republican soldiers standing to attention and others giving their clenched-fist anti-fascist salute. At the conclusion of La Pasionaria's public appearance, the Republican soldiers march away from the camera into the distance and out of the frame forever.

Joris Ivens and *The Spanish Earth*: The Delicate Balance between the Dramatization of Fiction Film and the Authenticity of Documentary

Surprisingly, apart from Shub's *Spain*, *The Spanish Earth* by Joris Ivens is one of the only other full-length documentaries on the Spanish Civil War readily available today. Made for the American market, primarily in order to raise funds for the war effort, it premièred in Hollywood in July 1937. Its format and approach are very different from that of Shub's.

The commentary of *The Spanish Earth* was both scripted and spoken by Ernest Hemingway in his role as a roving war correspondent. Hemingway's narration shows the writer as witness not only to the daily practice of the filmmaker (Ivens) and his camera operator (John Ferno) but also, more significantly, as a chronicler of the Spanish Civil War and the Republican cause. Therefore, it is a form of collaboration between two authors – Ivens as director and creator of the filmic vision and Hemingway as the writer and reader of the text. This mirrors Shub's collaboration with Vishnevsky.

However, Hemingway's journalistic style at times has a tendency towards overt subjectivity. As Joris Ivens noted when *The Spanish Earth* was screened:

'there were demands for more "objectivity". . . . My only answer was that a documentary filmmaker has to have an opinion on such vital issues as fascism or anti-fascism – he [sic] has to have feelings about these issues, if his work is to have any dramatic or emotional or art value.'[34]

In contrast to Shub, who doesn't use excessive dialogue to support her argument and prefers concise language, in *The Spanish Earth* Hemingway sometimes displays a propensity for a more romantic use of direct speech. Issues of impartiality aside, this mars his testimony as a witness. It is made obvious by the following examples, which show Hemingway in fictional mode rather than as a documentary observer in the field. A soldier parts from his wife and toddler – no words are necessary to convey these heart-wrenching images beautifully constructed by John Ferno. Occupying just a few frames, the visuals total no more than nine seconds. Yet Hemingway's narration, to accompany this man and woman seated next to their baby, carries on over multiple shots that follow. The dialogue between them is mere conjecture on his part.

Hemingway's conversation relating to this moment in time is as follows: 'They say the old goodbyes that sound the same in any language. She says she'll wait.' At this juncture the little family group is permanently out of the frame. Nonetheless, he continues: 'He says he'll come back. He knows she'll wait. Who knows what for or where the shelling is? Nobody knows if he'll come back. "Take care of the kid," he says. "I will," she says. They both know that when they move you on out in trucks, it's to a battle.' As can be ascertained from this quotation, Hemingway's accompanying script dilutes the power of the touching camera shots that render words redundant.

Similarly, a few segments prior to this, there are the expressive portraits of the faces of the people of Madrid during the evacuation of their city. We view mothers lifting their children onto a lorry being assisted by soldiers. There is footage of a grey-haired matriarch observing the proceedings. The pitiful mise en scène is composed with commanding artistry and needs no amplification. The audience sees an impactful public information poster with the words 'Evacuation of Madrid' written across it in a large bold font. This same frame is repeated and flashed across the screen at two separate intervals during this brief incident. The message is abundantly clear, and no oral interjection is necessary. In spite of this, Hemingway breaks the spell shrouding this poignant sequence. He intervenes and, acting as their mouthpiece, as he had done with the young soldier leaving his wife and infant, Hemingway constructs another imagined conversation: 'But where will we go? Where can we live? What can we do for a living? I won't go, I'm too old.' These musings are purportedly linked to the thoughts of the silent elderly lady, the spectator of this heartfelt scene.

Unlike Vishnevsky's restrained and non-emotive language, in these two instances Hemingway's conversational text is unnecessary. It would have been more appropriate in his famed novel *For Whom the Bell Tolls* rather than in a documentary. Yet there are moments in *The Spanish Earth* where his voice-over narration is ideal. By way of distinction, Shub's more measured approach in *Spain* is worthy of comparison. She has some heartrending scenes centred on the evacuation of children, and these segments contain minimal language. It is far more effective than Hemingway's use of the spoken word, poetic though it may be. In addition, Shub has a prolonged filmic episode concerning the tragedy of the refugees, and yet the only voice-over in this lengthy part of the action is a matter of a few short sentences interspersed amongst a plethora of images: 'With the arrival of the fascists, people are forced to leave their homes: the places where they have always lived. They go. They take such grief with them.' Vishnevsky's brevity is factual yet sensitive. And then later: 'The police search them at the French border with Spain.' His information is delivered succinctly and used with restraint, whereas Hemingway's commentary, in the extracts referred to, has far less impact.

Just as Hemingway's monologues occasionally seem contrived, similarly Ivens had no qualms about orchestrating or staging events to bring his story to life. As he asserted: 'I could not agree with the Vertov approach to this big question of documentary truth.'[35] Ivens's premise about Vertov's philosophy and the issue of fact and reality in nonfiction film is incorrect; indeed, it is false: although Vertov erroneously claimed that his scenes were unstaged. In direct contrast to this assumption, Vertov's blatant re-enactments were raised publicly in the film print media. As early as 1925, Viktor Shklovsky had been critical of Vertov and his Cine-Eyes in an article 'The Semantics of Cinema'. The plot, according to Shklovsky, was embedded in the essence of cinema. Where was Vertov's plot? Where was the meaningful presentation of reality? Furthermore, in 1926, Shklovsky challenged what he believed was the misrepresentation of fact versus fiction in Vertov's films in the journal *Soviet Screen*. The article was 'Where is Dziga Vertov Striding?' [Kuda shagaet Dziga Vertov?]. Added to this fact when Ivens went to study nonfiction film in the USSR, these controversies about truth and reality and Vertov's methodology were common knowledge in the film community.

In his film *Song of Heroes* [Pesn o geroiakh, 1932] made in the USSR, Ivens openly justifies the choreographing of a Komsomol 'storm night' 'in order to emphasize its real meaning. . . . This enabled us to take all the close ups and medium shots of the faces we wanted, to direct the movement of the trucks and the torches.'[36] Whatever his motivation, Ivens was not averse to re-staging a scene if it brought a greater 'authenticity' to his thematic approach. For him, 'the re-enactment introduces a very subjective and personal factor in making documentary films: the integrity of the director—his understanding and approach to reality . . . he is, as an artist, creating a new reality.'[37] This pronouncement is compatible with Vertov's melange of art and documented reality. Similarly, Ivens refers to *The Spanish Earth* as a 'subtle half-fiction, half-documentary'.[38]

Without a doubt, it is a splendidly filmed, engrossing and stimulating work. *The Spanish Earth* is to be applauded, but, as his declaration attests, Ivens's approach to nonfiction film differs radically from Shub's. Accordingly, Ivens combines fact with fiction effortlessly as he parallel cuts the story of the hamlet of Fuentidueña with the defence of Madrid and the Republican Army's fight for survival. East of Madrid, Fuentidueña is highlighted to show how the parched Spanish fields can flower by the simple act of installing irrigation. Moreover, as a result of this process, the villagers are now able to grow extra crops to support and feed beleaguered Madrid and the troops defending it. The overriding motif of the film is, of course, the vital importance of the Spanish earth: from the microcosm of the pro-Republican farmers cultivating the soil to the Popular Army's battle to retain the land. Like Flaherty and Buñuel before him, Ivens's scenes of village life are partially dramatized, and although overall they are extremely successful, sometimes they appear manufactured in their structural composition. Although diverging markedly from the methodology of Shub's nonfiction film, and only concentrating on a very select narrative rather than an overview of the Civil War, *The Spanish Earth* is a highly recommended and successful work combining fact and fiction.

'The End is yet to come'

With an often winning marriage of nonfiction and fiction film in order to accentuate his stance, Ivens's work is undeniably accomplished. However, Shub's unstaged documentary possesses a depth and added vibrancy not available to Ivens's and his partial rendition of the Civil War. Nevertheless, both filmmakers have a similarity of purpose, ideologically and politically. Consequently, centred on the collision of totalitarian fascism against the democratic ideals of republicanism, both Ivens and Shub's works are imbued with a message of hope and triumph.

Just as Shub's first image in *Spain* is of Mediterranean pines, she concludes her film with a frame containing a palm tree next to the Spanish flag. Both these specific genera of pines and palms flourished throughout the Republican strongholds of Spain. The palm tree is seen in shots of both Barcelona and Madrid and also lining the crucial arterial road linking Valencia with Madrid. During the conflict, the audience saw palm trees thriving in the streets of central Madrid, seemingly impervious to the bombing, as people raced in fear of their lives towards the underground shelters. These sturdy species, symbols of growth, renewal and shelter are still there despite the chaos and destruction of war. The trees stand firmly in the soil steadfastly grounded alongside the ravages of battle-scarred cities and the countryside. Shub may see them as life forces giving hope for the future. The Spanish flag proudly waves in the light breeze, and this is where Shub ends her saga. The last words of Vishnevsky after the fluttering flag on the black screen are 'the End is yet to come! . . .'[39]

The sobering thought for the contemporary viewer is the knowledge that, despite Shub's attempt at a buoyant and triumphant finale showcasing the departure of the valiant International Brigades, the Republicans were not to be victorious. On the contrary, all that they had fought for was in vain. Shub was aware that she was presenting a one-sided narrative, but there was little choice. She wanted to work and she wanted to live. Disconcerting though it may have been for her, a misleading commentary that suited the Kremlin and yet used authentic footage to substantiate this viewpoint was the only option. Vishnevsky's final words of optimistic and breathtaking misinformation show that he understood this painful reality too.

As a result, Shub gives no indication of the brutal realities ahead after the defeat of the Republican Popular Army and the beginning of Franco's dictatorship. Her necessarily skewed interpretation of the Spanish Civil had erroneously steered her audience to believe that the Republicans would live to fight another day. There is no mention of their resounding defeat by Nationalist forces that had ended in the complete capitulation of Madrid in March 1939. After three bitter years of conflict and savagery, all the cherished hopes for democratic rule were shattered. We are all too aware of the resultant decades of suppression, cruelty and misery under the repressive yoke of fascism and its implementer Franco.

Additionally, for a present-day audience, this ineluctable realization is also a grim reminder of the parallels to be drawn by the dictatorship of Franco and the steel boot of Stalin over his similarly downtrodden subjects.

Shub's dilemma aside, her panoramic interpretation of the Spanish Civil War provides a valuable historical perspective chronicling as it does a momentous event in twentieth-century history. Equally, *Spain* transcends the didacticism of a dry history lesson, and, justifiably, Jay Leyda regards this work of Shub's as 'one of the sure masterpieces of compilation – exquisitely precise in its thinking and cutting, from the quiet opening to the tragic end'.[40] Furthermore, he considers,

> Its brilliant execution is all to communicate a feeling, an experience – akin to a great work of history, not objective or rounded, but personal and passionate. Though inadequacy of material must often have compelled the elimination of certain sequences, one does not sense this in the finished film: every idea that is touched is touched fully, yet without the boredom that so often accompanies the thorough.[41]

In addition, Leyda believes that 'Its combination of passion and artistic control makes it an enduring work of art that should last as long as celluloid'.[42] Thus, in spite of the brutal subject matter, Shub's film is one of visual splendour and fascination. Her absorbing examination of a society, its mores and its politics has been embodied in this, her final nonfiction film of note. It is a remarkable full-length documentary on the Civil War and superior in many ways to Frédéric Rossif's deserved award-winning *Mourir à Madrid* [To Die in Madrid, 1963] made decades later: a work which was heavily influenced by Shub's film. In Leyda's opinion, Rossif's gloriously shot documentary owes much to Shub and is paying obvious homage to *Spain*. Rossif was nominated for an Academy Award for Best Documentary in 1965 and won the BAFTA for Best Documentary in 1967. In fact, Leyda considers that both Rossif's *Mourir à Madrid* and Annelie and Andrew Thorndike's *Das russische Wunder* [The Russian Wonder, 1964][43] 'are tributes to Shub, even to the point of borrowing ideas and sequences as well as footage from her work – but I believe that she also would have seen this as a tribute to her as a pioneer. More vitally, both films learned method, clarity and thoroughness from Shub.'[44] Made twenty-four years after Shub's *Spain*, Rossif's film is undeniably technically superior and some of the cinematography is of great beauty. However, it not only borrows extensively from Shub's documentary but also uses a very distinctive piece of music from her film, which Rossif inserts three times at various intervals. He never shows Diaz. Ibárruri is only glimpsed.

The content has none of Shub's depth and research. Narratively, *Mourir à Madrid* is not as well rounded or cohesive as Shub's chronicle of the Spanish Civil War.

Deserving of a wide audience *Spain* is an all-encompassing work of considerable value and, as such, is worthy of commendation and acclaim. Regrettably, due to circumstances beyond her control, Shub was never to reach such heights again, and the remainder of her career consisted of demoralizing and inferior work. Nonetheless, the five films contained within this book merit the full attention of not only film scholars and students but also anyone with an interest in cinema. Moreover, they deserve to be regularly screened as well as carefully preserved and commemorated as highly significant works in the history of documentary film.

Conclusion

Justifiably, despite Mayakovsky's praise for 'the extraordinary films created by Esfir Shub' and Eisenstein's unceasing support, Shub felt the immense frustration and disappointment of non-fulfilment and foiled opportunities.[1] To corroborate this, in his introduction to her book, *My Life – Cinematography* [Zhizn moya – kinematograf], published after Shub's death, the avant-garde artist and filmmaker Sergei Yutkevich examined Shub's disillusionment with what she believed was her lack of professional and public acknowledgement. Yutkevich asserted that 'in this book, the joy of accomplishment is mixed with the bitterness of non-recognition'.[2] This feeling of disenchantment is apparent when, in a letter that Shub sent to her friend, the celebrated artist and sculptor Vera Mukhina, in 1953, Shub wrote poignantly: 'I cannot help thinking that I have failed to contribute to the art of my homeland by even a tenth of what I really hoped to achieve. Cinema is, you see, my whole life. I didn't have the chance and now it is too late.'[3]

Correspondingly, Yutkevich summarizes Shub's occupational hardships in his overview of her career:

> The path that Esfir Shub walked was not 'strewn with rose petals'. Not only did she continue to struggle with the entrenched tendency to underestimate the value of her chosen area, but also the historical period itself constantly presented new demands. The socialist art of the mid-thirties presented her and all the artists of Soviet cinema with unique problems.[4]

The euphemistic expression 'unique problems', which Yutkevich could not elaborate on, can be readily interpreted as a thinly veiled reference to the perils of life under Stalin. Aesopian language was the norm for Soviet readers.

Hence, in this reappraisal of Shub's oeuvre, I have argued that she deserves a far more prominent place in the history of film studies. As a result, this monograph gives due recognition to Shub's pioneering introduction of the compilation genre, to her form of Constructivist nonfiction film and to her influential contribution to the development of documentary cinema.

Accordingly, it must be stated that the effect of Shub's Constructivist compilation methodology extends far wider afield than the USSR. In 1972 Sergei Yutkevich defined her global significance in the following terms:

> A wonderful discovery was made that is connected with the name of Esfir Shub. For several decades, movies assembled from old and new newsreels have been shown throughout the world. This genre is now universally recognised ... Joris Ivens, Frank Capra ... and other famous creators ... have used this method.[5]

Shub's marked impact on the direction of the documentary genre not only in the Soviet Union but globally may be said to derive primarily from her influence on Joris Ivens, the Dutch champion of socialist documentary. This contention is, of course, rendered problematic by the very scarcity of direct historical records that may support it. Nevertheless, by giving attention to the dialectics between the documented aspects of their historical circumstances and the films themselves, it is reasonable to suggest that, through Shub's early mentoring of Ivens and the latter's subsequent emergence as (in the opinion of the film scholar Robert Sklar) 'the most important political filmmaker of the decade – perhaps of the century', her approach to nonfiction film would have been assimilated into the early patterning of documentary cinema.[6]

While recalling in her memoirs that: 'Joris Ivens was as close to me as [Mikhail] Kaufman through his art work in combination with his social and political agitation', significantly, Shub describes the early work of Ivens as highly 'expressive and emotional'.[7] She observes that Ivens 'was very young when he came ... to our country', and his work, at that stage, comprised of imaginative romanticized odes such as his lyrical studies *The Bridge* [De Brug, 1928] and *Rain* [Regen, 1929].[8] *Rain* was made in Amsterdam in 1929, just prior to Ivens leaving for the Soviet Union. As a result, Shub's imprint on Ivens at this nascent stage of his career may be clearly identified with the fact that his work began to move, markedly, from the sensitive and artistic poetic étude to the overtly agitational nonfiction film (for which he was to become recognized as he worked his way across the globe). Shub was the leading exponent of this specific form of film genre in the USSR at the time of Ivens's film studies there. Not only this, but as mentioned earlier, in September 1932, Shub was appointed to the staff of VGIK [All-Union State Institute of Cinematography], where she taught montage studies. She also conducted workshops from 1933 to 1935. In addition, Shub was a mentor for graduating directors and advised on film scripts.

Moreover, Ivens's editor Helen van Dongen (1909–2006), who divulged in an interview in *Film Quarterly* that she 'began her career as general assistant and pupil to Joris Ivens on his films *De Brug* . . . and *Regen*', also showed evidence of Shub's cinematic perspective and technique.⁹ In fact, in his book *Films Beget Films* (an analysis of the compilation film genre), Jay Leyda makes a direct comparison between Shub and van Dongen, noting the similarity of their styles.¹⁰ It should be noted that van Dongen, possibly encouraged by Ivens's journey to the Soviet Union, visited there 'in the mid 1930s . . . to study with leading Soviet filmmakers', as expressed by Bob Mastrangelo, in his obituary on van Dongen.¹¹ This coincides with the time of Shub's tenure at VGIK.

While van Dongen was to end her career in the United States, where she collaborated with Robert Flaherty on *The Land* in 1942 and *Louisiana Story* in 1948, Ivens had already made an important contribution to left-wing documentary filmmaking in that country in the previous decade. In fact, Ivens has been credited as having been extremely 'influential' in the creation of Nykino's 'political film output' in the 1930s.¹² 'Dedicated to socialist principles', Nykino was a breakaway movement that resulted from the disbandment, due to unresolved internal disputes, of the Workers' Film and Photo League.¹³ Established in 1930 in New York City, and simply referred to as the Film and Photo League (FPL) by 1932, this was an agitational documentary group that 'sought to educate, inform and politicize' the working class.¹⁴ Significantly, 'Under the auspices of Workers' International Relief, an international communist organization that ran its own film studio in Moscow', members of the FPL came into contact with both the work and theories that Shub had been championing in the Soviet Union after she commenced production on her compilation trilogy in August 1926.¹⁵ When screened in New York, her documentary *Cannons and Tractors?* [*Today* in the Soviet Union] was said to have inspired the FPL.

Furthermore, Ivens and Nykino introduced Pare Lorentz to the nonfiction film form. According to the documentary historian Erik Barnouw, Lorentz (a writer and cinema enthusiast) had absolutely no experience in the skills of filmmaking.¹⁶ However, working with the foremost members of Nykino during 1936 and 1937, Lorentz was to become a major presence in American documentary. Like Shub before him, he 'tried to create films that provided ideological justification' for, in his case, agrarian reform, as highlighted by his compilation *The Plow That Broke the Plains* in 1936.¹⁷

Additionally, it should be noted that Leyda was a prominent associate of the FPL. After returning from the Soviet Union where his film studies with

Eisenstein had culminated in his work as an assistant cameraman on *Bezhin Meadow* [*Bezhin lug*, 1935–1937], he became a valued member of Nykino. It is feasible therefore that as a vocal supporter of Shub's compilation film form (and her documentaries of the 1930s), that Leyda may have discussed her highly relevant genre with this group of filmmakers. In fact, Leyda commends Lorentz's emerging compilations as 'newsreels skilfully cut' because 'in this context... the footage showed a strength that it had never shown in its original uses'.[18] Shub's successful expression of this precise feature in *The Fall of the Romanov Dynasty* in the previous decade (as well as her committed theorizing and advocating for the principles of nonfiction film both in written texts and public forums) should be acknowledged as comprising an essential part of the sources informing Lorentz's film learning via the influence of Ivens and Nykino, even if perhaps Lorentz was not aware of this fact himself.

Ivens, van Dongen and Lorentz aside, Yutkevich firmly believed that both *cinéma vérité* and direct cinema owed a debt to Shub. Yutkevich highlights her 'daring experiment,' a 'pioneering discovery' in documentary reporting that would not be used until three decades later by '[Jean] Rouch and [Chris] Marker'.[19] When Shub introduced 'synchronous filming' in her first sound film *K.Sh.E.* in 1932, she deviated stylistically from her earlier compilation genre, as there was no inclusion of archival footage in this documentary.[20] Nonetheless, with its use of a roving camera in reportage mode, *K.Sh.E.* continued to adhere strictly to Shub's filmic creed regarding the authenticity of its material. Thus, Shub welcomed the newly discovered science of film sound with zest. The arrival of this cinematic medium offered the potential to enhance the transmission of reality further in Shub's documentaries. Accordingly, she was opposed intensely to post-synchronized sound and other artificialities created in a studio. With specific reference to the success of *K.Sh.E.*, it was Sergei Drobashenko's belief that 'Shub's film became a document of the time'.[21]

When *K.Sh.E.* was screened in Ankara for the first president of modern Turkey, Mustafa Kemal Atatürk, Yutkevich was present.[22] In his analysis of *K.Sh.E.*, Yutkevich depicted it as representing Shub's 'next decisive step – from montage of documentary sequences filmed by others, to filming her own material'.[23] Yutkevich elaborates:

> [In *K.Sh.E.* Shub] conducts one daring experiment, the true originality of which would only be appreciated much later. Thirty years afterwards, foreign theoreticians would applaud the discovery of direct cinema, synchronous

reporting by [Richard] Leacock and [Robert] Drew, [Jean] Rouch and [Chris] Marker; forgetting the pioneering experiment by Shub, who dared to perform synchronous filming of a factory meeting using the heavy and unwieldy apparatus of the period. This is not a stilted official function but a passionate self-critical debate . . . the participants are young factory workers who do not pose for the camera and don't seek self-exposure. . . . The result is a collective portrait of the thirties, lively and authentic and therefore priceless evidence of the unrepeatable enthusiasm of the early Soviet years . . . Shub's achievement was that, without staging the meeting, she was able to present the event as totally real and recorded it with the exactness and care of a reporter.[24]

Cinéma-vérité is defined as 'a style of documentary filmmaking emerging in France at the end of the 1950s that emphasized the use of hand-held cameras and synchronous sound as technologies for filming "truth"'.[25] This movement's leader, Jean Rouch, acknowledged that, in his opinion, it was 'Dziga Vertov, who completely invented the kind of film that we do today'.[26] Although there is no known evidence of a direct link between Shub and Rouch, it was Shub, rather than Vertov (as inaccurately credited by Rouch), who first introduced 'hand-held cameras and synchronous sound' to Soviet film (the defining elements of *cinéma vérité* and direct cinema), in *K.Sh.E.* Accordingly, in verification of this claim, Lilya Kaganovsky confirms that Shub 'is credited with using the first ever sync-sound recording in the Soviet Union'.[27]

There is nothing to suggest that, given his familiarity with Vertov, Rouch was similarly conversant with Shub's films or written texts on film theory. It may be sheer coincidence that in Shub's journal article 'Non-acted Film' [Neigrovaya filma] in 1929, she discusses how her aim was 'filming real people in their everyday behaviour'.[28] Shub is not concerned 'that the various types of equipment will disrupt their normal behaviour because even if they are posing in front of the camera, even if they are "acting" they are showing themselves'.[29] In 1964 Jay Leyda was the sole curator of a film festival at London's National Film Theatre, which showcased the compilation film and foregrounded Shub. In the same year, Rouch was to reiterate the key argument of Shub's essay in an interview with James Blue. Rouch makes the following pronouncement: 'when people are being recorded, the reactions they have are always infinitely more sincere than those they have when they are not being recorded . . . they begin to express what they have within themselves'.[30] There is a correlation between Shub's essay and Rouch's interview. Although there is no tangible proof, Shub exerted an influence on Jean Rouch and *cinéma vérité*, even though her connection with

Rouch may have only been indirectly through Chris Marker. Marker, a fellow Frenchman, is often linked with Rouch because they were both participants in the groundbreaking French cinematic movement 'The New Wave' [La Nouvelle Vague] and pioneers of *cinéma vérité*.

Added to this, Joris Ivens eventually joined forces with Marker to make *Loin du Vietnam* [Far from Vietnam, 1967], a film in which Marker used contributions from leading directors of the New Wave, such as Jean-Luc Godard and Alain Resnais. In this collaboration, Marker was in complete harmony with Shub's fundamental ideals as he created 'collective film-making towards a political purpose ... [of] anonymity'.[31]

Furthermore, in 1993, Marker released *The Last Bolshevik* [Le tombeau d'Alexandre]. It was a compilation, which paid homage to the filmmaker Alexander Medvedkin.[32] At the beginning of this documentary, Marker uses a sequence used so ironically by Shub in *The Fall of the Romanov Dynasty* juxtaposed with segments from two fiction films: Medvedkin's *Happiness* [Schaste, 1935] and Yakov Protazanov's *Aelita* [1924].[33] Marker inserts the home movie footage of the tsar, tsarina, their children, family and courtiers dancing on the deck of their cruiser, which Shub had found and utilized with such impact in *The Fall of the Romanov Dynasty*. Marker then distorts the cavorting revellers as he dissolves the sequence into a dreamlike image. This transmutes into Shub's long procession of the privileged classes at the tercentenary festivities for the Romanov rulers, as they strut past the obedient plebs. In this way, Marker acknowledges and recycles Shub's first nonfiction film and in doing so creates a fresh and new compilation scenario. Therefore, Marker's bond with Rouch and *cinéma vérité*, his use of the compilation genre as both a film form and an ideological tool and his professional association with Ivens links him to the early nonfiction film of Shub, her cinematic theory and praxis.

In Leyda's film festival highlighting Shub's far-reaching impact on the compilation nonfiction documentary, he paid tribute to her considerable role in the formation of this genre. As he phrased it in his draft essay for the festival catalogue, every film that he 'chose for the series – whether by the Thorndikes [Annelie and Andrew] or [Erwin] Leiser,[34] whether from Ireland or Denmark or France – seemed [to be] a direct descendant from the pioneering work of Shub'.[35] Moreover, in reinforcement of Leyda's declaration, Drobashenko believes:

> Shub developed many modes of film journalism and documentary film journalism that are now widely used. The political method of compiling

archival footage found in the . . . work of filmmakers [such as] the Thorndikes, the Soviet director Medvedkin and many others has its roots in the historical documentaries made by Shub at the end of the 1920s.[36]

Furthermore, the film scholar and documentary maker Michael Chanan in his book on documentary film states that 'Andrew and Annelie Thorndike . . . assimilated the methods of Shub'.[37]

In light of my assertions regarding Shub's international influence, it is significant that the works in the National Film Festival specifically selected in this 'homage to Shub' (as Leyda phrased it) included the screening of films by both Joris Ivens and Chris Marker.

Correspondingly, a connection can be drawn between Shub and direct cinema. Robert Drew and Richard Leacock both appear side by side with Rouch and Marker in Yutkevich's quote linking them all to Shub. Direct cinema is defined as 'the name used in the United States, as an alternative for *cinéma vérité*, for new documentary practices of the 1960s using hand-held cameras with synchronous sound'.[38] The film scholar Paul Wells describes the methodology of Robert Drew and his direct cinema team (Richard Leacock, D. A. Pennebaker and Albert Maysles) in the documentary *Primary*. Made in 1960, *Primary* follows John F. Kennedy as he campaigns against Hubert Humphrey with both of these candidates competing for the Democratic Party's presidential nomination. As Wells perceives it, in *Primary*, by operating 'shoulder mounted camerawork . . . its intimacy and immediacy appeared to record "actuality" in a way that seemed to demonstrate historical authenticity and accuracy'.[39] Likewise this was precisely Shub's purpose, over thirty-five years before direct cinema, when she used a similar technique and motivation as she filmed *K.Sh.E.*

Both Yutkevich and Drobashenko consider, as does Chanan,[40] that *K.Sh.E.* is a milestone in documentary film practice. Moreover, with reference to *K.Sh.E.*, Chanan asserts that 'there is no other documentary of the time [that he is] aware of that works in quite this way'.[41] Within *K.Sh.E.* Shub conveys, as Drobashenko records, 'a single episode in the huge . . . reconstruction effort' of the Soviet Union.[42] There are several sequences where Shub and her crew travel from site to site, recording political gatherings and their speakers, using synchronous sound. Again, this is reflected in direct cinema, which likewise is 'heightening the idea that "reality" is being directly observed'.[43] Just as in direct cinema, 'Shub was not afraid to show people looking into the camera, frowning at the bright lights or faltering before the camera because the camera bothered them . . . their reaction to the camera... helps to enhance the credibility that the author sought to achieve.'⁴⁴ In Chanan's opinion, *K.Sh.E.* is 'a film, in which propaganda and artistic experiment are still combined in a Constructivist spirit, pointing way beyond the norms of documentary narrative in the 30s.'⁴⁵

Nonetheless, in an environment where Shub and her comrades wished for creative freedom, she was always optimistic for a better world. Waiting for the impossible, she believed that documentary could in fact demonstrate the longed-for Soviet utopia. Even more so and consequently, for her, nonfiction film was an everlasting historical document of incalculable importance.

This attitude can be detected in her article written in 1928. Here Shub referred to her film, the final part of her compilation trilogy (and yet in date sequence, the first), *The Russia of Nicholas II and Leo Tolstoy*. She affirmed that 'this montage must serve as an eloquent illustration of the fact that any available dramatised method for the historical film [acted film], no matter how good or how skilled, has only an ephemeral value in comparison with newsreel, which possesses a conviction that can never pale and can never age.'⁴⁶ Unfortunately, a complete copy of this film is no longer extant. Nevertheless, these remarks promote Shub's belief in the indelible value of nonfiction films.

Later in her career, through the demoralizing experience of having been denied permission for various film projects, which had the potential to give her a higher profile both at home and abroad, a wiser and self-critical Shub outlines a modified model for documentary:

> Now we don't have to prove that newsreels, both historical and current, are art. However, we still have not learned to film our contemporaries in the new way, even though this is the only method to relieve the monotony of documentaries. The problem of biography in film must be solved very differently. The topic must not just be about the dead and departed, but those living today. A film about... a worker, a farmer... an artist, must be approached differently. I believe that there will be major discoveries in this area. We must be brave, and then we will be able to clearly express our socialist epoch, see our culture, art, and nature in the new way.⁴⁷

Rainer Werner Fassbinder, the filmmaker and playwright who spearheaded New German Cinema, the post-war film movement in Germany, was interviewed on the essence of film in 1977. He made the following assertion: 'it is the entirety of the oeuvre that must say something special about the time in which it was made, otherwise it is worthless.'⁴⁸ Applying Fassbinder's criterion to Shub's filmic opus gives evidence of her value in the annals of cinema. Her oeuvre served to crystallize an era. Shub's films captured the mood of the vibrant avant-garde in the 1920s and encapsulated a period in history. Not only this, but she stood as a leading light in her vision for the documentary.

A possible cause of Shub's historical obscurity is that, since her death, her oeuvre may have been simplistically disregarded as propaganda.[49] While her films undoubtedly were overtly agitational and unashamedly presented as a promotion of socialist politics and culture, Shub's propagandist ideological montage (which was examined in my first chapter) is not only inextricably connected to her cinematic practice but also is an extension of her avant-garde Constructivist outlook on Soviet art and life.[50] She dared to admit that the filmmakers had been finding difficulty with dialectical materialism and its intricacies. Significantly, this observation by Shub demonstrates that her embracing of Marxist theory was critical rather than fundamentalist.[51]

These articulations of Shub's principles, formulated in her written texts, were to find full expression in her nonfiction films. Shub sought to educate the proletariat, thereby aspiring to bring about a transformation of society. This reawakening was to be achieved through radical experimentation in the arts, a process that in her eyes culminated in documentary. Significantly, it is the vitality of Shub's (and the avant-garde's) euphoria about both the revolution in the arts and the events of October 1917 that should hold the key to their considerable and ongoing influence on the art and cinema of today. For in this state of idealism and creative vibrancy, Shub and her comrades believed, with great conviction, that they could change the design of society. Indeed, they were fighting a public battle against the conventions of traditional high art. The passionate and dedicated belief of Shub and her compatriots in the ultimate success of their utopian quest gives their work universality. In fact, years later, Shub's comrade Alexander Medvedkin reflected on the unique nature of the cohorts participating in the vanguard of late 1920s cinema in Russia. As he was to muse: 'in the history of mankind [sic], there has never been a generation like ours.'[52]

Shub's cinematic philosophy was exemplified by her first work, *The Fall of the Romanov Dynasty*, that was not only the first compilation nonfiction feature film worldwide but also represented the essential criteria of non-dramatized documentary. Although of a slightly earlier period, Vertov's straightforward compilations, *The Anniversary of the Revolution* [Godovshchina revoliutsy, 1919] and *The History of the Civil War* [Istoriya grazhdanskoi voiny, 1921], were merely a direct transfer of newsreel footage from episodes of *Cinema Week* [Kino-nedelya].⁵³ *The Fall of the Romanov Dynasty*, on the other hand, was a fully realized and deeply considered narrative constructed from many sources (often only unlabelled fragments) of newsreel footage and then imbued with Shub's ideological montage. Moreover, Shub not only founded the compilation genre but, as a result of her decidedly negative experiences during the initial stages of research for material to construct *The Fall of the Romanov Dynasty*, she was instrumental in the establishment of film archives for documentary cinema.

As Leyda asserted, the compilation 'now in active use throughout the world, and accepted by [film] audiences and television viewers everywhere, was invented by . . . Shub.'⁵⁴ He states that in his extensive investigation of this subject, he had 'found no conscious, creative manipulation of raw newsreel material earlier than Shub's first work . . . Previously, only Dziga Vertov and Lev Kuleshov had treated newsreel material to gain its maximum dynamic effect and social purpose.'⁵⁵ However, in contrast to Shub, as Leyda elaborates, they merely:

> applied their principles to newsreels only as a step towards a more total control of their material – camera and studio as well as cutting room. . . . Shub, on the other hand, found her basic material – and her true inspiration – in the idea of shaping old newsreels to show history . . . To this aim she brought all her experience and skill and sensitivity to make the first socialist compilations – the first compilations in film history that are conscious works of art.⁵⁶

Reinforcing Leyda's pronouncement, Vlada Petric confirms, 'From today's perspective, it is clear that Shub was the initiator of the "compilation film" genre.'⁵⁷ Similarly, and far more recently, Lilya Kaganovsky declares that *The Fall of the Romanov Dynasty* 'is commonly thought of as the first compilation documentary ever produced'.⁵⁸ Additionally, with reference to Shub's debut as a director, Denise Youngblood acknowledges that, irrefutably: 'The nonfiction film had a new star in 1927.'⁵⁹ Youngblood regards Shub's first nonfiction film as a 'splendid example of the compilation documentary. Although Shub's material has intrinsic pictorial interest, it is her eye and flair for drama that makes this film a work of art *and* an important historical document. . . . It is a rare example of how interesting uncompromised realism could be.'⁶⁰

Several decades after her death, Leyda hailed the lasting contribution of Shub's trilogy, which he termed her 'first three precedent-forming films' adding that 'Shub's work provides many examples of a power too rarely used by the compilation film'.⁶¹ Honouring her as both a distinguished documentary filmmaker and the founder of the compilation genre, Leyda had confidently claimed in the 1960s that 'the place of... Shub in world film history is assured'.[62] However, in spite of praise from Jay Leyda, Vlada Petric and Graham Roberts, it is my conviction that the influence of Shub's films and her film texts, on the documentary methodology and theory of today, has not received the recognition it deserves.

Thus, I argue for the recovery and restoration of Esfir Shub to her rightful place in cinema's history as the foremost influence on the creation of the compilation genre, and its advancement, and one of the earliest contributors to the documentary film form both in her written theorizations and in her Constructivist practice.

Consequently, the book has focused on the reassessment and historical recovery of a unique filmmaker within a vibrant and exceptional avant-garde community. Indeed, I agree with Medvedkin that the cinematic vanguard, of which both he and Shub were prominent members, was unparalleled in the annals of revolutionary art.

My work has identified Shub as the only female director at the inception of the documentary film genre, who, correspondingly, was also the first of her gender to write critical cinema texts on nonfiction film (in conjunction with the establishing of a filmmaking career). Her active theorizing of her filmic practice requires recognition. No one has yet acknowledged that Shub was the sole woman in early Soviet cinema to actively contribute to the theoretical discourse of the day, thereby providing invaluable knowledge of cinematic principles. Shub's incisive essays were published in leading contemporary journals *Cinema* [Kino] and *New LEF* [Novyi Lef], where she stood as a solitary female voice in the cinematic debates that raged during that era.

Furthermore, I have presented Shub rather than Vertov as not only the founder of the compilation film genre, and an innovator in cinematic methodology, but also as the first Soviet filmmaker who actively championed the creation of a film archive. Thus, I have sought to examine and give recognition to Shub's role as a key figure in the early Soviet avant-garde, shaping her Constructivist nonfiction film as a foundational paradigm. Not only this but also Shub anticipated, by multiple decades, documentary film expressions such as *cinéma vérité* and direct cinema.

Accordingly, it has been argued that the doctrine of Constructivism was used cinematically by Shub in order to represent, although, through a somewhat naive sense of historical truth, the political and social transformation brought about by the revolutions of February and October 1917. Shub's Constructivist nonfiction film, as endorsed by the avant-garde, constituted the documentation of their historical reality. *The Fall of the Romanov Dynasty* was the embodiment of the tenets of her Constructivist template for ideological montage within the compilation film. In addition, as has been demonstrated, beyond its ideological and agitational functions, *The Fall of the Romanov Dynasty*, for example, illustrated a broader convergence between a modernist technological culture and the art of Constructivism.

As a result, despite Shub's compilation genre's glorification of the October Revolution, this film would nevertheless fall from favour. In spite of the fact that she had aimed simply to convey historical reality by means of newsreel footage, the contents of the archive, absorbed into Shub's compilation, became at variance with the cult of Stalin and his rewriting of history. Nonetheless, she never veered from her dedicated commitment to nonfiction film, although the professional consequences of this stance effectively destroyed her career. Even though Shub received vocal support from major avant-garde personalities, such as Lev Kuleshov, Vladimir Mayakovsky, Viktor Shklovsky and Sergei Eisenstein, she never believed that she had been permitted to realize her full potential, being thwarted in her aspirations during the 1930s. This is despite the undoubted virtuosity of *Today*, *K.Sh.E.* and *Spain* throughout this decade of increasing terror and dislocation.

Shub merits recognition as a crucial contributor to the historical development of the documentary film. This claim can be evidenced by *The Fall of the Romanov Dynasty*, *The Great Way*, *Today*, *K.Sh.E.* and *Spain*. These key cinematic works all encapsulate the creeds of Constructivism and observe the strictest adherence to nonfiction film in the construction of historical meaning. Each of the five films is worthy of a far more elevated position in the documentary canon. Shub and her unrivalled documentaries of a bygone era are deserving of far greater prominence. They should be both fully promoted and celebrated. Hopefully, in part due to this book, she will be accorded her deserved placing in the annals of film history. Her time has finally arrived.

Esfir Shub belongs to the world.

Notes

Introduction

1 Yakov Tolchan, cameraman and intimate friend of the filmmaker Alexander Medvedkin, interviewed by Chris Marker in *The Last Bolshevik* [Le tombeau d'Alexandre], [Documentary] dir. Chris Marker (France: Icarus Films, 1992). Alexander Medvedkin (1900–89), the director and scriptwriter, commenced his cinema career in 1927. Initially, he was the creator of a set of short agit-film farces for *Gosvoenkino* [State Military Cinema Organization]. Anatoly Lunacharsky praised them as noteworthy educational tools. Medvedkin is also known for his political satirical comedy *Happiness* [Schast'e, 1935]. The film historian Jay Leyda calls it 'one of the most original films in Soviet film history'. Jay Leyda, *Kino: A History of the Russian and Soviet Film* (London: Allen and Unwin, 1960; rev. ed. Princeton, NJ: Princeton University Press, 1983), 326. For the definitive work on Medvedkin, see Emma Widdis, *Alexander Medvedkin* (London and New York: I. B. Tauris, 2005).
2 Russia abandoned the Julian calendar and adopted the Gregorian calendar on 14 February 1918. In the nineteenth century dates in Russia were twelve days 'behind' Europe and much of the rest of the world. In the twentieth century the difference was thirteen days. Hence the October Revolution of 25 October 1917 (known as Old Style and abbreviated as O.S.) took place on a date known more widely as 7 November.
3 In the Russian census when Shub was three, the total population of Surazh was only 4000. Of these, the majority were Jewish (2400); the remainder were 1000 Belorussians and the rest, Russian.
4 Eisenstein's *Strike* was made in 1924 but not released until 1925.
5 My book endorses and extends Graham Roberts's stance in a journal article where he states that Shub 'has been sadly neglected'. See Graham Roberts, 'Esfir Shub: A Suitable Case for Treatment', *Historical Journal of Film, Radio and Television*, 11, no. 2 (1991): 149.
6 Russian does not have a definite or indefinite article. This renders it problematic when translating film titles into English. For ease of reading, I've inserted the definite article when referring to Shub's trilogy: thus *The Fall of the Romanov Dynasty* rather than *Fall of the Romanov Dynasty*.

7 Over a decade ago when trying to access *Spain*, I contacted a journalist in Madrid. She and her colleagues had never heard of Shub's film and were unable to source a copy.

8 Shub's anonymity in her own country was such that in 2000, Galina Tsykin, a Jewish intellectual who was a teenager in the Stalinist regime of the late 1930s and early 1940s, professed to never have heard Shub's name let alone having seen any of her films.

Chapter 1

1 Vladimir Mayakovsky (1893–1930) was simultaneously an artist, futurist poet (Shub and her friends at university recited his works by heart), playwright, painter, theatre and film theorist, actor (star of both stage and screen) and scriptwriter. He was the vital conduit linking and supporting the avant-garde in all of the arts, both prior to and after the Revolution. Shub was not a member of the CPSU [Communist Party of the Soviet Union], but she was to become ideologically engaged and politically connected through both her student years in Moscow and her film practice. Although Shub and Mayakovsky displayed a vastly differing response in their political commitment to Bolshevism, in their respective careers in the arts, they both aspired towards the showcasing and glorification of the socialist state.

2 Robert Chadwell Williams, *Artists in Revolution: Portraits of the Russian Avant-Garde, 1905–1925* (Bloomington: Indiana University Press, 1977), 143–4.

3 Vsevolod E. Meyerhold (1874–1940) the doyen of Russian avant-garde theatre directors who also directed films prior to the Revolution, Meyerhold's provocative masterpiece, a film version of Oscar Wilde's *The Portrait of Dorian Gray*, was the pinnacle of pre-Revolutionary cinema with spectacular lighting and use of atmospheric chiaroscuro. Taking the role of Lord Henry Wotton, Meyerhold was also the director.

4 Even Chagall's surreal *Self-Portrait with Seven Fingers* [1911] is clearly pointing the way forward, with its references to dislocation and alienation. This displacement is clearly visible in his montage-like juxtaposition of painted images. In this painting, the Eiffel Tower and Chagall's Belorussian village of Vitebsk are in opposite corners of the canvas – with the artist working at his easel, seated firmly between them.

5 Kazimir Malevich's work of 1914 allies him with the Cubo-Futurist writers Velimir Khlebnikov, Aleksei Kruchenykh and the concept of trans-rational poetry [*zaum*]. It was not just Malevich's artworks that influenced the avant-garde but also his passionate proclamations and booklets. In fact, Shub captures

the essence of his uplifting utopian texts when she exclaims: 'The old world has died . . . A new world is beginning . . . And in art the way is open. Ahead innovators, seekers of new paths! Cinema is the art of the future.' Esfir Shub, 'My School of Cinematography' [Moya shkola kinematografy], *In Close-up* [Krupnym planom] (Moscow: Iskusstvo, 1959) (henceforth known as *In Close-up*), 61.

6 Malevich's *An Englishman in Moscow* [1914] was a pictorial representation of the illogical reality and non-sense of Khlebnikov and Kruchenykh's poetry and prose. This painting, commenced in 1913, was a montage of seemingly unrelated images. Years ahead of its time and an obvious precursor to Dada and Surrealism, *An Englishman in Moscow* was startling in its originality and presented a deconstructed composition with objects nonsensically juxtaposed. Malevich was rejecting traditional modes of representation in the visual arts and his dislocated images also opened the way for Kuleshov.

7 Gustav Klutsis, 'Photomontage as a New Form of Agitational Art', in *Art into Life: Russian Constructivism 1914–1932*, exhibition catalogue (Seattle: Henry Art Gallery, University of Washington, 1990), 116.

8 Margit Rowell, 'Constructivist Book Design: Shaping the Proletarian Conscience', in *The Russian Avant-Garde Book 1910–1934*, eds. Margit Rowell and Deborah Wye (New York: Harry N. Abrams, 2002), 55.

9 Williams, *Artists in Revolution*, 85.

10 Sergei Yutkevich, 'Teenage Artists of the Revolution', in *Cinema in Revolution: The Heroic Era of the Soviet Film*, eds. Luda Schnitzer, Jean Schnitzer and Marcel Martin (London: Secker and Warburg, 1973), 29.

11 Alexander Matskin in Konstantin Rudnitsky, *Russian and Soviet Theatre: Tradition and the Avant-Garde* (London: Thames and Hudson, 1988), 22.

12 Alexander Golovin, a graduate of both the artist colony at Abramtsevo and Savva Mamontov's opera and theatre company (afterwards a highly sought-after stage designer), created breathtaking sets and costumes for *Masquerade*, adding a new dimension to the performances.

13 Rudnitsky, *Russian and Soviet Theatre*, 22–3.

14 Grigori Kozintsev, aged sixteen; the positively ancient Leonid Trauberg, aged nineteen; and the seventeen-year-old Sergei Yutkevich, who was to become a staunch supporter of Shub (and in fact was to write a glowing introduction to her *My Life – Cinematography* many years later), formed the delightfully exuberant and irreverent FEKS in 1921.

15 Kozintsev, 'A Child of the Revolution', in *Cinema in Revolution*, eds. L. Schnitzer et al., 95–6.

16 Grigori Kozintsev, Leonid Trauberg, Sergei Yutkevich and Georgi Kryzhitsky, 'Eccentrism', Petrograd, 1922, in *The Film Factory: Russian and Soviet Cinema in*

Documents 1896–1939, Richard Taylor, ed. and trans. Co-ed. and introduction Ian Christie (London: Routledge & Keegan Paul Ltd., 1988; rev. ed. London: Routledge, 1994), 62–3. Georgi Kryzhitsky, born the year after Esfir Shub, was only temporarily associated with FEKS. He was a theatre critic by profession.

17 Esfir Shub, 'The Path toward Choosing a Profession' [Put k vyboru professy], in *My Life – Cinematography* [Zhizn moya – kinematograf], (Moscow: Iskusstvo, 1972), 47. *My Life – Cinematography* (henceforth abbreviated to *My Life*).
18 Ibid., 46.
19 Ibid., 47.
20 Schnitzer et al., *Cinema in Revolution*, 9.
21 Shub, 'The Path toward Choosing a Profession', 51.
22 Ibid.
23 It should therefore come as no surprise that Eisenstein acknowledged having seen *Mystery-Bouffe* in rehearsal. See Sergei Eisenstein, *S.M. Eisenstein Selected Works Volume IV, Beyond the Stars: The Memoirs of Sergei Eisenstein*, ed. Richard Taylor, trans. William Powell (London: British Film Institute, 1995), 452.
24 Shub, 'First Work' [Pervaya rabota], 1928 in *My Life*, 250.
25 Lev Kuleshov, 'The Origins of Montage', in *Cinema in Revolution*, eds. L. Schnitzer et al., 67–8. Kuleshov's "Our First Experiences," written in 1934, reconfirms the date as 1917. However, there are conflicting dates given by *The Film Factory* as 1918, and Jay Leyda in *Kino*, who also cites the date of release as 1918. It seems likely that the film was completed before the Revolution and due to the ensuing conflict wasn't released until the following year.
26 Lev Kuleshov, 'Amerikanshchina', 1922, in *The Film Factory*, 73.
27 Lev Kuleshov, 'The Tasks of the Artist in Cinema', 1917, in *The Film Factory*, 41.
28 Ibid.
29 Lev Kuleshov, 'The Art of Cinema', 1918, in *The Film* Factory, 46.
30 Shub, 'My School of Cinematography', 71.
31 Ibid.
32 Ibid. Shub remembers that 'as far as . . . *By the Law* was concerned, I took every opportunity to be present at the rehearsals and the shoots which strictly followed a professionally formulated plan'. Ibid., 74.
33 Ibid., 73.
34 Ibid.
35 Shub, 'Non-acted Film', [Neigrovaya filma] in *My Life*, 264.
36 Kuleshov, 'Amerikanshchina', 73.
37 See Vsevolod Pudovkin, *Film Technique and Film Acting: The Cinema Writings of V. I. Pudovkin* (New York: Bonanza Books, 1969), 139–41; Schnitzer et al., *Cinema in Revolution*, 66–70; Richard Sklar, *Film: An International History of the Medium*

(London: Thames and Hudson, 1993), 151; Denise J. Youngblood, *Soviet Cinema in the Silent Era, 1918–1935* (Ann Arbor: UMI Research Press, 1985; rev. ed. Austin: University of Texas Press, 1991), 7; Neya Zorkaya *The Illustrated History of Soviet Cinema* (New York: Hippocrene Books, 1991), 49.

38 Sergei Eisenstein, 'The Montage of Film Attractions', 1924, in *The Eisenstein Reader*, ed. Richard Taylor and trans. Richard Taylor and William Powell (London: British Film Institute, 1998), 36.

39 Lev Kuleshov, 'The Screen Today', 1927 in *Lines of Resistance: Dziga Vertov and the Twenties*, ed. Yuri Tsivian and trans. Julian Graffy (Sacile: Le Giornate del Cinema Muto, 2004), 274.

40 Shub, 'Non-acted Film', 267.

41 Ibid.

42 Sergei Yutkevich, the title of his introduction to Shub's book is 'The Magician of the Editing Table' [Volshebnitsa montazhnogo stola], in *My Life*, 5.

43 Ibid.

44 Vlada Petric, *Constructivism in Film: The Man with the Movie Camera: A Cinematic Analysis* (Cambridge and New York: Cambridge University Press, 1987), 19.

45 Known as the Vasilev 'brothers', Sergei and Georgy were not actually related. In 1934, they directed one of the masterpieces of Socialist Realism: *Chapayev*. Shub, 'The Magician of the Editing Table', 9.

46 Ibid.

47 Shub, Letter 'A. I. Medvedkin – E. I. Shub', in *My Life*, 449. Shub was to die in September 1959.

48 Yutkevich, 'Teenage Artists of the Revolution', 16.

49 Yutkevich, 'The Magician of the Editing Table', 5–6.

50 Ibid., 6.

51 Ibid.

52 'Sergei Mikhailovich Eisenstein' [Sergei Mikhailovich Eizenshtein], *In Close-up*, 147–8.

53 Ibid.

54 Ibid., 141.

55 Ibid., 144.

56 Ibid., 120.

57 Ibid., 69.

58 Shub, 'Vladimir Mayakovsky' [Vladimir Maiakovsky], *In Close-up*, 95–111.

59 Petric, *Constructivism in Film*, viii, 25, and 35–6.

60 Sergei Eisenstein, 'Montage' 1938, in *S. M. Eisenstein Selected Works Volume II, Towards a Theory of Montage*, eds. Michael Glenny and Richard Taylor, trans. Michael Glenny (London: British Film Institute, 1994), 322.

61 Shub, 'Dziga Vertov' [Dziga Vertov], *In Close-up*, 75.
62 Growing up, Shub remembers that she 'often listened to music at home: violin, piano, singing. And in Moscow, I was mainly attracted to music . . . symphony concerts . . . free morning recitals . . . Rachmaninov and Scriabin.' 'A Diversion (A Tribute to My Youth): Moscow Higher Courses for Women' [Ostuplenie (dan moei molodosti): Moskovskie vysshie zhenskie kursy], in *My Life*, 25.
63 Ibid.
64 Mayakovsky's poem, *Kiev* is reproduced and quoted in full by Shub, 'My School of Cinematography', 64.
65 Viktor Shklovsky (1893–1984) was a Formalist theoretician and linguistics scholar who formed the Society for the Study of Poetic Language [OPOYAZ] with Osip Brik in St. Petersburg. Shklovsky was a prolific writer, literary critic and scriptwriter.
66 I travelled from Western Australia to the Pacific Film Archive, at the University of California – Berkeley, specifically to view this rare and enthralling film. Despite nine laborious reel changes, *Wings of a Serf*, one hundred and twenty-five minutes in length, was totally absorbing and captivating. Apart from its stunning aesthetic qualities, I felt completely engaged with both the narrative and its coherent plot: Shklovsky's philosophies put into practice.
67 Denise J. Youngblood, '"History" on Film: The Historical Melodrama in Soviet Cinema', *Historical Journal of Film, Radio and Television*, 11, no. 2 (1991): 177.
68 Youngblood, *Soviet Cinema in the Silent Era*, 98.
69 Yutkevich, 'The Magician of the Editing Table', 9.
70 Shub, 'My School of Cinematography', 73.
71 Ibid.
72 Ibid., 74.
73 Youngblood, '"History" on Film: The Historical Melodrama in Early Soviet Cinema', 177.
74 Like Eisenstein's *Ivan the Terrible*, the subtext of *Wings of a Serf* concerns the repression and death of creativity during the reign of a hated despot. Although contemporary parallels were patently clear, strangely this is not why it was singled out for damning criticism. *Wings of a Serf* was to be so publicly savaged, that it led to Shklovsky's recantation and attempted justification of the script. *Wings of a Serf* was unfortunately not an isolated example of an initially popular work later being accused of being decadent, vulgar or 'formalist'.
75 Shub, 'The Path toward Choosing a Profession', 64.
76 Shub, 'My School of Cinematography', 69.
77 Marcel Martin (April 1963), 'Les films de montage', Cinéma 63 in Jay Leyda, *Films Beget Films: A Study of the Compilation Film* (London: George Allen and Unwin, 1964), 27.

78 David Gillespie, *Early Soviet Cinema: Innovation, Ideology and Propaganda* (London: Wallflower Press, 2005), 9. Apart from a phrase in Leyda's *Kino*, 272 where he spells Frelikh as 'Froelich' and just records the name of the film, the only other reference that I could find regarding *Prostitutka* was a brief entry in Julie A. Cassiday and Leyla Rouhi, 'From Nevskii Prospekt to Zoia's Apartment: Trials of the Russian Procuress', *The Russian Review*, 58, no. 3 (1999): 413. Cassiday and Rouhi refer to the film as A Prostitute/ Crushed by Life [*Prostitutka/Ubitaia zhizn'iu*].

79 Aleksei Gan, 'Recognition for the Cine-Eyes', 1924 in *The Film Factory*, 107. Vertov 'became' his camera and enthusiastically proclaimed that as a mechanical instrument, he was the 'Cine-Eye.' Also, as Vertov exclaimed: 'I the machine show you the world as only I can see it.' This was Vertov's special and unique vision of the universe. Dziga Vertov, 'The Cine-Eyes. A Revolution', in *The Film Factory*, 93.

80 Ibid.

81 Shub, 'Dziga Vertov', 79.

82 Ibid. Like Malevich, the Weimar photomontagists (Hannah Höch, Raoul Hausmann, John Heartfield, and Kurt Schwitters) also influenced the cutting-edge design of Alexander Rodchenko – from his arresting graphic layouts in *LEF* (and later in *Novyi LEF*) to his collage illustrations for Mayakovsky's poetry and his film design for Vertov.

83 Maud Lavin, *cut with the kitchen knife: the weimar photomontages of hannah höch* (New HavenUniversity Press, 1993), 9. The 'Illustrierte' referred to by Lavin was the *Workers' Illustrated Newspaper* [Arbeiter-Illustrierte Zeitung], a leading German communist publication with magazine quality photographic images.

84 Shub, 'Sergei Mikhailovich Eisenstein', 113.

85 *Glumov's Diary*, which was Eisenstein's only other film work to that date was a film segment of a few minutes duration, initially supervised by Vertov, inserted into Eisenstein's theatre production in 1923 of Alexander Ostrovsky's play *Enough Folly in a Wise Man*.

86 Sergei Eisenstein, 'Through Theatre to Cinema', in Sergei Eisenstein, *Film Form: Essays in Film Theory*, ed. and trans. Jay Leyda (New York: Harcourt Brace Jovanovich, 1977 [orig. pub. 1949]), 11.

87 Yutkevich, 'The Magician of the Editing Table', 3.

88 Shub, 'My School of Cinematography', 74.

89 Apart from a fleeting reference by R. C. Williams, no other text has pinpointed (let alone alluded to) Shub's contribution to *Strike*. Yet, in the archives of the British Film Institute, Shub is in fact listed as *Strike*'s co-editor with Eisenstein.

90 Yutkevich, 'Teenage Artists of the Revolution', 16.

91 Williams, *Artists in Revolution*, 172.

92 Jay Leyda footnote, in Eisenstein, *Film Form: Essays in Film Theory*, 11.
93 For the depth of the relationship between Shub and Eisenstein, see a body of their personal correspondence from May 1928 to February 1946 in Jay Leyda, ed. and trans., *Eisenstein 2—A Premature Celebration of Eisenstein's Centenary* (Calcutta: Seagull Books, 1985), 31–58. Alternatively, a large number of their letters to each other (published after their deaths) can be found in *My Life*, 372–93.
94 Shub, 'My School of Cinematography', 74.
95 Sergei Eisenstein 'Laocoön', in *S. M. Eisenstein Selected Works Volume II*, eds. Glenny and Taylor, trans. Glenny, 178.
96 Similarly, in his 1926 polemic against Béla Balázs, Eisenstein had referred to Isaac Babel: using an example of his poetic text to illustrate his concept of 'contextual confrontation' and montage. Sergei Eisenstein, 'Béla Forgets the Scissors', 1926, in *The Film Factory*, 147. Béla Balázs (1884–1949) was a Hungarian writer of film scripts and theory, and also a director, who lived and worked in both Germany and Russia.
97 Eisenstein, *S. M. Eisenstein Selected Works Volume II*, 178.
98 Sergei Eisenstein, 'How I Became a Film Director', in *Notes of a Film Director*, trans. X. Danko (Moscow: Foreign Languages Publishing House, 1959), 14.
99 Trans. Youngblood in *Soviet Cinema in the Silent Era*, 83.
100 Trans. Taylor in Richard Taylor, *The Politics of the Soviet Cinema 1917–1929* (Cambridge: Cambridge University Press, 1979), 90.
101 Shub, 'Dziga Vertov', 75.

Chapter 2

1 The Imperial Academy of Fine Arts in St Petersburg dated back to the reign of the Empress Elizabeth in the eighteenth century.
2 Shub, 'A Diversion (A Tribute to My Youth)', 25. Of the writings of significant socialist figures of this era, it is the discourse of both Alexander Herzen and that of Nikolai Chernyshevsky that bears the greatest influence in terms of early women's liberation in pre-Revolutionary Russia. See Richard Stites, *The Women's Liberation Movement in Russia: Feminism, Nihilism, and Bolshevism 1860–1930* (Princeton: Princeton University Press, 1978), 29, 34–5, 46–8, 62, 122, 150, 249.
3 David Elliott, *New Worlds: Russian Art and Society 1900–1937* (London: Thames and Hudson, 1986), 8.
4 Eugenia Kirichenko, *The Russian Style* (London: Laurence King, 1991), 143.
5 Ibid.

6 'Why We Paint Ourselves' means precisely that. The leading avant-garde artists Mikhail Larionov and Natalia Goncharova and the leading Futurists Mayakovsky, Vasily Kamensky and David Burliuk regularly painted their faces. In 1913, Mayakovsky, Kamensky and Burliuk, in full war paint, fixed spoons to their lapels and strolled purposively to the Kuznetsky Bridge, where they dramatically recited their poetry. This performance art must be one of the earliest examples of twentieth-century street theatre, and these 'happenings' took place on a daily basis in front of outraged, bemused and curious members of the public, causing utter pandemonium. See Wiktor Woroszylski, *The Life of Mayakovsky*, trans. Boleslaw Taborski. (London: Victor Gollancz, 1972), 56–7. There was face painting in the first Futurist film *Drama in the Futurists' Cabaret No.13* [Drama v kabare futuristov No.13, 1913]. It starred Goncharova, who had her face and naked breast painted with an abstract face, and Larionov, who had green tears painted on his cheeks. It featured Mayakovsky and Burliuk, who were also the scriptwriters.

7 Ilya Zdanevich and Mikhail Larionov in John E. Bowlt, ed. and trans., *Russian Art of the Avant-Garde: Theory and Criticism 1902–1934* (New York: The Viking Press, 1976; rev. and enl., ed. London: Thames and Hudson, 1988), 81. Ilya Zdanevich, the co-signatory of Larionov's manifesto, was born in the same year as Esfir Shub. He was a poet and Futurist who wrote and published a critical work on Goncharova and Larionov under the nom de plume Eli Eganbyuri and was a great champion of Goncharova's art practice.

8 There is such a plethora of material on Tatlin, and although he is acknowledged as the originator of the birth of Constructivism, I agree with Maria Gough, who asserts that Tatlin was not 'present for the long haul', Maria Gough, *The Artist as Producer: Russian Constructivism in Revolution* (Berkeley: University of California Press, 2005), 18. For in-depth material on Tatlin, see John Milner, *Vladimir Tatlin and the Russian Avant-Garde* (New Haven: Yale University Press, 1983); *Art into Life: Russian Constructivism 1914–1932*; Christina Lodder, *Russian Constructivism* (New Haven: Yale University Press, 1990) and Camilla Gray, *The Russian Experiment in Art 1863–1922* (London: Thames and Hudson, 1962; rev. and enl. ed. London: Thames and Hudson, 1986).

9 Varvara Fedorovna Stepanova (1894–1958) was born in the same year as Shub. They were close friends. Stepanova wrote non-objective poetry in conjunction with non-objective art before the Revolution. In 1921 she contributed to an exhibition seen as the swansong of painting, called 5×5=25 with Rodchenko, the Constructivist artist and photographer; the artists Alexandra Exter and Liubov Popova and architect Aleksandr Vesnin. Stepanova presented a paper at the end of December 1922 on Constructivism. Together with Popova, Stepanova worked

for Meyerhold in the theatre after the Revolution. Stepanova created the sets and designed the costumes for Meyerhold's production of *Tarelkin's Death* in 1922.
10. Varvara Stepanova states the following: 'Constructivism is an ideology and not an artistic movement' in 'The General Theory of Constructivism'. Aleksandr M. Rodchenko and Varvara F. Stepanova, ed. Peter Noever, *The Future Is Our Only Goal* (Munich: Prestel Verlag, 1991), 174. Stepanova's proclamation is mystifying. It appears to be somewhat contradictory in terms of her theoretical assertions versus her principles, then translated into her creative output. In reality, Stepanova's Constructivist work included graphic art design in textile patterns, book designs, typography and illustrations (some of them using gouache, a basic artist's paint), linocuts, theatre sets with costumes and sports clothing. With the benefit of distance and painstaking research, unlike Stepanova, Maria Gough appraised the Constructivist movement as being the 'most groundbreaking development in the visual arts in the decade or so following the October Revolution of 1917'. Gough, *The Artist as Producer*, 1. I agree fully with Gough's evaluation.
11. Ibid., 49–50.
12. Ibid., 45.
13. Ibid., 48.
14. Shub, 'The Path toward Choosing a Profession', 50–1.
15. Vladimir Mayakovsky, 'Art of the Commune' [Iskusstvo kommuny] No. 1, 1918, in Gray, *The Russian Experiment in Art*, 219. In this first issue, Mayakovsky conveys the passion and enthusiasm of the artists after the founding of the new Soviet state. This is despite chronic food shortages, then famine and bitterly harsh winters without adequate fuel supplies as a direct result of the Revolution and ensuing Civil War that erupted in December 1917.
16. LEF, the acronym for *Levyi front iskusstv* translated as the Left Front of the Arts, was an avant-garde movement in the arts initiated by Mayakovsky in the early 1920s. It was an extension of the Russian Futurists, and in 1923 it first published its highly regarded journal, also called *LEF*. In 1927, *Novyi LEF* superseded the publication of *LEF*. Shub was one of the co-editors of *Novyi LEF* together with Mayakovsky and Osip Brik.
17. Woroszylski, *The Life of Mayakovsky*, 415.
18. Shub, 'The Path toward Choosing a Profession', 41.
19. Mayakovsky, as an avant-garde artist of stature, spent a considerable time with Fernand Léger, visited Picasso at his studio, had meetings with Jean Cocteau and attended Marcel Proust's funeral.
20. Woroszylski, *The Life of Mayakovsky*, 336.
21. Shub, 'Non-acted Film', 266.

22 Lev Kuleshov, 'Cinema as the Fixing of Theatrical Action', 1922, in *The Film Factory*, 67. The italic emphasis in the quote is Kuleshov's.
23 Aleksei Gan, 'The Cinematograph and Cinema' [Kinematograf i kinematografiya], 1922, in *The Film Factory*, 67.
24 Ibid., 68.
25 Ibid.
26 Shub, 'And Again – the Newsreel' [I opiat – khronika], 1929, 258.
27 Ibid., 262.
28 Shub, 'First Work', 251.
29 Ibid.
30 Shub, 'My School of Cinematography', *In Close-up*, 64.
31 Osip Brik (1888–1945) was a Formalist theoretician who founded the 'Society for the Study of Poetic Language' [OPOYAZ] with Viktor Shklovsky in 1916 in St. Petersburg. Brik was also a dramatist and literary critic, a member of both IZO Narkompros [Department of Fine Arts within Narkompros] and INKhUK [Institute of Artistic Culture]. Additionally, Brik was a stalwart supporter of the Constructivist movement and a friend of Shub. Brik, 'Odinnadtsatyi Vertova', in *Lines of Resistance: Dziga Vertov and the Twenties*, ed. Tsivian, 311.
32 Youngblood, *Soviet Cinema in the Silent Era*, 133–48.
33 Later Stalin would be portrayed in dramatized film histories, the new 'documentaries' of the Revolution (such as *Lenin in October* [Lenin v oktiabr] (1937), [Film] Dir. Mikhail Romm, USSR: Mosfilm) as Lenin's indispensable comrade in arms (his right hand). These films were seen as irrefutable evidence that Stalin was an instigator of the Revolution. It helped to instil and perpetuate the myths with which he surrounded himself. According to Yuri Buranov, a Party archivist, Stalin's 'role was quite insignificant. At the most decisive moment of the October takeover in 1917, he was nowhere to be found'. Yuri Buranov interviewed in *Stalin: The Myth*, Part One (2003), [TV programme], Channel 4. Dir. Peter Adler, UK, produced for British Television, in conjunction with the History Channel. This is further reinforced by Anton Antonov-Ovseenko, the son of the October revolutionary V. A. Antonov-Ovseenko (who led the Bolsheviks in the attack against the Winter Palace), who relates that 'On the night of the October uprising 25 October 1917 there was a tea party at the Alliluyev's apartment' (Stalin's wife's family). 'Stalin drank tea the whole night long, told amusing stories and his favourite Georgian jokes'. A. Antonov-Ovseenko interviewed in *Stalin: The Myth*, Part One.
34 'Shakespeare or a pair of boots' was the title of a pamphlet written in the second half of the nineteenth century by Nikolai Dobrolyubov, a member of the intelligentsia and a contemporary of Nikolai Chernyshevsky. See Gray, *The Russian Experiment*

in Art, 274. Shub would have been familiar with Dobrolyubov's pithy phrase and she writes enthusiastically of her time as a student absorbing the works of the great socialist intellectuals. As part of her political and ideological enlightenment in her early days in Moscow, Shub records that she 're-read Herzen, Dobrolyubov and Chernyshevsky and I started reading Plekhanov and any works of Lenin that I could obtain'. Shub, 'A Diversion (A Tribute to My Youth)', 32.

35 For the philosophy of Vasily Kandinsky (1866–1944), see Wassily Kandinsky, *Concerning the Spiritual in Art*, trans. Michael T. H. Sadler (New York: Dover, 1977).

36 Petric, *Constructivism in Film*, 5.

37 See Camilla Gray, Christina Lodder, John E. Bowlt and David Elliott.

38 See Naum Gabo, *Gabo, Constructions, Sculpture, Paintings, Drawings, Engravings* (London: Lund Humphries, 1957), 174.

39 Lodder, *Russian Constructivism*, 1.

40 Bill Nichols asserts, 'Malevich (in his late paintings) . . . [was] among the many artists who contributed to a Constructivist movement.' Bill Nichols, *Speaking Truths with Film: Evidence, Ethics, Politics in Documentary* (Oakland: University of California Press, 2016), 20. This is inaccurate. As Gilles Néret states in his work on Malevich: 'It should not be forgotten that Malevich remained viscerally anti-Constructivist. He had long denounced the perverse effects of Constructivist ideology placed at the service of the state, that is, of utopian perspectives.' Gilles Néret, *Kazimir Malevich 1878–1935 and Suprematism* (Cologne: Taschen, 2003), 80.

41 Maria Gough rightly paints Malevich as a spiritually inclined Suprematist. Gough, *The Artist as Producer*, 21–3. Nevertheless, although never a participant in the Constructivist movement, see early examples of Malevich's work to appraise my claim for Malevich as a major influence on the leading Constructivist artists Rodchenko, Popova and Olga Rozanova, in Néret, *Kazimir Malevich 1878–1935 and Suprematism*, 48–51, 54–61, 68–9; and in Jeannot Simmen and Kolja Kohlhoff, *Kasimir Malevich: Life and Work* (Bonn: Könneman, 1999), 46–51, 62–3. For Rodchenko's *Black on Black* (1918), see Lodder, *Russian Constructivism*, 24. Rodchenko's three canvases each a square of flat colour – *Pure Red Colour, Pure Yellow Colour and Pure Blue Colour*, 1921, were almost identical to Malevich's earlier yellow, red, black and white squares. See Alexander Rodchenko, in *Art into Life: Russian Constructivism 1914–1932*, 47; see Popova, 'Painterly Architectonics' of 1917 and 1918, in *Amazons of the Avant-Garde*, eds. John E. Bowlt and Matthew Drutt (New York: Harry N. Abrams, 2000), 206–7 and Rozanova's 'Non-Objective Compositions', of 1917, ibid., 236–9.

42 Apart from Tatlin and his contemporaries having exposure to significant artworks by Picasso in major Russian exhibitions between 1912 and 1914, Tatlin travelled

to Paris specifically to meet Picasso and to visit his studio. As a young university student in Moscow, Shub describes visiting the major collection by Picasso (forty pieces in all by 1913) housed in the famed galleries of the art patron Sergei Shchukin. Shub summed up the Picasso paintings as 'interesting but not entirely comprehensible'. Shub, 'A Diversion (A Tribute to My Youth)', 26.

43 The link between the assemblages of *objets-trouvés* and the compilation film can be illustrated by the work of the American artist Joseph Cornell, renowned for his evocative boxes of juxtaposed found objects. Cornell was introduced to the collages of the Surrealists, such as Max Ernst. In 1936 Cornell made his only compilation film, indeed his only film, *Rose Hobart*. See Robert Hughes, *American Visions: The Epic History of Art in America* (London: Harvill Press, 1997), 498–501.
44 Shub, 'And Again – the Newsreel', 259.
45 Gray, *The Russian Experiment in Art*, 180.
46 Stephen Bann, ed., *The Tradition of Constructivism: The Documents of Twentieth Century Art* (New York: Viking Press, 1974), xxiii.
47 Aleksei Gan, 'Constructivism in the Cinema', ibid., 131.
48 Ibid.
49 Ibid.
50 Ibid.
51 For the trials that beset nonfiction film, see Youngblood, *Soviet Cinema in the Silent Era*, 118, 138–43, and Shub, 'Non-acted Film', 262.
52 Shub, 'And Again – the Newsreel', 259.
53 For Leninist Film Proportion, see 'Vladimir Lenin: Directive on Cinema Affairs', *The Film Factory*, 56.
54 Shub, 'Non-acted Film', 269.
55 Ibid.
56 Jaroslav Andel, 'The Constructivist Entanglement: Art into Politics, Politics into Art', in *Art into Life: Russian Constructivism 1914–1932*, 227.
57 Graham Roberts, *Forward Soviet! History and Nonfiction Film in the USSR* (London: I. B. Tauris, 1999), 51.
58 'Programme of the Constructivist Working Group of INKhUK, 1921', in *Art Into Life: Russian Constructivism 1914–1932*, 67.
59 Gough, *The Artist as Producer*, 12.
60 According to Maria Gough, Karlis Johansons then 'Russifies his name to Karl Ioganson'. *The Artist as Producer*, 2. Gough spells his name 'Ioganson' as does Christina Lodder in *Russian Constructivism*. As all my references for this Latvian sculptor come from Gough and Lodder, I am leaving the spelling as it is given in their respective works.
61 Gan, 28 March 1921, in Gough, *The Artist as Producer*, 72.

62 'Constructivist Protocol No. 1, 1921' (document in private collection), in *Art into Life: Russian Constructivism 1914–1932*, 65.
63 Alexander Rodchenko, 'Liniya on the formation of the First Working Group of Constructivists', March 1921, in Lodder, *Russian Constructivism*, 27.
64 Boris Kushner (1888–1937) was a poet, founder of Communist Futurists [Komfut], literary critic and contributor to *LEF* and *Novyi LEF*. Imprisoned, Kushner died in the Gulag. Boris Kushner, 'The Divine Work of Art (Polemics)' Art of the Commune [Iskusstvo kommuny], 1919, in Bowlt, *Russian Art of the Avant-Garde*, 170.
65 Osip Brik, 'A Drain for Art' [Drenazh iskusstvu'], in Iskusstvo kommuny, 1918, in Lodder, *Russian Constructivism*, 76.
66 Ibid.
67 Aleksei Gan, 'Konstruktivizm', 1922, in Bowlt, *Russian Art of the Avant-Garde*, 221 and 223.
68 Aleksei Gan, 'Konstruktivizm', 1922, in Lodder, *Russian Constructivism*, 99.
69 Yakov Tugenkhold was an art critic, correspondent for the Russian art journal *Appollon* in Paris (1910–1911) and a vocal supporter of Marc Chagall. Yakov Tugenkhold in Bowlt, *Russian Art of the Avant-Garde,* xxxix.
70 Shub, 'Non-acted Film', 264.
71 Gustav Klutsis (1895–1944) was both an artist and a teacher. A contributor to *LEF*, Klutsis was at the forefront of early Soviet photomontage, leaving both Suprematism and Malevich to turn to Constructivism.
72 The well-known actress Zinaida Raikh, Meyerhold's wife, was murdered by the secret police.
73 Sergei Tretiakov (1892–1937), a Soviet avant-garde dramatist, futurist poet and literary and film critic, was born in Latvia. One of his proletarian plays, *Gas Masks*, was the last theatre production directed by Eisenstein before he left for a career in cinema. He died during the purges. Isaac Babel (1894–1940) playwright, scriptwriter and author was a literary giant of the twentieth century. Lauded by Maxim Gorky and André Malraux, Babel's short stories, such as the famed cycle called *Red Cavalry*, were deemed worthy successors to the oeuvre of Chekhov. Babel was executed in Lubyanka Prison.
74 Shub in Yutkevich's introduction, 'The Magician of the Editing Table', 12.
75 Shub, 'And Again – the Newsreel', 257.
76 El Lissitzky (1890–1941) was a typographer, graphic designer, photographer, architect and critic. He was also an illustrator and writer of children's books in Hebrew, Yiddish and Russian. He wrote an important Constructivist text on furniture production and design, *The Artistic Prerequisites for the Standardisation of Furniture*, in which he rejected the decorative and presented criteria and elements

of style linked to the industrial and technological. El Lissitzky also established a significant dialogue between the avant-garde in Russia and Dada, the Bauhaus and De Stijl in Europe.

77 See my book review. Ilana Sharp, 'Harmony + Dissent: Film and Avant-Garde Art Movements in the Early Twentieth Century', R. Bruce Elder in *Studies in Russian & Soviet Cinema*, 3, no. 3 (2009): 355–8.
78 Gough, *The Artist as Producer*, 1.
79 Shub, 'First Work', 251.
80 Lev Kuleshov, 'The Screen Today' [Ekran Segodnya], *Novyi LEF*, 4, 1927, in *Lines of Resistance*, 275.
81 Ibid., 272.
82 Ibid.
83 Ibid., 273.
84 Ibid., 274.
85 Ibid., 275.
86 In Chapter 3, I engage in a detailed examination of the sequences relating to the Tsar and his followers, and the Governor of Kaluga.
87 Shub, 'Non-acted Film', 263.
88 'An Interview with Mikhail Kaufman: Essays in Honour of Jay Leyda', *October*, 11 (Winter 1979): 61 in Kevin Macdonald and Mark Cousins, eds. *Imagining Reality: The Faber Book of Documentary* (London: Faber and Faber, 1998), 67.
89 *Man with a Movie Camera* is Vertov's personal ode of homage to the life and soul of a Soviet city and the lives of the people therein: as sheer cinematic poetry, as a lyrical symphony it is the antithesis of Constructivism. Petric, *Constructivism in Film*, x.
90 The narrator in Chris Marker's documentary *The Last Bolshevik* declares that 'propaganda was a continuation of war by other means', *The Last Bolshevik*. This theme is developed throughout my book with regard to both Shub and the avant-garde.
91 Walter Benjamin, 'The Artist as Producer', in *Art After Modernism: Rethinking Representation*, ed. Brian Wallis (New York: New Museum of Contemporary Art, 1995), 303.
92 Shub, 'Non-acted Film', 264.

Chapter 3

1 The release of *October* by Sovkino, took place on 14 March 1928.
2 Shub, 'The Film about Tolstoy' [Filma o Tolstom], in *My Life*, 260.

3 Shub, 'The Beginning of Fame for Soviet Cinematography' [Nachalo slavy sovetskoi kinematografii], *In Close-up*, 92.
4 Aleksei Gan, 'The Thirteenth Experiment', 1922, in *The Film Factory*, 78.
5 This scenario is fully described later in this chapter.
6 In this statement, Shub is referring specifically to her compilation trilogy. Shub, 'The Film about Tolstoy', 260.
7 Ibid.
8 John Reed (1887–1920) was an American journalist and war correspondent who had covered the Mexican War and World War I. His bestseller, *Ten Days That Shook the World*, published in 1919, became a political classic and was an account of the October Revolution as seen through idealistic Western eyes.
9 Esfir Shub, 'This Work Cries Out' [Eta rabota krichit], 1928, in *The Film Factory*, 217.
10 Ibid.
11 Ibid.
12 According to Victor Sebestyen, and unlike Eisenstein's portrayal of Kerensky as a whimpering coward, the latter was a man of courage with a keen sense of social justice. Kerensky 'went to Kuzhi, a small town near the Front in western Ukraine where Jews were being lynched . . . he pleaded with soldiers and local soldiers to stop their "barbarous and counter-productive actions". His intervention prevented what might have been a far bloodier pogrom.' In addition, 'He denounced anti-Semitism wherever he saw it – amid court circles or in the lower ranks of the army.' Victor Sebestyen, *Lenin the Dictator* (London: Weidenfield and Nicolson, 2018), 299.
13 Richard Abrahams, 'Provisional Government', in *The Blackwell Encyclopaedia of the Russian Revolution*, ed. Harold Shukman (Oxford: Blackwell Publishers, 1988), 124–5.
14 Ibid., 125.
15 Yuri Tsivian interview in *Eisenstein: The Little Boy from Riga* (1988), [TV programme] dir. Ian Potts, BBC1, 14 October.
16 Andrey Bely (1880–1934) and Alexander Blok (1880–1921), who was an acquaintance of Shub's, were the leading Symbolist poets of the second wave. For Shub on Bely, see 'A Diverson (A Tribute to My Youth)', 19–21 and Shub on Blok, in 'The Path to Choosing a Profession', in *My Life*, 40–1.
17 R. Bruce Elder, *Harmony + Dissent: Film and Avant-Garde Art Movements in the Early Twentieth Century* (Waterloo, Ontario: Wilfred Laurier University Press, 2008), 23–4, 304–17.
18 A more detailed account of this juxtaposed scenario between master and servant is provided later in this chapter.

19 Yuri Tsivian quoting Eisenstein, in *Eisenstein: The Little Boy from Riga*.
20 Nicholas Pronay and Derek W. Spring, eds., *Propaganda, Politics and Film 1918–1945* (London: Macmillan, 1982), 250.
21 André Bazin, 'The Ontology of the Photographic Image', in *What Is Cinema?* trans. Hugh Gray (Berkeley and Los Angeles: University of California Press, 1967), 12.
22 Ibid., 9.
23 Ibid., 14.
24 André Bazin, 'The Evolution of the Language of Cinema', in *What Is Cinema?*, 37.
25 Martin Stollery, 'Eisenstein, Shub and the gender of the author as producer', *Film History*, 14, no. 1 (2002): 95. There is a reference in Shub's memoirs to a female revolutionary, someone who, through political activism, forged the way for Shub and her peers. In *My Life*, she describes how she was taken to meet the now elderly Yekaterina Breshko-Breshkovskaya, who was known as the Babushka of the Revolution and, in 1878, had been the first female political prisoner banished to Siberia with hard labour. Shub, 'A Diversion (A Tribute to My Youth)', 31.
26 Youngblood, email to author, 10 December 2020.
27 Ibid.
28 On the perception of the storming of the Winter Palace scene in *October* as actual documentary footage, see Richard Taylor, 'From October to "October": The Soviet Political System in the 1920s and Its Films', in *Politics and The Media: Film and Television for the Political Scientist and Historian*, ed. M. J. Clark (Oxford: Pergamon Press, 1979), 31.
29 Shub, 'The Film about Tolstoy', 261.
30 The *Black Hundreds* were supported by the Slavophiles with the enthusiastic participation of the Grand Duke Nicholas Nikolaevich, a close member of the Tsar's family. Vehemently anti-Semitic and ultra-right-wing, the *Black Hundreds* like Konstantin Pobedonostev, Procurator of the Holy Synod (and the Tsar's valued confidante and mentor), firmly believed that the Jewish inhabitants of Holy Mother Russia were responsible for all her ills. Pobedonostev's chilling solution to the Jewish problem was threefold – assimilation by conversion to the Orthodox Church; exile by emigration; and finally, extermination through pogroms.
31 Shub, 'A Diversion (A Tribute to My Youth)', 24.
32 Ibid.
33 Reverend James Parkes, *A History of the Jewish People* (Harmondsworth: Pelican Books, 1967), 166.
34 According to James Parkes, Tsar Nicholas II not only supported the *Black Hundreds* but also publicly wore their badge. Ibid.
35 Shub, intertitle in *The Fall of the Romanov Dynasty*.

36 Benjamin, 'The Work of Art in the Age of Mechanical Reproduction', in *Illuminations: Essays and Reflections*. Ed. Hannah Arendt. Trans. Harry Zohn (New York: Schocken Books, 1968), 229.
37 Ibid., 231.
38 Ibid., 232 (italic emphasis is in the original).
39 The Smolnyi Institute, Lenin's headquarters, housed the Central Executive Committee of the Soviets, and the C.C. of the Bolshevik Party. It had previously been an exclusive school for 'well-born girls' established by Catherine the Great.
40 *The Fall of the Romanov Dynasty* was released on 11 March 1927, whereas Eisenstein didn't begin filming *October* until April 1927. See Norman Swallow, *Eisenstein: A Documentary Portrait* (New York: E. P. Dutton, 1977), 56.
During Eisenstein's and his cameraman Eduard Tisse's filming of *October*, Shub stayed in the same lodgings in Leningrad. She looked at their daily rushes and offered her support and advice. At this time, Shub was already filming sequences for *The Great Way*, but nonetheless she always found the time to offer encouragement to Eisenstein. As she recalls: 'After setting up the shot and the lighting, Sergei Mikhailovich invariably called me to the lens and, while executing one of the pre-shooting rehearsals, he would give me the opportunity to view it through the objective. He would always demand critical feedback.' Shub, 'My School of Cinematography', 102.
41 Shub, 'First Work', 251.
42 Ibid.
43 It is obvious that this intertitle is historically inaccurate. The farm labourers would not be peasants toiling on the landowner's fields. As this is post-emancipation of the serfs by many decades, they are working on a commune. Unfortunately, this would not correspond with Shub's overriding argument regarding the oppression of the workers by the wealthy capitalist landowners.
44 Leyda, 'Esther Shub', in *Sexual Stratagems: The World of Women in Film*, ed. Patricia Erens (New York: Horizon, 1979), 183.

Chapter 4

1 Shub, 'As a Reminder' [V poriadke napominaniya], in *My Life*, 287.
2 Brik, 'The Fixation of Fact', in *The Film Factory*, 185.
3 Kuleshov, 'The Screen Today', 274.
4 Bill Nichols, 'The Voice of Documentary', in *Film Quarterly: Forty Years—A Selection*, eds. Brian Henderson and Ann Martin (Berkeley: University of California Press, 1999), 248.

5 'Party Cinema Conference Resolution: The Results of Cinema Construction in the USSR and the Tasks of Soviet Cinema', in *The Film Factory*, 208.
6 Shub, 'On the Creative Method' [O tvorcheskom metode], in *My Life*, 276.
7 Ibid.
8 For verification of Lenin's forcible expulsion of intellectuals, whom he threatened with execution if they returned to Russia, see Dmitri Volkogonov, *Lenin: Life and Legacy*, ed. and trans. Harold Shukman (London: HarperCollins, 1994), 358–65.
9 In fact, Helen van Dongen, who worked closely with Flaherty on both *The Land* (1940) and *Louisiana Story* (1948), alleges: 'to me Flaherty is *not* a documentarian; he makes it all up. He does use the documentary style and background but, except for *The Land*, they are all, to a degree, stories.' Ben Achtenberg, 'Helen van Dongen: An Interview', *Film Quarterly* 30, no. 2 (Winter 1976-1977): 51. On these easily accessible documentaries by Flaherty, see Eric Barnouw, *Documentary: A History of the Nonfiction Film* (Oxford and New York: Oxford University Press, 1974; 2nd rev. ed., 1993), 36–48 and 97–9.
10 Shub, 'Non-acted Film', 262.
11 Shub, 'As a Reminder', 287.
12 Yutkevich, 'The Magician of the Editing Table', 11.
13 I discuss Shub's awareness of the issues attached to the cultural reception of nonfiction film later in this chapter.
14 Shub, 'First Work', 251.
15 Ibid., 259.
16 Esfir Shub, 'Road from the Past', Sovietskoye Kino, 1934 in Leyda, *Kino*, 224.
17 Shub, 'The Beginning of Fame for Soviet Cinematography', 90–1.
18 Roberts, *Forward Soviet!*, 51.
19 Shub, 'First Work', 251.
20 Shub, 'The Advent of Sound in Cinema' [K prikhodu zvuka v kinematograf], in *My Life*, 269.
21 Shub, 'The Beginning of Fame for Soviet Cinematography', 102.
22 Shub, 'First Work', 251.
23 Shub, 'And Again – The Newsreel', 258.
24 Shub, 'Vladimir Mayakovsky', 96.
25 Leyda, *Kino*, 224.
26 Shub, 'First Work', 251.
27 Shub, 'Non-acted Film', 263.
28 Shub, 'The Beginning of Fame for Soviet Cinematography', 92.
29 Roberts, *Forward Soviet!*, 56.
30 Shub, 'As a Reminder', 287.
31 Stollery, *Eisenstein, Shub and the gender of the author as producer*, 97.

32 Shub, 'Vladimir Mayakovsky', *In Close-up*, 101–2.
33 Vladimir Mayakovsky, 'Speech in Debate on "The Paths and Policy of Sovkino,"' 1927, in *The Film Factory*, 174.
34 Shub, 'Vladimir Mayakovsky', 96.
35 Ibid., 101.
36 Ibid.
37 Ibid., 102.
38 Shub, 'We Do Not Deny the Element of Mastery' [My ne otritsaem element masterstva], in *My Life*, 248.
39 Ibid., 249.
40 Boris Kushner, 'Art of the Commune', in Christina Lodder, *Russian Constructivism*, 76. For Boris Kushner, also see my chapter on Constructivism.
41 Shub, 'We Do Not Deny the Element of Mastery', 249.
42 Ibid.
43 Shub, 'The Magician of the Editing Table', 11.
44 Leyda, 'Bridge', in *Films Beget Films*, 28.
45 I found evidence of this in two films that have appropriated Shub's work. The first is a National Geographic documentary *The 1917 Revolution in Russia*. It contains scenes from *The Fall of the Romanov Dynasty* with no recognition of Shub's contribution either in the voice-over commentary or in the credits. Its director and producer Sidney Platt inserts, in precisely the same sequential order as in the original Shub film, the bucolic scene with the Governor of Kaluga and his wife, followed by the peasant women cutting and stacking sheaves and finally the landowner and his child 'inspecting' the furrows. Likewise, Hugh Brody and Michael Ignatieff's drama *1919/Nineteen Nineteen*, starring Paul Scofield, cuts a body of material directly from *The Fall of the Romanov Dynasty* without acknowledgement.
46 Mikhail Yampolsky, 'Reality at Second Hand', *Historical Journal of Film, Radio and Television*, 11, no. 2 (1991): 163.
47 Ibid.
48 Shub, 'First Work', 251.
49 Kuleshov, 'The Screen Today', 274.
50 Shub, 'My School of Cinematography', 65.
51 Although *The Russia of Nicholas II and Leo Tolstoy* preceded *The Fall of the Romanov Dynasty* chronologically and was in fact the first film in Shub's compilation trilogy, it was made after both *The Fall* and *The Great Way* and not released until October 1928.
52 Leo Tolstoy, *What is Art?* Trans. Aylmer Maude (Dublin: ROADS Publishing, 2014), 113.

53 Shub, 'First Work', 250.
54 Shub, 'On the Film "Today"' [O filme 'Segodnya'], in *My Life*, 277.
55 Born in Odessa, Roman Lazarevich Karmen (1906–1978) was a famed Soviet documentary filmmaker. He shot memorable war footage of revolutionary struggle, such as the Spanish Civil War where his brilliant camera work was utilized by Shub in her acclaimed film *Spain*, and Karmen also filmed Mao Tse-tung for a work called *In China* [1941]. Karmen, who was Jewish, also made a documentary of the trials at Nuremberg. Roman Karmen, 'Soviet Documentary', in *Experiment in the Film*, ed. Roger Manvell (London: The Grey Walls Press, 1949), 175.
56 Valeriya Selunskaya and Maria Zezina, 'Documentary Film—a Soviet Source', in *Stalinism and Soviet Cinema*, eds. Richard Taylor and Derek Spring (London and New York: Routledge, 1993), 175.
57 Shub, 'Non-acted Film', 262.
58 Ibid., 268.
59 Ibid., 272.
60 Ibid., 273.
61 Yampolsky, 'Reality at Second Hand', 162.
62 Ibid., 161.
63 In an essay by Viktor Shklovsky, he equates subject/theme [syuzhet] with plot and fable [fabula] with story. Thus we have the creation and introduction of two key markers. These signposts are formalist theoretical constructs, that is, principal cues that serve to denote, classify and describe perceptions of narration. They are analytical devices enabling the spectator through a myriad of signals and schemata to access and read the cinematic representations as they then unfold on the screen. It was Shklovsky's firm belief that 'cinema needs an accumulation of conventions that will replace its trusty terminations of language'. Shklovsky, 'Poetry and Prose in Cinema', 1927, in *The Film Factory*, 177.
64 Shub, 'And Again – The Newsreel', 258.
65 Ibid.
66 Trans. Youngblood, *Soviet Cinema in the Silent Era*, 118.
67 'To drink from the river named "Fact"' is a line from Mayakovsky's poem titled *Good*, quoted by Shub. *In Close-up*, 105.
68 Shub, 'First Work', 251.
69 Shub, 'And Again – The Newsreel', 259. Alexandra Tolstaya left the USSR in 1929 and lived in the United States until her death.
70 Ibid. The reference to sawing is to Tolstoy's staged performance: the cutting of timber for the camera in his forest at Yasnaya Polyana.
71 Ibid., 260.

72 To reinforce his public persona, Tolstoy dressed in rustic worker's garb and is magnificently portrayed in this 'costume' by one of the most technically gifted of all the Peredvizhniki, Ilya Repin. The new genre of visual realism was epitomized by Repin's narrative paintings whose content and form was mirrored in the realist literature of Dostoevsky and Tolstoy. These are early examples of both art and literature interpreting society mimetically. *Leo Tolstoy Barefoot*, Repin's nostalgic portrait of a shoeless Tolstoy communing with nature, was a painting known to Shub. It has an element of the pantheistic and shows the great literary figure as a man of the people with his naked feet on the bare earth. It was a choreographed portrait of Tolstoy as he wished to be seen. As Shub was to remark: 'Tolstoy's personality was undoubtedly duplicitous.' Shub, 'And Again – The Newsreel', 260.
73 Ibid., 257.
74 Ibid., 260.
75 Shub, 'The Film about Tolstoy', 262.
76 Leyda, 'In The Footsteps of Esther Shub', in *Jay Leyda Collection* (Manuscript dated London, 1964). 1. This quote is from a three-page-typed draft, with handwritten corrections, discovered by me in a box of un-catalogued papers in the Jay Leyda Collection, at the Tamiment Institute and Robert F. Wagner Labour Archives, Elmer Holmes Bobst Library, New York University in 2000. Unfortunately, after an intensive week's search from morning until night, sifting through all of his papers, this was the only major reference to Shub to be found in the whole archive.
77 Shub, 'Non-acted Film', 264–5.
78 Ibid., 262–9.
79 Shub, 'This Work Cries Out' [Eta rabota krichit], in *My Life*, 217.
80 Esfir Shub, 'We Do Not Deny the Element of Mastery', 1927, in *The Film Factory*, 186.
81 José de la Colina and Tomás Pérez Turrent, 'Conversations with Luis Buñuel', in *Imagining Reality: The Faber Book of Documentary*, eds. Macdonald and Cousins, 86.
82 Ibid.
83 Shub, 'Our Way' [Nash put], in *My Life*, 295.
84 Shub, 'Non-acted Film', 265.
85 Ibid.
86 Ibid.
87 Yampolsky, 'Reality at Second Hand', 161.
88 Ibid., 161–2.
89 Shub, 'Our Way', 295.
90 Shub, 'The Film about Tolstoy', 262.
91 Shub, 'Non-acted Film', 267.

92 Dziga Vertov, 'The Eleventh Year' Speech to ARK 1928, in *The Film Factory*, 203.
93 'Dziga Vertov', *In Close-up*, 76.
94 Brik, 'The Lef Ring', in *The Film Factory*, 226.
95 Ibid., 227.
96 Ibid., 230.
97 *The Secret Life of Sergei Eisenstein* (1987), [Documentary Film] Dir. Gian-Carlo Bertelli, UK, The British Film Institute in collaboration with SSR-RTSI.
98 Shklovsky, 'The Lef Ring; Comrades! A Clash of Views: The Reasons for Failure' 1928, in *The Film Factory*: 231.
99 Viktor Pertsov (1898–1980) was a poet and literary critic. Initially, Pertsov was employed in Ukraine by Narkompros prior to leaving there to make his mark in Moscow. He was a member of LEF and *Novyi* LEF. A passionate supporter of Mayakovsky, Pertsov wrote *Mayakovsky: His Life and Work* which was published in 1957.
100 Cited in and translated by Roberts, *Forward Soviet!*, 75.
101 Ibid., 56.
102 Shklovsky, 'The Temperature of Cinema' 1927, in *The Film Factory*, 163.
The Decembrists [Dekabristy] was a mediocre costume drama based on the famous uprising of 1825. To reinforce this less than flattering viewpoint and for more details, see Youngblood, *Soviet Cinema in the Silent Era*, 145–6.
The Decembrists was released in February 1927, a month before *The Fall of the Romanov Dynasty*.
103 Shklovsky, 'Screen', 1928, in *Realism and the Cinema: A Reader*, ed. Christopher Williams (London: Routledge and Kegan Paul, 1980), 121.
104 Viktor Pertsov, 'Literature and Cinema', 1927, in *The Film Factory*, 165.
105 Shklovsky, 'The Film Factory' (Extracts), 1927, in *The Film Factory*, 169.
106 Ibid.
107 Viktor Pertsov, 'Play and Demonstration', 1927, in Vlada Petric, *Constructivism in Film: The Man with the Movie Camera*, 19.
108 Youngblood, *Soviet Cinema in the Silent Era*, 140. The italic emphasis is in Youngblood's translation.
109 See Youngblood in *Soviet Cinema in the Silent Era*, where she refers to 'the Dziga Vertov scandal', 155, and for the full detailed narrative, see 138–42.
110 Pertsov, Play and Demonstration' in Vlada Petric, 'Esther Shub: Film as Historical Discourse', in *Show Us Life: Toward a History and an Aesthetics of the Committed Documentary*, ed. Thomas Waugh (Metuchen: Scarecrow Press, 1984), 39.
111 Ibid.
112 Shklovsky, 'The Temperature of Cinema', 163.
113 Ibid.

114 Ibid.
115 Leyda, *Kino*, 224.
116 Shub, 'And Again – The Newsreel', 261.
117 Yutkevich, 'The Magician of the Editing Table', 9.
118 Shub, 'Non-acted Film', 264.
119 Shub, 'The Magician of the Editing Table', 18.
120 Ibid.
121 Shub, 'First Work', 252.
122 Ibid.
123 Ibid.
124 Ibid.
125 Benjamin, 'The Work of Art in the Age of Mechanical Reproduction', 220–3.
126 Ibid., 223.
127 Ibid., 226.
128 Ibid., 238, quoted by Benjamin from *Scènes de la vie future*, printed in Paris in 1930.
129 Vladimir Mayakovsky, 'Theatre, Cinema and Futurism', 1913, in *The Film Factory*, 33.
130 Ibid., p. 33.
131 Charles Baudelaire, 'The Salon of 1859', in *Art After Modernism*, ed. Wallis, 144.
132 Ibid.
133 Kuleshov, 'For a Great Cinema Art: Speeches to the All-Union Creative Conference of Workers', in *The Film Factory*, 355.
134 Peter Kenez, 'Silencing Cinema: Film Censorship around the World', *Studies in Russian and Soviet Cinema*, 7, no. 3 (2013): 365.
135 Kuleshov, 'For a Great Cinema Art: Speeches to the All-Union Creative Conference of Workers', 354.
136 Williams, *Artists in Revolution*, vii.
137 Shub, 'First Work', 252.
138 'We Are Continuing the Struggle', Proletarian Cinema editorial 1932, in *The Film Factory*, 321.
139 Ibid., 322.
140 Ibid.

Chapter 5

1 Bill Nichols, *Representing Reality: Issues and Concepts in Documentary* (Bloomington and Indianapolis: Indiana University Press, 1991), 21.

2 Ibid., ix.
3 Shub, 'And Again—The Newsreel', 257.
4 Nichols, *Speaking Truths with Film*, 19.
5 See 'The Archive and Issues of Authorship', in Ilana Sharp, *Esfir Shub's Neigrovaia Fil'ma: The Constructivist Origins of Documentary Cinema* (PhD diss., 2007).
6 Shub's interview with V. Pfeffer, trans. Leyda in *Sexual Stratagems: The World of Women in Film*, 181.
7 Shub, 'Vladimir Mayakovsky', 102.
8 Ibid.
9 Grigori Boltyansky, 'Cinema and the Soviet Public', 1925, in *The Film Factory*, 134.
10 Youngblood, *Soviet Cinema in the Silent Era*, 155.
11 See Ilana Sharp (née Shub), 'The Fall of the Romanov Dynasty (1927): A Constructivist Paradigm for *Neigrovaia Fil'ma*', *Historical Journal of Film, Radio and Television*, 28, no. 2 (2008): 195–217.
12 Serena Vitale (trans. Jamie Richards), *Shklovsky: Witness to an Era* (London and Dublin: Dalkey Archive Press, 2012), 57.
13 Ironically, the monument to Tsar Alexander III, symbolic of Romanov power, was originally erected in a square in 1909 that, in 1918, was renamed Uprising Square [Ploshchad Vosstaniya]. It was done so to commemorate the civil unrest and violent clashes with tsarist authorities in that area in February 1917.
14 Shklovsky, 'Resurrecting the Word' 1914 and 'Technique of Writing Craft', 1927, in *Viktor Shklovsky: A Reader*, ed. and trans. Alexandra Berlina (New York and London: Bloomsbury Academic, 2017), 70 and 184.
15 Sebestyen, *Lenin the Dictator*, 34.
16 Ibid., 4.
17 Aristide Briand and Austen Chamberlain were leaders of the French and British delegation respectively who gathered in Locarno, Switzerland, in October 1925. Together with Germany's Gustav Stresemann, Briand and Chamberlain were instrumental in the successful negotiations leading to the Locarno Treaties of 1925. The formal signing took place in London that December. L.C.B. Seaman, *Post-Victorian Britain 1902-1951* (London: Routledge, 1968), 180–1.
18 Terry Martin, *The Affirmative Action Empire: Nations and Nationalism in the Soviet Union, 1923-1939* (Ithaca and London: Cornell University Press, 2001), 267.
19 Anna M. Cienciala, 'The Foreign Policy of Jozef Pilsudski and Jozef Beck, 1926 -1929: Misconceptions and Interpretations', *The Polish Review*, LVI, no. 1–2 (2011): 115.
20 Martin, *The Affirmative Action Empire*, 226.
21 Although he didn't consider himself a socialist, together with Alexander Ulianov, Pilsudski had been implicated in the attempted assassination of Tsar Alexander III and was banished to Siberia. See Sebestyen, *Lenin the Dictator*, 458.

22 Brik, 'Against Genre Pictures', 1927, in *Lines of Resistance*, 277.
23 Brik, 'The Lef Ring: Comrades! A Clash of Views', 1928, in *The Film Factory*, 227.
24 Krylenko's name was later expunged from the annals of Soviet history after his execution in 1938. Michael Perrins, 'Nikolai Vasilievich Krylenko', in *The Blackwell Encyclopedia of the Russian Revolution*, ed. Harold Shukman (Oxford: Basil Blackwell, 1988), 337–8 and Sebestyen, *Lenin the Dictator*, 429–30.
25 Vera Figner, a medical student and political activist, was sentenced to death for her role in terrorist activities and the assassination of Tsar Alexander II. Her death sentence was commuted to a total of almost twenty-two years in solitary confinement.
26 Roberts, *Forward Soviet!*, 58.
27 Abraham Ascher, *Russia: A Short History* (Oxford: Oneworld Publications, 2002), 167–8.
28 Instead, in *October*, Eisenstein used the actor playing Trotsky (who bore a startling resemblance to him) to discredit him by denigrating all Trotsky's considerable achievements.
29 Robert Service, *Stalin: A Biography* (London: Pan Macmillan, 2004), 51.
30 Ibid., 47–8, 50–1, 58–9, 66, 76, 97, 100–1.
31 Kuleshov, 'The Screen Today', 272.
32 Ascher, *Russia: A Short History*, 172.
33 Peter Kenez, *Cinema and Soviet Society: From the Revolution to the Death of Stalin* (Cambridge and New York: Cambridge University Press, 1992; rev. ed. London and New York: I. B. Tauris, 2001), 155–8.
34 Ian D. Thatcher, 'Trotskii and Lenin's Funeral, 27 January 1924: A Brief Note', *History* 94, no. 2 (2009): 194–202.
35 Sebestyen, *Lenin the Dictator*, 503.
36 Shub, 'Vladimir Mayakovsky', 104.
37 Ibid., 103.

Chapter 6

1 Shub, 'On the Film "Today"', 277.
2 Vsevolod Pudovkin, Esfir Shub et al., 'To All Creative Workers in Soviet Cinema', in *The Film Factory*, 322. Vsevolod Pudovkin (1893–1953) was a director, actor, theorist and maker of Soviet fiction films, including *The End of St Petersburg* in 1927. He collaborated with Shub on *Twenty Years of Soviet Cinema* in 1940.
3 Ibid., 323.
4 Shub, 'We Do Not Deny the Element of Mastery', in *My Life*, 249.

5. Sergei Tretiakov, 'Our Cinema', *October*, 118 (2006): 37. *JSTOR*, www.jstor.org/stable/40368441.
6. Anne Applebaum, *Red Famine: Stalin's War on Ukraine* (Milton Keynes: Penguin Random House, 2018), 140.
7. Ibid., 134.
8. Sergei Drobashenko, 'Soviet Documentary 1917–1940', in *Propaganda, Politics and Film 1918–1945*, eds. Nicholas Pronay and Derek W. Spring (London: Macmillan, 1982), 251.
9. Shub, 'On the Film "Today"', 277.
10. Nichols, *Representing Reality*, 4–5.
11. Ibid., 20.
12. 'Symposium on Soviet Documentary', trans. Elizabeth Henderson in *The Documentary Tradition: from Nanook to Woodstock*, ed, Lewis Jacobs (New York: Hopkinson and Blake, 1971), 34.
13. Roberts, *Forward Soviet!*, 70.
14. Leyda, *Kino*, 250.
15. Roberts, 70.
16. Zhemchuzhnyi, 'The Eleventh Year', in *Lines of Resistance*, 301.
17. Ibid., 302.
18. Commissioned by Sovkino but released by Soiuzkino who superseded Sovkino during the purges in the film industry in 1930.
19. Roberts, *Forward Soviet!*, 72.
20. Youngblood, *Soviet Cinema in the Silent Era*, 168.
21. Denise J. Youngblood, email to author, 4 October 2019.
22. Ibid., 189.
23. Jamie Miller, *Soviet Cinema: Politics and Persuasion under Stalin* (London and New York: I. B.Tauris, 2010), 72.
24. Youngblood, *Soviet Cinema in the Silent Era*, 157.
25. In the autumn of 1918, after being immersed in an academic and literary background, Shub was offered a position in the secretariat, working directly under Lunacharsky. She remained there until 1922.
26. Elliott, *New Worlds: Russian Art and Society*, 22.
27. Youngblood, *Soviet Cinema in the Silent Era*, 189. It was the eventual fall of Sovkino (1924–30) and the rise of Soiuzkino (1930–3).
28. Ibid., 190.
29. Ibid.
30. Shub, 'On the Film "Today"', 278.
31. ARRK was the Association of Workers in Revolutionary Cinematography.
32. Ibid., 277.

33 Ibid.
34 Ibid., 278.
35 Jeremy Hicks, *Dziga Vertov: Defining Documentary Film* (London and New York: I. B. Tauris, 2007), 106.
36 Lynne Attwood, ed., *Red Women on the Silver Screen: Soviet Women and Cinema from the Beginning to the End of the Communist Era* (London: Pandora Press, 1991), 57.
37 Writing about the end of the 1920s, Youngblood concludes, 'Cinema had indeed become a battle front, one lacking the enthusiastic idealism which had prompted ARK to change its journal's name to *Cinema Front* in 1926.' Youngblood, *Soviet Cinema in the Silent Era*, 238.
38 Lynne Attwood, 'The Stalin Era', in *Red Women on the Silver Screen*, 57.
39 Ibid.
40 Roberts, *Forward Soviet!*, 72.
41 Youngblood, *Soviet Cinema in the Silent Era*, 230–1.
42 Tony Shaw and Denise J. Youngblood, *Cinematic Cold War: The American and Soviet Struggle for Hearts and Minds* (Lawrence: University Press of Kansas, 2010), 38.
43 Roberts, *Forward Soviet!*, 140.

Chapter 7

1 Youngblood, *Soviet Cinema in The Silent Era*, 221.
2 Miller, *Soviet Cinema: Politics and Persuasion under Stalin*, 31.
3 David Bordwell, *On the Theory of Film Style* (Cambridge, MA and London: Harvard University Press, 1999), 46. Bordwell's translated quote is from Alexandre Astruc, *Écrits* (1942–1984) (Paris: L'Archipel, 1992), 269.
4 Shub, 'The Advent of Sound in Cinema', 269.
5 Bill Nichols, *Introduction to Documentary* (Bloomington: Indiana University Press, 2010), 26.
6 Lilya Kaganovsky, *The Voice of Technology: Soviet Cinema's Transition to Sound 1928–1935* (Bloomington: Indiana University Press, 2018), 72.
7 Laura U. Marks, *Touch: Sensuous Theory and Multisensory Media* (Minneapolis and London: University of Minnesota Press, 2002), 8.
8 Ibid.
9 Ibid., 13.
10 Kaganovsky, *The Voice of Technology: Soviet Cinema's Transition to Sound*, 71.
11 Ibid., 72.

12 Shub, 'The Theme of My Speech' [Tema moei rechi], in *My Life*, 281.
13 Kozintsev, Trauberg, Yutkevich and Kryzhitsky, 'Eccentrism', 64.
14 In a speech Lenin delivered to the Moscow Gubernia Conference of the R. C. P. (B.), 21 November 1920. *Lenin's Collected Works*, Volume 31, trans. Julius Katzer (Moscow, 1965). V. I. Lenin Internet Archive (www.marx.org) accessed 11 November 2002.
15 Albert Glinsky, *Theremin: Ether Music and Espionage* (Urbana, Chicago and Springfield: University of Illinois, 2005), 36.
16 Thomas P. Hughes, 'How America Helped Build the Soviet Machine', *American Heritage*, 39, no. 8 (1988): 4.
17 Kevin Bartig, 'The correspondence of Sergei Eisenstein and Gavriil Popov 1933–1939', *Studies in Russian and Soviet Cinema* 11, no. 2 (2017): 165.
18 Shub, 'The Theme of My Speech', 284.
19 Ibid.
20 Drobashenko, 'Soviet documentary film 1917–1940', 265.
21 Ian Christie, 'Making Sense of Early Soviet Sound', *Inside the Film Factory: New Approaches to Russian and Soviet Cinema*, eds. Richard Taylor and Ian Christie (London: Routledge, 1991), 185. For a definition of facture [faktura], see my chapter on Constructivism.
22 For further information, see Kenez, *Cinema and Soviet Society*, 123.
23 Glinsky, *Theremin: Ether Music and Espionage*, xi.
24 Professor Abram Fedorovich Ioffe, recognized as the father of Soviet physics, was a leading physicist and an academic supervisor to Theremin in his early career. Ioffe established the Physico-Mechanical/Technical Institute within the Leningrad Polytechnical Institute. Glinsky, *Theremin: Ether Music and Espionage*, 23.
25 Shub, 'Nato Vachnadze', in *My Life*, 225. Professor Alexander Alekseevich Chernyshev was a prominent expert in the field of electrical engineering and was responsible for the first high-frequency telephone connection in the USSR. Ioffe is seen towards the end of the film showing scientific experiments in electricity to Komsomol representatives. Nato Vachnadze's name is sometimes russifed as 'Nata.'
26 Drobashenko, 'Soviet documentary film 1917–1940', 264.
27 Shub, 'The Advent of Sound in Cinema', 269.
28 Hughes, 'How America Helped Build the Soviet Machine', 4.
29 Marietta Shaginyan's novel *Miss Mend* was adapted for the screen by Boris Barnet and released in 1926.
30 Shub, 'The Advent of Sound in Cinema', 270.
31 Ibid.
32 Shub, 'Nato Vachnadze', 225.
33 Drobashenko, 'Soviet documentary film 1917–1940', 265.

34 In addition, a loudspeaker can also be a transducer and convert electrical energy back into acoustical energy.
35 Glinsky, *Theremin: Ether Music and Espionage*, 108.
36 Ibid., 19. The word 'beloved' used to describe Ioffe is a quote from Theremin himself.
37 Shub, 'Nato Vachnadze', 225.
38 Ibid.
39 For a comprehensive volume on Vertov, see Jeremy Hicks, *Dziga Vertov: Defining Documentary Film*, (London, 2007), and the more recent publication by John Mackay, *Dziga Vertov: Life and Work* (Volume 1: 1896–1921) (Boston, MA: Academic Studies Press, 2018).
40 Hicks, *Dziga Vertov: Defining Documentary, Film*, 73.
41 Kaganovsky, *The Voice of Technology: Soviet Cinema's Transition to Sound*, 81–2.
42 Roberts, *Forward Soviet!*, 99.
43 Vertov, 'Speech to the First All-Union Conference on Sound Cinema', 1930 in *The Film Factory*, 301.
44 Hicks, *Dziga Vertov: Defining Documentary, Film*, 79.
45 Robert. A. Rosenstone, ed. Introduction to *Revisioning History: Film and the Construction of a New Past* (Princeton: Princeton University Press, 1995), 10.
46 Boris Shumiatsky, 'A Cinema for the Millions', in *The Film Factory*, 358.
47 Elena Stishova, 'The Mythologization of Soviet Woman', in *Red Women on the Silver Screen*, 179.
48 Attwood, 'The Stalin Era', 58.
49 Hughes, 'How America Helped Build the Soviet Machine', 5.
50 Drobashenko, 'Soviet documentary film 1917–1940', 264.
51 Ibid., 265.
52 For a comprehensive coverage of the major problems besetting the Soviet film industry in the transition to sound, see Youngblood, *Soviet Cinema in the Silent Era*, 221–232.
53 Peter Kenez, *Cinema and Soviet Society*, 123.
54 Youngblood, *Soviet Cinema in the Silent Era*, 221.
55 Roberts, *Forward Soviet!*, 99.
56 Hicks, *Dziga Vertov: Defining Documentary, Film*, 106.
57 Ibid., 90.
58 Attwood, 'The Stalin Era', 70.
59 Hicks, *Dziga Vertov: Defining Documentary, Film*, 105.
60 There were other films about Pushkin and Shub's friend Mayakovsky that never came to fruition. In addition, she took ample footage in Turkey for a vibrant travelogue that was not made. It not only contained footage of the magnificent

ancient architecture to be found in Istanbul (where her companion on location was Ilya Ehrenburg) but also fascinating images of the Greek ruins of Smyrna, which are part of modern-day Turkey.

61 Youngblood, *Soviet Cinema in the Silent Era*, 199.
62 'We Are Continuing the Struggle', 1932, Proletarian Cinema editorial in *The Film Factory*, 321.
63 Ibid., 322.
64 Evgeny Dobrenko, *Stalinist Cinema and the Production of History: Museum of the Revolution* (New Haven and London: Yale University Press, 2008), 5.
65 Stishova, 'The Mythologization of Soviet Woman', 179.
66 Kuleshov, 'For a Great Cinema Art: Speeches to the All-Union Creative Conference of Workers in Soviet Cinema', 354.
67 Ibid., 355. Another segment of Kuleshov's speech has been quoted in Chapter 4.
68 Shub, 'Our Way', 297.
69 Ibid. See endnote 60.
70 Roberts, *Forward Soviet!*, 140.
71 Shub, 'Non-acted Film', 285.
72 Ibid., 286.
73 Vera Kholodnaya was a leading screen idol, much loved by the public, who died tragically young during the influenza epidemic in 1919. For further information on Kholodnaya, see Denise J. Youngblood, *The Magic Mirror: Moviemaking in Russia, 1908-1918* (Wisconsin and London: The University of Wisconsin Press, 1999), 52-2, 84-5, 86-7. Also see Zorkaya, *The Illustrated History of Soviet Cinema*, 22, 33, 34, 35, 46-7.
74 Kolkhoz was a Soviet collective farm.
75 Shub, 'I Want to Make a Film about Women' [Khochu delat filmu o zhenshchine], in *My Life*, 256.
76 Ibid.
77 Maya Turovskaya, '"Women's Cinema" in the USSR', in *Red Women on the Silver Screen*, 145.
78 Ibid.
79 Ibid.
80 Ibid. Interestingly, long before Shub had submitted her script for *Women*, she had edited Oleg Frelikh's work *A Prostitute* in 1926. According to David Gillespie, Shklovsky's script for the film not only 'attacked social injustice' in general but the exploitation of women in particular. Gillespie, *Early Soviet Cinema: Innovation, Ideology and Propaganda*, 9.
81 Turovskaya, '"Women's Cinema" in the USSR', 145.
82 Ibid.

83 Shub, 'I Want to Make a Film about Women', 256. This final paragraph, where Shub appears to praise Stalin and his supportive perspective towards women workers at the kolkhoz, is profoundly ironic. According to Richard Stites, Stalin showed a traditional Georgian male chauvinist attitude in his dealings with women and was 'deeply anti-feminist.' Stites, *The Women's Liberation Movement in Russia*, 385. Unsurprisingly, 'Stalin was anti-abortion because for him it was the role of women to procreate and help to build a solid socialist labour force.' Stites, *The Women's Liberation Movement in Russia*, 385–6. More specifically, the anti-abortion policy was an attempt to redress the devastating decimation of human life and agricultural productivity resulting from his policy of collectivization. This catastrophic situation of famine aside, Stalin viewed women as breeding machines, domestic slaves and workers: objects to be used in Soviet production.

84 Shub, 'I Want to Work' [Khochu rabotat], in *My Life*, 288–91.

85 Ibid., 288.

86 Ibid.

87 Ibid., 291.

88 To add to her isolation, Shub had made a critical error of judgement. In 1934 the journal *Soviet Cinema* [Sovetskoe kino] published the obsequious *Film-Makers' Letter to Stalin* in their November/December issue. In a time of terror and with this document swearing devoted allegiance and genuflecting to Stalin, the filmmakers relinquished any last vestiges of artistic autonomy. As they declared: 'Our art . . . derives its strength from ideology . . . the greatest reconstruction of the world, the cause of the revolutionary Party of Lenin and Stalin . . . the slogan of our Five-Year Plan. . . . For this we are grateful to the Party and to you, its great Leader, Comrade Stalin.' *The Film Factory*, 337. Eisenstein, Tisse, Alexandrov, Dovzhenko, Kuleshov, Medvedkin, the Vasilievs, Yutkevich, Romm, Vertov and many other prominent figures in the industry were signatories to this letter. Conspicuous by her absence was Shub. In terms of her career, this was an ill-considered stance with consequences. It very likely accounted for the debacle surrounding *Land of the Soviets*.

89 Shub, 'The City Sleeps' [Gorod spit], in *My Life*, 342.

90 Roberts, *Forward Soviet!*, 4.

91 Ibid., 130.

92 Boris Shumiatsky was described by Denise Youngblood as 'a Party hack with absolutely no cinema experience' when he was elevated to the position of Chairman at the Central Soviet Cinema Organization [Soiuzkino] in 1930. Youngblood, *Soviet Cinema in the Silent Era*, 190.

93 Miller, *Soviet Cinema: Politics and Persuasion under Stalin*, 179–80.

94 See Roberts, *Forward Soviet!*, 4, 130–1, 143.

95 Miller, *Soviet Cinema: Politics and Persuasion under Stalin*, 180.
96 Shub, *My Life*, 211. Graham Roberts's translation of Shub's words in *Forward Soviet!*, 128.
97 Ibid., 69.
98 Ibid., 180.
99 Ibid.
100 Shub, 'A Diversion (A Tribute to my Youth)', 28.

Chapter 8

1 Antonio Prado, 'Anarchism and Counterinformation in Documentaries: From Civil War Spain to Post-2001 Argentina', *Latin American Perspectives*, 40, no. 1 (2013): 55.
2 Miller, *Soviet Cinema: Politics and Persuasion under Stalin*, 180.
3 Shub relates that when the film was completed and ready for editing, disappointingly, Karmen 'was supposed to work with us but he was already in China at the time.' Shub, 'Warrior and Poet–Vsevolod Vishnevsky' [Voin I poet–Vsevolod Vishnevsky], *In Close-up*, 160.
4 According to Shub, the initial concept of the film came from a meeting with the journalist Mikhail Koltsov. As leading foreign correspondent for *Pravda*, he had spent several months in Spain during 1936, sending regular bulletins back to Moscow. Koltsov 'called' Shub and Karmen into 'his editorial office at Pravda.' The dramatist Vishnevsky superseded Koltsov as the scriptwriter. Vishnevsky was a passionate supporter of Spanish people, had been to Spain during the conflict and 'could talk about it endlessly.' 'Warrior and Poet–Vsevolod Vishnevsky', 159–60. Another added advantage was Vishnevsky's esteem for Shub's work. In fact, Leyda states that Vishnevsky's 'admiration for Shub's work dates from its beginning: when *Fall of the Romanov Dynasty* first appeared, Vishnevsky saw it three times.' Leyda, 'The Lines Are Drawn', in *Films Beget Films*, 40.
5 Shub, 'Warrior and Poet–Vsevolod Vishnevsky', 159.
6 Ibid.
7 Shub praised not only Karmen's filming but also his bravery because, as she remarked admiringly, 'this amazing shooting relies on the reporter's skill and the fearlessness of Karmen, the camera operator. He's with the attackers.' 'Warrior and Poet–Vsevolod Vishnevsky', 166.
8 Miller, *Soviet Cinema: Politics and Persuasion under Stalin*, 89.
9 Ibid., 71.
10 Stanley G. Payne, *The Spanish Civil War, The Soviet Union, and Communism* (New Haven and London: Yale University Press, 2004), 129. Payne has been my primary

source although I have accessed Sebastian Balfour, *Spain: A History* (Oxford: Oxford University Press, 2000); Raymond Carr, ed., *Spain a History* (Oxford: Oxford University Press, 2000); Shelagh M. Ellwood, *The Spanish Civil War* (Oxford: Basil Blackwell, 1991); Lisa Kirschenbaum, *International Communism and the Spanish Civil War: Solidarity and Suspicion* (Cambridge and New York: Cambridge University Press, 2015); Michael Seidman's *Republic of Egos: A Social History of the Spanish Civil War* (Wisconsin: University of Wisconsin Press, 2002); Hugh Thomas, *The Spanish Civil War* (London: Eyre and Spottiswode, 1961; rev. edn, London and New York: Penguin Books, 2012).

11 Payne, *The Spanish Civil War, The Soviet Union, and Communism*, 129.
12 Ibid., 143.
13 Ibid., 125, 127, 129, 140–50, 157–8.
14 Ibid., 317.
15 Ibid., 126.
16 Eisenstein, 'My Subject Is Patriotism', in *The Film Factory*, 398.
17 Ibid., 400.
18 Ibid. The enemy forces, the Livonian Knights, were part of the Order of Teutonic Knights.
19 Ibid., 398.
20 Peter Wollen, *Signs and Meaning in the Cinema* (Bloomington: Indiana University Press, 1972), 123–4.
21 Shub writes that she and Vishnevsky wanted him to read the voice-over for *Spain*. As he had written the text, it seemed fitting that as the author, his voice should be heard. However, 'the studio management decided otherwise.' They determined that the speaker should be Yury Levitan, the well-known head announcer at Radio Moscow. However, after an audition, it was determined that Levitan was not the right option. Vishnevsky was chosen instead, and 'his narration was original and beautiful.' Shub, 'Warrior and Poet–Vsevolod Vishnevsky', 161.
22 Ibid.
23 Ibid.
24 Seidman, *Republic of Egos*, 3.
25 This technique of showing the old and the new, the primitive and repressive Russian world prior to the Revolution being contrasted with the modern technological marvels of the Soviet state is a thematic device applied to all of Shub's films. She extends this motif to *Spain*.
26 Balfour, *Spain: A History*, 254.
27 Shub, 'Warrior and Poet–Vsevolod Vishnevsky', 166.
28 Balfour, *Spain: A History*, 254.
29 Shub, 'Warrior and Poet–Vsevolod Vishnevsky', 168.

30 Ibid., 164.
31 Vishnevsky was later an active participant during the Siege of Leningrad from where he wrote letters to Shub in 1942. See 'Warrior and Poet–Vsevolod Vishnevsky', 179–82. They were close friends, and when Vishnevsky died in 1951 at the age of fifty, Shub recalled with poignancy: 'He left. Left too soon. My dear, beautiful friend. His memory is precious to me.' Ibid., 183.
32 Ibid., 161.
33 Shub, 'Warrior and Poet–Vsevolod Vishnevsky', 171.
34 Joris Ivens, *The Camera and I* (New York: International Publishers, 1969), 136.
35 Ibid., 75.
36 Ibid., 76.
37 Ibid., 77.
38 Ibid., 107.
39 Shub, 'Warrior and Poet–Vsevolod Vishnevsky', 164.
40 Leyda, *Films Beget Films*, 41.
41 Ibid.
42 This is an extract from the second page of an unpublished typed essay, with handwritten corrections, by Leyda. It was titled *In the footsteps of Esther Shub* and was found by me, in 2000, within a box of papers in the Tamiment Archives, Bobst Library, New York University.
43 The Thorndikes (Annelie and Andrew) were a documentary team working in West Germany after World War II, who made highly political nonfiction films.
44 Leyda, *Films Beget Films*, 141.

Conclusion

1 Vladimir Mayakovsky in *Show Us Life: Toward a History and an Aesthetics of the Committed Documentary*, 31.
   A lasting sorrow concerned Shub's proposed documentary paying homage to the career of Mayakovsky. Just prior to Mayakovsky's tragic suicide in 1930, Shub was given the funding to make a work on this outspoken and charismatic leader of the avant-garde. It was to be a unique opportunity to film the glorious idol of her student days. As Shub recounts: 'I was lucky to receive permission to film Vladimir Mayakovsky in connection with the twentieth anniversary of his literary activity . . . my last conversation with Mayakovsky was by telephone approximately four or five days before such an impossible ending to his life.' Shub, 'Vladimir Mayakovsky', 110.
2 Yutkevich, 'The Magician of the Editing Table', 7.

3 Shub, Letter 'E. I. Shub–V. I. Mukhina', in *My Life*, 448.
4 Yutkevich, 'The Magician of the Editing Table', 17.
5 Ibid., 7, Yutkevich is most probably referring here to Capra's documentary war series *Why We Fight*.
6 Sklar, *Film: An International History of the Medium*, 250.
7 Shub, 'Documentary Cinema: Affairs and People', [Dokumentalnoe kino: Dela i liudi] in *My Life*, 208.
8 Ibid.
9 Achtenberg, 'Helen van Dongen: An Interview', 55.
10 Leyda, *Films Beget Films*, 63.
11 Bob Mastrangelo, 'Obituary: Helen van Dongen', *The Guardian*, Friday, 10 November 2006.
12 Paul Wells, 'The Documentary Form: Personal and Social Realities', in *An Introduction to Film Studies*, ed. Jill Nelmes (London and New York: Routledge, 1996; rev. ed. London: Routledge, 2003), 199.
13 Ibid.
14 Ibid.
15 Sklar, *Film: An International History of the Medium*, 248
16 Barnouw, *Documentary: A History of the Nonfiction Film*, 114.
17 Wells, 'The Documentary Form: Personal and Social Realities', 181.
18 Leyda, *Films Beget Films*, 44.
19 Yutkevich, 'The Magician of the Editing Table', 17.
20 Ibid., 16.
21 Drobashenko, 'Soviet documentary film, 1917–40', 264.
22 Better known as Kemal Atatürk, after leading a revolution, he ruled Turkey until his death in 1938. A reformer and dictator, he westernized Turkey and gave emancipation to women.
23 Yutkevich, 'The Magician of the Editing Table', 17.
24 Ibid. For Robert Drew and Richard Leacock, see Barnouw, *Documentary: A History of the Nonfiction Film*, 235–8.
25 Sklar, *Film: An International History of the Medium*, 523.
26 G. Roy Levin, *Documentary Explorations: 15 Interviews with Film-makers* (Garden City: Doubleday, 1971), 135. Jean Rouch, one of the founders of *cinéma verité*, also worked on synchronized sound. His fellow Frenchman, Chris Marker, extended Rouch's principles of *cinéma verité* to make challenging documentaries, which, like Vertov's, were both political and poetic. For Jean Rouch, see Barnouw, *Documentary: A History of the Nonfiction Film*, 253–5.
27 Kaganovsky, *The Voice of Technology*, 93.
28 Shub, 'Non-acted Film', 265.

29 Ibid.
30 James Blue, 'Jean Rouch', in *Imagining Reality: The Faber Book of Documentary*, eds. Macdonald and Cousins, 268–9.
31 William F. Van Wert, 'Chris Marker: The SLON Films', *Film Quarterly*, 32, no. 3 (Spring 1979): 41.
32 Alexander Medvedkin died in 1989, four years after Marker's documentary was released.
33 For details of Medvedkin's *Happiness*, see endnote 1 in my Introduction. Yakov Protazanov's science-fiction film *Aelita* [1924] was based loosely on Aleksei Tolstoy's novel of the same title. Protazanov and his scriptwriters substantially altered and built on Tolstoy's text by layering it with added meaning and inserting an appropriate ideological framework. The film depicts divergent perspectives and a complexity of themes, including the Soviet Union of the early 1920s, science fiction, romantic interludes, scenes from contemporary life [byt], socialist ideology and utopian visions. Their dramatic sets for Mars were geometric, futuristic and monumental and have led to many arguments as to whether these structures are Constructivist in intent. Suffice to say that they are riveting avant-garde works of art with a strongly utilitarian function.
34 Annelie and Andrew Thorndike's work owes a great debt to Shub's pioneering work. Similarly, so did Erwin Leiser, who made a confronting compilation documentary about Hitler and the Nazi regime called *Mein Kampf*.
35 Leyda, 'In the Footsteps of Esther Shub', 1.
36 Sergei Drobashenko quoted in Vlada Petric, 'Esther Shub's Unrealized Project', *Quarterly Review of Film Studies*, 3, no. 4 (Fall 1978): 446.
37 Michael Chanan, *The Politics of Documentary* (London: British Film Institute, 2007), 261.
38 Sklar, *Film: An International History of the Medium*, 524.
39 Wells, 'The Documentary Form: Personal and Social Realities', 183.
40 Chanan, *The Politics of Documentary*, 121.
41 Ibid.
42 Drobashenko, 'Soviet documentary film, 1917–40', 264.
43 Wells, 'The Documentary Form: Personal and Social Realities', 183.
44 Drobashenko, 'Soviet documentary film, 1917–40', 264.
45 Chanan, *The Politics of Documentary*, 122.
46 Esfir Shub, 'How the Film Was Made', trans. Jay Leyda, in Leyda, *Films Beget Films*, 161.
47 Shub, 'A Diversion (A Tribute to my Youth)', 28.
48 Norbert Sparrow, 'I Let the Audience Feel and Think: An Interview with Rainer Werner Fassbinder', *Cinéaste*, 8, no. 2 (1977): 21.

49 For an incisive examination of propaganda, politics and film in the Soviet Union, see Richard Taylor, *Film Propaganda: Soviet Russia and Nazi Germany* (London and New York: I. B. Tauris, 1998), 3–62. Perhaps a possible clue to Shub's obscurity lies in the introduction to a film on the life and work of the English documentary filmmaker Humphrey Jennings (1907–1950). Jennings's oeuvre was sometimes compared with Jean Rouch and Joris Ivens. The voice-over narration asserts that Jennings had 'an extraordinary ability to capture truthful and spontaneous human moments.... But... perhaps because he worked in the unpromising and deeply unfashionable field of propaganda films, his name is virtually unknown except among cinephiles and those few survivors who knew and worked with him.' Possibly, in part at least, the theory behind this statement could also be applicable to Shub. *Humphrey Jennings: The Man Who Listened to Britain* (2000), [TV programme] Channel 4. Dir. Kevin Macdonald, UK.

50 The narrator in Chris Marker's documentary, *The Last Bolshevik*, declares that 'propaganda was a continuation of war by other means'.

51 Writing in 1931 in her sub-chapter 'On the Creative Method,' Shub confesses in her conclusion: 'It is necessary to talk about the shortcomings in Soviet cinematography as a whole.... As yet, none of us has satisfactorily mastered the method of dialectical materialism.' Shub, 'On the Film "Today"', 277.

52 Medvedkin interviewed in Paris by Chris Marker in 1984. *The Last Bolshevik*. It is my inclination to agree with Medvedkin that has energized my interest in Shub from the start. Indeed, the subtext of my thinking about her work, life and times is self-referential, for this exploration has also been a personal odyssey. It is highly probable that, by marriage, Esfir Shub was a member of my lost and dispersed Jewish forebears in Eastern Europe.

53 Seth R. Feldman, *Dziga Vertov: A Guide to References and Resources* (Boston: G. K. Hall, 1979), 5. 'Cinema Week' [Kino-nedelya] was the Soviet newsreel created under the auspices of the Moscow Cinema Committee of Narkompros and this was where Vertov first honed his skills.

54 Leyda, 'In the Footsteps of Esther Shub', 1.

55 Ibid.

56 Ibid.

57 Petric, *Constructivism in Film*, 20.

58 Kaganovsky, *The Voice of Technology*, 84. Added to Lilya Kaganovsky's pronouncement, as my book goes to print, Anastasia Kostina has unearthed *Manifesto*, the first film by Lidia Stepanova. A silent compilation, initially, the date given was 1927. However, its intertitles point to a release date of late 1928 (they speak of a year elapsing after the tenth anniversary of October Revolution). *Manifesto* was screened during a two-hour panel at the Women and the Silent

Screen Conference held at Columbia University. Anastasia Kostina. *The Art of Recycling: Early Soviet Compilation Film*. Women and the Silent Screen Conference, Columbia University, New York, 4 June 2021.
59 Youngblood, *Soviet Cinema in the Silent Era*, 155.
60 Ibid. The italic emphasis is Youngblood's.
61 Leyda, 'Esther Shub' in *Sexual Stratagems: The World of Women in Film*, 183.
62 Leyda, 'In the Footsteps of Esther Shub', 3.

Esfir Shub: Filmography

The Fall of the Romanov Dynasty [Padenie dinasty Romanovykh] 1927

Sovkino and the Museum of the Revolution
A chronicle of the years 1912 to 1917
In 7 parts
Length 2080 metres
Director Esfir Shub
Consultant Mark Tzeitlin

The Great Way [Veliky put] 1927

Sovkino and the Museum of the Revolution
A chronicle of the years 1917 to 1927
In 9 parts
Length 2350 metres
Director Esfir Shub
Scenarist Esfir Shub
Camera N. Sokolov
Consultant Mark Tzeitlin
Assistant directors Lev Felanov, Tatiana Kuvshinchikhova

The Russia of Nicholas II and Leo Tolstoy [Rossiia Nikolaya II i Lva Tolstogo] 1928

Sovkino
A chronicle of the years from 1897 to 1912
In 5 parts
Length 1700 metres
Editor Esfir Shub
Scenarist Esfir Shub

Consultant Mark Tzeitlin
Assistant director Lev Felanov
Additional camera work E. Schneider, D. Feldman, G. Bloom.

Today [Segodnya] 1930

Soiuzkino
In 6 parts
Length 2090 metres
Director Esfir Shub
Scenarists Esfir Shub and Mark Tzeitlin
Camera Stepanov and Stilianudis

K.Sh.E. Komsomol – Patron of Electrification [Komsomol-shef elektrifikatsy] 1932

Soiuzkino
In 6 parts
Length 2750 metres
Scenarist and director Esfir Shub
Assistant director Lev Felanov, N. Vachnadze
Camera V. Solodovnikov, A. Barkovsky
Composer Gavriil Popov

Moscow Builds the Metro [Moskva stroit metro] or *Metro by Night* [Metro nochiu] or *The City Sleeps* [Gorod spit] 1934

Moscow Kinokombinat
In 1 part
Length 400 metres
Director Esfir Shub
Camera V. Solodovnikov
Composer Gavriil Popov

Land of the Soviets [Strana sovetov] 1937

Mosfilm
In 8 parts
Length 1945 metres

Director Esfir Shub
Scenarists Boris Agapov and Esfir Shub
Editor Lev Felanov
Camera Eduard Tisse (Ukraine and Georgia), B. Krilov (Crimea), D Feldman (Moscow)
Musical production L. Shteinberg and N Kriukov
Song and lyrics Mikhail Svetlov with music by N. Kryukov

Spain [Ispaniya] 1939

Mosfilm
In 10 parts
Length 2090 metres
Director Esfir Shub
Co-director A. Frolov
Scenarist Vsevolod Vishnevsky
Camera Roman Karmen, Boris Makaseev
Composer Gavriil Popov
Narrator Vsevolod Vishnevsky

Twenty Years of Soviet Cinema [20 let sovetskogo kino] or *Our Cinema* [Nashe kino] 1940

Central Studio of Documentary Films
Scenarists and directors Esfir Shub and Vsevolod Pudovkin

Fascism Will Be Defeated [Fashizm budet razbyt] or *The Face of the Enemy* [Litso vraga] 1941

Mosfilm
In 6 parts
Director Esfir Shub.
Scenarists Boris Agapov and Esfir Shub
Narrated text Boris Agapov

Homeland [Strana rodnaya] 1942

Central Studio of Documentary Films
Director Esfir Shub
Scenarist Esfir Shub

Judgement in Smolensk (special release) [Sud v Smolenske (spetsvypoisk)] 1946

Central Studio of Documentary Films
Director Esfir Shub
Scenarist Esfir Shub

On the Other Side of the Araks River [Po tu storonu Araksa] 1947

Baku Film Studio
In 6 parts
Length 1946 metres
Director Esfir Shub
Co-director I. Efendev
Scenarists Esfir Shub and N. Shpikovsky
Cameramen M. Dalishev and O. Badalov
Narrator L. Kmara
Composer Niazin.

[See *My Life – Cinematography*, 470].

Select Filmography

1917: Revolution in Russia (1988). [TV programme], National Geographic Society.
Aelita [Aelita] (1924). Dir. Yakov Protazanov, USSR: Mezhrabpom-Rus.
Alexander Nevsky [Alexsandr Nevsky] (1938). Dir. Sergei Eisenstein, USSR: Mosfilm.
Arsenal [Arsenal] (1929). Dir. Alexander Dovzhenko, USSR: VUFKU.
Battleship Potemkin [Bronenosets Potemkin] (1926). Dir. Sergei Eisenstein, USSR: Goskino.
By the Law [Po zakonu] (1926). Dir. Lev Kuleshov, USSR: Goskino.
Chagall: To Russia, Asses and Others [Chagall à la Russie, aux ânes et aux autres] (2003). [TV programme], France 3 in association with France 5.
Cinema-Eye [Kino-glaz] (1924). Dir. Dziga Vertov, USSR: Goskino.
Dura Lex see *By the Law*.
Earth [Zemlya] (1930). Dir. Alexander Dovzhenko, USSR: VUFKU.
Eisenstein: The Little Boy from Riga (1988). [TV programme], BBC1.
The Eleventh Year [Odinnadtsatyi] (1928). Dir. Dziga Vertov, USSR: VUFKU.
The End of St. Petersburg [Konets Sankt-Peterburga] (1927). Dir. Vsevolod Pudovkin, USSR: Mezhrabpom-Rus.
Enthusiasm: the Symphony of the Donbass [Entuziazm: Simfoniya Donbassa] (1931). Dir. Dziga Vertov, USSR: Ukrainfilm.
The Extraordinary Adventures of Mr West in the Land of the Bolsheviks [Neobychainye prikliucheniya Mistera Vesta v strane bolshevikov] (1924). Dir. Lev Kuleshov, USSR: Goskino.
Humphrey Jennings: The Man Who Listened to Britain (2000). [TV programme], Channel 4.
Ivan the Terrible [Ivan Grozny]: Part One (1944). Dir. Sergei Eisenstein, USSR: Central Cinema Studio.
Ivan the Terrible [Ivan Grozny]: Part Two (1945 but not released until 1958). Dir. Sergei Eisenstein, USSR: Mosfilm.
The Jew on the Land [Yevrei na zemle] (1927). Dir. Abram Room, USSR: Sovkino.
Land Without Bread [Las Hurdes: Tierra Sin Pan] (1932). Dir. Luis Buñuel, Spain.
The Last Bolshevik [Le tombeau d'Alexandre] (1992). Dir. Chris Marker, France: Icarus Films.
Man of Aran (1934). Dir. Robert J. Flaherty, UK: Gainsborough Pictures.
Man with a Movie Camera [Chelovek s kinoapparatom] (1929). Dir. Dziga Vertov, USSR: VUFKU.

Mother [Mat] (1926). Dir. Vsevolod Pudovkin, USSR: Mezhrabpom-Rus.

Nanook of the North (1922). Dir. Robert J. Flaherty, France: Pathé Exchange and Revillon Frères.

Nineteen Nineteen/1919 (1985). Dir. Hugh Brody, UK: British Film Institute (BFI) Production Board and Channel Four Films.

October [Oktiabr] (1928). Dir. Sergei Eisenstein, USSR: Sovkino.

Primary (1960). [TV programme], Time Inc. (Time-Life Broadcasting).

The Secret Life of Sergei Eisenstein (1987). [TV programme], British Film Institute (BFI) in conjunction with SSR-RTSI.

A Sixth Part of the World [Shestaya chast mira] (1926). Dir. Dziga Vertov, USSR: Goskino (Kultkino).

The Spanish Earth (1937). Dir. Joris Ivens, USA: Contemporary Historians Inc.

Stalin: The Myth, Part One and Part Two (2003). [TV programme], Channel 4.

Strike [Stachka] (made in 1924 but not released until 1925). Dir. Sergei Eisenstein, USSR: Proletkult and Goskino.

Wings of a Serf [Krylya kholopa] (1926). Dir. Yury Tarich, USSR: Sovkino.

Zvenigora [Zvenigora] (1928). Dir. Alexander Dovzhenko, USSR: VUFKU.

Bibliography

Primary Sources

Bann, Stephen, ed. *The Tradition of Constructivism: The Documents of Twentieth Century Art*. New York: Viking Press, 1974.

Bartig, Kevin. 'The Correspondence of Sergei Eisenstein and Gavriil Popov 1933–1939', *Studies in Russian and Soviet Cinema* 11, no. 2 (2017): 163–77.

Bazin, André. *What Is Cinema?* Trans. Hugh Gray. Berkeley and Los Angeles: University of California Press, 1967.

Benjamin, Walter. 'The Artist as Producer', in *Art after Modernism: Rethinking Representation*. Ed. Brian Wallis, 297–309. New York: New Museum of Contemporary Art, 1995.

Benjamin, Walter. 'The Work of Art in the Age of Mechanical Reproduction', in *Illuminations: Essays and Reflections*. Ed. Hannah Arendt. Trans. Harry Zohn, 217–51. New York: Schocken Books, 1968.

Bowlt, John E., ed. and trans. *Russian Art of the Avant-Garde: Theory and Criticism 1902–1934*. New York: The Viking Press, 1976; rev. and enl. ed. London: Thames and Hudson, 1988.

Brecht, Bertolt. 'A Short Organum for the Theatre', in *Playwrights on Playwriting: The Meaning and Making of Modern Drama from Ibsen to Ionesco*. Ed. Toby Cole, 72–105. London: MacGibbon and Kee, 1960.

Chagall, Marc. *My Life*. Trans. Dorothy Williams. Oxford: Peter Owen, 1957.

Chicago, Judy. *Through the Flower: My Struggle as a Woman Artist*. London: The Women's Press, 1975.

Eisenstein, Sergei. *Eisenstein 2 – A Premature Celebration of Eisenstein's Centenary*. Ed. and trans. Jay Leyda. Seagull Books: Calcutta, 1985.

Eisenstein, Sergei. *The Eisenstein Reader*. Ed. Richard Taylor. Trans. Richard Taylor and William Powell. London: British Film Institute, 1998.

Eisenstein, Sergei. *Film Form: Essays in Film Theory*. Ed. and trans. Jay Leyda. New York: Harcourt Brace Jovanovich, 1977 [orig. pub.1949].

Eisenstein, Sergei. *Notes of a Film Director*. Trans. X. Danko. Moscow: Foreign Languages Publishing House, 1959.

Eisenstein, Sergei. *S. M. Eisenstein Selected Works Volume II, Towards a Theory of Montage*. Eds. Michael Glenny and Richard Taylor. Trans. Michael Glenny. London: British Film Institute, 1994.

Eisenstein, Sergei. *S. M. Eisenstein Selected Works Volume IV, Beyond the Stars: The Memoirs of Sergei Eisenstein*. Ed. Richard Taylor. Trans. William Powell. London: British Film Institute, 1995.

Ivens, Joris. *The Camera and I*. New York: International Publishers, 1969.

Kandinsky, Wassily. *Concerning the Spiritual in Art*. Trans. Michael T. H. Sadler. New York: Dover, 1977.

Lenin, Vladimir I. *Selected Works/ V. I. Lenin*. Moscow: Progress Publishers, 1971.

Lenin, Vladimir I. *What Is to be Done?: Burning Questions of Our Movement*. Moscow: Progress Publishers, 1970.

Mandelstam, Nadezhda. *Hope Against Hope: A Memoir*. London: Harvill Press, 1999.

McLellan, David. *Karl Marx: Selected Writings*. Oxford: Oxford University Press, 2000.

Metz, Christian. *A Semiotics of Film Language*. Chicago: The University of Chicago Press, 1974.

Nizhny, Vladimir B. *Lessons with Eisenstein*. Trans. and ed. Ivor Montagu and Jay Leyda. New York: Hill and Wang, 1962.

Pudovkin, Vsevolod. *Film Technique and Film Acting. The Cinema Writings of V. I. Pudovkin*. New York: Bonanza Books, 1969.

Shklovsky, Viktor. *Mayakovsky and His Circle*. Ed. and trans. Lily Feiler. New York: Dodd, Mead and Company, 1972.

Shklovsky, Viktor. *Theory of Prose*. Trans. Benjamin Sher. London and Dublin: Dalkey Archive Press, 2015.

Shklovsky, Viktor. *The Third Factory* [Tretya fabrika]. Ed. and trans. Richard Sheldon. Ann Arbor: Ardis, 1977.

Shklovsky, Viktor. *Viktor Shklovsky: A Reader*. Ed. and trans. Alexandra Berlina. New York and London: Bloomsbury Academic, 2017.

Shostakovich, Dmitri. *Testimony: The Memoirs of Dmitri Shostakovich*. New York: Harper and Row, 1979.

Shub, Esfir Ilinichna. *In Close-up* [Krupnym planom]. Moscow: Iskusstvo, 1959.

Shub, Esfir Ilinichna. *My Life – Cinematography* [Zhizn moya – kinematograf]. Moscow: Iskusstvo, 1972.

Taylor, Richard, ed. and trans. Co-ed. and introduction Ian Christie. *The Film Factory: Russian and Soviet Cinema in Documents 1896–1939*. London: Routledge & Keegan Paul Ltd., 1988; rev. ed. London: Routledge, 1994.

Tolstoy, Leo. *What is Art?* Trans. Aylmer Maude. Dublin: ROADS Publishing, 2014.

Tsivian, Yuri, ed. *Lines of Resistance: Dziga Vertov and the Twenties*. Trans. Julian Graffy. Sacile, Pordenone: Le Giornate del Cinema Muto, 2004.

Vertov, Dziga. *The Writings of Dziga Vertov*. Ed. Annette Michelson. Berkeley: University of California Press, 1984.

Vitale, Serena. *Shklovsky: Witness to an Era*. Trans. Jamie Richards. London and Dublin: Dalkey Archive Press, 2012.

Wollen, Peter. *Signs and Meaning in the Cinema*. Bloomington: Indiana University Press, 1969.

Secondary Sources

Achtenberg, Ben. 'Helen van Dongen: An Interview', *Film Quarterly* 30, no. 2 (Winter 1976–1977): 46–57.

Altschuler, Bruce. *The Avant-Garde in Exhibition: New Art in the 20th Century*. New York: Harry N. Abrams, 1994.

Applebaum, Anne. *Gulag: A History of the Soviet Camps*. London: Penguin Books, 2004.

Applebaum, Anne. *Red Famine: Stalin's War on Ukraine*. Milton Keynes: Penguin Random House, 2018.

Art into Life: Russian Constructivism 1914–1932, exhibition catalogue. Seattle: Henry Art Gallery, University of Washington, 1990.

Ascher, Abraham. *Russia: A Short History*. Oxford: Oneworld Publications, 2002.

Attwood, Lynne, ed. *Red Women On the Silver Screen: Soviet Women and Cinema from the Beginning to the End of the Communist Era*. London: Pandora Press, 1993.

Aumont, Jacques. *Montage Eisenstein*. Trans. Lee Hildreth, Constance Penley and Andrew Ross. London and Bloomington: BFI Publishing and Indiana University Press, 1987.

Balfour, Sebastian. *Spain: A History*. Oxford: Oxford University Press, 2000.

Barna, Ion. *Eisenstein*. London: Secker and Warburg, 1973.

Barnouw, Erik. *Documentary: A History of the Nonfiction Film*. New York: Oxford University Press, 1974; 2nd rev. ed., 1993.

Barooshian, Vahan D. *Russian Cubo-Futurism 1910–1930: A Study in Avant-gardism*. The Hague: Mouton, 1974.

Beattie, Keith. *Documentary Screens: Nonfiction Film and Television*. Basingstoke: Palgrave Macmillan, 2004.

Blue, James. 'Jean Rouch', in *Imagining Reality: The Faber Book of Documentary*. Eds. Kevin Macdonald and Mark Cousins, 268–70. London: Faber and Faber, 1998.

Bolton, Richard, ed. *The Contest of Meaning: Critical Histories of Photography*. Cambridge, MA and London: MIT Press, 1989.

Bordwell, David. *On the History of Film Style*. Cambridge, MA and London: Harvard University Press, 1997.

Bordwell, David. *The Cinema of Eisenstein*. Cambridge, MA: Harvard University Press, 1993.

Borzello, Frances. *A World of Our Own: Women as Artists Since the Renaissance*. New York: Watson-Guptill Publications, 2000.

Bowlt, John E. and Matthew Drutt, eds. *Amazons of the Avant-Garde: Alexandra Exter, Natalia Goncharova, Liubov Popova, Olga Rozanova, Varvara Stepanova, and Nadezhda Udaltsova*. New York: Harry N. Abrams, 2000.
Brewster, Ben. 'The Soviet State, the Communist Party and the Arts', *Red Letters: Communist Party Literature Journal* 3 (1976): 3–9.
Buckley, Mary. *Women and Ideology in the Soviet Union*. Hemel Hempstead and New York: Harvester Wheatsheaf, 1989.
Bürger, Peter. *Theory of the Avant-Garde*. Minneapolis: University of Minnesota Press, 1984.
Carr, Raymond, ed. *Spain A History*. Oxford: Oxford University Press, 2000.
Cassiday, Julie A. and Leyla Rouhi. 'From Nevskii Prospekt to Zoia's Apartment: Trials of the Russian Procuress', *The Russian Review* 58, no. 3 (1999): 413–31.
Caygill, Howard. *Walter Benjamin: The Colour of Experience*. London and New York: Routledge, 1998.
Chadwick, Whitney. *Women, Art and Society*. London: Thames and Hudson, 1990.
Chanan, Michael. *The Politics of Documentary*. London: British Film Institute, 2007.
Christie, Ian and David Elliott, eds. *Eisenstein at Ninety*. Oxford and London: Museum of Modern Art and British Film Institute, 1988.
Christie, Ian and John Gillett, eds. *Futurism/ Formalism/FEKS: 'Eccentrism' and Soviet Cinema 1918–1936*. London: British Film Institute, 1987.
Christie, Ian and Richard Taylor, eds. *Eisenstein Rediscovered*. London and New York: Routledge, 1993.
Cienciala, Anna M. 'The Foreign Policy of Józef Piłsudski and Józef Beck, 1926–1939: Misconceptions and Interpretations', *The Polish Review* LVI, nos 1–2 (2001): 199–226.
Clark, M. J., ed. *Politics and The Media: Film and Television for the Political Scientist and Historian*. Oxford: Pergamon Press, 1979.
Dabrowski, Magdalena. *Contrasts of Form: Geometric Abstract Art 1910–1980*. New York: The Museum of Modern Art, 1985.
Dobrenko, Evgeny. *Stalinist Cinema and the Production of History: Museum of the Revolution*. New Haven and London: Yale University Press, 2008.
Donald, James, Anne Friedberg and Laura Marcus, eds. *Close Up: 1927–1933: Cinema and Modernism*. London: Cassell, 1998.
Eagleton, Terry and Drew Milne, eds. *Marxist Literary Theory: A Reader*. Oxford: Blackwell, 1996.
Elder, R. Bruce. *Harmony + Dissent: Film and Avant-Garde Art Movements in the Early Twentieth Century*. Waterloo, Ontario: Wilfred Laurier University Press, 2007.
Elliott, David. *New Worlds: Russian Art and Society 1900–1937*. London: Thames and Hudson, 1986.
Ellwood, Shelagh M. *The Spanish Civil War*. Oxford: Basil Blackwell, 1991.

Erens, Patricia, ed. *Sexual Stratagems: The World of Women in Film*. New York: Horizon, 1979.

Feldman, Seth R. *Dziga Vertov: A Guide to References and Resources*. Boston: G. K. Hall, 1979.

Figes, Orlando. *A People's Tragedy: The Russian Revolution 1891–1924*. London: Jonathan Cape, 1996.

Figes, Orlando. *Natasha's Dance: A Cultural History of Russia*. New York: Picador, 2002.

Fitzpatrick, Sheila. *The Commissariat of Enlightenment. Soviet Organization of Education and the Arts under Lunacharsky, October 1917–1921*. Cambridge: Cambridge University Press, 1970.

Fitzpatrick, Sheila. *The Russian Revolution*. Oxford: Oxford University Press, 1994.

Fitzpatrick, Sheila, ed. *Stalinism: New Directions*. London: Routledge, 2000.

Fitzpatrick, Sheila, Alexander Rabinowitch and Richard Stites, eds. *Russia in the Era of NEP: Explorations in Soviet Society and Culture*. Bloomington: Indiana University Press, 1991.

Frascina, Francis and Jonathan Harris, eds. *Art in Modern Culture: An Anthology of Critical Thought*. London: Phaidon, 1992.

Gabo, Naum. *Gabo: Constructions, Sculpture, Paintings, Drawings, Engravings*. London: Lund Humphries, 1957.

Gibian, George and H. W. Tjalsma, eds. *Russian Modernism: Culture and the Avant-Garde 1900–1930*. Ithaca: Cornell University Press, 1976.

Gillespie, David. *Early Soviet Cinema: Innovation, Ideology and Propaganda*. London: Wallflower Press, 2005.

Gillespie, David. *Russian Cinema*. Essex and New York: Longman, 2003.

Gleason, Abbott, Peter Kenez and Richard Stites, eds. *Bolshevik Culture: Experiment and Order in the Russian Revolution*. Bloomington: Indiana University Press, 1985.

Glinsky, Albert. *Theremin: Ether Music and Espionage*. Urbana, Chicago and Springfield: University of Illinois, 2005.

Goscilo, Helena and Beth Holmgren, eds. *Russia, Women, Culture*. Bloomington: Indiana University Press, 1996.

Gough, Maria. *The Artist as Producer: Russian Constructivism in Revolution*. Berkeley: University of California Press, 2005.

Gray, Camilla. *The Russian Experiment in Art 1863–1922*. London: Thames and Hudson, 1962; rev. and enl. ed London: Thames and Hudson, 1986.

Greer, Germaine. *The Obstacle Race. The Fortunes of Women Painters and Their Work*. New York: Farrar, Straus and Giroux, 1979.

Grierson, John. *Grierson on Documentary*. Ed. Forsyth Hardy. London: Faber and Faber, 1966.

Guynn, William H. *A Cinema of Nonfiction*. Rutherford: Fairleigh Dickinson University Press, 1990.

Henderson, Brian and Ann Martin, eds. *Film Quarterly: Forty Years — a Selection*. Berkeley: University of California Press, 1999.

Hickey, Michael. "'People with Pure Souls": Jewish Youth Radicalism in Smolensk, 1900-1914', *Revolutionary Russia* 20, no. 1 (2007): 51-73.

Hicks, Jeremy. *Dziga Vertov: Defining Documentary Film*. London and New York: I. B. Tauris, 2007.

Hirsch, Joshua. *Afterimage: Film, Trauma and the Holocaust*. Philadelphia: Temple University Press, 2004.

Hooks, Margaret. *Tina Modotti*. Cologne: Könemann, 1999.

Hughes, Robert. *American Visions: The Epic History of Art in America*. London: Harvill Press, 1997.

Hughes, Thomas P. 'How America Helped Build the Soviet Machine', *American Heritage* 39, no. 8 (1988): 1-8.

Jacobs, Lewis, ed. *The Documentary Tradition: from Nanook to Woodstock*. New York: Hopkinson and Blake, 1971.

Kaganovsky, Lilya. *The Voice of Technology: Soviet Cinema's Transition to Sound 1928-1935*. Bloomington: Indiana University Press, 2018.

Kamensky, Aleksandr. *Chagall: The Russian Years 1907-1922*. London: Thames and Hudson, 1989.

Kaufman, Mikhail. 'An Interview with Mikhail Kaufman: Essays in Honour of Jay Leyda', *October* 11 (Winter 1979): 54-76 in *Imagining Reality: The Faber Book of Documentary*. Eds. Kevin Macdonald and Mark Cousins. London: Faber and Faber, 1998.

Kenez, Peter. *Cinema and Soviet Society from the Revolution to the Death of Stalin*. Cambridge and New York: Cambridge University Press, 1992; rev. ed London and New York: I.B.Tauris, 2001.

Khan-Magomedev, Selim O. *Rodchenko: The Complete Works*. London: Thames and Hudson, 1986.

Kirichenko, Eugenia. *The Russian Style*. London: Laurence King, 1991.

Kirschenbaum, Lisa. *International Communism and the Spanish Civil War: Solidarity and Suspicion*. Cambridge and New York: Cambridge University Press, 2015.

Koenig-Quart, Barbara. *Women Directors: The Emergence of a New Cinema*. New York: Praeger, 1988.

Kostyrchenko, Gennadi. *Out of the Red Shadows: Anti-Semitism in Stalin's Russia*. New York: Prometheus Books, 1995.

Lavin, Maud. *cut with the kitchen knife: the weimar photomontages of hannah höch*. New Haven: Yale University Press, 1993.

Lavrentiev, Alexander. *Rodchenko: Photography 1924-1954*. Cologne: Könemann, 1995.

Lavrentiev, Alexander. *Varvara Stepanova: A Constructivist Life*. Ed. John E. Bowlt. London: Thames and Hudson, 1988.

Lawton, Anna, ed. *The Red Screen. Politics, Society and Art in Soviet Russia*. London and New York: Routledge, 1992.

Levin, G. Roy. *Documentary Explorations: 15 Interviews with Film-makers*. Garden City: Doubleday, 1971.

Leyda, Jay. 'Esther Shub', in *Sexual Stratagems: The World of Women in Film*. Ed. Patricia Erens,179–84. New York: Horizon, 1979.

Leyda, Jay. *Films Beget Films: A Study of the Compilation Film*. London: George Allen and Unwin, 1964.

Leyda, Jay. *In the Footsteps of Esther Shub*. Typed draft with handwritten corrections, in the *Jay Leyda Collection*, Tamiment Institute, Elmer Holmes Bobst Library, New York University. Manuscript dated London, 1964.

Leyda, Jay. *Kino: A History of the Russian and Soviet Film*. London: Allen and Unwin, 1960; rev. ed. Princeton: Princeton University Press, 1983.

Leyda, Jay and Zina Voynow. *Eisenstein at Work*. New York: Pantheon Books, 1982.

Lodder, Christina. *Russian Constructivism*. New Haven: Yale University Press, 1990.

Lucie Smith, Edward. *Art of the 1930s. The Age of Anxiety*. London: Weidenfield and Nicolson, 1985.

Macdonald, Kevin and Mark Cousins, eds. *Imagining Reality: The Faber Book of Documentary*. London: Faber and Faber, 1998.

Malitsky, Joshua. *Post-Revolution Nonfiction Film: Building the Soviet and Cuban Nations*. Bloomington and Indianapolis: Indiana University Press, 2013.

Manvell, Roger, ed. *Experiment in the Film*. London: The Grey Walls Press, 1949.

Markov, Vladimir. *Russian Futurism: A History*. Berkeley: University of California Press, 1968.

Marks, Laura U. *The Skin of the Film: Intercultural Cinema, Embodiment, and the Senses*. Durham: Duke University Press, 2000.

Marks, Laura U. *Touch: Sensuous Theory and Multisensory Media*. Minneapolis and London: University of Minnesota Press, 2002.

Martin, Terry. *The Affirmative Action Empire: Nations and Nationalism in the Soviet Union, 1923–1939*. Ithaca and London: Cornell University Press, 2001.

Mastrangelo, Bob. 'Obituary: Helen van Dongen', *The Guardian*, Friday 10, November 2006. https://www.theguardian.com/news/2006/nov/10/guardianobituaries.obituaries?. CMP=share_btn_link (accessed 11 November 2007).

Mayne, Judith. *Kino and the Woman Question: Feminism and Soviet Silent Film*. Columbus: Ohio State University Press, 1989.

Miller, Jamie. *Soviet Cinema: Politics and Persuasion under Stalin*. London and New York: I.B.Tauris, 2010.

Milner, John. *Vladimir Tatlin and the Russian Avant-Garde*. New Haven: Yale University Press, 1983.

Montefiore, Simon Sebag. *Stalin: The Court of the Red Tsar*. London: Weidenfeld & Nicolson Ltd, 2003; rev. ed. London: Phoenix, 2004.

Montefiore, Simon Sebag. *Young Stalin*. London: Phoenix, 2008.
Néret, Gilles. *Kazimir Malevich 1878–1935 and Suprematism*. Cologne: Taschen, 2003.
Nichols, Bill. *Introduction to Documentary*. Bloomington: Indiana University Press, 2010.
Nichols, Bill. *Representing Reality: Issues and Concepts in Documentary*. Bloomington and Indianapolis: Indiana University Press, 1991.
Nichols, Bill. *Speaking Truths with Film: Evidence, Ethics, Politics in Documentary*. Oakland: University of California Press, 2016.
Nochlin, Linda. *Women, Art, and Power and Other Essays*. Boulder and Oxford: Westview Press, 1998.
O'Mahony, Mike. *Sergei Eisenstein*. London: Reaktion, 2008.
Parker, Rozsika and Griselda Pollock. *Old Mistresses: Women, Art and Ideology*. London and Henley: Routledge and Kegan Paul, 1981.
Parkes, Reverend James. *A History of the Jewish People*. Harmondsworth: Pelican Books, 1967.
Parton, Anthony. *Mikhail Larionov and the Russian Avant-Garde*. Princeton: Princeton University Press, 1993.
Payne, Stanley G. *The Spanish Civil War, The Soviet Union, and Communism*. New Haven and London: Yale University Press, 2004
Petric, Vlada. *Constructivism in Film: The Man with the Movie Camera: A Cinematic Analysis*. Cambridge and New York: Cambridge University Press, 1987.
Petric, Vlada. 'Esther Shub: Cinema Is My Life', *Quarterly Review of Film Studies* 3, no. 4 (Fall 1978): 429–48.
Petric, Vlada. 'Esther Shub: Film as a Historical Discourse', in *Show Us Life: Toward a History and an Aesthetics of the Committed Documentary*. Ed. Thomas Waugh, 21–46. Metuchen: The Scarecrow Press, 1984.
Petric, Vlada. 'Esther Shub's Unrealized Project', *Quarterly Review of Film Studies* 3, no. 4 (Fall 1978): 449–56.
Pipes, Richard. *Russia Under the Bolshevik Regime 1919–1924*. London: Harvill Press, 1997.
Pipes, Richard. *The Russian Revolution 1899–1918*. London: Collins Harvill, 1990.
Plantinga, Carl R. *Rhetoric and Representation in Nonfiction Film*. Cambridge and New York: Cambridge University Press, 1997.
Pollock, Griselda. *Differencing the Canon: Feminist Desire and the Writing of Art's Histories*. London and New York: Routledge, 1999.
Prado, Antonio. 'Anarchism and Counterinformation in Documentaries: From Civil War Spain to Post-2001 Argentina', *Latin American Perspectives* 40, no. 1 (2013): 50–9.
Pronay, Nicholas and Derek W. Spring, eds. *Propaganda, Politics and Film 1918–1945*. London: Macmillan, 1982.
Reed, John. *Ten Days that Shook the World*. London: Penguin Books, 1977.

Roberts, Graham. 'Esfir Shub: A Suitable Case for Treatment', *Historical Journal of Film, Radio and Television* 11, no. 2 (1991): 149–58.

Roberts, Graham. *Forward Soviet! History and Nonfiction Film in the USSR*. London: I. B. Tauris, 1999.

Roberts, Graham. 'The Great Way', *History Today* 47, no. 11 (1991): 39–44.

Rodchenko, Aleksandr M. and Varvara F. Stepanova. *The Future Is Our Only Goal*. Ed. Peter Noever. Munich: Prestel Verlag, 1991.

Rogovin, Vadim Z. *1937 Stalin's Year of Terror 1937-1938: Political Genocide in the USSR*. Trans. Frederick S. Choate. Oak Park: Mehring Books, 1998.

Romberg, Kristin. *Gan's Constructivism: Aesthetic Theory for an Embedded Modernism*. Oakland: University of California Press, 2018.

Rosenstone, Robert A., ed. *Revisioning History: Film and the Construction of a New Past*. Princeton: Princeton University Press, 1995.

Rouch, Jean. *Ciné-Ethnography*. Ed. and trans. Steven Feld. Series 'Visible Evidence' 13. Minneapolis: University of Minnesota Press, 2003.

Rowell, Margit. 'Constructivist Book Design: Shaping the Proletarian Conscience', in *The Russian Avant-Garde Book 1910–1934*. Eds. Margit Rowell and Deborah Wye, 50–9. New York: Harry N. Abrams, 2002.

Rudnitsky, Konstantin. *Russian and Soviet Theatre. Tradition and the Avant-Garde*. London: Thames and Hudson, 1988.

Rzhevsky, Nicholas, ed. *The Cambridge Companion to Modern Russian Culture*. Cambridge and New York: Cambridge University Press, 1998.

Schnitzer, Luda, Jean Schnitzer and Marcel Martin, eds. *Cinema In Revolution. The Heroic Era of the Soviet Film*. London: Secker and Warburg, 1973.

Seaman, L. C. B.. *Post-Victorian Britain 1902–1951*. London: Routledge, 1968.

Sebestyen, Victor. *Lenin the Dictator*. London: Weidenfield and Nicolson, 2018.

Seidman, Michael. *Republic of Egos: A Social History of the Spanish Civil War*. Madison: University of Wisconsin Press, 2002.

Service, Robert. *Stalin: A Biography*. London: Pan Macmillan, 2004.

Seton, Marie. *Sergei M. Eisenstein: A Biography*. London: Dobson, 1978.

Sharp, Ilana. 'A New History of Documentary Film', Betsy A. McLane in *Studies in Russian & Soviet Cinema* 7, no. 3 (2013): 363–4.

Sharp, Ilana. 'Harmony + Dissent: Film and Avant-Garde Art Movements in the Early Twentieth Century', R. Bruce Elder in *Studies in Russian & Soviet Cinema* 3, no. 3 (2009): 355–8.

Sharp, Ilana. 'Spain', in *Directory of World Cinema: Russia 2*. Ed. Birgit Beumers, 323–5. Bristol and Chicago: Intellect, 2015.

Sharp (née Shub), Ilana. '*The Fall of the Romanov Dynasty* (1927): A Constructivist Paradigm for *Neigrovaia Fil'ma*', *Historical Journal of Film, Radio and Television* 28, no. 2 (2008): 195–217.

Shaw, Tony and Denise J. Youngblood. *Cinematic Cold War: The American and Soviet Struggle for Hearts and Minds*. Lawrence: University Press of Kansas, 2010.

Shub, David. *Lenin: A Biography*. Harmondsworth: Penguin Books, 1971.

Shukman, Harold, ed. *The Blackwell Encyclopedia of the Russian Revolution*. Oxford: Basil Blackwell, 1988.

Shukman, Harold. *Stalin*. Gloucestershire: Sutton Publishing, 1999.

Simmen, Jeannot and Kolja Kohlhoff. *Kasimir Malevich: Life and Work*. Bonn: Könneman, 1999.

Sklar, Richard. *Film: An International History of the Medium*. London: Thames and Hudson, 1993.

Sparrow, Norbert. ' I Let the Audience Feel and Think: An Interview with Rainer Werner Fassbinder', *Cinéaste* 8, no. 2 (1977): 20–1.

Spring, Derek and Richard Taylor, eds. *Stalinism and Soviet Cinema*. London: Routledge, 2013.

Stishova, Elena. 'The Mythologization of Soviet Woman', in *Red Women On the Silver Screen: Soviet Women and Cinema from the Beginning to the End of the Communist Era*. Ed. Lynne Attwood, 175–85. London: Pandora Press, 1993.

Stites, Richard. *The Women's Liberation Movement in Russia: Feminism, Nihilism, and Bolshevism 1860–1930*. Princeton: Princeton University Press, 1978.

Stollery, Martin. 'Eisenstein, Shub and the gender of the author as producer', *Film History, Sydney* 14, no. 1 (2002): 87–99.

Swallow, Norman. *Eisenstein: A Documentary Portrait*. New York: E. P. Dutton, 1977.

Tatlin, Vladimir E. *Tatlin*. Ed. Larissa A. Zhadova. London: Thames and Hudson, 1988.

Taylor, Richard. *Film Propaganda: Soviet Russia and Nazi Germany*. London and New York: I. B. Tauris, 1998.

Taylor, Richard. *The Politics of the Soviet Cinema 1917–1929*. Cambridge: Cambridge University Press, 1979.

Taylor, Richard and Derek Spring, eds. *Stalinism and Soviet Cinema*. London and New York: Routledge, 1993.

Taylor, Richard and Ian Christie, eds. *Inside the Film Factory: New Approaches to Russian and Soviet Cinema*. London: Routledge, 1991.

Thomas, Hugh. *The Spanish Civil War*. London: Eyre and Spottiswode, 1961; rev. ed. London and New York: Penguin Books, 2012.

Tsivian, Yuri. *Early Cinema in Russia and Its Cultural Reception*. Ed. Richard Taylor. Trans. Alan Bodger. London and New York: Routledge, 1994.

Turovskaya, Maya. 'Women and the "Woman Question" in the USSR', in *Red Women On the Silver Screen: Soviet Women and Cinema from the beginning to the end of the Communist Era*. Ed. Lynne Attwood, 133–40. London: Pandora Press, 1993.

Van Wert, William F. 'Chris Marker: The SLON Films', *Film Quarterly* 32, no. 3 (Spring 1979): 38–46.

Volkogonov, Dmitri. *Lenin: Life and Legacy*. Ed. and trans. Harold Shukman. London: HarperCollins, 1994.

Vorontsov, Yuri and Igor Rachuk. *The Phenomenon of the Soviet Cinema*. Moscow: Progress Publishers, 1980.

Wallis, Brian, ed. *Art after Modernism: Rethinking Representation*. New York: New Museum of Contemporary Art, 1995.

Walther, Ingo F. and Rainer Metzger. *Marc Chagall, 1887–1985 Painting as Poetry*. Cologne: Taschen, 1987.

Walworth, Catherine. *Soviet Salvage: Imperial Debris, Revolutionary Reuse, and Russian Constructivism*. University Park: Pennsylvania State University Press, 2017.

Waugh, Thomas, ed. *Show us life: Toward a History and an Aesthetics of the Committed Documentary*. Metuchen: Scarecrow Press, 1984.

Wells, Paul, 'The Documentary Form: Personal and Social Realities', in *An Introduction to Film Studies*. Ed. Jill Nelmes, 188–211. London and New York: Routledge, 1996; rev. ed. London: Routledge, 2003.

Widdis, Emma. *Alexander Medvedkin*. London and New York: I. B. Tauris, 2005.

Willett, John. *The New Sobriety 1917–1933: Art and Politics in the Weimar Period*. London: Thames and Hudson, 1978.

Williams, Christopher, ed. *Realism and the Cinema: A Reader*. London: Routledge and Kegan Paul, 1980.

Williams, Robert Chadwell. *Artists in Revolution: Portraits of the Russian Avant-Garde*. Bloomington: Indiana University Press, 1977.

Winston, Brian. *Claiming the Real: the Griersonian Documentary and Its Legitimations*. London: BFI Publishing, 2001.

Woroszylski, Wiktor. *The Life of Mayakovsky*. Translated by Boleslaw Taborski. London: Victor Gollancz, 1972.

Yampolsky, Mikhail. 'Reality at Second Hand', *Historical Journal of Film, Radio and Television* 11, no. 2 (1991): 161–71.

Youngblood, Denise J. '"History" on Film: The Historical Melodrama in Soviet Cinema", *Historical Journal of Film, Radio and Television* 11, no. 2 (1991): 173–84.

Youngblood, Denise J. *The Magic Mirror: Moviemaking in Russia 1908–1918*. Madison: The University of Wisconsin Press, 1999.

Youngblood, Denise J. *Movies for the Masses: Popular Cinema and Soviet Society in the 1920s*. New York: Cambridge University Press, 1992.

Youngblood, Denise J. *Soviet Cinema In the Silent Era 1918–1935*. Ann Arbor, MI: UMI Research Press, 1985; rev. ed. Austin: University of Texas Press, 1991.

Zorkaya, Neya. *The Illustrated History of Soviet Cinema*. New York: Hippocrene Books, 1991.

Index

Page numbers in italics refer to illustrations.

Abraham, Richard   65
Abramtsevo   36–7
Aelita (Protazanov film)   258, 301 n.33
Aleksandrov, Grigory   64
Aleksandrov, Ivan Gavrilovich   195
Alexander Nevsky (Eisenstein film)   222
All-Union Creative Conference of Workers in Soviet Cinema (1935)   123, 209
Andel, Jaroslav   47
The Anniversary of the Revolution (Vertov film)   261
anti-Semitism   73–4, 280 n.12, 281 n.30
Antonov-Ovseenko, Vladimir   135
Applebaum, Anne   155–6
ARRK [Association of Workers of Revolutionary Cinematography]   180
Astruc, Alexandre   185
Atatürk, Mustafa Kemal   256
Attwood, Lynne   181, 206, 207–8
authentic [podlinny] material   3, 41, 45, 51, 57, 59, 65, 96, 110, 113, 116, 124, 145, 256. *See also* Shub
authorship, questions of   103; author as producer 104; issues for Shub 3, 93, 99–104
avant-garde   2–3, 7, 8, 10, 11, 15, 19, 24, 27, 31–2, 35, 36, 37, 39, 41, 43–4, 50, 59, 62–3, 69, 91, 93, 105–6, 108, 110, 116, 124–5, 179, 253, 263–4, 266 n.1, 266 n.3, 273 n.6, 274 n.16, 274 n.19, 278 n.73, 279 n.76, 299 n.1, 301 n.33; denunciation of Eisenstein, Kuleshov, Shub, Vertov et al. 68, 209–16; draconian artistic repression 208–10; flowering in the 1920s 122, 185, 261; in the 1930s, impact of Socialist Realism 5, 42, 50–1, 123, 180, 183
Azaña, Manuel, Prime Minister   226

Babel, Isaac   51, 272 n.96
Baird, John Logie   190
Bann, Stephen   45
Barnouw, Erik   255
Battleship Potemkin (Eisenstein film)   17
Baudelaire, Charles   122
Bazin, André   68–9, 72
Bely, Andrei   66, 280 n.16
Benjamin, Walter   52, 59, 80; 'The Work of Art in the Age of Mechanical Reproduction' 78, 120–1
Bezhin Meadow (Eisenstein film)   256
Black Hundreds   73–5, 281 n.30
Blok, Alexander   66
Bolshevik Revolution   2, 27, 37, 61
Bourke-White, Margaret   206
Brest-Litovsk, Treaty of   135–6
Briand, Aristide, Prime Minister   54, 132
The Bridge (Ivens film)   254
Brik, Osip   42, 48, 57, 93, 100, 105, 110, 114–15, 116, 120, 134, 168, 274 n.16, 275 n.65
Buñuel, Luis   111–12, 249; intensifying 'authenticity' in *Land Without Bread* 111–12
Burch, Noël   186
By the Law (Kuleshov film)   13, 22, 268 n.32

Casado, Segismundo   244
censorship   95, 123, 214
cento   30. *See also* Eisenstein, Sergei
Chagall, Marc   8
Chamberlain, Austen   132–3
Chanan, Michael   259–60
Chapayev, Vasily   139, 243; *Chapayev* [Chapaev] (Vasilev 'brothers' film) 123, 243, 269 n.45; *Chapayev* (Dmitry Furmanov book) 139

Chernyshevsky, Nikolai   36, 276 n.34; *The Aesthetic Relations of Art and Reality* (essay) 36; *What Is To Be Done?* (novel) 36
Christie, Ian   189
Cine-Eye   114, 204, 248, 271 n.79. See also Vertov, Dziga
Cinema (journal)   263
Cinema Front (journal)   182, 208, 292 n.37
Cinema Gazette (journal)   13
Cinema-Photo (journal)   40. See also Gan, Aleksei
cinéma-vérité   107, 113, 124, 256–9, 263
circus   9–12
Cocteau, Jean   274 n.19
compilation genre (*also* compilation nonfiction film)   2, 14, 23, 27, 30, 32, 33, 35, 41, 43–5, 47, 48, 50, 51, 60, 62, 63, 65, 67, 84, 90, 93, 96, 99–100, 102–3, 106, 110–11, 113–14, 117–18, 120, 121, 124, 129, 145, 147, 181, 200, 251, 253–4, 255–8, 260, 263–4, 277 n.43, 301 n.34; Shub as founder 1–3, 52, 90, 93–4, 119, 253, 254, 261, 262
Constructivism: anti-art stance   36, 42–3, 50, 122; art as production 36–8, 43; as an art form 44–5, 264; construction [konstruksiya] 47–8; European variant 53; facture [faktura] 47–8, 189; Gan 38, 48–50; interpretations of 43–5; Mayakovsky 38–40, 121–2; Rodchenko *The Constructivist Party* (photograph) 38, *39*; Shub 3, 7, 11, 30, 33, 35, 41, 52, 59–60, 61, 84, 120, 187, 224, 263–4; Stepanova 38, *39*, 44, 105, 274 n.10; Tatlin 44–5, 47, 273 n.8; tectonics [tektonika] 47; Working Group of Constructivists (Moscow) 38, 47. See also *Constructivism* [Konstruktivizm] (Gan book)
Cooper, Hugh Lincoln   195, 201–2
Cornell, Joseph   277 n.43

Dadaist photomontage   8, 24
The Decembrists (Ivanovsky film)   116, 287 n.102
De Chirico, Giorgio   238

defamiliarization [ostranenie]   8, 63, 130. See also Shklovsky, Viktor
Deleuze, Gilles   186
Diaz Ramos, José (Diaz)   231, 233–4, 239, 242, 244, 251
direct cinema   107, 113, 124, 256, 257, 259
displacement [sdvig]   8, 25
Diterikhs, Mikhail K., General   136
Dneprostroi Dam (*also known as* Dnieper Hydroelectric Station)   174, *194*, 195
Dobrenko, Evgeny   208–9
'documentarism'   124, 208
documentary film   5, 32, 59, 95, 186, 255, 259; criticism of 208; death of 212–16; and newsreel 41, 45, 46, 52, 56, 59–60, 61, 62, 63, 69, 95–6, 102, 106, 107, 110–12, 117, 119–21, 125, 127–8, 134, 171, 215, 218, 254, 260, 262, 264; 'truth' 57, 107. See also compilation genre; nonfiction film
Dovzhenko, Alexander   255
Drew, Robert   257, 259; direct cinema 259; *Primary* (film) 259
Dr. Mabuse (Lang film)   29
Drobashenko, Sergei   158, 189, 194, 200, 206, 256, 258–9
Dubrovin, A. I.   73, 74
Duchamp, Marcel   45
Duhamel, Georges   121
Duma   68, 72–3, 83, 104
The Dynamic City (Klutsis photomontage)   8
Dzoraget Hydroelectric Power Station   197, 199

'Eccentrism' (manifesto)   10–11
Eisenstein, Sergei   1, 3, 7, 17, 19, 90, 100, 115, 180, 188, 253, 264, 268 n.23, 271 n.85, 272 n.96, 278 n.73, 296 n.88; anti-Constructivism 31; cento, linking of it with Shub's montage 30; *Dr. Mabuse*: Shub's re-editing of 29; tutelage by 16, 29; fact versus fiction 68; *Film Form* (book) 29; films cited: *Alexander Nevsky* 222; *Battleship Potemkin* 17; *Bezhin Meadow* 256;

October 60, 61, 64, 68, 88, 103, 112, 282 n.40, 290 n.28; *Strike* 2, 10, 12–14, 17, 23, 27–33, *31*, 265 n.4; and Meyerhold, Vsevolod 9, 10, 51; montage, use of 12–14, 15, 25, 29, 30, 32, 124; 'My Subject is Patriotism' (essay) 222; *Notes of a Film Director* (book) 30–1; *October* versus *The Fall of the Romanov Dynasty* 61, 65, 68, 72, 80–1; realism, approach to 68; Shub, collaboration with 2, 18, 22, 23, 27–9, 30, 32, 101: comparison with 64, 67, 68, 69, 81, 83, 111, 118, 122, 135, 136; storming of the Winter Palace re-enactment 68, 72, 95; Symbolist allegory, use of 66–7

Eisler, Hanns 193

Elder, R. Bruce 66

Elegance and Poverty (Modotti photomontage) 26–7, *26*

The Eleventh Year (Vertov film) 114, 170–1

Elliott, David 179

Engineer Prite's Project (Kuleshov film) 12

Enthusiasm: the Symphony of the Donbass (Vertov film) 4, 186, 203–7

The Extraordinary Adventures of Mr. West in the Land of the Bolsheviks (Kuleshov film) 13

fable [fabula] 107. *See also* Shklovsky, Viktor

facture [faktura] 47–8, 189. *See also* Constructivism

fact versus fiction 61–8. *See also* historical truth; Party propaganda and ideology

The Fall of the Romanov Dynasty (Shub film) 3–4, 8, 14, 15, 20, 22–4, 26–8, 30–1, 33, 35, 41, 44–5, 47–8, 51–60, 61–91, *71, 74, 76, 79, 87, 88,* 93–125, *101,* 127–31, 134–5, 145, 147, 149, 154, 162, 167, 178, 182, 208, 217–18, 223–6, 229, 235–6, 238, 240, 242, 256, 258, 261–2, 264, 284 n.45

Fascism will be Defeated (Shub film) 215

Fassbinder, Rainer Werner 260

February Revolution 9, 27, 52, 61, 63, 69, 70–2, *71,* 75, 79, 97, 127, 264

FEKS [Factory of the Eccentric Actor] 10–11, 28, 188; anti-art stance 10–11; avant-garde, allegiance to 10–11; 'Eccentrism' (manifesto) 10–11

Ferno, John 246, 247

fiction film [igrovaya filma] 2

Figner, Vera Nikolaevna 71, 135

Film and Photo League (FPL) 255

Film Truth [Kino-pravda] 57–9. *See also* Vertov, Dziga

Five Year Plan 4, 148, 154, 158, 159, 175, 182, 192, 193, 199, 202, 205, 209

Flaherty, Robert 95, 249, 255; films cited: *The Land* 255; *Louisiana Story* 255; *Man of Aran* 95; *Nanook of the North* 95

formalism 51, 124, 180, 208

Franco, Francisco 219, 221, 225, 227, 231–2, *232,* 234, 235, 236, 239, 240, 241, 242, 243, 244, 245, 246, 250–1

Franz Joseph, Emperor 54

Frelikh, Oleg 2; *A Prostitute* (film) 2, 24

Frunze, Mikhail 139

Fuchs, Georg 9; *Theatre of the Future* 9

Gabo, Naum 43–4, 49; 'The Realistic Manifesto' 43–4. *See also* Pevsner, Antoine

Gan, Aleksei 2, 8, 38, *39,* 40, 47–8, 51, 105; Shub, writing about 45–6: 'The Cinematograph and Cinema' (essay) 41; *Constructivism* (book) 48–51, *49*; 'Constructivism in the Cinema' (essay) 45. *See also Cinema-Photo*

George V, King 54

Glinsky, Albert 190

Godard, Jean-Luc 258

GOELRO [State Commission for the Electrification of Russia] 195

Golovin, Alexander 10

Goncharova, Natalia 273 nn.6–7

Goskino [the state film trust] 2, 18. *See also* Sovkino; Soiuzkino

Gosvoenkino [State Military Cinema Organization] 265 n.1

Gough, Maria 38, 47, 53

The Great Way (Shub film)   4, 71, 101, 106, 115–18, 127–45, *131*, *140*, *144*, 148, 149, 155, 164, 178, 188, 191, 193, 208, 213–14, 217–19, 264
GTK [State Cinema Technical Institute]   46
Guadalajara, Battle of   239–40

Happiness (Medvedkin film)   258, 265 n.1
haptic elements in relation to sound cinema   186–7, 190–1, 195, 199. See also *Enthusiasm: the Symphony of the Donbass* (Vertov film); *K.Sh.E.* (Komsomol Patron of Electrification) (Shub film)
Hausmann, Raoul   8, 25, 271 n.82
Heartfield, John   8, 25, 52, 271 n.82
Hemingway, Ernest   246–8
Hermitage (journal)   40
Hicks, Jeremy   181, 203, 204, 207, 208
historical truth   3, 45, 64, 66, 68, 73, 80, 93, 118, 121, 123, 263; and notions of reality 95, 109–14. See also fact versus fiction; Party propaganda and ideology
The History of the Civil War (Vertov film)   261
Hitler, Adolf   231, 242
Höch, Hannah   8, 24–5, 26, 52, 271 n.82
Homeland (Shub film)   215
Hoover, Herbert, President   161, 169

Ibárruri, Dolores   228–9, *229*, 231, 239, 242, 243–6. See also Pasionaria, La
Imperial Academy of Fine Arts (St. Petersburg)   36
In Close-up (Shub book)   1, *16*, 19, 58, *101*
INKhUK [Institute of Artistic Culture]   275 n.31
Ioffe, Abram Fedorovich   190, 202
Ioganson, Karl   38, 47, 59
Ivens, Joris   5, 246, 248–9, 250, 254–5, 256, 258, 259; films cited: *The Bridge* 254, 255; *Rain* 254, 255; *Song of Heroes* 249; *The Spanish Earth* 5, 249
IZO Narkompros [Department of Fine Arts within Narkompros]   275 n.31
Izvestiya (newspaper)   221

Jewish   1, 73, 265 n.3, 266 n.8, 281 n.30, 285 n.55, 302 n.52; quotas   2
Joffre, Joseph, General   54

Kaganovsky, Lilya   186–7, 203, 204, 257, 262
Kalinin, Mikhail   144
Kandinsky, Vasily   43, 48
Karmen, Roman   105–6, 217, 218, 219, 225, 227, 240, 241, 242
Katovis, Steve   170
Katsman, (Comrade) Evgeny   212–13
Kaufman, Mikhail   24, 58, 114, 118, 171, 254
Kenez, Peter   123, 207
Kerensky, Alexander   64–5, 66, 68, 88, 113, 134
Khlebnikov, Velimir   8, 267 n.6
Kholodnaya, Vera   211
Kinoki   114
Klutsis, Gustav   8–9, 47, 51, 52
Kolli, Nikolai   198
Komsomol   145, 187, 189, 192, 194, 196, 197, 202, 203, 205, 249
Kovalsky, Konstantin   190–1, 193
Kozintsev, Grigory   10–11
Kruchenykh, Alexander   8, 266 n.5, 267 n.6
Krupskaya, Nadezhda   *140*, 141
Krylenko, Nikolai   135
K.Sh.E. (Komsomol Patron of Electrification) (Shub film)   4, 174, 185–216, *192*, *194*, *197–8*, 219, 256–7, 259–60, 264
Kulaks   148, 155, 157, 175
Kuleshov, Lev   3, 7, 13, 25, 26, 30, 32, 56, 93, 123, 124, 208, 209, 262, 264, 267 n.6, 268 n.25, 296 n.88; 'Cinema as the Fixing of Theatrical Action' (essay) 40–1; films cited: *By the Law* 13, 22, 268 n.32; *Engineer Prite's Project* 12; *The Extraordinary Adventures of Mr. West in the Land of the Bolsheviks* 13; founder of Soviet montage theory 12, 15; principles 14; 'Kuleshov effect' 14–15; support for *The Fall of the Romanov Dynasty*: authentic images, real events and people as opposed to the artifice of staged theatre 104, 106, 137

Kushner, Boris   48, 102
Kuvshinchikova, Tatiana   *16*

The Land (Flaherty film)   255
Land of the Soviets (Shub film)   213–15, 296 n.88
Land Without Bread (Buñuel film)   111–12
Lang, Fritz   29; *Dr. Mabuse* 29
Larionov, Mikhail   37, 273 nn.6–7; 'Why We Paint Ourselves: A Futurist Manifesto' 37. *See also* Zdanevich, Ilya
The Last Bolshevik (Marker film)   84, 258
Lavin, Maud   24
Leacock, Richard   257, 259
LEF [Left Front of the Arts]   39, 40, 51, 57, 62–3, 68, 100, 103, 104, 114, 115, 116, 117, 120, 124
LEF (publication)   7, 51, 271 n.82, 274 n.16, 278 n.64. *See also* New LEF
Léger, Fernand   274 n.19
Lenin, Vladimir   4, 42, 46, 57, 63, 65, 68, 69, 82–4, 121, 128, 130, 133–4, 135, 137, 138–9, *140*, *144*, 155, 188, 203, 209, 220, 223, 235, 275 n.33, 276 n.34, 282 n.39, 283 n.8, 296 n.88; cult of 95, 145; funeral of 131, 141–3, 191–2
Leonidov, Leonid   21–2
Leo Tolstoy Barefoot (Repin painting)   286 n.72
Lermontov, Mikhail   9; *Masquerade* 9–10
Letatlin 45. *See also* Tatlin, Vladimir
Leyda, Jay   29, 90, 98–9, 102–3, 110, 118, 251, 255, 256, 257, 258, 259, 262, 263
life caught unawares [zhizn vrasplokh]   103
Lissitzky, El   52
Lister, Enrique, General   239–40, 242
Lodder, Christina   43, 44, 51
Loin du Vietnam (Marker film)   258
Lorentz, Pare   255–6; *The Plow That Broke the Plains* 255
Louisiana Story (Flaherty film)   255
Lunacharsky, Anatoly   2, 38, 134, 179–80

MacDonald, Ramsay, Prime Minister   161
Maginot, André, Minister   168
Makaseev, Boris   218, 227

Malevich, Kazimir   3, 7–8, 11, 25, 32, 121, 271 n.82; *Black Square* 44; *Darkness in Parts, Composition with Mona Lisa* 8; *An Englishman in Moscow* 267 n.6; *Lady by the Advertising Pillar* 8; *Warriors of the First Division* 8
Mallarmé, Stéphane   30
Mamontov, Savva   37
Man with a Movie Camera (Vertov film)   124, 204, 279 n.89
Marker, Chris   256, 257, 258–9; films cited: *The Last Bolshevik* 84, 258; *Loin du Vietnam* 258
Markov, P.A.   11
Marks, Laura U.   186–7, 199
Martin, Marcel   23
Martin, Terry   133
Marty, André   235, 242
Marxist discourse (*also* Marxism)   38, 50, 52, 53, 61–2, 65, 69, 70, 76, 77, 106, 130, 137, 148, 163–4, 225, 261
Masquerade (Meyerhold drama)   9–10
Mastrangelo, Bob   255
Mayakovsky, Vladimir   3, 8, 32, 36, 38–9, 40, 98, 105, 110, 115, 122, 128, 253, 264, 266 n.1, 271 n.82, 274 n.15, 287 n.99, 294 n.60; characterization, approach to experimental theatre 9, 11–12, 273 n.6; and on Eisenstein's *Strike* 12; LEF 7, 39, 116, 274 n.16; *Mystery-Bouffe* 10, 11–12: major influence on FEKS 10; newsreel, views on 101; poetry as inspiration for the montage of Shub, Eisenstein and Vertov 19, 20, 30; rejection of the theatricality of the stage for the reality of cinema 40; suicide 124, 299 n.1; vociferous support for Shub's recognition as author-producer of *The Fall of the Romanov Dynasty* 30, 57, 100–1; and Walter Benjamin 120
Maysles, Albert   259
Medunetsky, Konstantin   38, 47, 59
Medvedkin, Alexander   16, 258, 259, 261, 263, 265 n.1, 269 n.47, 296 n.88, 301 n.32, 302 n.52; *Happiness* 258, 265 n.1

Meyerhold, Vsevolod 2–3, 8–9, 12, 15, 32, 36, 51, 266 n.3, 274 n.9; circus and music hall 10–11; Eisenstein, Sergei, influence on 9, 28; *Masquerade* 9–10; Radlov, Sergei, influence on 9–10; 'Theatrical October' 9–12, 38–9; Yutkevich, Sergei, influence on 9
Miaja, José 244
Miller, Jamie 179, 185, 213–15, 217, 220
Millerand, Alexandre 54
Modotti, Tina: *Elegance and Poverty* (photomontage) 26–7, 26
Molotov, Vyacheslav 142, 148, 149, 214
montage. *See* Eisenstein's *October*; and Shub's contribution to *Wings of a Serf*; *Strike*; art, in 7–9, 25, 32; authenticity 63, 68, 115, 117; documentary film 63, 102, 121, 134; Eisenstein, Sergei 13, 19, 23, 27–33, 124; for montage in specific films (*see* Shub's *The Fall of the Romanov Dynasty*; *The Great Way*; *K.Sh.E*; *Spain*; *Today*); Kuleshov, Lev 12–15, 56; nonfiction film 23, 32, 67, 121; politics 25, 261; roots 2–3, 7–9, l25; Shub 12, 15–19, 21–5, 27–33, 47, 52, 63, 67, 68, 75, 84, 90, 96, 113, 115, 117, 124, 181, 260, 262, 264; Soviet film theory 7, 12–15, 185; theatrical antecedent 9; Vertov, Dziga 19, 20, 24
Monument to the Third International 44–5. *See also* Tatlin, Vladimir
Morris, William 37
Moscow Builds the Metro (Shub film) 213
Mourir à Madrid (Rossif film) 251–2
Mukhina, Vera 253
music hall 10, 11
Mussolini, Benito 132, 167
My Life – Cinematography (Shub book) 1, 17, 73, 110, 253, 281 n.25
Mystery-Bouffe (Mayakovsky drama) 10, 11–12, 268 n.23

Narkompros [the People's Commissariat of Enlightenment] 2, 179, 275 n.31, 287 n.99, 302 n.53
National Film Theatre (London) 257
New German Cinema 260

New LEF (journal) 263, 271 n.82, 274 n.16, 278 n.64, 287 n.99
New Spectator (journal) 32
newsreel 25, 46, 48, 50, 51, 56, 59–60, 62, 63, 64, 69, 72, 78, 95–7, 100, 101–3, 106, 110–13, 116–20, 123, 127–8, 134, 137, 183, 215, 254, 260, 264; manipulation of 95–6, 262; use as propaganda 46, 62, 121, 124
New Wave (French cinema) 258
Nichols, Bill 127, 163–4, 186, 276 n.40
Nicholas II, Tsar 4, 55, 62, 63, 73, 75, 80, 89, 90, 95, 98, 130, 132, 134, 236
nonfiction film [neigrovaya filma] 2, 32, 257; non-acted nonfiction film versus acted fiction film 107, 112–13
Nykino 255–6

October (Eisenstein film) 60, 61, 64, 68, 88, 103, 112, 282 n.40, 290 n.28
October Revolution (*also* October 1917) 8, 11, 12, 35, 41, 53, 61, 63–4, 65, 72, 80, 95, 115, 127–8, 131, 133–4, 137, 147, 182, 241, 261, 264, 265 n.2, 274 n.10, 274 n.15, 275 n.33, 280 n.8, 302 n.58
[OPOYAZ] the Society for the Study of Poetic Language 270 n.65, 275 n.31

Paramonova, Katya 189
Party Conference on Cinema (1928) 94, 179
Party propaganda and ideology 3, 94, 125, 205, 209, 221. *See also* archival footage; fact versus fiction; historical truth
Pasionaria, La (Dolores Ibárruri) 228–9, 229, 231, 239, 242, 243–6
Payne, Stanley 220–1, 297 n.10
Peirce, Charles 223
Pennebaker, D.A. 259
People's Commissariat of Enlightenment (Narkompros) 2, 179, 275 n.31, 287 n.99, 302 n.53
Peredvizhniki 35–7, 42, 286 n.72
Pertsov, Viktor 115, 116–17, 287 n.99
Petric, Vlada 16, 19, 43, 59, 262, 263
Petrograd 9, 10, 72, 132, 134

Pevsner, Antoine   43–4, 50
Photography and Charles Baudelaire   122
photomontage: Constructivist foundations   44, 50, 52; *The Dynamic City* 8; Gan, Aleksei 8; Höch, Hannah 8, 24–6; Klutsis, Gustav 9, 52, 278 n.71; Malevich, Kazimir 8; in prerevolutionary Russia 8; Rodchenko, Alexander 8, 9, 26, 52; in the Weimar Republic 271 n.82. *See also* Dadaist photomontage
Picasso, Pablo   45, 229, 274 n.19, 276–7 n.42
Pilsudski, Marshal Josef   132–3
Pletnev, Valerian   29
plot [syuzhet]   107, 285 n.63
The Plow That Broke the Plains (Lorentz film)   255
Poincaré, Raymond, President   54, 132, 137
Pope Pius XI   167
Popov, Gavriil   188; film scores: *K.Sh.E* 188–9, 193, 197, 199, 200; *Spain* 224
Popova, Liubov   44, 158, 177, 273 n.9, 276 n.41; *Spatial-Force Construction* (painting) 31
Popular Comedy Theatre   9, 10
Popular Front   225–6, 228, 232, 234, 236, 242
Prado, Antonio   217
Pravda (newspaper)   11, 104, 221, 297 n.4
Primary (Drew film)   259
Proletarian Cinema (film journal)   124, 147, 148, 208
Proletkult [Proletarian Culture Organization]   29
propaganda   12, 46, 52, 59, 62, 74, 88, 90, 93, 94, 108, 109, 121, 124, 133, 145, 174, 182, 205, 209, 213, 221, 225, 239, 260, 261, 279 n.90, 302 n.49, 302 n.50. *See also* Party propaganda and ideology
A Prostitute (Frelikh film)   2, 24
Protazanov, Yakov   258; *Aelita* 258, 301 n.33
Proust, Marcel   274 n.19

Pudovkin, Vsevolod   147–8, 154, 290 n.2; *Twenty Years of Soviet Cinema* (film co-scripted and co-directed with Shub) 215
Purishkevich, V.M.   73–4, 74

Radlov, Sergei   9, 28; and Meyerhold, Vsevolod 9, 10; Popular Comedy Theatre 9, 10
Rain (Ivens film)   254, 255
RAPP [Russian Association of Proletarian Writers]   94, 179, 181
Realist Manifesto   43
Reed, John   64, 280 n.8; *Ten Days That Shook the World* 64, 280 n.8
Regler, Gustav   234, 240, 242
Repin, Ilya   286 n.72; *Leo Tolstoy Barefoot* 286 n.72
Resnais, Alain   258
Riefenstahl, Leni   145
Roberts, Graham   47, 97, 116, 135, 170–1, 178–9, 182, 183, 203–5, 207, 210, 213, 263, 265 n.5
Rodchenko, Alexander   8–9, 24, 26, 38, 44, 47–8, 52, 53, 59, 105, 132, 177, 240, *241*, 271 n.82, 273 n.9, 276 n.41; *The Constructivist Party* (photograph) 38, *39*
Rosenstone, Robert   205
Rosicrucianism and Eisenstein   66
Rossif, Frédéric   251; *Mourir à Madrid* 251–2
Rouch, Jean   256, 257–8, 259, 300 n.26, 302 n.49
Rozanova, Olga   44, 276 n.41
Rudnitsky, Konstantin   9
Russia: folk arts and crafts, revival of   36–7; literature 2; Symbolist poets 66, 280 n.16
The Russian Banner (newspaper)   74–5
The Russia of Nicholas II and Leo Tolstoy (Shub film)   4, 101, 105, 107, 109, 118, 260, 284 n.51
Das russiche Wunder (Thorndike Film)   251

Schwitters, Kurt   8, 25, 271 n.82
Sebestyen, Victor   130, 280 n.12

Seidman, Michael   225
Selunskaya, Valeriya   106
Shaginyan, Marietta   198–9, *198*, 293 n.29
Shklovsky, Viktor   100, 105, 115, 129, 270 n.65, 275 n.31; fable [fabula] 107, 285 n.63; formalist theory of defamiliarization [ostranenie] 8, 63, 130; screenplays: and *A Prostitute* 24, 295 n.80; *Wings of a Serf* 20, 21, 270 n.66; 'The Semantics of Cinema' (journal article) 248; subject/theme [syuzhet] 107, 285 n.63; support for Shub and nonfiction film 110, 116, 118, 120, 264; 'The Temperature of Cinema' (journal article) 116, 118; 'Where is Dziga Vertov Striding?' (journal article) 248
Shorin, Alexander   189–90, 193
Shostakovich, Dmitry   *19*
Shub, Esfir Ilinichna   16, *19*, *58*: books: *In Close-up* 1, 16, 19, *58*, *101*; *My Life – Cinematography* 1, 17, 73, 110, 253, 281 n.25; censorship in the 1930s 123, 214–15: cancelling Shub's documentary 'truth' 208–13; the purges 180–1, 183, 185resultant decline in career 215–16, 252, 253; rewriting of history 42, 264 (*see also* Shub's 'On the Film "Today"'); Constructivist principles 7, 25, 38, 47, 57–60, 62, 84, 93, 145, 224; authentic [podlinny] material 57; author as producer issues 99–104; authorship 93, 100, 103, 104; compilation film, founder of 1–3, 52, 90, 93–4, 119, 253, 254, 261, 262; and Eisenstein, Sergei: differences, in approach 30, 61–9, 72, 80–4, 90, 95, 111–12, 118, 122, 136; working on *Strike* 2, 27–33; essays and articles quoted: 'The Advent of Sound in Cinema' 97–8, 185, 195, 200; 'A. I. Medvedkin – E. I. Shub' (letter) 16; 'And Again – the Newsreel' 41, 45, 46, 51, 98, 107, 108, 109, 110, 118, 127, 286 n.72; 'As a Reminder' 93, 96, 99–100; 'The Beginning of Fame for Soviet Cinematography' 62, 97, 98, 99; 'The City Sleeps' 231; 'A Diversion (A Tribute to my Youth): Moscow Higher Courses for Women' 19, 36, 73, 74, 215, 260, 270 n.62, 276 n.34, 277 n.42, 280 n.16; 'Documentary Cinema: Affairs and People' 214, 254, 297 n.96; 'Dziga Vertov' 19, 24, 32, 114; 'E. I. Shub – V. I. Mukhina' (letter) 253; 'The Film about Tolstoy' 62, 63, 73, 110, 114; 'First Work' 12, 41, 53, 84, 97, 98, 99, 103, 105, 109, 119, 120, 124; 'How the Film Was Made' 260; 'I Want to Make a Film About Women' 211, 212; 'I Want to Work' 212–13; 'My School of Cinematography' 13, 20, 21, 22, 23, 29, 30, 42, 104, 267 n.5; 'Nato Vachnadze' 191, 200, 202, 203; 'Non-acted Film' 14, 15, 40, 46, 50, 57, 59, 96, 99, 106, 111, 112–13, 114, 119, 210–11, 257, 277 n.51; 'On the Creative Method' 94; 'On the Film "Today"' 105, 147, 154, 158, 180, 181, 261, 302 n.51; 'Our Way' 112, 113, 209–10; 'The Path toward Choosing a Profession' 11, 22–3, 38, 40, 280 n.16; 'Road from the Past' 97; 'Sergei Mikhailovich Eisenstein' 17, 18, 27;'The Theme of My Speech' 187, 189; 'This Work Cries Out' 64, 111; 'To All Creative Workers in Soviet Cinema' (with Pudovkin, et al.) 147; 'Vladimir Mayakovsky' 98, 100–2, 128, 145; 'Warrior and Poet – Vsevolod Vishnevsky' 217, 218, 219, 224, 232, 240, 241, 244, 245, 250; 'We Do Not Deny the Element of Mastery' 102, 111, 154; feminism: Höch, Hannah 8, 24–5; influence on young filmmakers 16–17; Jewish heritage 1, 73; LEF 68, 90–1, 100, 103–4, 115; Lenin's and Stalin's patriarchal and misogynistic views on women 69; Lunacharsky, Anatoly 2, 38, 134; Mayakovsky, Vladimir 10, 12, 19–20, 39–40, 57, 98, 100–1, 110, 115, 116, 120–1, 124, 128, 253, 264, 266 n.1, 270 n.64, 274 n.16, 285 n.67, 294 n.60, 299 n.1; Meyerhold, Vsevolod 2, 11–12, 28,

36, 38; Modotti, Tina 26–7; notions of 36, 69; films: *The Fall of the Romanov Dynasty* [Padenie dinasty Romanovykh] (1927) 3–4, 8, 14, 15, 20, 22–4, 26–8, 30–1, 33, 35, 41, 44–5, 47–8, 51–60, 61–91, *71*, *74*, *76*, *79*, *87*, *88*, 93–125, *101*, 127–31, 134–5, 145, 147, 149, 154, 162, 167, 178, 182, 208, 217–18, 223–6, 229, 235–6, 238, 240, 242, 256, 258, 261–2, 264, 284 n.45; *The Great Way* [Veliky put] (1927) 4, 71, 101, 106, 115–18, 127–45, *131*, *140*, *144*, 148, 149, 155, 164, 178, 188, 191, 193, 208, 213–14, 217–19, 264; *The Russia of Nicholas II and Leo Tolstoy* [Rossiia Nikolaya II i Lva Tolstogo] (1928) 4, 101, 105, 107, 109, 118, 260, 284 n.51; *Today* [Segodnya] (1930) 4, 111, 118, 147–83, *152*, *153*, *155*–*7*, *159*, *161*, *174*, *178*, 193, 207–8, 215, 217, 219, 255, 264; *K.Sh.E.* (Komsomol Patron of Electrification) [Komsomol shef elektrifikatsy] (1932) 4, 174, 185–216, *192*, *194*, *197*–*8*, 219, 256–7, 259–60, 264; *Moscow Builds the Metro* [Moskva stroit metro] or *Metro by Night* [Metro nochiu] or *The City Sleeps* [Gorod spit] (1934) 213; *Land of the Soviets* [Strana sovetov] (1937) 213–15, 296 n.88; *Spain* [Ispaniya] (1939) 5, 23, 105, 111, 217–52, *229*, *232–8*, *241*, 264; *Twenty Years of Soviet Cinema* [20 let sovetskogo kino] or *Our Cinema* [Nashe kino] (1940) 215; *Fascism Will Be Defeated* [Fashizm budet razbyt] or *The Face of the Enemy* [Litso vraga] (1941) 215; *Homeland* [Strana rodnaya] (1942) 215; Goskino/Sovkino, tenure at 2, 18, 100–1, 104, 109; public criticism of *Today*: *Cinema Front* 182, 208; Sutyrin 179–82, 207–8; sound in film 185–207, 224, 226–7: comparison between Shub's *K.Sh.E* and Vertov's *Enthusiasm* 203–7; utopian vision 25, 43, 57, 90–1, 99, 219; and Vertov, Dziga 3, 16, 19–20, 24–5, 57–8, 70, 117, 170–3, 186–7, 203–7, 257, 262–3; interview quoted: Interview with V. Pfeffer, *Soviet Screen*, November 1 (1927) 128; legacy 253–64; montage: editing foreign films 2, 29; experimentation with Lev Kuleshov 13–15; ideological montage 7, 14–15, 23–4, 26, 28–30, 32–3, 47, 62–3, 67, 84–91, 95, 117, 119, 124, 229, 261–2, 264; Shub's contribution as editor on: *A Prostitute* 2, 24; *Strike* 12, 28–9, *31*, 32, 271 n.89; *Wings of a Serf* 2, 20–4; Moscow State Circus 11; fact versus fiction 61–77, 179 (*see also* Shub's 'The Manufacture of Facts'); newsreels 41, 51–2, 56–7, 61, 96, 98–9, 102–3, 110, 120, 123, 127–45, 215, 218, 260, 262; propagandist, role as 62, 129, 183, 222, 261: endorsement of revolutionary project 62; recycling of reality 78–80, 118, 218; socialist ideals of 40, 143, 209; Shub as pioneer of synchronized sound in the USSR 199–200, 256–7 (*see also* Shub's 'The Advent of Sound in Cinema'); VGIK, tenure at 18, 254–5; *Women*, script of 110, 210–12; and its rejection 210, 212; representation of 211–12 (*see also* Shub's 'I Want to Make a Film About Women' and 'I Want to Work'); Women's Institute of Higher Learning, studies at 1–2, 36; Jewish quota 2; People's Commissariat of Enlightenment [Narkompros], work at 2; TEO [Theatre Department of Narkompros], work at 2, 11, 27

Shumiatsky, Boris   105, 206, 213–14, 220, 296 n.92

A Sixth Part of the World (Vertov film)   117

Sobchack, Vivian   186

Socialist Realism   32, 42, 50, 93, 124, 147, 180, 183, 215, 269 n.45. *See also* avant-garde

Soiuzkino   180, 291 n.18, 291 n.27, 296 n.92. *See also* Sovkino; Goskino

Sokolov, Ippolit   117

Song of Heroes (Ivens film)   249

Soviet Screen (film journal)   108, 115–16, 248

Sovkino 2, 18, 100–1, 104, 109, 178, 180, 271 n.1, 291 n.18, 291 n.27. *See also* Goskino; Soiuzkino
Spain (Shub film) 5, 23, 105, 111, 217–52, *229, 232–8, 241*, 264
The Spanish Earth (Ivens film) 5, 249
Stalin, Joseph 5, 51, 65, 69, 90, 114, 123, 125, 131, 133, 135–7, 141–2, 148–9, 159, 179–80, 181, 183, 195, 202, 210, 212–14, 217, 219, 220–3, 208–9, 233, 243, 251, 253, 266 n.8, 296 n.83
Stalinist mythology 42, 264, 275 n.33
Stenberg brothers, Georgy and Vladimir 38, 47, 59
Stepanova, Varvara 38, *39*, 44, 53, 105, 273 n.9, 274 n.10
Stishova, Elena 206, 209
Stollery, Martin 69, 100
story [fabula] 107, 285 n.63
Strike (Eisenstein film) 2, 10, 12–14, 17, 23, 27–33, *31*, 265 n.4
subject/theme [syuzhet] 85 n.63, 107. *See also* Shklovsky, Viktor
Sutyrin, Vladimir 179–82, 207–8
Sverdlov, Yakov 135
Svilova, Elizaveta 114

Tager, Pavel 190
Talashkino 37
Tarich, Yury 2, 20–2; *Wings of a Serf* 2, 20–4, *21*, 102, 270 n.66
Tatlin, Vladimir 38, 40, 47, 122, 273 n.8, 276 n.42; *Letatlin* 45; *Monument to the Third International* 44–5
Taylor, Richard 32, 72
Ten Days That Shook the World (book) 64, 280 n.8. *See also* Reed, John
TEO [Theatre Department of Narkompros] 2, 11, 27
Theatre Courier (journal) 11
Theatre of the Future 9. *See also* Fuchs, Georg
Theremin 190–1, 193, 200, 201. *See also* K.Sh.E.
Theremin, Leon 190
Thorndike, Annelie and Andrew 251, 258–9, 299 n.43, 301 n.34

Three Songs of Lenin (Vertov film) 207
Today (Shub film) 4, 111, 118, 147–83, *152, 153, 155–7, 159, 161, 174, 178*, 193, 207–8, 215, 217, 219, 255, 264
Togliatti, Palmiro 220
Tolstaya, Alexandra 109, 285 n.69
Tolstoy, Leo 109, 118, 285 n.70; complexities of contradictory behaviours 110; *Leo Tolstoy Barefoot* 286 n.72; *What is Art?* 105
Trainin, Ilya *58*, 100
trans-sense [zaum] 8, 266 n.5
Trauberg, Leonid 10–11, 267 n.14
Tretiakov, Sergei 51, 100, 154, 220, 278 n.73
Trotsky, Leon 65, 136, 139, 141, 214, 290 n.28
Tsivian, Yuri 66, 67
Tugenkhold, Yakov 50, 278 n.69
Turovskaya, Maya 212, 213
Twenty Years of Soviet Cinema (Shub film) 215

Ulianov, Alexander 130, 133, 289 n.21
USA personifying the evils of capitalism 160–70, 172–3. *See also* Today
USSR a socialist utopia for the proletariat 174–8. *See also* Today

Vachnadze, Nato 191, *192*, 293 n.25
Van Dongen, Helen 255, 256, 283 n.9
Vasilev 'brothers', Georgy and Sergei 16, 269 n.45
Vertov, Dziga 1, 3, 7, 12, 14–16, 25, 32, 36, 43, 57, *58*, 59, 68, 98–9, 107, 115, 174, 179–81, 186–7, 205, 208, 249, 257, 262–3, 271 n.79, 271 n.82, 271 n.85, 287 n.109, 296 n.88, 300 n.26; Cine-Eye 114, 204, 248, 271 n.79; criticism of 58–9, 106, 117, 207–8, 248; dramatizing the facts 117, 171, 205; films cited: *The Anniversary of the Revolution* 261; *The Eleventh Year* 114, 170–1; *Enthusiasm: the Symphony of the Donbass* 4, 186, 203–7; *The History of the Civil War* 261; *Man with a Movie*

Camera 124, 204, 279 n.89; *A Sixth Part of the World* 117; *Three Songs of Lenin* 207; and Shub 16, 19–20, 24, 27, 70, 170–1, 203–7; views on nonfiction film and 'Film Truth' 24, 57–9, 103–4, 117–18, 204, 248
Vesnin, Viktor 198
VGIK [All-Union State Institute of Cinematography] 18, 254–5
Vishnevsky, Vsevolod 218, 224, 225, 226, 232, 236, 240–1, 244, 246, 248, 250, 297 n.4, 298 n.21, 299 n.31

Wells, Paul 259
Wilhelm II, Kaiser 54, 136, 137
Williams, Robert C. 7, 8, 29, 123, 271 n.89
Wings of a Serf (Tarich film) 2, 20–4, *21*, 102, 270 n.66
Wollen, Peter 235
Women's Institute of Higher Learning (Moscow) 36
Workers' Illustrated Newspaper 24, 271 n.83

Workers' International Relief 255
working class 4, 12, 28, 31, 83, 105–6, 128, 148, 155, 166, 173, 209, 220, 222, 255
Working Group of Constructivists (Moscow) 38, 47

Yampolsky, Mikhail 103, 106–7, 113; 'Reality at Second Hand' 103, 113
Yasnaya Polyana 109, 285 n.70
Youngblood, Denise J. 20, 22, 31, 69, 108, 129, 179, 183, 185, 207, 208, 262, 292 n.37, 296 n.92
Yutkevich, Sergei 9–11, 15–17, 20–1, 22, 29, 96, 119, 253–4, 256–7, 259, 267 n.14, 269 n.42, 296 n.88

Zalka, Máté 240, 242
Zdanevich, Ilya 37, 273 n.7; 'Why We Paint Ourselves: A Futurist Manifesto' 37. *See also* Larionov, Mikhail
Zezina, Maria 106
Zhemchuzhnyi, Vitaly 171
Zhordania, Noe 136–7

www.ingramcontent.com/pod-product-compliance
Lightning Source LLC
Chambersburg PA
CBHW052145300426
44115CB00011B/1520